Sun, Sea, and Sound

Sun, Sea, and Sound

Music and Tourism in the Circum-Caribbean

EDITED BY TIMOTHY ROMMEN

AND

DANIEL T. NEELY

OXFORD
UNIVERSITY PRESS

OXFORD
UNIVERSITY PRESS

Oxford University Press is a department of the University of
Oxford. It furthers the University's objective of excellence in research,
scholarship, and education by publishing worldwide.

Oxford   New York
Auckland   Cape Town   Dar es Salaam   Hong Kong   Karachi
Kuala Lumpur   Madrid   Melbourne   Mexico City   Nairobi
New Delhi   Shanghai   Taipei   Toronto

With offices in
Argentina   Austria   Brazil   Chile   Czech Republic   France   Greece
Guatemala   Hungary   Italy   Japan   Poland   Portugal   Singapore
South Korea   Switzerland   Thailand   Turkey   Ukraine   Vietnam

Oxford is a registered trademark of Oxford University Press
in the UK and certain other countries.

Published in the United States of America by
Oxford University Press
198 Madison Avenue, New York, NY 10016

Library of Congress Cataloging-in-Publication Data
Sun, sea, and sound: music and tourism in the circum-Caribbean / edited by
Timothy Rommen and Daniel T. Neely.
pages cm
Includes bibliographical references and index.
ISBN 978-0-19-998885-3 (hardback: alk. paper)—ISBN 978-0-19-998886-0
(pbk.: alk. paper)   1. Music and tourism—Caribbean Area.   2. Music—Social aspects—Caribbean
Area.   I. Rommen, Timothy.   II. Neely, Daniel Tannehill.
ML3917.C38S86 2014
306.484209729—dc23
2013041311

9 8 7 6 5 4 3 2 1
Printed in the United States of America
on acid-free paper

In memory of our friend and colleague, Katherine J. Hagedorn

CONTENTS

FOREWORD

You're in Jamaica, come on and smile…
Said I see you're having fun,
Dancing to the reggae rhythm,
Oh, island in the sun
    —Bob Marley, *"Smile Jamaica" (1976)*

Tourism in the Caribbean is often represented in stark terms, and for good reason. After more than a century of experience with touristic enterprises of one kind or another, many in the region continue to view their position on the receiving end of the tourist industry with wary ambivalence. By now, most are aware that promised economic boons seldom come without a hefty price tag. When it comes to unbridled mass tourism, the downsides—among them environmental ravages and future unsustainability—are increasingly evident.

But what of the ostensibly kinder, gentler paradigms of community-based eco-tourism and cultural tourism that appear to be on the upswing? These are, of course, fraught with problems of their own. My own ethnographic field notes contain rather stark examples of the unsettling effect of the smaller-scale touristic gaze on rural Caribbean communities on the cusp of cultural commodification. In 1978, for instance, I sat in on a council meeting in the Jamaican Maroon community of Accompong, during which an enterprising Maroon youth with connections to the tourist industry caused consternation by blithely suggesting that the sacred private portion of the January 6th rites to the Maroon ancestors, from which non-Maroons had always been strictly excluded, be opened—subject to an admission fee—to the limited but growing number of tourists who every year made the trek to Maroon country to attend the annual celebrations. The elders on the council were shocked that one of their own would advocate the "commercialization" (as they put it) of private offerings made at the graves of ancestors.

A few years later, in 1984, soon after arriving in the rain forest territory of the Aluku Maroons on the border of French Guiana and Suriname—some 155 miles from the more populous coastal region and reachable only by river or air—I noted disparaging remarks among my Maroon neighbors about the new phenomenon of the *tuwisi* (a recent Aluku coinage, from French, *touriste*). These uninvited visitors, I was told (and as I was soon to witness), would occasionally show up in motorized canoes along with their hired guides, gawking at the few remaining bare-breasted women out and about in public, and making unseemly offers of French francs for woodcarvings or other artifacts of Aluku domestic life. In many other parts of the circum-Caribbean, of course, exoticizing imagery, cultural othering, cultural commodification, and exploitative economic practices had been commonplace on a much larger scale for decades, as part of long histories of institutionalized tourism. In booming centers of touristic development like Jamaica, such themes provided grist for resident cultural critics and were effectively satirized in local productions such as the 1976 film *Smile Orange* (based on an earlier play by Trevor Rhone).

Since the heady days of the 1970s, musical tourism has emerged, largely without official support or sanction, as a distinct form of cultural tourism with potentially enormous appeal, further complicating the cultural ambiguities alluded to above. In some parts of the circum-Caribbean region—Jamaica being a case in point—local music has become a primary draw for visitors from abroad. So one might ask: when viewed through a specifically "musical" lens—whether our focus is on musical production itself, or on music as soundtrack to other attractions and encounters—might tourism in the Caribbean take on a somewhat different appearance? By asking just this question, and tying it to an explicitly theorized concept of music touristics, this book opens a new area of critical inquiry in the field of tourism studies.

When investigations of tourism place music and musicians at the center, and when a certain ethnographic sensitivity comes into play, things that once seemed clear and simple can suddenly appear rather "messy," as Tim Rommen suggests in his introduction to this volume. Unexamined assumptions and preconceived notions (for cultural critics, most often negative ones) about the relationship between music and tourism can be thrown into question. The stark terms in which the cultural dimensions of tourism are often portrayed may no longer seem adequate without further qualification.

Once again, Jamaica provides us with a helpful example. In the minds of many across the globe, few musics are as clearly associated with protest against social injustice as reggae (especially the variety of "roots reggae" that flourished during the 1970s). The elevation of Bob Marley to iconic status helped to cement the idea that reggae and Rastafarian consciousness were inseparable—a notion that continues to hold considerable sway, contradictory elements of more recent Jamaican dance-hall music notwithstanding. Owing to a complex mix of translocal politics, mass-mediated communications, and niche marketing, Jamaican popular music on the whole has come to be viewed by many as an inherently "revolutionary" expression of resistance to structural inequality, black (and other) disenfranchisement, poverty, and oppression more generally. If there is any room for tourism in this imaginary, it is as the antithesis of genuine reggae.

And one can see why. In its starker guises, the musical face of organized tourism can be cynically dissembling, doing its best to avoid acknowledgment of harsh social and economic realities. Smiling mento musicians in straw hats and bright shirts are typically thrust into the spotlight. Rastas, when admitted, are most often reduced to mellow, weed-happy bohemians with little bark and less bite. Marley's "One Love" and "Three Little Birds" (often in mento, or "calypso," versions) play interminably in airport welcoming zones and at poolside bars, while his "Burning and Looting" and "Ambush in the Night" are actively forgotten. It is easy to see why, for certain defenders of reggae authenticity, tourism is quite simply the enemy, part and parcel of Babylon.

Not all of the facts of Jamaican music, however, lend support to such starkly oppositional imagery. Truth to tell, there is plenty of evidence—when one digs deep enough—that Jamaican popular music from its earliest days has been enmeshed in complex ways with the business of tourism. Not only most of the early recording artists working in the urbanizing mento idiom of the 1950s but also several of those who made important contributions to Jamaica's first bona fide urban popular form, ska, spent portions of their early years performing for tourists. Key figures in early Jamaican popular music such as saxophonist Tommy McCook (of the Skatalites), guitarist Ernest Ranglin (dean of Jamaican studio musicians), bandleader and arranger Carlos Malcolm (of the Afro-Jamaicans), guitarist Dwight Pinkney (of the Sharks), singer and bassist Boris Gardiner (of the Boris Gardiner Happening), and saxophonist Cedric Brooks (eventual cofounder, with drummer Count Ossie, of the Mystic Revelation of Rastafari), cut their musical teeth playing in hotels and clubs both in Jamaica and during stints in the Bahamas in the 1950s or early '60s. Others, such as seminal drummer Lloyd Knibb (of the Skatalites), opted for employment on cruise ships. While in Nassau, Freeport, or on the high seas, these foundational Jamaican figures mingled with other Caribbean performers and professional musicians from many other parts of the world. Upon their return, they applied some of the cosmopolitan lessons learned on the international tourist circuit to the new sounds they were helping to fashion in the burgeoning studios of Kingston.

The tourist trade was implicated in the full-fledged reggae explosion that was soon to follow as well. While collecting oral histories over the last decade from a large number of the session musicians responsible for the birth of the new genre of reggae in the late 1960s and its flowering in the 1970s, I was surprised to learn how many of these pioneers, at one time or another, had fallen back on the expanding tourist economy as a means of guaranteeing or supplementing their income. Although the amounts of time and the degree of exposure varied, virtually every one of these musicians had played at one point or another in hotels or tourist-friendly clubs, whether in Kingston or on the tourism-saturated north coast of the island. This was no less true of Rasta rebels hailing from the tough streets of West Kingston than of those from more comfortable, middle-class backgrounds. Even those session musicians and vocalists identified with the "roughest," "rawest" forms of grassroots reg-gae—players and singers such as Leroy "Horsemouth" Wallace (of the Black Disciples), Bertram "Ranchie" McLean (of the Revolutionaries), Vin Morgan (of the Soul Defenders), or Joseph Hill (of Culture)—had chalked up sub-stantial experience performing in tourist (or mixed) venues before becom-ing mainstays in the studios. Indeed, quite a few of reggae's founding fathers spent good portions of their careers alternating between studios, clubs, and hotels. Moreover, even during the period when hardcore Rastafarian "roots" music dominated, there were certain live performance settings where mixing between foreign tourists and Jamaican patrons was more common than is gen-erally recognized.

It is difficult to assess the impact of such experiences performing in touristic (or tourist-influenced) contexts on the recorded output of studio musicians. Some interviewees mentioned the beneficial effect of having to keep on top of the varied tastes of foreign visitors, in the process enlarging their repertoires and the range of stylistic resources they would be able to draw on in future. One could sense that some of these musicians felt a certain pride in the musical versatility they had acquired in such contexts as a matter of necessity. As the veteran session player (bassist and guitarist) Ranchie McLean told me in 2008, "You used to have more tourists ina town [i.e., Kingston], you know. When they come a night club, a elder couple [might] say, 'do you know "Fly Me to the Moon?"' I say, 'you want to hear it?' And we come up with it, and we play it. So we play *every*thing." Drummer and keyboardist Vin Morgan, a fixture at Coxsone Dodd's legendary Studio One during the 1970s, spoke in a similar vein of one of several "mixed" clubs in the north coast resort town of Ocho Rios, where he used to play regularly: "You would find tourist in there too [alongside locals]. Because we were playing all type of music. We knew that we had to know the influence of songs on the radio—that means the R&B and all those songs that were played. We had to know these songs for people to get attracted and come to our shows. So we tried to learn a lot of R&B, and even different kind of traditional folk songs. *All* of these things they wanted."

Such memories hint at a part of the history of Jamaican popular music that remains underexposed, whether because of its uncomfortable fit with narratives that stress the authenticity of reggae as the unadulterated voice of the "sufferer," or because most of the music's chroniclers have simply not thought to ask musicians about such things. Imagine how much more would be understood now about the interface between tourism and popular music in Jamaica during the critical years of the 1960s and '70s had one or two ethnographically minded observers recorded from close up, and over an extended period, the actual substance of encounters between active studio musicians and the audiences they entertained from time to time in spaces defined as touristic, as well as other places where the boundaries between residents and "guests" were more porous than usual. This is not to suggest that the resulting knowledge would fundamentally alter our view of reggae as predominantly a product of the underclass of "downtown" Kingston, intended at first primarily for local consumption. Nor is it to grant tourism a central role. Rather, it would simply help us refine our understanding of Jamaican popular music over time in all its varied dimensions. A full account of the development of this music would include both its ongoing susceptibility to the tourist gaze and its power to affect that gaze. Such an account would certainly lead to a more nuanced view of the musical dimensions of tourism than the one many proponents of reggae authenticity seem to hold.

A similar rationale guides the present book. Regardless of the particular circum-Caribbean site under consideration, all of the contributors seek to highlight the actual actors—foremost among them musicians and songwriters, their audiences, and their communities—who inhabit (or once inhabited) the physical and imagined spaces in which tourism and music are (or have been) mutually constructed. In this framing of music touristics, the focus is as much on questions of local agency and active meaning-making as on imposed stereotypes and other imported forms of cultural othering. Likewise, performers' responses to economic exploitation are as important as the fact of exploitation itself. By the same token, the actual motivations behind local musical performance and production, and the meanings attached to these, hold at least as much interest as more abstract questions centering on, for instance, musical marketing, reception, and the large-scale structural forces that constrain or encourage creativity.

Apprehending how those who participate in touristic musical contexts actually create, perform, and think about their music requires us first to identify the actual spaces in which such endeavors take place and are interpreted. This in turn forces us to recognize the existence of varying modalities of tourism. One of the great strengths of this volume, in addition to the ethnographic approach it favors, is the degree of variation it reveals in types of tourism and the kinds of music associated with these. Once we grasp how multifaceted a beast "tourism" truly is, we begin to see how much adjustment may be required before coming to conclusions about the musical parameters of tourism. The lines between "tourists" and "locals," "insiders" and "outsiders," may, at least in certain times and places, become much fuzzier than usually thought. The connotations of "Yellow Bird," "Day O," or "Island in the Sun" may change entirely, depending on where, when, by whom, and for whom they are performed. Scholarly conversations about the significance and authenticity of music created and played in touristic contexts may now need to sample, compare, and contrast a wider range of voices—including, for instance, those of *rara* celebrants and *twoubadou* revivalists in Haiti and the diaspora, "vintage" *soneros*, trendy *timberos*, and possessing orishas in Cuba, returning Garifuna expatriates in Belize, or erotic dancers and sex workers across the region. Then, and only then—as we see in this volume—do the human subtleties concealed behind the caricatures in which tourism has often trafficked begin to be apparent.

The Caribbean region bears deeper scars than most other parts of the world from the devastation wrought by the European imperial projects that helped to produce the scourges of slavery, colonialism, and ongoing underdevelopment. It is a region of vexing contradictions and glaring contrasts, and the cruder forms of touristic exploitation that have been heaped upon this historical burden in many areas perhaps justify the stark terms in which Caribbean tourism is often portrayed by critics. Yet, as the chapters that follow show, the relationship between music and tourism in a region as musically rich and dynamic as the Caribbean also deserves a second, closer look. Though the idea that music identified with (or touched by) tourism is worthy of more serious consideration has special meaning in the countries and territories of this particular region, it will no doubt resonate elsewhere as well. One hopes that this book will help spur further research and reexamination along similar lines wherever in the world music and tourism have been conjoined.

—*Kenneth Bilby*
Smithsonian Institution

ACKNOWLEDGMENTS

This volume, like many such projects, I suspect, started over a beer at a conference. Daniel Neely and I were wrestling with what we saw as a real lack of literature and scholarship specifically treating the relationship of music and tourism, and this especially as it related to our own current work in the Caribbean. In the process of shaping this idea into a concrete reality, Daniel and I have had the distinct pleasure to draw on a wide range of resources and to interact with a host of wonderful individuals. To those scholars who have thought about music and tourism in their own work, and to those many who have consistently wrestled with the difficult questions related to tourism from the vantage point of other disciplines, we, along with the contributors, owe a debt of gratitude. This volume moves in new directions in large part because of the signposts scattered throughout such earlier work.

To the musicians, officials, travelers, scholars, and other interlocutors who animate the ethnographic case studies in this volume, we all offer our profound thanks. The insights and new ideas generated in and through our interactions with these individuals constitute the main motivation for and substance of this collection. In this connection, Daniel and I also wish to thank the contributing authors to this collection. We have been continually impressed by their scholarship and have learned a great deal from their work in the process of assembling this volume.

The external readers offered invaluable advice and suggestions on the manuscript and we thank them for their time, efforts, and insights. Thanks also go to Bo Kyung Blenda Im, who prepared the volume's index. Finally, the wonderful team of editors and staff at Oxford University Press has been a pleasure to work with, and Daniel and I especially thank Suzanne Ryan, Adam Cohen, and Molly Morrison of Newgen for their diligence and enthusiasm throughout the publishing process.

CONTRIBUTORS

Kenneth Bilby is Research Associate in the Department of Anthropology at the Smithsonian Institution. An anthropologist, ethnomusicologist, and cultural historian, he has carried out fieldwork in various parts of the Caribbean and in West Africa. He has published widely on music, language, history, and the politics of culture in the Caribbean. He is co-author, with Peter Manuel and Michael Largey, of *Caribbean Currents: Caribbean Music from Rumba to Reggae* (1995, 2006). In 2004 he was awarded a Guggenheim Fellowship to research a book (forthcoming) on the vital role of historically deep rural musical traditions in the development of urban popular music (including ska, reggae, and dance-hall) in Jamaica. His book, *True-Born Maroons* (2005)—a study of Jamaican Maroon oral narratives based on fieldwork spanning nearly three decades—won the American Historical Association's Wesley-Logan Prize. His most recent book (co-authored with Jerome Handler) is *Enacting Power: The Criminalization of Obeah in the Anglophone Caribbean, 1760–2011* (2012).

Jerome Camal Jerome Camal earned his PhD in Musicology with a specialization in ethnomusicology from Washington University in St. Louis. He went on to teach at UCLA for two years where he joined the Mellon Postdoctoral Program in the Humanities, Cultures in Transnational Perspectives. He is currently Assistant Professor of Anthropology at the University of Wisconsin–Madison and working on a book manuscript tentatively entitled *The Distant Drum: Musical Paths towards a Creole Postnationalism.*

Oliver N. Greene, Jr. is Associate Professor of Music at Georgia State University where he teaches courses on traditional world music, the popular music of Africa and the Middle East, carnival traditions of Trinidad and Brazil, and the origin and development of popular American music. His documentary film, *Play, Jankunú Play: The Garifuna Wanaragua Ritual in Belize"* has been shown in New Zealand, Brazil, Belize, Serbia, the US Virgin Islands, and at numerous festivals and universities in the United States. He has published articles in the book *The Garifuna: A Nation Across Borders, Senderos* (Revista de Etnomusicologia), *Black Music Research Journal*, the *Continuum Encyclopedia of Popular Music of Music*, the *Concise Garland Encyclopedia of World Music*, and the *Garland Encyclopedia of World Music*. He has also created a web site on Garifuna music and ritual arts traditions for La Médiathèque Caraïbe in Guadeloupe, French West Indies.

Jocelyne Guilbault is Professor of Music at the University of California, Berkeley. She specializes in theory and method in popular music studies, politics of aesthetics, and issues dealing with power relations in music production and circulation. Since 1980, she has done extensive fieldwork in the French Creole- and English-speaking islands of the Caribbean on both traditional and popular music. She published several articles on ethnographic writings, aesthetics, the cultural politics of West Indian music industries, and world music. She is the author of *Zouk: World Music in the West Indies* (1993) and the co-editor of *Border Crossings: New Directions in Music Studies* (1999–2000). Her last main publication is entitled *Governing Sound: The Cultural Politics of Trinidad's Carnival Musics* (2007).

Katherine J. Hagedorn, PhD, was Professor of Music and Director of the Ethnomusicology Program at Pomona College in Claremont, California, and she published widely on Afro-Cuban ritual and folkloric music. Her book *Divine Utterances: The Performance of Afro-Cuban Santería* (2001) won the Alan P. Merriam Prize for the best ethnography. Professor Hagedorn taught courses in the performance traditions of Latin America and the African diaspora, Roma performance, as well as ethnomusicology in theory and practice. In 2000, Professor Hagedorn was named California Professor of the Year by the Carnegie Foundation for the Advancement of Teaching. In 2002, Pomona College awarded her a Wig Teaching Award, and in 2005 she won a coveted Mellon New Directions Fellowship for her book project, *Toward a Theology of Sound*. Trained as a classical pianist, she performed Afro-Cuban, West African, and Indonesian percussive traditions for over twenty years. A former member of the Board of Directors of the national Society for Ethnomusicology, Dr. Hagedorn served as Associate Dean of Pomona College, where she taught from 1993 until her passing in 2013.

Sydney Hutchinson is Assistant Professor of Ethnomusicology at Syracuse University. She is the author of an award-winning book on Mexican American dance and youth culture as well as numerous articles in journals like *Ethnomusicology, Journal of American Folklore, Centro Journal, e-misférica, Folklore Forum*, and *Popular Music*. A former Humboldt Fellow at the Berlin

Phonogramm-Archiv, she is also the current book reviews editor for the Yearbook for Traditional Music. Hutchinson is working on a book based on her ten years' research into Dominican merengue típico and she enjoys yodeling in her spare time.

Darien Lamen is ACLS New Faculty Fellow in Ethnomusicology at the University of Wisconsin–Madison where he specializes in issues of circulation, labor, and technology in Brazil and the circum-Caribbean. He earned a PhD from the University of Pennsylvania in 2011 and received a Social Science Research Council fellowship for his doctoral research on the Caribbeanization of Brazilian popular music. He is currently developing an ethnographic history of work and sound design in the informal sound system economy of Belém do Pará (Brazilian Amazon).

Michael Largey is Professor and Chair of Musicology at Michigan State University. He is an ethnomusicologist and folklorist specializing in the music and culture of Haiti. He is the author of *Vodou Nation: Haitian Art, Music, and Cultural Nationalism* (University of Chicago Press, 2006) that was a co-winner of the Alan P. Merriam Prize from the Society for Ethnomusicology for the most distinguished book in the field of ethnomusicology. He is also a co-author with Peter Manuel and Kenneth Bilby of the revised and expanded edition of *Caribbean Currents: Caribbean Music from Rumba to Reggae* (Temple University Press, 2006). The first edition of *Caribbean Currents* won the Gordon K. Lewis Award for Caribbean Scholarship from the Caribbean Studies Association and was a Choice Outstanding Title in 1996. His most recent book is Haitians in Michigan (Michigan State University Press, 2010). Largey has conducted extensive research on Haitian Rara and has been a member of Rara Ti Malis Kache in Léogâne since 1995.

Ruthie Meadows is a PhD Candidate in Ethnomusicology at the University of Pennsylvania. Her research focuses on poetics and aurality in the Hispanophone- and circum-Caribbean, including the interplay between new media and queer poetics in literature, poetry, and popular musics, the transnationalized nature of the Dominican popular musical sphere, Afro-religious sensorial poetics within Cuban popular musics, and the historical interconnectedness of New Orleans and Havana as Afro-sensorial and Afro-Caribbean poetic and religious spaces. Her research furthermore incorporates ethnographic film and aural narrative as a means of examining the ethics of and mediations inherent to ethnomusicological research.

Daniel T. Neely received a PhD in Music from New York University and wrote his dissertation on Jamaican *mento* music. His writing has appeared in *Caribbean Studies, Caribbean Quarterly, Nieuwe West-IndischeGids, Ethnomusicology*, and the *Yearbook for Traditional Music*. He is co-author (with Kenneth Bilby) of "The English-Speaking Caribbean: Re-Embodying the Colonial Ballroom" in *Creolizing Contradance in the Caribbean* (Temple University Press, 2009), and he was the music director and banjoist on the Jolly Boys modern mento album *Great Expectation*. In addition to his work in Jamaica, he is the author of "Ding, Ding!: The Commodity Aesthetic of Ice Cream Truck Music" in the *Oxford Companion to Mobile Music Studies* (Oxford University Press, 2014), he is the traditional music columnist for the *Irish Echo* newspaper, and he is the leader of the Washington Square Harp and Shamrock Orchestra, an Irish music group based in New York City.

Vincenzo A. Perna holds a degree in music from the University of Bologna and a PhD in Ethnomusicology from the School of Oriental and African Studies, University of London (SOAS). He is the author of the book *Timba. The Sound of the Cuban Crisis* (Ashgate 2005, honorable mention at Alan Merriam Prize, Society for Ethnomusicology 2006). He has contributed to the report *Music in Europe* (European Music Office/European Commission 1996) and written about Western and non-Western popular music and jazz for Italian and international encyclopedias (*Enciclopedia Italiana, Nova Utet, Enciclopedia di Repubblica, Encyclopaedia Britannica, The Continuum Encyclopaedia of Popular Music of the World, Greenwood Encyclopedia of Latin American Popular Music*). Among the books on popular music that he has edited and translated is the Italian version of the volume *Shoot the Singer! Music Censorship Today* (M. Korpeed), Freemuse-Zed Books, 2004. As a freelance journalist, he has contributed since 1990 to the Italian music newsmagazine *Il Giornale della Musica* and to various other Italian and foreign publications. He presently works as a lecturer and music journalist, and he is secretary of the Italian branch of IASPM.

Timothy Rommen is Associate Professor of Music at the University of Pennsylvania. He specializes in the music of the Caribbean with research interests that include folk and popular sacred music, popular music, critical theory, ethics, diaspora, tourism, and the intellectual history of ethnomusicology. His first book, entitled *"Mek Some Noise": Gospel Music and the Ethics of Style in Trinidad* (University of California Press, 2007), was awarded the Alan P. Merriam Prize by the Society for Ethnomusicology in 2008. He is also the author of *Funky Nassau: Roots, Routes, and Representation in Bahamian Popular Music* (University of California Press, 2011). He is co-editor of the Chicago Series in Ethnomusicology, published by the University of Chicago Press. He is also a contributing author to and the editor of *Excursions in World Music*.

Matthew J. Smith is a Senior Lecturer in History at the University of the West Indies, Mona in Jamaica. His main area of research is Haitian politics and society after the U.S. Occupation (1915–1934) and Haitian regional migration in the nineteenth and early twentieth century. He is the author of *Red and Black in Haiti: Radicalism, Conflict, and Political Change, 1934-1957*, and several articles on Haitian political and social history.

Mimi Sheller is Professor of Sociology and Director of the Center for Mobilities Research and Policy at Drexel University. She is also Senior Research Fellow and former co-Director of the Centre for Mobilities Research at Lancaster University (UK) and founding co-editor of the journal *Mobilities*. She is the author of the books *Democracy After Slavery* (Macmillan, 2000); *Consuming the Caribbean* (Routledge, 2003); and forthcoming *Citizenship from Below* (Duke University Press, 2012). She is co-editor with John Urry of *Mobile Technologies of the City* (Routledge, 2006), *Tourism Mobilities* (Routledge, 2004), and a special issue of *Environment and Planning A* on "Materialities and Mobilities." She has held recent Visiting Fellowships in the Davis Center for Historical Studies at Princeton University (2008–2009); Media@McGill in Montreal (2009); the Center for Mobility and Urban Studies at Aalborg University, Denmark (2009); and the Penn Humanities Forum at the University of Pennsylvania (2010–2011).

Sun, Sea, and Sound

Introduction

Music Touristics in the Circum-Caribbean

TIMOTHY ROMMEN ∎

What is the earthly paradise for our visitors? Two weeks without rain and a mahogany tan, and, at sunset, local troubadours in straw hats and floral shirts beating "Yellow Bird" and "Banana Boat Song" to death. There is a territory wider than this—wider than the limits made by the map of an island—which is the illimitable sea and what it remembers.

—DEREK WALCOTT, *Fragments of Epic Memory*

The circum-Caribbean, has long served as a hot spot for travelers, both in terms of actual travel and in terms of the tourist imagination. Beginning in the nineteenth century, a tourist industry emerged throughout the region—an industry that has developed myriad and idiosyncratic ways of tailoring encounter and experience to desire and expectation. Shaped along the paths of colonial and postcolonial power, this industry continues to exert itself in the contemporary moment, attracting millions of visitors to the region each year. As such, it is hardly possible to encounter the region musically without encountering it also as a collection of leisure destinations or, as Mimi Sheller has aptly phrased it, as "places to play."[1]

And yet, in spite of the ubiquitous presence of tourism throughout the region, the roles and importance of music and musical performance within the tourism sector are generally overlooked by scholars. The local music makers and entertainers that provide vacationers with sound tracks to their leisure often remain little more than invisible women and men—unknown, undocumented, and under-theorized. The epigraph to this chapter illustrates this point nicely. Walcott's troubadours are one of the signs of the earthly paradise for visitors to the Caribbean. That they are included in a list including "two weeks without rain and a mahogany tan"—that they are subjected, that is, to a process that Aimé Cesaire once described as "thingification"—is significant here (Cesaire 1955 [2000]). So, too, is the fact that the songs these troubadours sing are named, whereas the musicians themselves receive no such recognition (though their clothing does). *wow!!*

In the end, the musicians feature as extras on the set, providing a rather thoughtless sound track to tourists' leisure. And yet these troubadours are, in fact, performing sonic emblems of the region. There are concrete reasons why Walcott can mobilize "Yellow Bird" and the "Banana Boat Song" as caricatures—reasons that are generally taken for granted in the process of making larger points about tourism or, from the perspective of music scholars, in the process of passing over these performances in favor of attending to other musical practices. The contributors to this volume, however, pause at this particularly fraught juncture of sound and context—the moment at which musical performances meet and merge with or challenge tourist experiences—in order more adequately to address the dynamics that make songs such as "Yellow Bird" and troubadours in straw hats so ubiquitous while simultaneously rendering them invisible (extras, thingification, and the like). Walcott's passage, then, helps us interrogate the extent to which musicians are understood to be part of the conditions of tourism itself rather than as active and individuated voices negotiating their place within the context of tourism. In so doing, it puts a finger on the two principal motivations for assembling this volume: (1) a felt need to more carefully think about the relationship between tourism and music; and (2) a desire to unpack what we mean by tourism in the first place, given that Walcott's passage highlights but one vector (among many) of tourist experience in the circum-Caribbean—that of mass tourism.

MUSIC/TOURISM

This book has taken shape in large measure because of a deep sense that music and tourism are too often thought as separate entities with only ancillary connections to each other, especially within the circum-Caribbean. Scholars who spend a great deal of their time thinking about and researching tourism tend to do so through the productive analytical lenses of mobility studies, leisure studies, or cultural geography.[2] Others address the topic from the perspectives of history or anthropology, offering particularly important readings of tourism and its itineraries and actors.[3] And yet, while these scholars certainly do notice music and musicians from time to time and occasionally even devote a few pages to thinking about the role of music in a given context, they tend, by and large, to write about other aspects of the tourist experience (i.e., economic policy, sustainability, demographics, political implications, and the like.), leaving any substantive discussion of music to the music scholars, as it were. A review of the articles published in the flagship journal of tourism studies—the Annals of Tourism Research—rather definitively confirms this state of affairs. Only two examples of scholarship aimed at wrestling explicitly with the connection between music and tourism have been included in this journal's very busy, forty-year career.[4]

Conversely, scholars who think about music in places where tourism is a major part of the economic and social fabric tend to approach their work from the perspective of ethnomusicology and folklore and thus often seek an understanding of musical life as it connects to other concerns—to questions of nationalism, authenticity, neocolonialism, power relations, heritage, and appropriation, to name only a few among many possibilities—rather than delving explicitly or directly into the relationship between tourism and musical performance. Put otherwise, for music scholars, tourism has often been ancillary—sometimes even understood as threatening—to their own research concerns, and it has thus often been relegated to cursory or otherwise incomplete treatment. Restricting myself for the moment to the circum-Caribbean, some of the best scholarship throughout the region has readily acknowledged tourism while simultaneously resisting a focus on its import for and relationship to musical practices (c.f. Dudley 2007; Moore 2006; Guilbault 1993, 2007; Austerlitz 1997). I should clarify that I do not mean to criticize these excellent projects in any way, but I am instead attempting to illustrate the fact that tourism is ever-present in Caribbean contexts—so much so that it is, more often than not, virtually woven in—and yet, despite this fact, it has not generated much scholarship or sustained attention. It is as if tourism and its relation to music is not yet widely accepted as a viable research paradigm for ethnomusicologists working in the region. In the main, then, just as tourism scholars tend to neglect music and musicians, so too do music scholars often miss the opportunity to engage with tourism in their work—leading both streams of scholarship to remain, too often, impoverished for lack of nuanced engagement with a constituent other.

And yet, several notable exceptions to this trend have been published, and I highlight a few (though certainly not all) of these here to point out the possibilities for such research and to clarify the aims of this volume. A collection of papers from the 1986 ICTM Colloquium in Jamaica, entitled *Come Mek Me Hol' Yu Han'*, was published by the Jamaica Memory Bank in 1988. It contains three parts, concerning the Caribbean and Latin America, Asia and the Pacific, and Europe, respectively. Each of the chapters deals with the impact of tourism on traditional music and does so with a view toward analyzing the extent to which tourism and traditional musics are intertwined with and affected by each other. It constitutes a landmark publication primarily because it stands virtually alone in addressing the interactions of music and tourism in the literature of the 1980s. That it devotes fully seven chapters to case studies in the Caribbean and Latin American region, moreover, is, itself, a major contribution, given the general dearth of scholarship on this topic within the circum-Caribbean. The present volume, then, seeks to provide a new set of case studies for consideration that, building on the model provided by *Come Mek Me Hol' Yu Han'*, extend the conversation through new methodological and theoretical lenses. I will return to this later.

Chris Gibson and John Connell, both cultural geographers, have offered an important contribution to the nexus of music and tourism. Their book, *Music and Tourism: On the Road Again* (2005), offers a broad framework for thinking about the many levels at which music is implicated in tourism as an industry. Surveying the roles that music fulfills in tourism markets, they ably describe how music is bent to the tasks of animating marketing campaigns, managing tourist expectations, generating authenticity, calibrating identity, and producing nostalgia and pleasure. The book accomplishes this through a series of short case studies that consider both actual and virtual forms of musical travel—both live performances and digital contexts for engagement—thereby exploring many of the parameters impacting the lives of musicians and communities living in tourist destinations. That said, the book also reproduces one of the lacunae found in much of the literature on tourism—that is, it lacks analyses dealing with the broad range of complexities facing musicians within these contexts. Although the book certainly touches on the lives of the musicians who service the tourism industry, it does so mostly through recourse to an economic lens and, as such, it fails to offer a sustained exploration of the dynamics attendant to their everyday movement between their local communities and the contexts in which they are asked to perform. The authors of the present volume seek to build on Gibson and Connell's excellent work and to do so by focusing more attention on the musicians, their performances, and their communities.

Several other projects offer important ethnographic perspectives on the relationship between music and tourism, serving as models for how to combine a focus on tourism studies with an emphasis on the music and musicians that people these contexts. The first of these is an ethnography penned by Ruth Hellier-Tinoco entitled *Embodying Mexico: Tourism, Nationalism, and Performance* (2011). This book tackles questions of tourism, nationalism, and performance by focusing attention on the long histories of the Dance of the Old Men and the Night of the Dead of Lake Pátzcuaro, both of which have become emblems of national folk life and major tourist attractions within and outside of Mexico. This book offers a richly historical exploration of the shifting meanings and uses of these traditions during the twentieth century and Hellier-Tinoco grounds these explorations in analyses of these performance practices in the contemporary moment. As such, this book illustrates the extent to which attention to music and tourism (and, in this case, dance and dramaturgy) can afford insights into the complex interactions between nationalism, the mobilities of performers (and, in this case, films), and tourists.

Adam Kaul has written an ethnography entitled *Turning the Tune: Traditional Music, Tourism, and Social Change in an Irish Village* (2009) that explores the intersections between traditional music, tourism, and social change in an Irish village. By exploring the ways in which tourism shifts the experience, economics, and performance of traditional music in Doolin, Kaul presents readers with a working model of how music and tourism can be thought together and what they can offer in terms of insights into musicians, their audiences, and their communities. More important for the authors in this volume is the fact that he does so with recourse to an ethnographic lens, developing his perspective through extended interactions with musicians, audiences, tourists, and officials.

Finally, Philip Hayward's *Tide Lines: Music, Tourism, and Cultural Transition in the Whitsunday Islands* (2001) is perhaps the most sustained example of the kind of scholarship that the authors in the present volume are striving for in their own work. Hayward blends careful historiography with sensitive ethnography, creating an engaging and musician-centered account of the encounters between tourists and musicians in this small "place to play" off the coast of Australia. Taking into account the long history of encounter between Aboriginal Australians and Europeans in and around the Whitsunday Islands, he traces the beginnings of the tourist industry in the early twentieth century; the rise of resort tourism and "tropical music" in the middle decades of the century; the maturation of that industry in the later decades of the century; attempts at a reclamation of Aboriginal space in the early twenty-first century; and the social and musical changes that all of these opportunities and challenges effected. Perhaps most significantly for the authors of this volume, Hayward is able to keep the generations of musicians and the multiplicity of musical styles they command central to his analytical lens throughout the book.[5]

MODALITIES OF TOURISM

A second reason for pursuing this project stems from the very real need further to delineate the various modalities or vectors of tourism that confront musicians and their audiences in the contemporary moment. Although many musicians perform in contexts marked by the economic dependencies created through mass tourism, many other forms of tourism exist that are, as often as not, occluded from view. These other vectors through which tourism touches ground in local, musical lives include at least festival tourism; intra-regional tourism; expatriate tourism; internal and heritage tourism; cruise ship tourism; eco-tourism; sex tourism; and spiritual tourism. Each of these vectors has generated a stream of scholarship, and yet, music has not factored centrally in these niche-literatures within tourism studies and leisure studies. A lack of research delineating and unraveling the musical dynamics peculiar to each of these modalities of tourism has contributed to a state of affairs that finds the relationship between music and tourism significantly under-theorized and generally neglected in the literature. An additional area of inquiry requiring a more sustained exploration involves the patterns of circulation that tourism instantiates, and this with regard both to material and immaterial objects. As such, we are interested in thinking about the mobility of instruments and recordings, for instance, as well as in attending to the circulation of songs (even genres) as sonic emblems in their own right.

The circum-Caribbean, as it turns out, plays host to all of these forms of tourism and circulation, offering ample contexts within which to explore the challenging and complex interactions between music and tourism. Walcott's vignette is, once again, instructive here: His description of the homogenized earthly paradise consumed by tourists and marketed in tourist brochures, offering "images of service that cannot distinguish one island from the other" is, on the one hand, an apt one. It is certainly the case that the many discreet locations throughout the Caribbean have consistently mobilized the homogenized "sun, sea, and sand" model that Walcott invokes in order to attract visitors and to build their tourism sectors. However, the realities on the ground afford a far richer and more nuanced picture of just how this "earthly paradise" is consumed and presented, for the dynamics in play on cruise ships, during festivals, or in mass tourism contexts (to name just three possibilities) are quite distinct from each other and offer unique insights into the particular forms of agency that local musicians and their communities bring to bear on their day to day experiences within local tourist economies. The contributors to this volume are committed to moving toward a richly grounded and comparative reading of these discreet and varied encounters, and it is for this reason that this volume foregrounds a consideration of the multiple tourism modalities throughout the region.

MUSIC TOURISTICS

The common thread that holds the essays in this volume together is the concept of "music touristics." Music touristics focuses the scope of our inquiries directly on the dynamics attendant to music prepared for the purpose of performance or sale within tourist networks and, by extension, on the musicians, audiences, communities, and media involved in these networks.[6] Music, when inserted into these networks, is often intended (and interpreted) as a sonic signifier of otherness (as a marker of difference), and consumed as such both locally and translocally. And yet, music touristics, more often than not, addresses itself to contexts within which musical performances are anything but straightforward in this regard. The general messiness and ambivalence inherent in tourist contexts is, in fact, the most salient aspect of what we are here calling music touristics.

How, for instance, do we think through the complexities of a Trinidadian calypso from the 1930s ("Love Alone"), recorded in Nassau during the 1950s and incorporating significant sonic markers of Cuban popular music, and then promoted by an artist self-consciously rejecting the calypso label in favor of a local term—goombay (George Symonette)? The song can, at one level, certainly stand as a marker of otherness for the tourist, but it is also a project that raises interesting questions for the local scene. How does otherness factor for Bahamians here? What possibilities (musical, economic, political, and so on) does this performance of localized otherness open up for them? How are the markers of Cuba and Trinidad interpreted by Bahamians, and to what ends and effect is a term like goombay employed at the local level?

Take another example from the Bahamas: how do we think through the complexities engendered by a Haitian troubadour (André Toussaint), performing a song written by a New Yorker who often wintered in the Bahamas (Alice Simms), complete with lyrics trading on exoticisms (audiences were encouraged to "beat the drum again, drink the rum again, and do what the natives do"), and doing so from a standing gig in a Nassau nightclub? Toussaint wasn't Bahamian and could have attempted to align himself with the tourists while singing this song about exotic others. And yet, he would not have been able to do so unambiguously, and this not least because he also played for local, Bahamian audiences and with local musicians. How did Toussaint negotiate the expectations of these competing audiences and of his fellow musicians? What did Bahamian audiences take away from Haitian performances of exoticized lyrics about Bahamians? What, moreover, are we to make of the fact that the song in question ("Calypso Island") was featured in the repertoires of most Bahamian entertainers of the day as well?[7]

Music touristics affords us a shorthand for addressing these kinds of complexities within tourist contexts, and the contributors to this volume use it to varying degrees in approaching a series of questions, such as the following: As tourism expands into emerging marketplaces, how do musicians adapt themselves to these shifts? How do we think about tourism in places that are not over-determined by the nation or the state—in places like cruise ships and private resort islands, owned and operated by multinational corporations, or in spaces such as music festivals? What can a careful exploration of expatriate tourism help us understand about the complicated relationship between travel and the sounds of nostalgia? And, why is intra-regional tourism so crucial to understanding the movement not only of people but also of music itself?

Music touristics also affords the contributors here a ground from which to approach anew questions that remain pressing throughout the region (and within ethnomusicology)—questions about representation; local, national, and regional identifications; aesthetics; race; gender; ethnicity; and class. As such, this approach offers a lens through which to ask both new and old, but nevertheless important, questions throughout the circum-Caribbean. Finally, music touristics focuses attention on the dynamics attendant to and the consequences growing out of such service relationships. In this way, music touristics provides a means of extending the critical reach and specificity of other important modes of inquiry throughout the region—particularly of travel, mobility, and diaspora. The contributors, moreover, approach the subject of music touristics from several disciplinary backgrounds, including ethnomusicology, anthropology, sociology, and history, making this volume rich in analytical perspectives and broad in methodological scope.

ORGANIZATIONAL PLAN AND CHAPTERS

This book does not treat the circum-Caribbean region comprehensively, whether in terms of locations or language blocs. Some of this was shaped deliberately: Readers will notice, for instance, that we have not included a chapter on Trinidad Carnival in this volume. This decision stems from the fact that a great deal of literature already exists on carnival cultures throughout the circum-Caribbean, some of which explicitly address music and tourism (c.f. Green and Scher 2007). We also decided not to include chapters dealing with diasporic or expatriate communities in metropoles such as New York, Paris, or London, again principally due to the already rather substantial amount of scholarship available on these topics elsewhere (c.f. Allen and Wilcken 1998; Foner 2001; Flores 2000). Conversely, we have attempted to draw the circum-Caribbean meaningfully into the conversation about the region, including chapters on music and tourism in New Orleans, Northeastern Brazil, and Belize.

As with any edited volume, however, the book's final form has also taken shape in certain respects despite our best efforts: For instance, we were not able to include a chapter on Barbados, even though a festival like Crop Over is an obvious and wonderful context within which to think music and tourism together. A chapter on music and tourism in the Dutch Caribbean also proved impossible to include. Similarly, chapters on Costeño music in Colombia and the Caribbean coast of Costa Rica, which would have added significantly to the circum-Caribbean dimensions of this volume, also eluded us. In structuring this volume, then, we hope that the broad themes announced in and through the chapters included here will serve as models for ongoing work in other contexts—perhaps even in places like Bridgetown or Barranquilla.

In this spirit, we have chosen to organize the book around the various modalities of tourism present throughout the region. To make this logic explicit, the book is organized into five parts. Part I, Music, Musicians, and Mass Tourism Markets, includes two chapters that address the dynamics of mass tourism and that develop case studies in Jamaica and Cuba, respectively. Daniel Neely's chapter explores the articulation between Jamaica's mento musicians and the business of tourism. Starting his inquiry in the 1930s, Neely reveals the extent to which many of mento's major stylistic developments have been predicated on marketing strategy. Illustrating how these dynamics have continued to shape the marketing of mento into the contemporary moment, Neely sheds light on the flexibility and strategic flair with which musicians in Jamaica have prepared at various times to be seen by the Other. Vincenzo Perna's essay offers a nuanced comparative reading of Timba musicians and their interactions with tourists since the 1990s and the dynamics attendant to the musicians who cater to the increasing number of tourists arriving to hear Buena Vista Social Club-style performances. By thinking about these two very different contexts for tourist interactions, Perna is able to offer insights into the musicians' careful calibration of their product to expectations and the consequences of tourist desires on musicians and their communities.

Part II, Material and Immaterial Patterns of Circulation and Music Touristics, includes two chapters, each of which deals with the relationship between music and tourism as expressed in and through the circulation of sound souvenirs. The first chapter in this section finds Mimi Sheller exploring the explicit use of music and art in the mid-twentieth century marketing campaigns of the Alcoa Steam Ship Company. Sheller illustrates the degree to which the emblems of the region, combined with the material culture of mail-in LPs and their liner notes, complete with sketches, created both recognition (of exotic tropical locations and sounds) and desire (to experience these locations), thereby filling their cruise ships with passengers who already had a very good idea of what they were expecting to find upon arriving in the Caribbean.

Michael Largey's chapter also explores the material culture of tourism, focusing on the circulation of souvenir recordings within the rara community in Haiti and in the United States. Drawing on extensive fieldwork with rara bands, he suggests that the CDs they produce to elevate their standing locally and to raise money in the form of sales and remittances from abroad also serve to instantiate instances of sonic tourism for members of the community—especially for those residing in the United States. Largey argues that these CDs should be read not as objects of nostalgia, but rather as active interventions in the contemporary moment that afford knowledgeable listeners the chance to participate in rara in spite of distance.

Part III, Sites and Sounds of Intra-regional, Expatriate, and Insider Tourism, comprises three chapters and concerns the rather slippery category of the tourist per se. Matthew Smith's chapter focuses on the long history of travel and musical interaction between Haiti and Jamaica and is a groundbreaking study of interregional travel in the northern Caribbean. Focusing on the long career of Eric Deans and his Orchestra, Smith illustrates the musical exchanges that occurred in the course of his long engagements in Haiti, pointing toward processes of change that shifted the horizon of possibilities against which later generations of Jamaican and Haitian artists calibrated their own performances. A chapter by Sydney Hutchinson details the importance of return migrants and dominicanos ausentes as key tourist demographics in the Dominican Republic. Hutchinson illustrates the disjuncture between official visions of tourism and the more informal economy of actual travelers by focusing on the audiences for traditional merengue típico ensembles and the musicians involved. Oliver Greene's chapter, exploring the role of tourism in the Garifuna Arrival Day celebrations of Belize, analyzes the importance of expatriate visitors to Belize, their complicated relationship to local Garifuna, and the increasing presence of non-Garifuna tourists at this festival of remembrance. Greene illustrates that the growth of tourism in this context is tightly controlled by the local Garifuna themselves, creating conditions conducive to sustainable indigenous tourism.

Part IV, Festivalizing Music Touristics, comprises two chapters and concerns itself specifically with the context of festival tourism within the circum-Caribbean. The first chapter, written by Jerome Camal, is a study focused on the annual Gwoka Festival in Guadeloupe—a festival intended for and marketed to Guadeloupeans themselves. This chapter explores the myriad opportunities and challenges (both political and economic) that emerge in the course of planning and funding an event that eschews tying itself into the official tourism channels already established in Guadeloupe. Camal also explores the extent to which anticolonialism and the Nation are in play in this context. Ruthie Meadows's chapter on the history of tourism in New Orleans argues that the history of music and tourism in New Orleans must be read by conceptualizing New Orleans as an aurally and historically Afro-Caribbean city, in which the audibility of Afro-Caribbean sounds has long been not supplemental to but constitutive of New Orleans's "uniqueness" and, concomitantly, of tourist production, desire, and consumption. Meadows explores this claim by focusing on three intertwined vernacular practices—the second line parades associated with Social Aid and Pleasure Clubs, second line brass bands, and the Mardi Gras Indians—all of which concretized in the late nineteenth century with strong aesthetic, linguistic, and religious ties to Cuba and Haiti. She traces the music touristics of these three practices through the twentieth century, concluding her chapter with a reflection on their role in New Orleans's post-Katrina tourist geography.

The intersections between music and sex tourism as well as music and spiritual tourism occupy the authors of Part V, On the Music Touristics of Sex and Spirituality. Darien Lamen's chapter interrogates the musical negotiations attendant to sex tourism in Fortaleza, Brazil. His careful approach to thinking about the different sites and contexts within which sex tourism occurs (clubs, brothels, and the like) leads him to a nuanced exploration of the sound tracks attendant to these diverse sites, an exploration that generates insights into the use of pan-Caribbean, tropical tropes of leisure in northeastern Brazil. The second chapter, contributed by Katherine Hagedorn, focuses on tourism and *Regla de Ocha (Santería)* in Cuba. Hagedorn, exploring the small but growing number of spiritual seekers traveling to Cuba, convincingly argues for a critical reassessment of the rather one-dimensional way tourists are often caricatured—as unsustainable, insatiable "consumers." Spiritual seekers, traveling to Cuba from the United States, in particular, seem to confound this easy essentialism. By exploring the dynamics attendant to spiritual seekers' involvement in the drumming and singing at the *tambores* of *Regla de Ocha* in Cuba, Hagedorn illustrates the powerful solidarities, both musical and spiritual, that emerge in this context, pointing the way toward the possibility of a sustainable form of music touristics in Cuba.

A final chapter, penned by Jocelyne Guilbault, brings the book full circle, providing some critical reflections on the reasons (disciplinary, political, geographic) why music and tourism have tended to be thought of separately. Her critical interaction with the history of scholarship in the region, moreover, provides the context for Guilbault to offer some final thoughts on new directions in music touristics—to point out that this volume should be read as a beginning rather than an arrival. The chapter closes with a call for more research that actively thinks about the lives of musicians, their products, their audiences, and their communities in relation to the unique demands that arise in the postcolonial contact zones of circum-Caribbean tourism destinations.

I close this introductory chapter by returning, once more, to the epigraph, for, as Walcott concludes: "There is a territory wider than this—wider than the limits made by the map of an island—which is the illimitable sea and what it remembers." This wider territory—the sea and what it remembers—is, I would argue, precisely the geography explored in this volume. By focusing on forms of circulation (what Kamau Brathwaite has called tidalectics); by attending to the travel of musicians, songs, and commodities, and not just of tourists; by addressing the questions surrounding just who is or can be considered a tourist (insiders, outsiders, expatriates, transmigrants, and so on); and by reminding ourselves that there are multiple forms of tourism, each with its own set of opportunities and challenges on the ground, the authors of this volume seek to re-member the invisible musicians and the spaces in which they "play"— to re-sound their contributions to and explore the itineraries they chart as they move within and without these often caricatured and always contested destinations.

NOTES

1. See Mimi Sheller's *Consuming the Caribbean* (2003) and Krista Thompson's *An Eye for the Tropics (2006)* for excellent studies of the long history of tourism in the region.
2. For excellent examples amidst a rapidly growing literature, see Minka and Oaks 2006; Baver and Deutsch Lynch 2006; Gibson and Connell 2005; Scheller and Urry 2004; Sheller 2003; Hanna and Del Casino 2003; Rojeck and Urry 1997; and Patullo 2005.
3. Examples of this literature include Thompson 2006; Strachan 2002; Bruner 2005; Clifford 1997; Gmelch 2003; Taylor 1993; and Crick 1989, among many others.
4. Gordon Waitt and Michelle Duffy's, "Listening and Tourism Studies," (2010); and Kaley Mason's "Sound and Meaning in Aboriginal Tourism," (2004).
5. The excellent contributions made by Heidi Feldman in *Black Rhythms of Peru: Reviving African Musical Heritage in the Black Pacific*; by Timothy Cooley in *Making Music in the Polish Tatras: Tourists, Ethnographers, and Mountain Musicians*; and by Geoffrey Baker in *Buena Vista in the Club* have also significantly influenced this volume's approach to music and tourism.
6. I want to take this opportunity to thank Daniel Neely who, during the planning stages of this project, suggested this formulation as a way of addressing the topic efficiently.
7. For a more extensive discussion of these examples, see Rommen 2011.

REFERENCES

Allen, Ray, and Lois Wilcken, eds. 1998. *Island Sounds in the Global City: Caribbean Popular Music and Identity in New York*. New York: New York Folklore Society Institute for Studies in American Music, Brooklyn College.

Austerlitz, Paul. 1997. *Merengue: Dominican Music and Dominican Identity*. Philadelphia: Temple University Press.

Baker, Geoffrey. 2011. *Buena Vista in the Club: Rap, Reggaetón, and Revolution in Cuba*. Durham, NC: Duke University Press.

Baver, Sherrie, and Barbara Deutsch Lynch, eds. 2006. *Beyond Sun and Sand: Caribbean Environmentalisms*. New Brunswick: Rutgers University Press.

Bruner, Edward M. 2005. *Culture On Tour: Ethnographies of Travel*. Chicago: University of Chicago Press.

Césaire, Aíme. 2000 [1955]. *Discourse on Colonialism*. New York: Monthly Review Press.

Clifford, James. 1997. *Routes: Travel and Translation in the Late Twentieth Century*. Cambridge, MA: Harvard University Press.

Cooley, Timothy. 2005. *Making Music in the Polish Tatras: Tourists, Ethnographers, and Mountain Musicians*. Bloomington: Indiana University Press.

Crick, Malcolm. 1989. "Representations of International Tourism in the Social Sciences: Sun, Sex, Sights, Savings, and Servility." *Annual Review of Anthropology* 18: 307–344.

Dudley, Shannon. 2007. *Music From Behind the Bridge: Steelband Aesthetics and Politics in Trinidad and Tobago*. New York: Oxford University Press.

Feldman, Heidi. 2007. *Rhythms of Black Peru: Reviving African Musical Heritage in the Black Pacific*. Middletown, CT: Wesleyan University Press.

Flores, Juan. 2000. *From Bomba to Hip Hop: Puerto Rican Culture and Latino Identity*. New York: Columbia University Press.

Foner. Nancy, ed. 2001. *Islands in the City: West Indian Migration to New York*. Berkeley: University of California Press.

Gibson, Chris, and John Connell, eds. 2005. *Music and Tourism: On the Road Again*. Buffalo, NY: Channel View.

Gmelch, George. 2003. *Behind the Smile: The Working Lives of Caribbean Tourism*. Bloomington: Indiana University Press.

Green, Garth L., and Philip W. Scher. 2007. *Trinidad Carnival: The Cultural Politics of a Transnational Festival*. Philadelphia: Temple University Press.

Guilbault, Jocelyne. 1993. *Zouk: World Music in the West Indies*. Chicago: University of Chicago Press.

——. 2007. *Governing Sound: The Cultural Politics in Trinidad's Carnival Musics*. Chicago: University of Chicago Press.

Hanna, Stephen, and Vincent Del Casino, Jr., eds. 2003. *Mapping Tourism*. Minneapolis: University of Minnesota Press.

Hayward, Philip. 2001. *Tide Lines: Music, Tourism, and Cultural Transition in the Whitsunday Islands*. Lismore, NSW: Music Archive for the Pacific Press, Southern Cross University.

Hellier-Tinoco, Ruth. 2011. *Embodying Mexico: Tourism, Nationalism, and Performance*. New York: Oxford University Press.

Kaul, Adam. 2009. *Turning the Tune: Traditional Music, Tourism, and Social Change in an Irish Village*. New York: Berghahn Books. 978 – 08574 58087

Lewin, Olive, and Adrienne Kaeppler, eds. 1988. *Come Mek Me Hol' Yu Han'*. Jamaica: Jamaica Memory Bank.

Mason, Kaley. 2004. "Sound and Meaning in Aboriginal Tourism." In *Annals of Tourism Research* 31(4): 837–854.

Moore, Robin. 2006. *Music and Revolution: Cultural Change in Socialist Cuba*. Berkeley: University of California Press.

Minca, Claudio, and Tim Oakes, eds. 2006. *Travels in Paradox: Remapping Tourism*. New York: Rowman and Littlefield.

Patullo, Polly. 2005. *Last Resorts: The Cost of Tourism in the Caribbean*. 2nd edition. New York: Monthly Review Press.

Rojeck, Chris, and John Urry, eds. 1997. *Touring Cultures: Transformations of Travel and Theory*. New York: Routledge.

Rommen, Timothy. 2011. *Funky Nassau: Roots, Routes, and Representation in Bahamian Popular Music*. Berkeley: University of California Press.

Sheller, Mimi. 2003. *Consuming the Caribbean: From Arawaks to Zombies*. New York: Routledge.

Sheller, Mimi, and John Urry. 2004. *Tourism Mobilities: Places to Play, Places in Play*. New York: Routledge.

Strachan, Ian Gregory. 2002. *Paradise and Plantation: Tourism and Culture in the Anglophone Caribbean*. Charlottesville: University of Virginia Press.

Taylor, Frank. 1993. *To Hell With Paradise; A History of the Jamaican Tourist Industry*. Pittsburgh, PA: University of Pittsburgh Press.

Thompson, Krista. 2006. *An Eye for the Tropics: Tourism, Photography, and Framing the Caribbean Picturesque*. Durham, NC: Duke University Press.

Waitt, Gordon, and Michelle Duffy. 2010. "Listening and Tourism Studies." *Annals of Tourism Research* 37(2): 457–477.

Walcott, Derek. 1992. *The Antilles: Fragments of Epic Memory, the Nobel Lecture*. New York: Farrar, Straus and Giroux.

PART I

Music, Musicians, and the Mass Tourism Market

Modern Mento

The Emergence of Native Music in Jamaica Tourism

DANIEL T. NEELY ■

Much of the fascination which the Caribbean and Latin America hold for the American and European tourist, lies in the entertainment, the age-old customs or rituals, and to a greater extent in the slightly exotic neo-primitive qualities found in the music and dances of the islands.

Thus, much of Havana's fame was built on the overnight success that greeted the introduction of the Rhumba into American ballroom, the French Riviera, and continental café society. Brazil took on a more potent lure with the Samba.

Haiti, traditionally thought the home of Voodoo and Zombies, had a difficult task unshackling the impression that there one found 'walking dead' parading the streets by day, and at night the only entertainment to be had was pagan rituals. Throughout other Latin countries, the unaccustomed sights and uninhibited revelry of "Carnival Time" has been a means of attracting millions of Americans.

Trinidad, within recent years, has ditched the application "Home of the Hummingbird" for "Home of the Calypso," and the amazing popularity with which this new-found musical specie swept the North American continent has created a salutary effect on the other West Indian islands awaking them to the realization that their folk music and folk lore was not only an important part of their culture, but a significant asset to the entertainment of visitors to their shores.

—"Music Comes Out Happy When We Smile,"
MoBay Times, 1949.

Mento is one of Jamaica's great social dance musics. It's also the name of a song type, a specific rhythm, a dance style, a dance event, and the generic local name for small, rustic community-based bands. Although now widely distributed throughout Jamaica, such bands have only been known to tourism since the 1930s, when they first started to appear in various iterations in nightclub floor shows and resort area beaches. Since then, they have been one of Jamaica's identifying sounds, a regular feature in tourism marketing, and an important articulation point between tourists and the people of Jamaica.

Hidden behind the smile and the breezy tropical demeanor that often characterizes those who play mento is a complex history of strategic adaptation shaped by foreign expectation in which the circulation and strategic mobilization of inter- and intra-regional sounds plays a prominent role in creating a sense of place. Kenneth Bilby's (1985) work, for example, has stressed how common such circulations are in the Caribbean. In describing the deep influence geography, tourism, and political history have had on Bahamian musical life, Timothy Rommen has looked at how such circulations have affected the trajectories of rake-n-scrape music (Rommen 2009, 161). In Cuba, Robin Moore (1997) has explored how they have led to musical adaptations with class associations and thus part of the country's vexed national narrative. Herbie Miller's (2007) work on jazz in the region shows its influence on the creation of cultural sensibilities, while Guilbault (2001) has looked at its articulations with world music marketing. In terms of material circulations, Dennis Howard's work on jukeboxes in Jamaica (2007) sheds direct light on where sound took root, whereas Michael Eldridge (2002), looks at this process in reverse, exploring calypso's relationship to American pop culture in the 1930s.

However, in tourism—and especially Jamaica tourism—sound has historically been part of a marketing strategy in which style and heritage are treated fungibly and mobilized as necessary to create a continually changing sense of place. Rommen (2009; see also 2011) has argued that "place" is the active point of engagement that allows one to think of location as itinerary rather than bounded site. With this in mind, the strategic role marketing plays in determining itinerary becomes much clearer and suggests the value sound has in reinventing "space" as required. Despite the massive amount of energy that's been devoted to understanding and refining how Jamaica's tourism product is marketed, little attention has been given over to exploring how marketing has driven stylistic change. In this chapter, then, I examine music's role in early Jamaica tourism, paying particular attention to the period 1934–1955, a time when Jamaica's importance as a vacation destination increased and when primitivist African-influenced indigenous practices and exotic foreign styles first became features of nightclub entertainment. I will argue that a marketing strategy that capitalized on how music circulated regionally played a major role in the construction of a marketable Jamaican identity, and that this strategy not only was a primary determinant of local musical style with respect to mento music, it had a longstanding effect on Jamaican musical identity.

THE JOLLY BOYS: A CONTEMPORARY CASE

The Jolly Boys are a well-known and currently active group whose relatively accessible history and ready successes allows easy insight into tourism's traditional marketing approach. A stalwart of Port Antonio's tourist entertainment, the group has existed in various iterations for more than fifty years and weathered the trade's many changes. Led by banjo player and guitarist Moses Deans until his passing in 1998, the group began in the early 1950s as the Navy Island Swamp Boys and gained early notoriety playing for Errol Flynn's parties aboard his yacht, the *Zaca*.

Band lore holds that Flynn, sometimes referred to as "Jamaica's greatest tourist," renamed the group the Jolly Boys around 1955 because it reflected the good feelings he had when he heard them play. Since then, the Jolly Boys have become a tourist favorite and have weathered the industry's many changes. They've performed at every local hotel and over the years have played for tens of thousands of tourists. Further, they have worked with the numerous different development and tourism organizations in the area that help keep Port Antonio as one of the world's finest vacation destinations, and they have built a hard earned and richly deserved reputation of excellence in their community.

Over the course of the group's existence, the Jolly Boys's music has been framed in at least three ways. Early photos of the band reveal that they cloaked themselves in the trappings of the pan-Caribbean calypso craze that informed so much of tourism's marketing in the late 1950s and 1960s. Current Jolly Boys singer Albert Minott recounts those days of performing in floor shows as part of a dance troupe, when his act was to wear nothing more than white skeleton body paint, a breadfruit leaf, and a pair of swim trunks, and to swallow fiery, kerosene dipped sticks while the Jolly Boys band played and sang. Images like these resonated with tourists and locals alike and helped buttress the group's local identity as a "calypso band" into the 1990s (*Daily Gleaner* 1990).

In 1988, American singer, songwriter, and producer Jules Shear was on vacation at Port Antonio's Trident Hotel and saw the group perform. The Jolly Boys' dynamic performance inspired him to produce a studio album, *Pop "N" Mento*, the first of four released between 1989 and 1997 that reframed the group's musical identity. In *Pop "N" Mento's* liner notes, the Jolly Boys's music is presented in the language of tourism. We learn that they're from "one of the most beautiful spots on Earth" that provides "nothing but spotless white sand, cloudless blue sky and tropical sunshine hot enough to make your troubles fade and your skin glow." There, our ears will be "teased" by familiar syncopated melodies that include "a hint of reggae, a touch of calypso, a vaguely African rhythm, the words of a British sea chanty and a Latin drum beat." But we are also told that this is *mento* music and, rather than be mired in the north coast's common practice, that the Jolly Boys "mix and match the traditions of mento's past with the sounds of today to create music that will sound as fresh in a hundred years as it does right now" (Jolly Boys 1989).

These four albums came out as the world music phenomenon was cresting. The marketing emphasis on the word mento was an indigenizing move, one that authenticated the encounter between consumers and Jamaican music's "real" roots and influenced the way people from abroad got to know them. Becoming a "mento band" helped the Jolly Boys. It not only raised their profile with the Jamaica Tourist Board (which helped the band facilitate overseas publicity trips) but it also led to a measure of international success few mento bands will ever know, including several tours, regular profiles in trade magazines, and even a feature in *The Mighty Quinn*, a Hollywood film starring Denzel Washington.

Today, the Jolly Boys are the house band at Geejam, a luxury resort and recording studio based in the Portland Parish district of San San. Geejam is managed and co-owned by Jon Baker, a savvy ex–music industry executive who, inspired by current lead singer Albert Minott's powerful stage personality, suggested the band record an album of rock, new wave and country covers. Baker and Geejam's in-house producer Dale "Dr. Dizzle" Virgo came up with the idea of using the album to introduce a "modern mento" concept, one in which a more contemporary musical aesthetic would supplement the music's traditionally rustic sound. Shortly after work started, Baker and Virgo contacted me to play banjo, act as the project's musical director, and work with the band to hone their live show.

This work resulted in an album called *Great Expectation* (Jolly Boys 2010), as well as a sophisticated marketing strategy that purported not only to reinvent the band but the genre itself. "Featuring vocalist Albert Minott's limitless charisma and extraordinary originality," our press copy read, "*Great Expectation* breathes powerful creative life into a carefully selected collection of rock classics and slams the tradition's creative doors open to a new generation of fans." This modern mento sound that Baker, Virgo, the Jolly Boys, and I developed drew heavily on modern studio techniques and the musical vocabularies of rock and dance-hall music. It was intended to appeal to a cosmopolitan (and not necessarily Jamaican) musical sensibility.

Marketed this time as a pop act and tied to the Geejam brand, the Jolly Boys relaunched in dramatic fashion. *Great Expectation* peaked on the BBC's indie charts at no. 5 and its national album chart at no. 48. The band itself was profiled in the UK's *Guardian* and *Telegraph* newspapers, *MOJO* magazine, the BBC Online, and Sky News, and was featured on the *Jools Holland Show*, ITV, and in several major European pop festivals. Baker was also careful to partner with the Jamaica Tourist Board, apprising them of the Jolly Boys's "modern" activities. As a result, the JTB's *Visit Jamaica* brand was included in the CD's packaging, and the group appeared in some of *Visit Jamaica's* collateral marketing pieces and web spaces. *Great Expectation* was a marketing success not only for the group itself, but for Geejam and Jamaica tourism.

All of this seems very unremarkable until one realizes that mento has been a recognizable genre within Jamaican music since the late nineteenth century. Why would the group ever need to identify as a calypso band, or need to be reintroduced as a mento act? It raises the further question, when did local music become a feature in Jamaica tourism, and more specifically, what role did musicians familiar with mento music have in determining what Jamaica should sound like to outsiders?

MUSIC AND EARLY TOURISM

Frank Fonda Taylor identified the Jamaica International Exhibition of 1891 as "the first intensive effort to promote tourism in the island" (Taylor 1993, 56). The organizers' primary interest was economic: it was hoped that the exhibition would alert people in Jamaica to the value of their own resources while simultaneously attracting outsiders to Jamaica's industrial potential. The secondary interest, however, was to promote Jamaica's climate as a vacation destination and heath spa. The exhibition brought people to Jamaica who would learn about and spread word of its climate and, to accommodate these people, the first hotels were built.

An examination of newspaper advertisements from that year reveals a large number of publicly advertised musical performances to commemorate the exhibition, which gives us an indication of how Jamaicans wished their country to be represented in sound to visitors (*Daily Gleaner* 1891). For example, at the exhibition's opening, a local choir sang the *Hundredth Psalm* accompanied by the West Indian Regiment band for Prince George of Wales (Taylor 1993, 64). Several pieces of souvenir sheet music were published in Jamaica for the occasion, including *Xaymaca Waltz, Jamaican Sketches*, and *Mountain Pride,* all of which embraced a romantic pastorality resonant with continental musical tastes, while one piece, *La Belle Jamaique, Valse, par Crèole,* was prepared especially for the exhibition's opening and was both stylistically akin to a Souza brass band arrangement and reminiscent of the kind of continental dance sequences one would expect from the time.

As Jamaican tourism began to grow in subsequent years, so too did the demand for an entertainment style appropriate to a traveling, upper class, and largely white Victorian clientele. Music was not common to every hotel, but some used it to attract Jamaica's elite and connect them with well-to-do visitors. In her book *Jamaica As It Is, 1903*, for example, Bessie Pullen-Burry wrote that the music at Kingston's Constant Spring Hotel was "supplied by . . . four musicians who are engaged to play every afternoon in the hotel drawing-room, a pianist, a violincello player, and two violinists," and noted that "some pretty frocks were worn, many of the girls appearing in delicate muslin gowns, evidently locally made, but quite adequate to the occasion" (Pullen-Burry, 60). Herbert DeLisser also described this sort of weekly public dance, first in 1910:

There are all sorts of dances. In the tourist season, which in Jamaica lasts from January to April, the big hotels give balls to which hundreds of fashionable folks are invited. At these balls one meets a representative crowd of people belonging to the upper classes of Jamaica society, and the gathering is, I think, one of the prettiest things Jamaica has to show. (107)

And again in 1913:

To return to the hotels, it may be said that they serve a double function: the first, naturally, is to cater for guests, and this they do in a manner creditable to them; the other function is the organizing of public dances, and in this they also succeed admirably. Balls are frequently given by them, and at some of these you will find hundreds of handsomely dressed people—Jamaica's best—and will get some idea of what a social function in the West Indies is like. On the whole, there is nothing quite so lively in the way of public entertainment as the dances arranged by these hotels, and their foreign guests seem to enjoy them thoroughly. They afford the average visitor the only chance he will have of meeting at close quarters the better class of Jamaicans. (76)

Much of this moment's hotel-based music was performed by musicians brought in from abroad, and period advertisements suggest they played modern light classical fare and popular ballroom dance music, such as mazurkas, schottisches, waltzes, and the like.[1]

Further, it appears that tourists were actively dissuaded from searching down "native" amusements outside class-appropriate contexts. For example, period travel writer John Henderson (1906, 55–60) described being part of a British touring group in Kingston that visited a "dignity dance," a social gathering where white and light-skinned men could go and, for a fee, dance with Jamaican women who had aspirations to whiteness and claimed high-class status. There, Henderson described the dancing he witnessed as "something like the visiting and Grand Chain in our lancers" and neither "fascinating or unique," adding that "a similar scene could be witnessed in any European ballroom." The music for this revelry, he noted, was "delivered in European concert fashion."

Dissatisfied with the Jamaican simulacra of European amusement that he encountered at the dance, he mentions asking "a supercilious half-breed, who wore an evening suit and a crimson necktie where [they] could hear some native singing."

> "If," said he, "you refer to the songs of the negroes, I can only indicate the low rum shops, and even there it is not permitted.
> Evidently his opinion of the musical abilities of the black man was not a high one. (59)

Henderson's party was not dissuaded and nevertheless "journeyed to the rum shops" where they "put [their] heads in the doors of many [and] never heard native music." This group seems to have been unusually intrepid as tourists go. Indeed, Henderson's complaints that Kingston lacked any sort of theatrical amusement and that its deserted streets left it a "cold and deathly place at night," suggests a virtually nonexistent market for tourist entertainment (Henderson 1906, 55–60).

NATIVE BELIEFS AND PRIMITIVE RHYTHMS: TOURISM'S FIRST ENCOUNTERS WITH JAMAICA'S FOLKLORE AND CUSTOMS

While the image of Jamaica presented to outsiders changed little in the first decade of Jamaica's tourism industry, several publications emerged shortly after the exhibition ended that introduced Jamaica's mostly white, monied tourists to the beliefs and customs of its African-descended population. One important early example was Hesketh J. Bell's *Obeah: Witchcraft in the West Indies* (1893), a book that explored and examined an African-derived practice of spiritual power in the Caribbean. The book was based largely in the author's experience in Grenada (not Jamaica), and in it, Bell (who had worked for several years in the British Colonial Service of the West Indies) presented obeah as a retiring practice of witchcraft, sorcery, and fetishism through a series of illustrative vignettes as a way of "[altering] some of the ideas prevalent 'at home' about the climate and state of the West Indies, and to induce lovers of travel and of beautiful scenery to visit these charming colonies, and so contribute to their prosperity" (Introduction, n.p.).

Obeah turned out to be a very popular volume that went through several printings. First published in London in 1889, period newspapers show that it was not only available in Europe throughout the 1890s to potential travelers, but in Jamaica as well, where visitors could find it with relative ease. Its popularity and availability in both contexts doubtlessly went a long way in apprising a generation of travelers to obeah's existence.

The first such book with a concentration on music was Walter Jekyll's 1907 publication, *Jamaica Song and Story*. Born in Surry in 1849, Jekyll was an English nobleman who received a master of arts degree from Cambridge. Upon graduating he entered the Episcopal ministry and apostatized around 1880, when he found his philosophical beliefs (influenced by Kant, Hegel, Nietzsche, and especially Schopenhauer) had overtaken his spiritual beliefs. After his mother died in 1895, he moved to Jamaica to relieve his asthma and settled in Mavis Bank, a community in Jamaica's Blue Mountains. In Mavis Bank, he wrote and conducted music research, culminating in *Jamaica Song and Story*, a publication that contains 144 digging, ring, and dance melodies, as well as 51 Anancy stories, many of which include short tunes. It was a landmark publication in the study of Jamaican traditional music and lore.

Reviewers wrote enthusiastically about the book's folkloric content. The *Daily Gleaner's* review correctly stated it would be *the* work consulted in the future for knowledge about Jamaica lore (*Daily Gleaner* 1907). However, in the context of tourism, *Jamaica Song and Story* had little effect—it presented Jamaican music and lore in mediated fashion, largely stripped of meaningful context, and it does not seem to have been very popular outside Jamaica.

Neither of these books advocated bringing tourists into direct contact with folk musicians or spiritual workers. However both—and I think especially Jekyll's—inspired local intellectuals to explore Jamaica's beliefs and customs in more depth. One of the most notable of these was Astley Clerk, a middle class poly-aesthete and music store owner well known for his interest in philately, poetry, and bird watching. Clerk believed in the value of local expression and was likely the first native-born Jamaican not only to attempt to identify systematically African elements in local music but also to encourage their appreciation. Clerk felt that music was not simply a crucial aspect of a Jamaican national culture, but that its so-called peasant music (which included mento) could and should be elevated to the level of fine art—that it was something of value to be presented to outsiders, including tourists.

Clerk owned a music store in Kingston and did his part to encourage amateur performance but, more importantly, from as early as 1913 until his death in 1944, Clerk lectured on the music and musical instruments of vernacular Jamaica. His research was largely historical: he kept notebooks in which he collected and analyzed any and all literary references to Jamaican music, and he

lectured around Kingston from these books. However, he supported his historical findings at these lectures with performances by invited local musicians of
different social strata. These lectures were intended not only to demonstrate the
cultural richness of the largely black lower classes, but legitimate them by fostering the idea that Jamaicans could produce something of value that the upper
classes could in turn embrace as an outward symbol of Jamaica.

Clerk applied his forward-looking ideas to music publication and was
responsible for introducing an early craze for "Jamaican" dance music in hotels,
with his *Mongoose Fox Trot* (1921), a dance piece based on the very well-known
mento song "Sly [or "Slide"] Mongoose." Its popularity—particularly at the
fashionable Constant Spring Hotel's society dances—was such that an anonymous letter to the editor of the *Daily Gleaner* publicly congratulated the hotel,
saying "at last some right appreciation of the popular native music is being
shown" (*Daily Gleaner* 1921).

Although the *Mongoose Fox Trot's* popularity was relatively short-lived,
Clerk's aggressive support of Jamaica's indigenous cultural forms continued
well afterward. In addition to his lecturing, he staged a popular concert series,
he was the Second Vice President of the Poetry League at its formation in 1924,
and he took an active role in its annual competitions. (In that capacity he was
an ardent supporter of poets who wrote in patois, including Claude McKay and
Una Marson, and he had planned to write Jamaican dialect dictionary with
Louise Bennett.) Because his was Kingston's biggest music store at the time,
Clerk not only had an active voice (although not an administrative role) in the
biennial music competitions (referred to as "festivals") started in 1929 by the
Musical Society of Jamaica, but he also used the competitions as a platform
to agitate for the increased recognition and cultivation of local folk music.[2]
For example, on the occasion of planned visits from the Dukes of Kent and
Gloucester in 1935, Clerk wrote the following to the *Jamaica Times* newspaper:

> I would be so bold as to say that our Royal visitors, who are expected
> soon, might well be interested to hear a short selection of our folk songs
> which so well reflect the traditions and history of our people. It might
> even be possible to prepare souvenir copies of the music which they could
> graciously be asked to accept. If our Royal guests were to show an interest
> in these folk songs our own people might quit looking down on them as
> something of which they need be ashamed.
>
> Again, one of the composition classes in the forthcoming Festival might
> be to write a piano arrangement or an orchestral arrangement of one of
> the folk songs. Why not? Last year there was a class for folk dancing in
> the syllabus yet it did not seem to occur to anyone that there are Jamaican
> folk dances.

Then, an effort might be made to have some of them published so as to make them readily available both to local people and to tourists. (Clerk 1935; c.f. *Jamaica Times* 1934)

Clerk was one of several who saw value in what Jamaica had to offer, and by the early-1930s, local support for the idea that Jamaican music and customs could be the basis for touristic presentation was clearly growing.[3] Tourist demand was increasing as well. In his 1933 book, for example, former Jamaican governor Sydney Olivier complained about the preoccupation of "the tourists and journalists who on their visits to Jamaica to-day conceive the Maroons and Obeah to be chief topics of social interest in the Island."[4] The following year, a piece on Jamaica's future as a tourist resort in the *Jamaica Times* seemed to take into account this changing tourist expectation:

> ...native dances or other functions with appropriate settings, would fill a breach and also provide opportunities for local entertainers. Other ideas could be worked up to meet the demand for night life very well, at the same time giving that "national atmosphere" until we can provide the cabarets and other attractions which some people declare are needed. (Lindsay 1934)

This would become a productive direction, as the dearth of locally derived entertainment for the tourist market risked Jamaica's long-term future in West Indies tourism and threatened to put it at a competitive disadvantage.

THE ULTRA-MODERN: RUMBA, VOODOO AND FLOOR SHOW TOURIST ENTERTAINMENT

Between 1929 and 1935, Jamaica tourism more than doubled, from 18,613 arrivals to 49,800. The colony's natural beauty and its proximity to the United States made an attractive destination for budget-minded tourists looking for a fulfilling tropical vacation. The rise of fascism in Europe and the 1933 overthrow of Cuban President Gerardo Machado certainly helped intensify Jamaica's appeal among American and European tourists (Taylor 1993, 144–145), but these events also happened to coincide with the 1933 passage of the Twenty-first Amendment repealing Prohibition in the United States. In this period, entertainment became a much more important means for private entrepreneurs to engage with the volatile tourist market and, as a result, the nature of tourist entertainment changed. No longer was the ideal to mimic continental style—rather, the modern expectation was that entertainments should reflect local styles and customs. The more primitive, it seemed, the better.

In the late 1920s, musical demand during the tourist season was robust, especially at hotels or clubs which held nightly dances that featured either local musicians or cruise ship orchestras (in some cases, both). And, although very popular with Kingstonian revelers and tourists alike, these dances had a reputation for ending early. With increased tourism in the early 1930s, demand for late night cabaret entertainment increased. Some older establishments, like Kingston's Bournemouth Club, adapted their entertainment offerings to a limited degree, but new venues, like the Silver Slipper nightclub (which opened on May 23, 1931), represented a major change in direction.

Owned by Victor Lindo, the Silver Slipper was named after the notorious New York City nightclub and was set next door to another of Lindo's establishments, the Tiger Bar, a drinking venue that received regular media attention for its late night, alcohol-fueled altercations. The upscale Silver Slipper would be open "all day and night for the convenience of its members" (*Daily Gleaner* 1931a) and together with the Tiger Bar, it developed a tantalizing notoriety that paralleled that of its American namesake.

The Silver Slipper had a reputation for presenting quality entertainment and appears to have been among the first to primarily feature jazz-oriented dance music. It was also the first to flirt with presenting rumba, a fusion of Afro-Cuban (including *son,* the similarly named *rumba, guaracha, and pregon*) and foreign influences (including vaudeville, ragtime, and early jazz) that enjoyed international prominence. In the late 1920s, rumba had become synonymous with fashionable entertainment the world over. Its foreign renown far exceeded that of marginally similar dance musics in Jamaica, like mento and shey shay (Moore 1977, 105–6) and, although audiences in Jamaica would have had some familiarity with rumba through commercial recordings (for example, the *Peanut Vendor* "rumba fox trot" by Don Azpiazu and his Havana Casino Orchestra, was available there as early as 1931), the music was largely stigmatized, as we see in this 1933 editorial pleading for the music's acceptance among Jamaica's middle and upper classes:

> Don't be afraid of the Rumba . . . you can't keep your feet still when you listen to the new Rumbas. They just pick you up and carry you round the floor.
> This dance is liked by those who know it and by those who don't. Whether you shuffle along happily or do the right steps, the music is cheery enough to make you sorry when the dance is over. (F.N. 1933)

Rumba's international stature and success elsewhere in Caribbean tourism was hard to dismiss. Its actual role in places like the Silver Slipper was small, but had the potential for growth.

It was not until 1934 that Cuba's signature sound first began to make substantial inroads into Jamaica with the *Jamaica and Empire Trade Exhibition and
Fair*. Organized by a small group of Jamaican entrepreneurs in 1933, it was
one of the colony's largest organizational efforts ever undertaken. Its intention
echoed that of the 1891 *Jamaica International Exhibition* in that its aim was
to develop "native trade" by "show(ing) the world what we [Jamaica] can produce" (*Daily Gleaner* 1933a). In preparation, organizers toured the country to
promote the fair and to generate broad support for its goals, presenting tourism
as a vehicle for industrial growth. At one such event, I. G. Aarons, one of the
exhibition's touring directors, explained that they "expect to have a good lot of
tourists calling at the Exhibition, [and] are not aiming so much on their paying
us a mere visit; but it is the impression that will be made in their minds and
the possibility of investing capital in this island that we feel so very particular
about" (*Daily Gleaner* 1933b).

The fair, which took place between February and March 1934, attracted
thousands of visitors and was a success for tourism and a terrific showcase for
local industry. However, with the repeal of Prohibition in the United States,
one industry group—the rum producers—received a disproportionate amount
of advance attention. Foreign investors recognized the industry's huge potential, but realized it needed more development. One critique was that Jamaican
rum and its marketing and presentation were deficient and that better care and
attention to it would not only be good for the rum business, but for tourism as
well. On the subject, one US-based investor wrote the following:

> It seems to me this is a good opportunity for Jamaica making a bold bid
> to capture the tourist trade, particularly in view that the tourists are not
> going now to Cuba as a consequence of the unrest there. It seems to me
> that a little more interest should be paid to the tourist trade by Jamaica.
> There should be an effort to get things typical of the Colony to offer tour-
> ists. They want to see things of native colour and the typical customs of the
> people. I am sure that if that is done this year you will get a lot of people
> next year for the season for it must be remembered that each tourist that
> comes here will be a potential advertiser of the Colony.—Manuel Noriega
> (*Daily Gleaner* 1934a)

The idea of showcasing "local color" was already a concern with liquor retail-
ers and festival organizers and fit well with the Fair's intended purpose. Rather
than finding Jamaican performers, however, the organizers instead featured a
Cuban son band, doubtless a concession to modern taste, and proudly proclaimed they had lived up to the "Rumba Age" because "for the first time [in
Jamaica], real Cuban Rumba music will be played: real Cuban Rumba songs

will be rendered by a real Cuban Rumba band."[5] In a very real sense, the band's feature at the *Jamaica and Empire Trade Exhibition and Fair* cultivated the association between music, rum, and industries like tourism in Jamaica.

But rumba's identification with Jamaica was solidified in the 1934 season in a breakthrough performance that ran concurrent to the *Jamaica and Empire Trade Exhibition and Fair* called *Jamaican Burro*.[6] Held in the John Crown Mountain district of Portland Parish, it comprised an exoticized, folklore-driven variety floor show featuring performers from the John Crown area along with the visiting Cuban rumba band. Ultimately, *Jamaican Burro* was styled to remind viewers not simply of the West Indies, but of "primitive Africa." Presented at the behest of several travel businesses that ran trips throughout the Caribbean, it appears to have been the first show in Jamaica to present an invented "native" Caribbean identity strictly for tourist consumption. One commentator wrote the following upon seeing it:

> I delved into the Jamaica of 1700 and saw moving pictures of the days of yore when tribal rites were featured in the heart of Jamaica's jungle country. I saw enacted shifting scenes from real Baile, Voodoo and Mento rhythm, pocomania and Tribal Ackee suppers and even Santiago Rumba.
>
> There was no silver screen, no film projection. It was a motion picture in the flesh, a relic of the days when Captain Kidd, Sir Henry Morgan and Blackbeard made the island their rendezvous.
>
> [. . .]
>
> It is at the request of the Cruise Directors of the Kungholm, the Dutchess of Bedford, and others of the tourist liners that these shows are tried out as they say that American visitors want to see some of the real rhythm of the people of Jamaica.
>
> A Jamaican who has spent some years abroad in Cuba, Haiti and the United States, with the cooperation of an Englishman and a Santiago rumba dancer is producing these shows.
>
> Many of the various tourist agencies in the United States, Canada and Europe have been longing for ideas to inspire tourists to come to Jamaica.
>
> When the come to the West Indies, care free tourists say they are filled with the tropical air of buccaneers and the tales of voodoo and obeah, a mixture of magic and superstition of the bygone days of these Colonies and want to see these things enacted in these days which the young describe as ultra-modern. (*Daily Gleaner* 1934b)

"Hundreds" of tourists watched this so-called ultra-modern spectacle, and its success inspired the producers to present it to local audiences less than a week later. "Don't expect spectacular costumes" the *Daily Gleaner* (1934d) article advised, "and bring the ladies at their own risk."

The 1934 tourist season became a watershed moment for tourism and also made not just rumba but any adaptable local "exotic" form marketable and a potential portal for performers because it resembled Jamaican forms (like mento) that already existed. What followed were substantial changes to tourist entertainment for the 1935 season, most notably marked by the opening of two nightclubs that marketed "native" floor shows to white tourists. The first club was the Glass Bucket, which opened on December 22, 1934. Promising "something new in the West Indies," its manager Joe Abner was intent on providing upper-class white Jamaicans and tourists alike with a cosmopolitan nightclub experience, and he consequently put a great deal of effort into thinking through his entertainment strategy. Comprised of a mix of foreign and local cabaret performers, the Glass Bucket's band was modeled after the American big band the Dorsey Brothers, and it played contemporary standards and jazz-based arrangements of local mento music, when a primitivist turn was required. To celebrate the club's opening, Abner featured thirteen local vaudeville artists, the Dan Williams Rhythm Raiders dance orchestra, and a "coolie dance" with "local Indians." (*Daily Gleaner* 1934f) By all accounts, it was an impressive gala opening. An American living in Jamaica, Abner had a keen understanding of tourist expectation. His staff included an American chef who served American foods like hot dogs, hamburgers, and ice cream to suit the tastes of tourists who weren't ready for Jamaican food and Jamaicans who wanted a taste of foreign fare. He brought performers over from the United States for two or three week engagements to work with the local artists and performers, and presented these performers between native-themed floor shows.

Notably, however, Abner was an employee of the United Fruit Company, an enterprise Lorenzo D. Baker founded in 1899, which not only was an early player in Jamaica tourism, but which also upon its founding quickly and successfully integrated all aspects of tourism, including transport, lodging, and catering (Taylor 1993, 46). So, with the opening of the Glass Bucket, the United Fruit Company could bring tourists to Jamaica, house them at the Myrtle Bank Hotel (which the UFC acquired in 1918) and entertain them in a largely closed system. This not only helped make the Glass Bucket a dominant force in tourist entertainment for decades, it also made its entertainment style a model for other nightclub entrepreneurs, like Lindo at the Silver Slipper, who borrowed Abner's approach.

The Glass Bucket also seems to have been the early model for resort-based entertainment, especially as it developed along Jamaica's north coast. In addition to tourists, the Glass Bucket attracted people from Kingston's wealthy merchant class, including several who would later become important players in tourism, notably Abe Issa, who in 1948 opened Jamaica's first year-round resort, the Tower Isle Hotel, in Ocho Rios, and who later pioneered the "all-inclusive" concept with Couples Resort; Stuart Sharpe, who ran guided tours of Kingston and Montego Bay in the 1930s, managed several prominent hotels in the 1940s and 1950s, including the Tower Isle, the Silver Seas, and the Falcondip, and who ultimately became Jamaica's Director of Tourism in 1967; and Stanley Motta, a businessman who owned department stores, was the director of Jamaica's Chamber of Commerce from 1947–74, was a board member of the Jamaica Tourist Board in the mid-1950s, and who founded Jamaica's first commercial record label (discussed later) which made records for hotels in Kingston, Montego Bay, and Ocho Rios. Throughout their careers, these individuals not only emphasized local entertainment's place in Jamaica's tourism product, but each seems to have followed Abner's pioneering tourist entertainment model in whatever managerial context they oversaw.[7]

The other new venue that year was the Sugar Cane Nightclub, which opened fairly late in the season, on May 18, 1935. It was the first major club to solely feature exotic (but like the Glass Bucket, largely jazz-based) entertainment as a matter of policy. Their early advertising boasted that they could "attract residents and tourists alike" with "voodoo" and "shey shay" dancing, and boldly stated "they have got the material with which to do it" (*Daily Gleaner* 1935; "shey shay" is an archaic Jamaican music and dance form related to mento). Because the Sugar Cane Nightclub quickly became the Glass Bucket's primary competition, it was not long before Abner adjusted his floor show marketing strategy to feature more folklore-inspired fare such as "duppy dances," "pocomania," "mento dances," and "shey shays."

The success of these clubs not only inspired others in Kingston (such as T. E. Legore, the manager of Rousseau Casino), but also led to expansion into Montego Bay, Jamaica's other major resort area. One of the earliest venues there was the Equator Club, which operated throughout the 1936 season and had an entertainment policy loosely modeled on that of the early Silver Slipper. Halfway through the 1936 season, however, Joe Abner (in partnership with an entrepreneur named Johnny Pike) bought the Equator Club and rechristened it the Wattle and Daub, which became home to saxophonist and bandleader Cyril Beckford and featured a floor show, likely led by comedian and vaudevillian Elkana "Worm" Chambers.[8] By January 1937, there were several venues in Montego Bay, including the newly opened Jolly Roger club and the Casa Blanca and Chatham hotels, that offered entertainment options to tourists (Constadt 1937).

When the British mystery writer Sax Rohmer proudly declared that he wanted three things on his 1936 visit to Jamaica—"rum, Voodoo and Obeah"—he was certain to find some version of all of them (*Daily Gleaner* 1936a). By this time, tourism's marketing more fully integrated Jamaica's sensual opportunities into a identifiable brand. People were sent to places like Kingston's "Sugar Wharf" to buy inexpensive rum with names like Rumba and Dagger. They could also drink it at nightclubs while watching sensational "native" entertainments that concatenated West Indian cultural forms. Both itineraries were part of a fashionably modern tourist experience, as suggested in the following description of the Springfield Club's "blood curdling Fire Dance," which purported depicting a "voodoo" ritual involving the sacrifice of a young girl; it was a hit during the 1939 season:

> Steadily, the troupe who performed the "Fire Dance" moved into the spotlight, whirling and circling until something of the fear which their postures indicated was communicated to the crowd who watched. In fact, drinks were forgotten, half-tasted as the menacing, gaunt high priest let his eyes rove around the circle of voodoo worshippers. Towering above them he lifted his knife while the chant of hypnotised savages rent the air with doleful sound.
>
> [...]
>
> Such is the realistic "Fire Dance" that Springfield's management is offering to visitors and local people who long for something truly different and interesting. Truly an interesting innovation in smart West Indian nightlife, these revived dances which depict savage customs force us to ask, "How much of our history do we know?"
>
> Seeing the "Fire Dance" is a stimulating experience guaran'eed to thrill even the most blasé bon homme or travelwise tripper. (*Daily Gleaner* 1939)

More importantly, however, the forms these shows presented (many of which were not endemic to Jamaica) started to index as "Jamaican" and so became the primary means for marketing Jamaican culture to tourists. That this had implications for local musicians was an especially important realization, one alluded to by the itinerant mento singers Slim and Sam in a editorial letter sent to the *Daily Gleaner* newspaper in 1936, protesting the aversion they saw to strictly "Jamaican" music:

> We, the undersigned, claim to know plenty about this Jamaica song affair, because for years we have been dealing in them, professionally. We have been using and keeping alive lots of old Jamaica tunes (and sometimes words) and have been actually writing and singing new ones, scores of them, words and music. Plainly, we earn our livelihood to-day by composing, singing, and selling (very cheaply) strictly Jamaica songs, on street and stage. We specialize in writing songs on the latest sensational topics of the day—serious or humorous.... During these years we have naturally learned a lot regarding Jamaica songs, and how they affect the various

people with whom we come in contact around Jamaica. We find there is a type of Jamaican who does not seem to like, even to hear, much more to sing, whistle, or even hum native songs or tunes. They seem to consider it degrading, or uncouth, indulging in a Jamaica melody. They would not think of dancing a native mento or shay-shay. No, Sir, why? That wouldn't be Londonish or New Yorkish, or foreignish anyhow. (Beckford and Blackwood 1936)

Rumba's international profile and the sense that it was the "modern" sound gave it a marketing advantage to which many Jamaican musicians would respond. Prior to rumba's popularity, there were certainly Jamaican dance bands that paralleled Cuban son groups in scale and focus. However, their instrumentation bore little resemblance in sound and repertory to the Cuban model, typically comprising homemade instruments such as horse jawbones, iron triangles, graters, bamboo fifes, cellos, and fiddles, as well as mass produced instruments like concertinas, melodeons and clarinets.[9] With changes in the nature of tourist entertainment, musicians predisposed to mento or shey shey who wanted to become involved soon realized that identifying as rumba musicians—at least sometimes—attracted more opportunity. This generally meant adapting the look and sound of Cuba through the use of clavés, castanets, and marimbulas (known in Jamaica as "rumba boxes"), by the wearing the ruffled vests and sleeves of the *guaracheros* in Cuba's *teatro vernáculo,* and even by borrowing some of the musical trappings of Cuba's *conjuntos de son,* most notably in the use of common introductory and closing melodic figures.

Rumba was part of a cutting edge and decidedly "modern" 1930s Jamaica tourism that changed the face of the colony's entertainment product and helped its industry grow. But the expansion of tourism around the Caribbean, not only in the north but also in places like Trinidad, was taking place amidst an increasingly complex geopolitical situation that would eventually culminate in World War II. Any regression in the industry's growth required a response, and when this began to happen, Jamaica's entertainment entrepreneurs began looking for the next new sound.

THE HOME OF CALYPSO: A GENERATIONAL SHIFT AND THE NEW MODERN

Jamaica's association with rumba seems to have hit its zenith in 1939, in part due to the international success of Arthur Benjamin's *Jamaican Rumba,* a piano piece based on the Jamaica mento melody "Gimme Back Me Shilling." However, growing international interest in Trinidadian calypso in the late 1930s led to

new ideas about what tourists might consider "modern" in West Indian entertainment and, in time, the musical product marketed to tourists was changed
to "calypso." This was an important development, as calypso's relevance to the
marketing of Jamaica's tourism product would last for more than four decades.

Calypso has a long history as commercial world music. Indeed, Donald
Hill (1993) detailed a small group of frontier performers—including Lionel
Belasco, Wilmoth Houdini, and Sam Manning—who established Anglophone
Caribbean music's and especially calypso's presence in the United States before
1930.[10] More pertinent, however, is the ten-year period 1934–44 which John
Cowley identified as the blossoming of calypso's international appeal. During
this time, the number of calypso recordings grew, and their increased availability found a receptive audience not only among immigrant West Indian communities in the United States, but also among tourists to Trinidad and Tobago, and
later among Allied military stationed throughout the Caribbean (Cowley 1993,
6). Hill (131) identifies 1937, the year RCA Victor and Decca each released an
unusually large number of calypso recordings, as having been a particularly
crucial turning point in that music's growth because it catalyzed an international vogue for Trinidadian calypso. This in turn yielded a flurry of articles
around the world that helped publicize that colony's "native" music to a far
greater extent than ever before.[11]

The Jamaican media quickly took notice of the attention being accorded to
Trinidad. In October 1937, the *Daily Gleaner* reprinted an article about calypso
music originally published in London's *Daily Express* (Hughes 1937). Then,
in September 1938, an article from the August issue of *Time* magazine that
showcased calypso's potential in tourism was reprinted in the *Jamaica Standard*
newspaper. With passages touting its "jerky rhythms and insinuating tunes
[that] suggest Africa and South America as well as the West Indies, [that] tell of
local and world news events [and] celebrate such universal subjects as women
and drink" (*Jamaica Standard* 1938a), the article painted a picture which articulated well with the primitivist reductionism upon which Jamaican floor show
entertainments were based. More important, however, was the article's suggestion there was money to be made from the style: "Tourists long ago discovered
Calypso, found it fun to pay a few dollars to have themselves described in an
impromptu ballad" (ibid.).

What would this mean for the future of tourism and marketing? Could
calypso really represent a new fashion in Jamaica's tourist entertainment? The
media seemed eager to push a connection. A *Daily Gleaner* article published
in October 1938 proclaimed "calypso singers the troubadours of Trinidad,"
explaining "to an accompaniment of rumba rhythms, they comment in suc-
cinct doggerel on all the news of the day" (Fletcher 1938). What's interesting is
that by grafting calypso's lyrics onto rumba's rhythm, the article elided calypso's

stylistic peculiarities for the sake of tourist expectation. However, in light of the *Time* magazine piece, this construction simultaneously invoked the compositional approach of mento singers (like Slim and Sam) and the style of some period nightclub comedians (like Ernest M. Cupidon and Kid Harold), which likely attracted the notice of the nightclub community: if tourists were interested in calypso, they could already find it in Jamaica and need not travel as far as Trinidad.

Less than a month after this *Gleaner* piece, the *Jamaica Standard* (1938b) in fact ran a photograph of Slim and Sam that (perhaps to their horror) referred to them as "calypso singers." It was the first time any Jamaican musician had been associated with calypso in print, and very clearly suggested a new stylistic direction for tourist entertainment.

Although the outbreak of World War II slowed Jamaica tourism, a military presence arrived that kept demand for nightclub entertainment strong. The use of the word calypso as a marketing term sprouted during the war years (fostered by the global popularity of the Andrews Sister's 1943 recording, "Rum and Coca Cola"), but it blossomed at war's end when investment in tourism resumed. Entrepreneurs acted quickly to capitalize on calypso's worldwide popularity and make it the premiere building block in entertainment moving forward.[12] This began in late 1945 with the arrival of two Trinidadian calypsonians, Sir Lancelot to the Springfield Club in November (*Daily Gleaner* 1945a) and Caresser to the Glass Bucket in December (*Daily Gleaner* 1945b; 1945c).[13] The critical success of these performers likely inspired many prominent Jamaican nightclub and cabaret performers who had flirted with calypso during the war years (including Lord Fly, Ben Bowers, and Tony Johnson) to model themselves even more explicitly on a Trinidadian model by borrowing more of its better-known repertory and introducing elements of the music into their compositional approach. It also created greater demand for the small "orchestras" that had become increasingly common in touristic contexts:

From across the valley comes the strumming of a guitar, the grit-grit of a grater and the humming of a comb covered with fine paper. It is a peasant orchestra...From my window I see a rosebush laden down with dewy pearls, glistening in the misty shadows as "Mango Time" crashes through with a mighty crescendo. The tempo is there; I listen; but the tune is changing almost imperceptibly to "Sandy Gully Man," modulating to a major key with rich shaded, colourful cadences so typical of our native digging songs. (Stewart 1944)

Although mento and rumba remained tried and true marketing terms, calypso flourished as the new sound of post-war Jamaican tourism. This importance intensified in late 1947 with the arrival of Lord Kitchener and Lord Beginner, two well-known Trinidadians who stayed in Jamaica for much of the 1947–1948 tourist season on their way to England via the ship the *Windrush* (*Daily Gleaner* 1948). During their visit, they were showcased in two Kingston nightclubs, Beginner at Wickie Wackie and Kitchener at the Sugar Hill Club, and each enjoyed great popularity (*Jamaica Daily Express* 1947a; 1947b). Kitchener, was particularly successful and performed alongside a cadre of Jamaican floor show entertainers, many of whom would later rise to prominence. The most important of these local entertainers was Norman Thomas, billed as the 14-year-old "Calypso Sensation."

Thomas, who became better known as Lord Flea, grew up steeped in mento music and became an important player on Jamaica's tourism-driven nightclub scene in the late 1940s. By the time he died of Hodgkins disease in 1959, he was well-versed in the stakes and strategies of tourist entertainment:

> In Jamaica...we called our music "mento" until very recently. Today the name calypso is beginning to be used for all kinds of West Indian music. This is because it's become so commercialized there. Some people like to think of West Indians as carefree natives who work and sing and play and laugh their lives away. But this isn't so. Most of the people are hard-working folks, and many of them are smart businessmen. If the tourists want calypso, that's what we sell them. (Lord Flea, quoted in Engel, 1957)

Flea's emergence in the late 1940s and early 1950s sheds powerful light on this important transitional moment in tourist entertainment. Not only was he different from other, earlier performers in that he was among the first of a younger generation of "Jamaican calypsonians" to come up after World War II knowing the previous era's performance conventions only as inherited tradition, but he was also one of the first to be recorded for commercial release.

When Beginner and Kitchener arrived, the young Flea was learning the ropes of nightclub entertainment as a member of the veteran comedy duo Bim and Bam's floor show.[14] However, Kitchener's success inspired Flea to go to Montego Bay to cut his teeth busking for tourists in the latter part of the 1948 tourist season. He returned to Kingston later that year and worked in local dance-halls like Success and Adastra Gardens through 1949, performing alongside acrobats, magicians, dance bands, and, of course, "torrid" rumba dancers in an effort to better learn the business.[15] Later in 1949, he participated in a talent competition at the Sugar Hill Club that resulted in a nearly year-long engagement where he was billed as the "Calypso King." His stint at the Sugar Hill lasted until mid-1950 at which point he moved to the Wickie Wackie (another, slightly more upscale, Kingston nightclub that specialized in staging exotic native floorshows). In the first half of 1951, he moved on to the illustrious Silver Slipper Club, which by then had become one of Kingston's ritziest venues.

Throughout this time, Flea's popularity was on the rise and he eventually attracted the attention of two local businessmen, Alec Durie and Ken Khouri. Durie owned and operated Kingston's Times department store, while Khouri owned a small business making private recordings. Durie and Khouri recognized the potential of commercial recordings and approached Flea about making a few sides. In August 1951, the two released a series of so-called calypso records on the Times Store label that featured Flea performing with a group called the "Jamaican Calypsonians." Although the records comprised songs from both the Jamaican mento and Trinidadian calypso repertoires, Jamaica's musical identity was hidden.

These records (along with a few later sides on the "Calypsotime" label) galvanized Flea's reputation and propelled his career. He spent the 1952 and 1953 seasons performing in the Glass Bucket's floor show. By then, the Bucket was Kingston's most exclusive nightclub and attracted a fairly high profile tourist clientele. Among them was Bill Saxon, the owner of Club Calypso on Biscayne Boulevard in Miami, who saw Flea and signed him to an extended engagement in the United States (*Star* 1953). Beginning in 1954, Flea found great subsequent success performing throughout the US, a tenure that yielded the *Swingin' Calypsos* LP on Capital Records (1957) and two films (*Bop Girl Goes Calypso* and *Calypso Joe,* both 1957).

Flea's participation in Jamaica's early recording era was crucial to this process, as was how his music—and that of his colleagues—was framed. I've argued elsewhere that the choices early record producers made in marketing music at the dawn of Jamaica's recording era emphasized its accessibility to foreign tastes, because tourists represented their most important revenue source (Neely 2007). Indeed, a comparison of Flea's output to that of artists whose first recordings were made contemporaneous to his own shows a consistency in presentation that illustrates how important and all-encompassing "calypso" had become to the way Jamaica's musical identity was being presented and sold.

Further, Jamaica's very first commercial record label was Stanley Motta's MRS (Motta's Recording Studio), an enterprise that grew out of the one-off recording service offered in Motta's downtown Kingston department store. Motta was a savvy and well-connected businessman, and in selecting performers to feature on his records, he opted for those with long experience in tourism entertainment. Motta's first sides appeared in December 1950, and featured Lord Fly and Dan Williams, both veterans of nightclub entertainment. These records—like those of many he recorded—were marketed very widely and obscured a strictly Jamaican musical identity with labels describing the music as "Jamaican Calypsos" or "Jamaican Mento-Calypsos," an approach consistent with how Times Store marketed their records. This led several hotels to realize how important branded albums of their in-house calypso bands could be to marketing and several made records. This practice not only flourished in the 1960s and 1970s, but it attracted the attention of the Jamaica Tourist Board, which would later sponsor some of these "souvenir" records.

Following the establishment of the Jamaica Tourist Board in 1955, calypso was poised to become a much more important piece in Jamaica's tourism marketing. As Flea was on his way to a promising career in the United States, other groups began to circulate abroad, most notably the Silver Seas Calypso Band, the first of several to travel on promotional trips sponsored by the Jamaica Tourist Board (JTB).[16] As the business of Jamaica tourism was poised to double by 1960 (Taylor 1993, 165), calypso's value increased. The marketing strategy that pitched Jamaica as the "land of the calypso," not only led to more bands going on JTB tours but to the global circulation of Jamaican music in tourism's image.

CONCLUSION

> In Jamaica an amazing transformation has taken place. Where American jazz and dance music once held complete sway, today on every street corner, in every bar or cafe, at every amusement park, dance hall, in the night clubs or hotel ballroom, even in the sanctum sanctorum of private homes, one hears the nostalgic and intriguing melodies of the Jamaican Mento, the digging melody, or the so-called Cudjoe-songs.
>
> Out of this musical maturity (for maturity it certainly is, in the sense that the people have grown to appreciate what is inherently their own) have sprung up numerous little groups, five piece orchestras, trios, quartets, small ensembles using ingeniously native-made instruments, male and mixed choirs, group harmonizers, and café serenaders, all of whom devote considerably more time to acquiring reputation as experts in native music, this in spite of 'boogie' and "be-bop." …Listening to them for the first time, you are immediately titillated by the provocative rhythm with its strong pulsating beat, and underscoring it the melodic line and the intricate phrasing. Imperceptibly, you are prompted to move to the tricky tempo, to hum the catchy tunes. (*MoBay Times* 1949)

I started this chapter with a long meditation on the Jolly Boys, a group with a great track record of success, in whose performances one can hear the echoes of 1960s calypso exuberance, see the kinesthetic patterns of the fire dance, and feel the vibes of the local mento music tradition. All these are traces of earlier practice and represent the complex constellation of foreign and local influences that many tourist groups share, and all of which I believe are informed by decades of marketing strategy. While the Jolly Boys' "modern mento" concept may seem incongruous with past practice, it is indeed very much a natural extension of tourism's representational trajectory.

To understand why this is the case, one must turn to the moment when local artists and tourism entrepreneurs first embraced the music and sounds considered "inherently their own." In many ways it was, as the quote above suggests, an outward sign of maturity. But what was the value of being strictly "Jamaican" in a touristic context? In this chapter, I have shown how the appropriation and assimilation of foreign styles was the basis for expressive diversity in Jamaica's nightclubs and floor shows and a major reason for tourism's success. I described how seasonal marketing campaigns led to stylistic shifts, largely by embracing the exotic and capitalizing on translocal cultural similarity. Non-Jamaican forms like rumba, calypso, and Voodoo—and their associated cultural expectations—were grafted onto Jamaican forms like mento because they fueled tourist interest and could help drive innovation in the industry. Marketing strategy became the basis for progressive modernity and, thus, stylistic change.

Today's tourist entertainers require a far more transnational and cosmopolitan outlook to remain modern. As far as mento bands go, only the Jolly Boys have had the benefit of a forward-looking marketing campaign. Ultimately, however, their success is rooted in the lessons learned from the marketing strategies of Jamaica tourism's past. With these lessons filling their sails, they have driven the mento-based tourism entertainment's reinvention, for better or worse, following in the entrepreneurial footsteps of those that came before.

NOTES

1. DeLeon (1936) suggests that the unemployment of local musicians was rampant into the 1930s.
2. This music festival had upwardly mobile aspirations and was an important part of the larger movement that began in the 1890s to improve the state of music in Jamaica. The repertory adjudicators expected was in the European classical model. Categories included (but were not limited to) piano forte and violin divided by age groups. The repertory included Beethoven, Schumann, and Brahms (among others).
3. Potential talent certainly existed. For example, the Ward Theater staged a large variety show loosely based on the Ziegfeld Follies, Geraldo Leon (whose brother Bertie Lyon would become famous as the mento personality Lord Fly) ran a thirty-artist cabaret called the Vanities, and Marcus Garvey, who ran the popular Edelweiss Amusement Company, organized vaudeville revues at Edelweiss Park, advertising the intention of "[making] Jamaica more like America, England and France in Amusements" by offering training for performers (*Daily Gleaner* 1931b). But these variety shows were large, and seem to have been prepared for largely working class

patois-speaking Jamaican audiences in touch with local tastes and current events (Taylor 1931).

4. Olivier 1933, quoted in Bilby 2006.

5. (Daily Gleaner 1934c; Daily Gleaner 1934e). Local coverage failed to reveal the group's specific identity, but a published photo of the band playing at the Fair showed it was a son sexteto that included a pair of string instruments, a single hand drum, a marimbula, a clave player, and a singer.

6. A burro is a kind of drum associated with pocomania (Neely, Lewin, and Averill 2008, 282; Lewin 2000: 189–197)

7. Issa and Sharpe (along with Ferdie Martin and John Pringle) are considered fathers of modern Jamaica tourism and it is important to note that these four—and especially Issa and Sharpe—helped make mento-based entertainment an important part of Jamaica tourism's legacy. For his input on Abner and Issa's influence, I am deeply grateful to musician, engineer, inventor, and longtime president of the Jamaica Federation of Musicians, Hedley Jones.

8. *Daily Gleaner* (1936b; 1958). Beckford and Chambers both became icons of north coast entertainment. Beckford led several successful dance bands and later went on to become an officer for the Jamaica Federation of Musicians, while Chambers built his reputation as the leader of a troupe of dancing girls and then later with the "Worm Chambers Showboat," a group of actors who performed "voodoo dances" and swallowed fire in boats along the waterfront in Montego Bay for the exclusive entertainment of tourists.

9. Such groups are described fairly widely, for example in *Daily Gleaner* (1897), Jekyll (1907, 216–217) and Roberts (1921, 20).

10. Incidentally, Manning performed in Jamaica in 1929 with the "Sam Manning Variety Company," a company owned by Marcus's Garvey's wife Amy Ashford Garvey. During his visit, he was billed as an actor and a comedian, never as a calypsonian. In addition, this appearance is not included in my analysis because there is no indication Manning was performing for tourist audiences; each of the venues he performed in catered to a working class Jamaican clientele.

11. For an excellent analysis of calypso's transnational emergence at this time, see Eldridge, 2002.

12. For a detailed analysis of "Rum and Coca Cola's" history, see Cowley 1993.

13. Lancelot, a Trinidadian who in the early 1940s was studying medicine in New York, was an interesting choice because he was a virtual unknown in Trinidad; indeed, his reputation as a calypsonian was made largely through American films (Hill 1993, p. 186–192). Although better known in Trinidad, Caresser was one of several Trinidadian calypsonians who went to New York in 1937. Based on his subsequent experience, he brought a similar international, cosmopolitan West Indian style that seems to have galvanized the lure of calypso in Jamaica and set the tone for how nightclub entertainments would happen for the next several years.

14. Bim and Bam (aka Edward Lewis and Aston Wynter) broke into the entertainment business in 1937 with the help of Slim and Sam, who, in addition to their songwriting activities, directed a theatrical troupe. Bim and Bam typically performed in blackface in the American minstrel tradition. Their reputation grew considerably in the 1940s with help from promoters like Eric Coverley, and they entered into

show business full time in 1947. With this, they staged several small-scale theatrical productions, often in nightclubs alongside mento and calypso-themed floor
shows. Their first was Rhygin's Ghost, a show based on a gun-toting Robin Hood–
like outlaw named Ivan Rhygin who was the basis for Jimmy Cliff's character in the
1973 film The Harder They Come (*Daily Gleaner* 1979).

15. Ruth Grant, interview with author, July 2004.
16. In 1955, the Silver Seas visited the United States, performed around New York
    City, and appeared on NBC's Home and Steve Allen shows (Daily Gleaner 1955).
    Notably, the Silver Seas Calypso Band formed in 1952—likely at the behest of
    Stuart Sharpe—as Reynolds Calypso Clippers to make records for Stanley Motta.
    Virtually all of the group's members had at least a decade of experience in tourist
    entertainment, some in the cabarets and nightclubs of the 1930s, others got their
    start in the 1940s. For more on this group's history, see *Daily Gleaner* 1947, *Star*
    1955, and *Sunday Gleaner* 1982.

REFERENCES

Beckford, Slim, and Sam Blackwood. 1936. "Jamaica Folk Songs." *Daily Gleaner*. August
    13, 17.
Bell, Hesketh J. 1893. *Obeah: Witchcraft in the West Indies*. London: Sampson Low,
    Marston & Company.
Bilby, Kenneth M. 1985. "The Caribbean as a Musical Region." In *Caribbean Contours*,
    edited by Sidney W. Mintz and Sally Price, 181–218. Baltimore, MD: Johns Hopkins
    University Press.
——. 2006. *True-Born Maroons*. Kingston, Jamaica: Ian Randle Publishers.
Clerk, Astley. 1935. "Suggests Short Group of Folk Songs Might Be Sung for Royal
    Visitors." *Jamaica Times*. January 26, 17.
Constadt, Joseph. 1937. "With Us in Montego Bay." *Daily Gleaner*. February 13, 21.
Cowley, John. 1993. "L'Année Passée: Selected Repertoire in English-Speaking West
    Indian Music, 1900–1960." *Keskidee: A Journal of Black Musical Traditions* 3: 2–43.
Daily Gleaner. 1891. "Recitals." March 30, 2.
Daily Gleaner. 1897. " 'The Light Fantastic Toe': How Our People Learn Dancing."
    October 6, 1.
Daily Gleaner. 1907. "Some New Dances." August 19, 3.
Daily Gleaner. 1921. "So-called 'Shay-Shays.' " July 23, 10.
Daily Gleaner. 1931a. Ad. "The Silver Slipper." May 30, 15.
Daily Gleaner. 1931b. Ad. "The Edelweis Amusement Company, Ltd." August 12, 4.
Daily Gleaner. 1933a. "S. Mary Hears of Purpose of Island Fair." August 18, 12.
Daily Gleaner. 1933b. "Meeting in Support of Coming Exhibition Held at Mo-Bay."
    August 25, 13.
Daily Gleaner. 1934a. "Bottle Jamaican Run More Attractively for United States."
    January 25, 3.
Daily Gleaner. 1934b. "Tourists See Scenes from a 1700s Jamaica." March 1, 3.
Daily Gleaner. 1934c. "Great Fireworks Display To-night at the Exhibition." March 3, 7.
Daily Gleaner. 1934d. "Riot of 'Burro.' " March 5, 10.
Daily Gleaner. 1934e. "Indian Tattoo at the Exhibition To-night." March 6, 16.

Daily Gleaner. 1934f. "The Glass Bucket, New Night Club, To Be Opened Saturday." December 20, 5.

Daily Gleaner. 1935. "Sugar Cane Starts Off with A Bang." May 18, 4.

Daily Gleaner. 1936a. "Obeah, Voodoo, Rum!—Sax Rohmer's Quest!" March 4, 5.

Daily Gleaner. 1936b. "New Night Club Opened at Mo-Bay." December 29, 17.

Daily Gleaner. 1939. "'Fire Dance' Thrills at Springfield Club." March 15, 16.

Daily Gleaner. 1945a. "'Sir Lancelot' Great Calypso Interpreter Makes Jamaican Debut This Week." November 5, 12.

Daily Gleaner. 1945b. "'Caresser' Is Unique Calypso Artiste." December 10, 4.

Daily Gleaner. 1945c. "'Lord Caresser' Draws Big Crowd to Bucket." December 17, 13.

Daily Gleaner. 1947. "Four Keys Featured at Sugar Hill Tonight." July 12, 14.

Daily Gleaner. 1948. "355 Going Deck to England." May 13, 1, 3.

Daily Gleaner. 1955. "Silver Seas Band Wins U.S. Applause." May 28, 12.

Daily Gleaner. 1958. "Cyril Beckford's Band at Gloucester House for Season." January 25, 10.

Daily Gleaner. 1979. "The Earthy Comic Duo of Bim and Bam." September 9, viii and 40.

Daily Gleaner. 1990. "Portland Roundabout." July 16, 39.

DeLeon, Beryl. 1936. "Why Are American Dance Bands Brought Here for the Season?" *Jamaica Times.* January 25, 21.

De Lisser, Herbert G. 1910. *In Jamaica and Cuba.* Kingston, Jamaica: The Gleaner Company.

——. 1913. *Twentieth Century Jamaica.* Kingston: The Jamaica Times Limited.

Eldridge, Michael. 2002. "There Goes the Transnational Neighborhood: Calypso Buys a Bungalow." *Callaloo* 25(2): 620–638.

Engel, Lyle Kenyon. 1957. "Lord Flea." *Calypso Stars* 1: 44–47.

F.N. 1933. "New Dance Steps." *Daily Gleaner.* November 11, 26.

Fletcher, Stuart. 1938 "Mack and Fippence Is Their Cry." *Daily Gleaner.* October 24, 17.

Guilbault, Jocelyn. 2001. "World Music." In *The Cambridge Companion to Pop and Rock*, edited by Simon Frith, Will Straw, and John Street, 176–192. Cambridge, UK: Cambridge University Press.

Henderson, John. 1906. *Jamaica.* London: Adam and Charles Black.

Hill, Donald R. 1993. *Calypso Calaloo: Early Carnival Music in Trinidad.* Gainesville: University Press of Florida.

Howard, Dennis. 2007. "Punching for Recognition: The Juke Box as a Key Instrument in the Development of Jamaican Popular Music." *Caribbean Quarterly* 53(4): 32–46.

Hughes, Spike. 1937. "They Sing News: Trinidad Troubadours of the Twentieth Century." *Daily Gleaner.* October 21, 16.

Jamaica Daily Express. 1947a. "Calypso Singer." December 8, 4.

Jamaica Daily Express. 1947b. Advertisement. "The Sugar Hill Presents a Week-End of Thrills." December 11, 2.

Jamaica Standard. 1938a. "In the West Indies: Calypso Singers of Trinidad." September 3, 6.

Jamaica Standard. 1938b. "Calypso Singers." Photograph. November 15, 9.

Jamaica Times. 1934. "Effort to Preserve Jamaica Folk Songs." December 15, 31.

Jekyll, Walter. 1966 [1907]. *Jamaica Song and Story.* New York: Dover Publications.

Jolly Boys. 1989. *Pop "n" Mento.* Rykodisc 10185.

——. 2010. *Great Expectation*. Geejam/Wall of Sound WOS079CD.

Lewin, Olive. 2000. *Rock It Come Over. The Folk Music of Jamaica*. Kingston, Jamaica: The University of the West Indies Press.

Lindsay, Maurice. 1934. "Jamaica's Future as a Tourist Resort." *Jamaica Times Christmas Number*. December 8, 18.

Miller, Herbie. 2007. "Syncopating Rhythms: Jazz and Caribbean Culture." *Jazz Studies Online*. Center for Jazz Studies at Columbia University. http://dev.jazzstudiesonline. org.

MoBay Times. 1949. "Music Comes Out Happy When We Smile." October 29, 2.

Moore, Robin. 1997. *Nationalizing Blackness: Afrocubanismo and Artistic Revolution in Havana, 1920–1940*. Pittsburgh, PA: University of Pittsburgh Press.

Neely, Daniel T. 2007. "Calling All Singers, Musicians, and Speechmakers: Mento Aesthetics and Jamaica's Early Recording Industry." *Caribbean Quarterly* 53(4): 1–15.

Neely, Daniel T., Olive Lewin, and Gage Averill. 2008. "Jamaica." In *Garland Encyclopedia of World Music*, condensed Version, 281–288. New York: Routledge.

Olivier, Lord. 1933. *The Myth of Governor Eyre*. London: Leonard and Virginia Woolf.

Pullen-Burry, Bessie. 1903. *Jamaica As It Is, 1903*. London: T. F. Unwin.

Roberts, Helen H. 1921. *Song Hunting in Jamaica*. Unpublished MS. Roberts MSS/YU, group 1410.

Rommen, Timothy. 2009. "'Come Back Home': Regional Travels, Global Encounters, and Local Nostalgias in Bahamian Popular Musics." *Latin American Music Review/ Revista de Música Latinoamericana* 30(2): 159–183.

——. 2011. *Funky Nassau: Roots, Routes, and Representation in Bahamian Popular Music*. Berkeley: University of California Press.

Star. 1953. "Miami Calling Calypso Bands." December 17, 3.

——. 1955. "Silver Seas Calypsos Play for Princess." February 22, 6.

Stewart, Sgt. Maj. R. McKinnon. 1944. "Jamaica Christmas Concerto." *North Caribbean Star*. December 22, 7.

Sunday Gleaner. 1982. "Monty Reynolds Recalls MRS Label Recordings." Motta's 50s Anniversary Supplement. March 7, 21.

Taylor, Frank. 1931. "Search for 200 Vaudeville Artists: A Candid Criticism of some Jamaican talent." *Daily Gleaner*. August 24, 6.

Taylor, Frank Fonda. 1993. *To Hell With Paradise: A History of the Jamaican Tourist Industry*. Pittsburgh, PA: The University of Pittsburgh Press.

Selling Cuba by the Sound

Music and Tourism in Cuba in the 1990s

VINCENZO A. PERNA ∎

The world is as taken with Buena Vista Social Club as it is with Fidel Castro.

> —F. McAuslan and M. Norman, *Cuba. The Rough Guide*

And when we make the *chen* [exchange]
How would you like me to pay you, baby?
With a cheque or in cash?
Or if you like, I'll give you a receipt[1]

> —La Charanga Habanera, *"Hagamos un chen"*
> *(Dedicated to all the tourists who visit Cuba)*

Popular music has long worked as an international ambassador for Cuba. In the 1870s, the Cuban *habanera* was already fashionable worldwide. As the island developed into a destination for wealthy US citizens in the first half of the twentieth century, Cuba's depiction as a land of sea and palms blended with echoes of rhythms and images of dark bodies. Between the 1920s and the 1950s, Cuban music and fiery *mulatas* became an inextricable part of the international representation of the "pleasure island" (Schwartz 1997).

The case of music and tourism in contemporary Cuba is therefore particularly challenging, because it connects past representations of the island with recent decisions taken by the Cuban socialist government, which, after actively discouraging foreign tourism for decades, was forced to rely again on international visitors by the unpredictable turn of post-1989 world events. After the collapse of the Soviet Union and the end of its economic patronage in the early 1990s, mass tourism has become for Cubans a highly strategic economic resource and an everyday reality.

International tourism generally entails traveling to certain places in search of some kind of special, extraordinary experience (Urry 2002). It involves anticipating the event, often going to some exotic country, and returning home. In such a process, representations of the country disseminated by the media in the form of pictures, films, sounds, and narratives take on paramount importance (see chapter 3) to the point that, it might be argued, contemporary traveling does not mainly consist in getting to know new places, but in actually experiencing something we think we already know. Among those signs, local musics, as "one means by which places can be represented in wider mediascapes" (Gibson and Connell 2005, 221), have been increasingly orienting tourists' tastes and decisions.

This has certainly been the case with Cuban popular music, which has proved central to the images that attract millions of tourists to the Caribbean island. In a nation that is world-renowned as a music powerhouse—as *la isla de la música*[2]—music has been used both to keep tourists entertained and to spread images and ideas about the country. As Robin Moore has remarked, visitors to Cuba "are welcomed with open arms and the island [is] described in promotional material as a haven of music, dance, and fiestas" (2006, 231).

In this chapter I will discuss how Cuban music has helped to sell Cuba on international tourist markets, shape tourists' expectations, mediate their experiences there, and build an avenue for their contacts with locals. As tourism itself has significantly affected the circumstances of Cuban music, I will also look at how musicians have adapted to the impact of mass tourism, and how their music has changed as a result.

My discussion will focus on the 1990s, a decade of acute economic crisis and deep changes for Cuba. During that decade, the island's forced engagement with global markets led to the rapid development of mass tourism. This created an environment favorable to Cuban popular music and, in particular, to two very different types of sounds. The first was *timba*, a type of Afro-Cuban dance music loosely similar to salsa. Born in Cuba for Cuban tastes, by the mid-1990s timba was being exploited by the tourism industry to promote a sexy image of Cuba. It dominated the Cuban airwaves and was on the verge of breaking into the international market.

The second type of sound coming out of the island was that of "traditional" music as represented by the *Buena Vista Social Club*. At the end of the 1990s, the album and the film had become a global sensation that almost completely redefined the world's perception of Cuban music: whereas Cuba had previously been identified with beach paradises and hot dancing, it came now to be defined by images of crumbling Havana and lively *viejitos*. In the words of one US commentator, *Buena Vista* became "the catalyst for Cuba's cultural boom abroad" (Sweig 2009, 141).

My analysis here will not consider in the strictest sense music tourism, a type of niche tourism that surely plays an important part in today's Cuba, on both a formal and an informal basis (for example, with foreigners attending music festivals, and individuals and groups traveling to Cuba to study folk music and dancing). Rather, I will focus my attention on the role played by music in relation to "generic" tourists, that is, to people with no specific interest in music, but whose visions and experiences of Cuba are nonetheless mediated by Cuban sounds.

I will argue that timba and Cuban "traditional music" have been paradigmatic of different relationships between music, tourism, and globalization. They have competed with different sounds and ideologies for international attention, have been used to articulate diverging images of the island, and have enjoyed distinctive commercial and political fortunes. Those two types of sounds are clearly not the only types of music that have been coming out of Cuba during the last two decades: yet, they have played a critical role in capturing and polarizing much of the foreign attention for local culture that continues to shape and feed tourism to Cuba.

Cuba's recent efforts to develop tourism and make the most of local music appear to have been powerfully conditioned by its own history. Black music and dance have been employed to sexualize Cuban women and attract men, just as they had been fifty years before, and the "alternative" tourist script generated by *Buena Vista Social Club* has been entirely pieced together with nostalgic sounds and images (the old music, the faded colonial building, the vintage American cars). In its attempts to capitalize on the rich heritage of Cuban music, it seems, the Cuban tourism industry has been unable to disentangle itself from the ghosts of its pre-revolutionary past.

CUBA UNDER THE SPECIAL PERIOD

> We have no oil, or diamonds, or gold, or silver. We have sun, sand, sea, pristine nature, culture, social stability, and a friendly, healthy, educated people.
>
> —A. Pozo, *"Necesario Turismo," Bohemia*

At the beginning of the 1990s, Cuba went from being a stable, relatively developed country dependent on trade with the Eastern European socialist bloc to a nation on the brink of collapse. In 1991, the disintegration of the Soviet Union shattered the Cuban economy and threw the island into chaos, threatening the very survival of the revolution. Oil shortages and a dramatic drop in industrial and agricultural production brought about a virtual standstill in public transportation, long power blackouts, and severe food and medicine shortages, along with widespread disease and malnutrition (Azicri 2000). Cubans learned from Fidel Castro that the island had entered a *período especial en tiempo de paz* (special period in time of peace), a period of wartime-like scarcity, rationing and sacrifices.[3]

The severity of the crisis compelled the Cuban government to make radical decisions, such as introducing elements of market economy, allowing limited forms of self-employment, and legalizing foreign remittances and the circulation of US currency. In an attempt to find new ways of bringing in hard currency and making the economy attractive to foreign investment, the government turned its attention toward the exploitation of Cuban shores. Western beach tourism became the leading force in the effort to avoid the meltdown of the Cuban economy, and the ultimate hope of salvation for the revolution (Espino 2008). Fidel Castro declared: "I envision the entire highway system north of Villa Clara, Ciego de Ávila, and Camagüey lined with hundreds of hotels" (Castro 1990).

Accordingly, international tourism in Cuba has grown at an extremely fast rate, eventually becoming "the preferred panacea for surviving the economic crisis" (Sanchez and Adams 2008, 32).[4] After an historic low of 3,000 visitors in 1968, foreign tourists in Cuba went from 340,000 (1990) to 750,000 (1995) and 1.2 million (1997), reaching 2.5 million in 2010, making Cuba into one of the main destinations in the Caribbean.[5] Over the period 1993–2003, overall international arrivals in the Caribbean grew at the annual rate of about 4 percent, while the Cuban share of those tourist arrivals went from 3 percent in 1990 to 11 percent in 2003 (Colantonio and Potter 2006). Most of the new visitors were males coming from North America and Western Europe (Cabezas 2009).

In the view of the Cuban government, market reforms and tourism were meant to work essentially as an emergency measure and mainly on an institutionally controlled level. Since airlines, travel companies, beach resorts, hotels, and restaurants were controlled by state entities or joint ventures, they were supposed to collect all the hard currency brought in by Western tourists and funnel it to the Cuban state. At the time, the Cuban authorities did not take into account the social impact of tourism and the effects produced by the "trickle down" of foreign money through the informal economy, which would later cause a political and economic backlash.

During the early years of the Special Period, therefore, Cubans experienced simultaneously the shock of the economic crisis and the sudden impact of mass tourism. While the crisis touched virtually every aspect of social life—impoverishing citizens, reducing state services, exacerbating social and racial inequalities, breaking families, increasing the level of crime and corruption, and shattering revolutionary idealism—tourism put young Cubans in contact with foreigners as never before, bringing about visions of affluence and hopes of expatriation (Centeno and Font 1997; Azicri 2000; Sweig 2009).

As the new "economic locomotive" of the island, however, tourism produced deeply divisive social effects. People who worked in contact with tourists and had access to foreign currency, for example, could get much-needed services and imported goods, while ordinary people who earned a living in devalued pesos kept struggling. On another level, the development of beach resorts and tourist enclaves meant that Cubans who did not work there were effectively banned from areas of their own country.[6] For Cubans with few opportunities at home and no family remittances from abroad, and particularly for Afro-Cubans, foreigners became a primary resource in their *lucha* (struggle) to keep afloat (Fernández 1999; Bisogno 2009).

MUSIC AND TOURISM ON THE *ISLAND OF MUSIC*

> Out of all the islands in the Caribbean, Cuba is renowned for having the best nightlife, and it is hard not to be caught up in the intoxicating rhythms and hip-swaying movements that permeate the many local music venues in every city.
> —*CUBA*. THOMAS COOK TRAVELLER GUIDES, *2008*[7]

In Western imagination, the notion of music, and particularly of dance music, is frequently tied to ideas of immediacy, emotion, and pleasure (DeNora 2000). In the case of Caribbean countries, as CD sleeves and tourist brochures show, music is often identified with dancing and images of partying and dark bodies. In that sense, Cuba could count on its preexisting depictions as the island of sea, hot rhythms, and sensual adventures. It was an image of hedonism that had its roots in Euro-American literary pictures of "Edenism" in the Caribbean (Sheller 2004) and that had been cultivated by US popular culture throughout the 1940s and the 1950s (Pérez 1999).

In the early 1990s Cuban economic planners and tourist managers sought to mobilize Cuban music for tourist purposes by capitalizing on these earlier representations of Cuba, and more generally of the Caribbean region. Predictably, they chose dance music, or *música bailable* (MB), seen as the most natural means to fulfill the industry's need for entertainment and foreigners' expectations of festive, rhythmic sounds. Cuba had plenty of professional musicians who had previously enjoyed state salaries and pensions, who were now

Figure 2.1 Among various tourist activities, a board inside Havana's Hotel Capri advertises "NG La Banda and guests." (© photo Vincenzo Perna)

encouraged to sell their services for dollars. Their cheap musical labor could be used to revive the faded entertainment industry and spice up the tourist experience (see Figure 2.1).

By the mid-1990s, tourists were packing old and new state-run, dollar-only clubs in Havana and Varadero (the main Cuban seaside resort), where MB offered them the main socializing ground for their nights of excitement and provided employment for hundreds of musicians. These musicians established a functional relationship with the venues: bands brought with them a loyal following of young fans (mostly dark, pretty *cubanas*), who would in turn attract tourists and try to "make friends" with them, making dance clubs thrive. It seemed a situation where everyone profited, or was at least satisfied: musicians played for much-needed dollars; state-run venues filled their coffers; young Cubans danced and engaged with foreigners; hookers and hustlers conducted their business (see chapter 10). Foreign tourists footed the bill, but they were happy for their wild night out or for the affair that developed as a result.

But music and dance took on a growing strategic role—a role that went beyond that of local economics—in that it also became a market differentiator for the projection of a touristically appealing, sexy image of Cuba. Alongside images of beaches and palms, guides and brochures of international tour operators began to be filled with pictures of musicians and drums, and images of the "explosive curves" of Cuban women (Holgado Fernández 2000). Any Caribbean destination could offer white sands and blue seas, but Cuba was different: unlike the rest of the Caribbean, not only was Cuba a land of spectacular beaches, but it was also the island of athletic *mulatos* and curvy *mulatas* dancing to burning beats. The return to pre-revolutionary modes of tourist marketing was perhaps most visible in the new fortunes enjoyed by the glitzy music-and-dance shows of the old Cabaret Tropicana. As the club spokesman, J. C. Aguilar stated that tourists flocked to this old-fashioned, expensive Havana nightclub to enjoy its "beautiful, well-endowed and sensual" (and mostly dark-skinned) showgirls (Arrington 2004).

Within the tourist industry, dance music became at the same time an instrument and an agent. From one of many attractions, it turned into a major means for shaping the international image of Cuba and the type of tourists traveling to the island. In those years, mostly working-class males longing for cheap sun, sea, and sexual adventure, might well choose to travel to Cuba based on such fantasies about music and dance (see Figure 2.2). This enhanced role of dance

Figure 2.2 Black, female, and dancing. The appeal of Afro-Cuban culture and the promises of tourist promotion. "Merengue dancer in Santiago de Cuba," from Italian travel magazine *Airone*, May 1997. (Courtesy of Danilo Pellegrini)

music was made possible by the popular notion that dancing is a natural way to let oneself go, but also by the central cultural and social role played by dancing in Cuba. For many foreigners, thus, nightclubbing and dancing became central to their experience of Cuba.

DANCE MUSIC FOR THE FOREIGN MASSES

> Cubans love to dance and whatever their taste in music . . . they can all dance salsa.
> —F. McAuslan and M. Norman, *Cuba. The Rough Guide, 2010*[8]

The development of a lucrative music scene produced remarkable economic benefits for a small number of popular artists. It rewarded established names of Cuban musical entertainment, such as the veteran dance band Los Van Van, while also benefiting new or emerging artists such as MB crooners Issac Delgado, Paulito FG, and Manolín (Manuel González), aka *El Médico de la Salsa*. Delgado, for example, left his band in 1992 to pursue a solo career and sign a contract with a foreign record label.[9]

Among the emerging names of MB in the early 1990s, two bands stood out. NG La Banda was originally a funk-jazz supergroup born from the jazz band Irakere, but its leader, José Luís Cortés, soon turned it into one of the most successful Havana dance bands. La Charanga Habanera was the brainchild of composer David Calzado, who returned to Cuba from an engagement abroad to set up a new, funky, sexy male band. Despite their differences in style and image, NG and La Charanga were both virtuosic, virtually all-black bands who played a heady mixture of Cuban dance music, funk, and jazz that was initially called *salsa cubana,* and later timba.[10] As the new, hot MB of the 1990s, this music became enormously popular with young Cubans, and particularly with Afro-Cubans. By the mid-1990s, it dominated the Havana music scene, ruled the airwaves, and was heavily promoted by state agencies. Its stars could be seen performing almost every night in tourist venues such as El Palacio de la Salsa, La Cecilia, El Papa, the Discoteca of the Hotel Comodoro, the Casa de la Música in Miramar, and the Café Cantante.

The economic reforms bestowed on successful musicians great economic and social power, enabling them to extend their networks of patronage and earn substantial amounts of money. In 1996, for example, a popular singer working in the capital's tourist clubs could earn thousands of US dollars a month, while a Cuban doctor made the equivalent of 15 dollars (Perna 2005). With flamboyant lifestyles and an image of affluence and extravagance, the stars of MB became part of the Cuban nouveaux riches and new role models for Cuba.

Amid general scarcity, they were seen in the streets of Havana driving their new cars and sporting fashionable clothing, golden chains, and mobile phones.

Why did timba become so popular? Its success, undoubtedly, depended on the convergence of the opportunities created by the reforms with the presence of masses of foreigners hungry for entertainment. Because timba songs were reminiscent of *salsa* (itself deriving from *son* and regarded by many as a music of Cuban descent), they managed to sound familiar enough to foreign ears to satisfy expectations without becoming disorienting. Timba's great popularity with young Cubans, however, stemmed from its topical content, its street language, and its musical continuity with the son and *rumba* tradition familiar to black Cuban dancers, as well as from a "modern" attitude that sought to incorporate elements of international black styles such as funk and rap.

Timba, in fact, was largely made by black bands, and employed black musical forms and black youth's language to tell stories largely seen from a black *barrio* perspective. Its name was an Afro-Cuban word for rumba, and its songs often celebrated African roots, contributing to the powerful revival of Afro-Cuban culture during the Special Period. The popularity of timba with black audiences confirmed the perceived Cuban association of MB with Afro-Cubans, but reinforced also the racial clichés that stereotyped black people "as more 'authentic' in terms of musical (and sexual and sporting) expressions of the body" (Gibson and Connell 2005, 157). Timba's ostensible ethnic character, thus, became an important selling point with tourists looking for tropical exoticism. Such character was further emphasized by timba's female dancing style, which added to the music's "African" appeal (see the following).

The engagement of Cuban dance musicians with tourism, moreover, was not confined to Cuba. During the 1990s, successful bands embarked on long international tours acquiring more money and additional fans abroad, and minor bands and musicians took residence for purpose of work throughout Europe and the Americas. In this role, musicians effectively became an integral part of the musical promotion of Cuba, in a circular process whereby foreigners went to Cuba and got to know Cuban music and dance and, upon returning home, went to listen and dance to Cuban music, which in turn promoted the image of Cuba abroad, possibly persuading new individuals to visit the island. The establishment of foreign independent labels in Cuba and the sale of Cuban recorded music abroad, another novelty of the Special Period, resulted in the further spread of Cuban sounds and images worldwide, raising the hopes of MB promoters and performers for international success.

The radical changes taking place in the economy of music of the 1990s, however, did not benefit all Cuban professional musicians. In fact, they penalized all those artists whose work depended on institutional support and was not marketable to foreigners. On an island that was strongly committed to live music, these changes also caused significant shifts in music consumption. As MB grew in popularity, it became less accessible to the local population, because dance bands, when not on tour abroad, played in Cuba mainly in tourist clubs, where most Cubans could not afford the ten or twenty dollar entrance fee.

A NIGHT IN HAVANA

In mid-1990s Cuba, therefore, dance music was one of the very limited options available to foreigners for entertainment. A casual Westerner arriving in Havana at that time and inquiring about where to go at night would be directed by hotel concierges, bed-and-breakfast establishments, and taxi drivers to the clubs where the best dance bands played, which were located in the upmarket areas of Playa and Vedado and were sometimes part of hotel complexes.

At the entrance of one of those clubs, the visitor would notice white middle-aged foreign males queueing up with their young Cuban fiancèes and friends, often of dark complexion. On the street, young black and mulatto women in sexy attire would be chatting up casual foreigners, trying to scrounge themselves an entrance ticket and a "lift" into the club.

Inside, a band would be playing onstage to a dancing crowd. The band would appear unusually large, numbering fifteen male, mostly black musicians, playing a sort of funky salsa dominated by singers (usually three), horns, and percussion—timba.

The band's lengthy songs would frequently follow a rough model. In the first section, the singer would croon a romantic theme reminiscent of salsa ballads, while Cubans male and female tried to persuade even the most reticent of tourists to dance. At that stage people would dance in the Cuban *casino* style, that is, couples dancing salsa- like with turns and whirls. Foreigners who did not know how to dance or did not want to engage would remain seated at the tables around the dance floor, drinking, chatting, and watching.

After a short rhythmic break, the song would suddenly give way to a markedly different second part, a lively section that set up a play of choral refrains (*coros*) and solo responses, interspersed with funky, virtuoso horn instrumental riffs. This part was the dancing acme of the song, and also its musical and semantic center of gravity. Much longer than the first section, this second part offered an adjustable space to accommodate vocal improvisations and impromptu commentaries which often made the song last up to more than thirty minutes.

The second part of the song was marked as well by a change in dancing style. Couples split and the attention focused on the women as they performed a series of sexually-provocative motions that included exaggerated pelvic movements such as the *batidora* ("blender"), with quick pelvic rotations, or the *tembleque* ("shaking"), where the body trembles as if electrocuted. Some women jumped onstage to perform the *batidora* in front of the band and to a cheering crowd, who loudly sang along the *coros*. At that stage, several foreigners often joined the dancing on the floor.[11]

To those who could understand Spanish, this part of the song also offered a distinctive narrative break, where the sentimental theme of the first section could be contradicted by the *coros*, which often gave vent to the narrator's anger for his woman's duplicity. While singers were calling young Cuban women treacherous and greedy, those very women danced eagerly to the driving timba rhythm and were being celebrated by the music.

Thanks to such paradoxical interaction of meanings and actors, timba bands were able to articulate contradictory messages and adapt dialogically to their composite audiences. To foreigners, they offered a recognizable sound and music structure that enhanced their tourist experience, staging shows of tropical sensuality and building a space where tourists could progress from entertainment to personal engagement with locals. For Cubans, they created a context that effectively transformed local people into a part of the show, but also provided a space for articulating meta-commentaries that called into question the very situation they were in (see Figure 2.3).

Around the mid-1990s, tourism appeared to be making an impact on live and recorded dance music in terms of both content and form. As tunes

Figure 2.3 Pedrito Calvo, former singer with Los Van Van, inspects the style of a female dancer onstage in Havana, 1999. (© photo Vincenzo Perna)

were making more room for *coros* and topical commentaries, their structure showed a marked shift away from the narrative *tema* and toward an expanded second part. This shift was a clear reflection of the way songs were becoming more formulaic, seeking to accommodate increasing participation by foreign audiences.

Music and dance, therefore, became central in setting up a festive mood, organizing tourists' encounters with Cubans, and eventually leading foreigners into a liminal state that seemed to open up new possibilities. Simoni (2009) has explored in detail the ways in which, in both state-run clubs and at spontaneous parties, Cubans would mobilize music and dance to engage foreigners into various forms of personal and economic exchanges, in "liquid" interactions where boundaries between dancing and seduction became blurred, and where social hierarchies between tourists and Cubans were dissolved and reorganized in favor of locals. For many young Cubans, music and dancing provided a highly-effective way to meet tourists, bring down their resistance, and seduce them.[12]

THE PEAK AND FALL OF *MÚSICA BAILABLE*

> Look, Nené, my suggestion is:
> find yourself a sugardaddy, but one with money
> —LA CHARANGA HABANERA, *"El temba"*[13]

The advent of the Special Period had brought to Cuba less state control and, if not real freedom of expression, a "conditional freedom" (Padura Fuentes 2008), and a desire to challenge official clichés and orthodoxies. The defiant behavior of timba stars was often matched by the daring content of their songs. Around the mid-1990s, timba tunes were offering topical commentaries on issues such as consumer culture ("La Chopimaniaca," Los Van Van), food policies ("Picadillo de soya," NG La Banda), Afro-Cuban culture and religion ("Soy todo," Los Van Van)—all commentaries were related in various ways to official policies and could be read as veiled criticisms of the state and the Communist Party.

A number of timba lyrics dealt more or less obliquely with issues of "dollarization" and tourism, the impact of which was causing a veritable earthquake in Cuban lives and minds, particularly with sex tourism. That was the case with Los Van Van's "La fruta," Manolito Simonet's "Amor matemático," and La Charanga Habanera's "Superturística" and "Hagamos un chen."[14] In a few instances, song content became openly controversial, almost explicitly challenging the Cuban establishment. In NG's "La bruja" (literally "The witch"), for example, the narrator lashed out at a woman who ignored him and traveled by foreigner-only taxis, thus implicitly calling her a whore. In La Charanga Habanera's "El temba," the male narrator, after praising a beautiful woman and lamenting that he had no material means to satisfy her, suddenly invites the woman to find herself a suitable middle-aged man, in yet another reference to young *cubanas* who dated older foreign men. The song was all the more provoking because it was a parody of *Tengo*, a well-known poem written by Afro-Cuban poet Nicolás Guillén in the early sixties to celebrate the achievements of black people under the revolution.

To be sure, most timba songs depicted women as unfaithful lovers and venal and easy objects of desire, sharing with much Cuban and Latin American popular music a fair amount of machismo. In the particular context of the economic crisis and of the tourist boom, however, timba's misogyny indirectly pointed to the demise of the role of the Cuban male and the rising power of young *cubanas* who stood on the front line of the tourism industry and were becoming the new breadwinners of the Special Period (Perna 2005).

The presence of tourism did not deter timba bands from their confrontational attitudes, but actually encouraged them. Popular bands became more and more audacious and took their critique to venues full of unsuspecting tourists, where singers would sometimes launch into context-sensitive, biting commentaries. S. Fernandes recalls how the singer of a dance band, while performing in a venue full of foreigners and *jineteros*,[15] adapted some verses from "Atrevido," a tune by the rap band Orishas, and added them to his song:

> The singer would call out, "Everything she asked for," and the Cuban audience members would reply, "The idiot paid for it"; then the singer would say, "A pretty room at the Cohiba" [a luxury Havana hotel], and the audience would sing, "The idiot paid for it." The Cubans were dancing, clapping, and singing along loudly to the chorus, especially the jineteros. There was a solidarity among all Cubans dancing and singing along in a shared recognition of their position in relation to the foreigners who had paid for their cover charges and drinks, and most likely for other things as well. The foreigners, dancing along too, had no idea what the lyrics meant. (2006, 126)

Such strategies, which clearly evaded Western notions of politically engaged music, suggest that the same song could be experienced very differently by foreigners and Cubans, resulting in radically diverging, and even subversive, meanings. The challenges presented by MB, furthermore, went far beyond the lyrics. As an extremely popular expression of Afro-Cuban identity and pride, timba hinted by its very existence at persisting racial inequalities, undercutting official discourses about social justice in Cuba.

It was a visibly dangerous game in which timba bands that profited massively from tourism were nevertheless candid about and critical of sex tourism in the very dance clubs that had become obvious pick-up places. As one embarrassed Cuban music executive put it to me, those places were "socially contaminated areas." He explained that, "What is called Cuban salsa has been linked very much to the Cuban tourism industry.... You find a lot of prostitutes linked to these shows of dance music. That is very important for them because . . . dance music enables them to 'show off their merchandise' . . . They sell their wares by using music" (Faya 1997).

Scholars have been debating whether those sexual encounters must be considered as outright prostitution or rather as a form of "tactical sex" (Cabezas 2009).[16] In the mid-1990s, at any rate, international scholars and journalists were quick to stress the resurgence of sex tourism in Cuba (O' Connell Davidson 1996). As foreign visitors arrived in the millions, the situation in dance clubs became increasingly grotesque, with bands inciting women to strip naked and inviting audiences to throw dollars to young women performing the best *batidora* onstage (Perna 2005).

With the recovery of the economy taking place in the second half of the 1990s, the Cuban government seemed to take a new authoritarian course, seeking to re-centralize the economy, fight corruption, restrict self-employed work, and repress dissent (Henken 2008). Not surprisingly, MB musicians came under attack from local journalists and institutional entities for their confrontational approach, their functional relationship with the tourist economy, and their proto-capitalist attitude. In July 1997, after an "offensive" performance given at a televised mass concert, La Charanga Habanera, the most popular timba band, was banned from performing and touring abroad for six months. Between 1997 and 1998, the police repeatedly raided dance venues in Havana and Varadero, arresting Cuban women and ultimately shutting down various tourist clubs. The institutional reaction made popular bands such as La Charanga yield and singers like El Médico go into exile. Despite timba's enduring popularity among young Cubans and its remarkable success in Latin music circles abroad, by the end of the 1990s timba appeared to have been brought fully under control.

WELCOME TO THE ISLAND OF NOSTALGIA. *BUENA VISTA SOCIAL CLUB*

Music is a treasure hunt. You dig and dig and sometimes you find something. In Cuba the music flows like a river. It takes care of you and rebuilds you from the inside out.

—Ry Cooder, *liner notes to Buena Vista Social Club,* 1997

The phenomenal success of the album [*Buena Vista Social Club*] seems to me to flow from that backward glance, the rediscovery of timeless, sensual places where dreams and desire merged in a comfortable, evocative music. It was not the real Cuba, of course, either then or now—though the Cuban government is happy for the burgeoning tourist industry to enjoy the fruits of this confusion.

—M. GONZALEZ, *"Music, Dream, and Desire"*[17]

TITLE: Havana—Crumbling colonial splendour
COMMENT: Existing in a time warp since the 1950's, Cuba is on the verge of change, and now is the perfect time to visit before its distinctive character is altered forever. This tour [is] designed to offer a flavour of the authentic Cuba.
PICTURE: Two US vintage cars with Havana's Capitolio in the background

—*THE OBSERVER, advertisement, 2009*[18]

Figure 2.4 Visit Cuba before it's too late. The *Buena Vista* promotional effect according to a brochure by Travel Editions (http://www.traveleditions.co.uk/). The travel package was advertised around 2009 to the readers of British newspapers *The Independent* and *The Guardian*. (Photo David Barham)

In the second half of the 1990s, with the Cuban economy slowly recovering and dance musicians increasingly under pressure from the authorities, new sounds and pictures of Cuban music started to surface in the international arena. The *Buena Vista Social Club* (BV) album contained a type of music that was not literally new, but that owed its appeal to styles and artists born in pre-revolutionary times. The CD was casually recorded in Havana with an assorted group of aging Cuban artists and released in 1997 by World Circuit, a small British world music label. In 1999, the album reached the top of international world music charts. By 2012, it had sold more than 8 million copies worldwide.

The popularity of BV has been all the more exceptional considering that the album did not involve international superstars or major record labels, and because it was stylistically remote from Anglo-American musical canons. Its success, in fact, was largely due to Wim Wenders's 1999 film of the same title, where images of old musicians and Havana's decaying grandeur mixed with a sense of musical intimacy and nostalgia, offering an extremely seductive portrayal of Cuba. Although the film told the story of the recording of a different album (that of Ibrahim Ferrer), many people in the West did not seem to make a distinction between the album and the movie, which, in their minds, became almost a single thing. A UK advertisement for the film, published in *Time Out* magazine, for example, quoted *The Times* exclaiming, "The album opened your ears—the film will touch your soul."[19]

Thrilled by the exoticism of the story, many Westerners were led to believe that the music of BV was everywhere in Cuba. But, at the end of the 1990s, there was hardly any sight of that musical scene on the island: the film was not in cinemas, the music was not on the radio, and there weren't any BV CDs to be bought or bands to be seen. Cubans, like other Latin Americans, knew about those songs and artists, but simply considered them passé and listened to entirely different music. BV's success was therefore an eminently foreign affair that had little impact on local popular tastes.

The only musical area where that impact was felt in Cuba was in the activity of musicians that locals derogatorily called *músicos de sopa* ("soup musicians") and who played for tourists in streets, hotels, and restaurants, where a flood of "traditional" outfits have appeared specifically to satisfy foreigners' expectations created by BV (Garlitz 2005). In 2006, the British magazine *The Economist* remarked: "In the tourist quarters of Old Havana it can seem at times as if every Cuban with a guitar has come out to sing the songs that *Buena Vista* made famous. It's as if you were to go to Liverpool and find bands singing Beatles songs on every street corner." This unstaged context of musical performance, which tourists hear and absorb while strolling through old Havana, has in a sense naturalized the music, fixing it as an indissoluble part of Cuban life and landscape, as the sonic sign of Cuba.

Despite all its calls to tradition and claims about rediscovering Cuba's for-gotten musicians, however, the music of BV was a highly heterogeneous prod-uct, a collection of disparate styles and artists pasted together by Ry Cooder's production. BV became a brand for bands with shifting personnel set up for international tours, which played only sporadically in Cuba and, even then, mainly for foreign audiences. Well into 2010, after most of its stars have died, one "Orquesta BV" and various other BV-branded bands were still touring the world (Voss 2010).

The main problem with BV was not a lack of artistic lineage or its tenuous connection to traditions, but rather its emphatic claims to authenticity, con-structed through a nostalgic portrait of Cuba that measured its distance from the West in terms of place (the secluded island) and time (the forgotten artists, crumbling Havana, collapsing socialism). Conceived by Ry Cooder and Nick Gold, two professional revivalists with experience in the mediation and mar-keting of Third World musics to Western audiences, the album could perhaps best be described as a form of *tourist art*, a local product made on assumptions about the aesthetic expectations of the foreign market (Kirschenblatt-Gimblett and Bruner 1992). To make the album's "classic" repertoire attractive to Western ears, for instance, Cooder chose to give the recording an archaic ambience in the form of a "vintage" sound obtained by recording the band live in the studio with just two microphones, rather than opting for the more analytical, crisp sound produced by modern techniques such as overdubbing and close-miking. According to BV musician Juan de Marcos González, Cooder's method fash-ioned "a sound that was very attractive for Europeans. . . . I'm a producer and musician myself . . . but it would never have occurred to me to make a record with that kind of sound, with such a *roomy* [English in the original text] con-cept" (De Marcos González 1999).

BV's connections to tourism, therefore, have been complex and powerful. The music of the album has clearly influenced the type of sound that tourists today hear and ask for on the streets and in the bars of Cuba's historic cities—but, unlike timba, it has never played a role in Cuban dance clubs or directly generated much income for the Cuban state. Tourism, however, is based upon a quest for difference of places, people, and signs that is largely constructed by the media and internalized by tourists *before* traveling, through a mechanism simi-lar to what Colin Campbell once defined as "imaginative hedonism" (1987). It is on this symbolic and ideological level that the impact of BV has been most pronounced. Thousands of articles published by the Western press in the early 2000s witness how the film and the album resulted in a single, gigantic adver-tisement for Cuba, which sparked a worldwide interest among audiences with middle-class tastes and a curiosity for local cultures. The imaginary Cuba of BV, however, couldn't be further removed from the here-and-now, provocative attitude of MB, from its sexual innuendos and its connections to morally dubi-ous activities. Whereas dance music required foreigners to engage in some form or fashion with the people and the place, BV offered tourists the experience of Walter Benjamin's *flâneur* (2002), that of detached observer, who could safely gaze at Cuba from afar, even when in Cuba.

A cursory look at travel websites in 2013 shows how radically BV has affected the marketing of Cuba. "Buena Vista Cuba" is the name of a package tour offered by Australian tour operator Contours Travel. Under images of vintage American cars in bustling Cuban streets, a commercial site aimed at North Americans who travel independently to Cuba reads:

> Cuba is almost the last place on earth to be kept under wraps, in a virtual time warp.. . . The vintage cars, street banter and slow pace of life; these disappeared from much of the modern world long ago. . . . Welcome to Havana, a city like no other in the world today. (www.havana-unwrapped.com)

This narrative of BV fed both the anti-modern ethos of Western tourism and the "forbidden fruit" syndrome of American audiences who were banned from traveling to Cuba by the US embargo. But it also matched the new touristic vision of Cuba as a cultural heritage destination that the Cuban authorities were seeking to project at the end of the 1990s, bolstering a reified image of Cuban history and identity that could be easily packaged and sold to tourists to gener-ate income for Cuba.[20]

MUSIC AND TOURISM IN THE STRUGGLE FOR CUBAN IDENTITY

During the last two decades, music has proved central to foreigners' experience of Cuba and to the strategies of the local tourism industry. The BV affair per-haps suggests that music can be much more than *one* of the elements support-ing the promotion and the practices of tourism. As the routine identification of certain nations with distinct music styles—say, Ireland and its traditional dance music, Brazil and samba, Argentina and tango—music can literally invent a place, define a location, and situate it within the global flow of tourist desti-nations. By acting as a sign of difference and otherness, music can shape our imagination and experience of a foreign place—more so because its persuasive-ness is grounded in pleasure and the body, thereby enabling sound to afford an immediacy to the tourism industry's representations, conferring depth, or an illusion of it, to the flatness of the "tourist gaze."

In the 1990s, the emergence of two distinctive, almost antithetical Cuban sounds were functional to diverging visions of tourism and helped to articulate different ideas of Cuban national identity. When struggling Cuba aimed to sell cheap vacations to undemanding foreigners, MB served to exhibit Cubans' exuberant sensuality. Under improved economic conditions, BV helped to project the island as a unique, especially humane place that foreigners could consume as a nostalgic fantasy and then, perhaps, experience in person. It was the symbolic power of music as "sonic tourism" (Taylor 1997) that Cooder was clearly aware of: "People want to go somewhere and stay at home, to travel in their armchair. That's fine. Journey with us now for an hour or so and that's enough" (Williamson 1999).

MB and BV eventually came to articulate different clichés about Cuba, feeding diverging, albeit specular fantasies about Cubans: the hypersexualized visions of Afro-Cubans, open to conquest and romance, as staged by timba, and the laid-back, romantic, sexually unchallenged characters of BV, feeding nostalgia for a colonial past populated by deferent, cigar-puffing others. Both visions ultimately helped to construct Cubans as Others and were "accompanied by assumptions that the 'natives' were available to serve tourists . . . and become part of the scenery" (Sheller 2004, 29).

Babb has noticed how "[p]eoples and nations that increasingly look to tourism for economic and political stabilization frequently refashion their cultural identities and histories to draw travellers" (2010, 173). By building a sense of nostalgia that encompassed both the pre- and post-revolutionary past, the revival of "traditional" music in Cuba has not only offered tourism a major focus of attraction, but also engendered a complex renegotiation of national identity, in which the Cuban government has actively engaged in "reimagining Cuba's history in such a way that the 'bourgeois' pre-revolutionary period may be viewed as the logical precursor to the triumph of the revolution" (ibid., 21). Despite Havana and Miami's conflicting agendas—and although the reemergence of Cuba's golden past may have reinforced in the northern side of the Florida Strait the view of the Cuban revolution as an accident of history—the raptured reception of BV in the United States, including in Florida (Levine 1999), suggests that nostalgia may have helped to cast an idea of *cubanidad* that reaches beyond the borders of the island (Ferguson 2003).

Given world music's emphatic celebration of hybridity (Stokes 2004), it is remarkable to notice how the international media that has enthused about Wender's film has remained virtually blind to the cosmopolitan and politically challenging facets of timba. BV's traditionalist fantasies, thus, underscore the politically regressive, but touristically effective role of world music, its "longing for what is not Europe or North America . . . [and] flight from the Euro-self at the very moment of that self's suffocating hegemony" (Brennan 2001). As

Gibson and Connell notice, those fantasies are part of a trend "most evident in some forms of tourism, which exaggerate, reify and romanticise the extent to which any culture, and place, is isolated from others" (2005, 157).

Originally, timba and BV had little in common: but in the complex cultural and political discourse of late 1990s Cuba, they became connected in the way they refracted conflicting ideologies and took on opposite political connotations. Whereas MB was portrayed as materialistic, unruly, foreign-leaning, and ultimately politically dangerous (Pérez 1997), BV came to be appropriated by cultural nationalists and celebrated, at least for a while, as the triumph of the true Cuban musical traditions against the "deviant" attitudes of dance musicians (Godfried 2000).

Such political positioning was, in some respects, ironic. If BV owed its merits to the charm of its musicians, the ability of Cooder and Wenders, and the cleverness of its marketing, its success on a global scale was made possible precisely by the fact that the project, being entirely foreign-produced, remained out of the tangles of the embargo. Timba's international diffusion, by contrast, was hampered by the obstacles that the embargo presented to the establishment of US companies in Cuba, by the limits that it imposed on the circulation of Cuban commercial records and artists, and by anti-Castro pressures from Miami. How the nostalgic trend affected other musicians in Cuba becomes clear from a casual statement made to me in the UK by the leader of a visiting band:

> Cuban music hasn't stopped in the 1940s, as most people think, "Guantanamera" and so on. Cuban music has evolved a lot . . . People over here are forty or fifty years back in relation to contemporary Cuban music. They should listen more to contemporary Cuban music, and those who are promoting Cuban traditional music should think about investing money into new things, into the development of music. (Kemell 1998)

CONCLUSIONS

It is perhaps only seemingly paradoxical that foreign-produced BV has come to embody a nationalist reaffirmation of *cubanidad* at a stage when international tourism has become Cuba's national salvation, and almost every young Cuban aspires to leave the island. MB was (and lent itself to be) used by the Cuban tourist industry as an instrument to tickle tourists' sexual fantasies, but it presented subversive aspects (such as its carnival spirit, mockery of power, and celebration of black identity) that Cuban authorities found extremely difficult to control. More annoyingly, because of its functional ties with the informal economy and sex tourism, MB inevitably called into question the role and poli-cies of the state-controlled tourism industry.

One striking aspect of Cuban tourist policies is the fact that they do not seem to differ much from pre-revolutionary ones. They entail attracting foreign companies to invest in Cuba, developing beach tourism to cater to Western tastes, making Cubans into servants to tourists' necessities, paying locals mea-ger wages, and excluding them from tourist resorts. Cuba's tourism industry employed images of music, dance, and black bodies to promote travel in the 1990s in much the same fashion as it did fifty years before, showing that the legacy of the island's neocolonial past was still very much in place. The emer-gence of a thriving sex tourism industry during the 1990s showed that those images were not lost on foreigners, and that Cuban politicians considered such tourism as a necessary evil.[21]

Aside from the necessities of the crisis, the policies adopted by the tourism industry have also echoed the conservatism of Cuban institutions in matters of race, gender, and culture. The idea that black dance bands and audiences would offer a platform to articulate the exuberant nature of Cubans fit the inherently racist perception of blacks among the white population and the Cuban ruling elite (De la Fuente 2001). It reflected as well a widespread institutional view of dance music as escapist, with no intellectual value—a view that has been strongly called into question by timba's politics of provocation, and then by its censorship.

So, despite the decline of timba's popularity, the context for timba and sex tourism that occurs around MB remains largely intact. Among the various types of Cuban music heard and consumed today in Cuba by tourists, dance music has not disappeared: after all, as tourist guides would have it, Cubans "can all dance salsa." Nor, unfortunately, has sex tourism disappeared. In fact, as Jiménez notices, the "tourist-oriented entertainment industry has contributed largely to the hyper-sexualization and objectification of Cuban women" (2007, 149). And despite the boom of Cuban rap and *reguetón* at the beginning of the new millennium, MB bands continue to work and operate in Cuban tourism alongside "traditional" bands, catering in different places to different groups of tourists—or, possibly, to different moments in their encounters with Cubans.[22]

It is reasonable to argue that the success of BV may have led to a partial refocusing in the marketing targets of Cuban tourism, from all-inclusive beach vacationers to relatively more independent, heritage-minded (and spending) travelers. Maybe its different portrait of Cuba has brought in a more respectful type of tourist, one who consumes places rather than bodies. Nonetheless, it has locked the island in an image of the past where locals, as Cuban musician X Alfonso once put it, "are fighting against the mythological vision of the old Cuba, the Cuba of the Tropicana Club and old cars" (Thigpen 2001).

Has the presence of mass tourism changed Cuban music? Certainly not in the sense of generating some sort of bland "tourist music" molded on Western tastes. Given Cuba's strong musical traditions, its high level of musicianship, and its cultural nationalism, most of the music heard and consumed by Cubans and tourists in Cuba still appears to be firmly local. During the Special Period, however, tourism did affect local music and musicians. On the positive side, it completely transformed the economy of Cuban music; it empowered popular musicians, overturning previous cultural hierarchies between serious and popular music; it brought about more venues and performances; it attracted foreign record labels and media, and helped to project Cuban music and musicians to worldwide audiences.

Before BV, for example, people working in the Cuban music business seemed to have no precise idea about what type of local music could be marketed to foreigners. People I talked to in Cuba seemed to assume that music had to be either utterly modern and entertaining (eg, MB) to be sold, or else culturally "valuable" (eg, *nueva trova*, Afro-Cuban folk or jazz, progressive rock). And although some people did recognize the charm of traditional *son*, almost everyone thought that it was a music of the past with no commercial value (hence BV's claims about the "forgotten" musicians). The international success of BV, thus, came as a total surprise in Cuba.

On the other hand, the divisive effects of tourism, its janus-faced character and its limited positive impact on Cubans' everyday life (Kempadoo 2004; Sanchez and Adams 2008; Cabezas 2009) has been tangible in music as well. Tourism may have made some popular musicians rich and famous, but it has ignored most of their colleagues; it has contributed to essentializing local music, focusing on certain styles at the expense of others; it has reinforced racial and gender stereotypes; it has changed the patterns of live music consumption on the island, concentrating resources on music for export and limiting Cubans' access to live music. If the success of old-fashioned sounds has made Cuban musicians more aware of their own music's potential, it has also persuaded many of them to work for tourists along remarkably narrow notions of tradition. Tourism has created new opportunities for artists, but these have been "driven largely by economic necessity rather than thoughtful consideration" (Moore 2006, 249).

In the foreseeable future, Cuba probably will not be able to survive without tourism. While the island remains nominally committed to socialism, it will still have to deal with the pervasive presence of foreign visitors. These—for both practical and symbolic reasons, and for better or worse—will continue to occupy a special place in Cuban society, bringing Cubans a little money and some chance for interactions that entail encounter, exchange, and struggle. This last word perhaps best defines the prospects of music *vis-à-vis* tourism on the island. If foreign tourism continues to fill the paramount economic and symbolic role it has acquired, Cuban musicians are likely to continue to struggle to get a share of the economic benefits that tourism brings in, struggle to evade the stereotypes that tourism imposes on them, and struggle to get access to the outer world that tourism represents.

NOTES

1. Y cuando hagamos un chen/como tú quieres que te pague, mami?/en cheque, o en efectivo?/o si tú quieres te paso un recibo (*Tremendo delirio*, CD, 1997).
2. The title of a documentary film made by Santiago Alvarez (2003).
3. The end of the Special Period was officially proclaimed by Fidel Castro in 2004. At the beginning of 2010, however, the economic and social context of the Special Period was still very much in place (Espina, Rodriguez, Triana, and Hernández, 2011).
4. In 2007, Cuban revenues from foreign tourism were overtaken by those from the extraction of nickel. "Cuba Nickel Industry Beats Tourism," *Cuba MinRex* (February 4, 2008).
5. For a quick comparison, in the same years Jamaica received respectively 1, 1.1, 1.2, and 1.9 million tourists (sources: Caribbean Tourist Organization http://www.onecaribbean.org/statistics/; Jamaica Tourist Board). The number of 2.5 million visitors to Cuba reached in 2010, however, was quite far from the 5 million forecast by the government at the beginning of the decade.
6. So-called *tourism apartheid* was ended by Raúl Castro in 2008. Even today, however, most Cubans cannot afford to patronize those places.
7. M. Hastings. *Cuba. Thomas Cook Traveller Guides.* Petersborough, UK: Thomas Cook Publishing (2008).
8. F. McAuslan and M. Norman (2010). *Cuba: The Rough Guide.* London: Rough Guides.
9. In 2001 and 2006, respectively, Manolín and Delgado have defected to the United States.
10. In this article I employ the term *música bailable* and *timba* interchangeably. In a strict sense, however, timba is a contemporary style of MB.
11. Timba's dance figures have now been somewhat accepted and normalized. They are, in fact, quite similar to reggaeton's *perreo,* and appear routinely in the dancing of *reguetón* (Cuban reggaeton). Interestingly, many of the cultural contentions and social stigmas attached to timba in the 1990s are now attached to *reguetón* (Gámez Torres, 2012). For a view of Cuban women performing the *batidora* onstage in 2008, see Asi baila una cubana. http://www.youtube.com/watch?v=tlnSjHAmumg&feature=related.
12. Simoni (2009) notices how, recently, seduction strategies in Cuban dance venues have taken different musical paths: while male Cubans continue to entice female foreigners by employing the gallantry codes of MB, female Cubans tend to use the more explicit dance style of *reguetón,* which enables them to make direct body contact and arouse male dance partners.
13. Oye, Nené, yo te aconsejo/que te busques un temba, pero que tenga.
14. *Tremendo delirio* (1997).

15. Generically meaning "hustlers," persons who "ride" tourists extracting some economic gain from them. More specifically, especially referred to women, "prostitutes" (*jineteras*).

16. According to Cabezas, the description of affairs between foreign men and third-world women as outright prostitution may be simplistic, as it makes no room for the "multivalent meanings, and fluctuating situations" typical of *any* relationship (2009, 118). The notion of "tactical sex" is therefore "part of a complex circulation of sex and affect to cultivate social relations with foreigners . . . [and] captures the sporadic and strategic use of sexuality" (ibid., 120).

17. Gonzalez (2004).

18. "The Observer Holiday Offer." *The Observer* (June 21, 2009).

19. *Time Out*. No. 1519, September 29, 1999.

20. In 1998, economic strategist Carlos Lage declared that "culture must become the great mark of Cuba as a tourist destination" (García and Pérez Mok, 2001).

21. Lage stated that prostitution was "the social price we pay for development" (Molyneaux 1996).

22. Babb suggests that the "authentic" Cuba appeals to older travelers, while the young are attracted to the island by the idea of romance and adventure (2010).

REFERENCES

Azicri, M. 2000. *Cuba Today and Tomorrow: Reinventing Socialism*. Gainesville: University Press of Florida.

Babb, F. E. 2010. *The Tourism Encounter: Fashioning Latin American Nations and Histories*. Stanford, CA: Stanford University Press.

Benjamin, Walter. 2002. *The Arcades Project*. Edited by Rolf Tiedemann. Translated by Howard Eiland and Kevin McLaughlin. New York: Belknap Press.

Bisogno, F. *Vivere nell'informalità: luchar nella Cuba post-sovietica*. PhD thesis, Dipartimento di Scienze umane per la formazione, Università Milano Bicocca, 2009.

Brennan, T. 2001. "World Music Does Not Exist," *Discourse* 23(1): 44–62.

Cabezas, A. L. 2009. *Economies of Desire. Sex and Tourism in Cuba and the Dominican Republic*. Philadelphia: Temple University Press.

Campbell, C. 1987. *Romantic Ethic and the Spirit of Modern Consumerism*. Oxford, UK: Basil Blackwell.

Castro, F. 1990. "Events Relating to 7th ANPP Assembly Session." *Castro Speech Data Base*. http://lanic.utexas.edu/project/castro/db/1990/19900712-1.html.

Centeno, M. A., and M. Font. eds. 1997. *Toward a New Cuba? Legacies of a Revolution*. Boulder, CO: Rienner.

Colantonio, A, and R. B. Potter. 2006. *Urban Tourism and Development in the Socialist State: Havana during the "Special Period."* Burlington, VT: Ashgate.

De la Fuente, A. 2001. *A Nation for All: Race, Inequality, and Politics in Twentieth-Century Cuba*. Chapel Hill: University of North Carolina Press.

De Marcos González, J. Interview by the author, London, November 1999.

DeNora, T. 2000. *Music in Everyday Life*. Cambridge, UK: Cambridge University Press.

Espino, M. D. "International Tourism in Cuba: An Update." Proceedings of the 18th Annual Meeting of the Association for the Study of the Cuban Economy (ASCE), Vol 18, August 5–7, 2008.

Faya, A. 1997. *Interview with the author*. Havana, Cuba.

Ferguson, R. J. 2003. "The Transnational Politics of Cuban Music and Cuban Culture." *The Culture Mandala: The Bulletin of the Centre for East-West Cultural and Economic Studies* 1(3).

Fernandes, S. 2006. *Cuba Represent! Cuban Arts, State Power, and the Making of New Revolutionary Cultures*. Durham, NC: Duke University Press.

Fernández, N. 1999. "Back to the Future? Women, Race, and Tourism in Cuba." In *Sun, Sex, and Gold. Tourism and Sex Work in the Caribbean*, edited by K. Kempadoo, 81–89. Lanham, MD: Rowan & Littlefield, Lanham.

García, A., and M. Pérez Mok. "La importancia del turismo en el desarrollo futuro de la economía cubana en las condiciones de globalización de la economía." Paper presented at XXIII Congreso Internacional *Latin American Studies Association*, Washington, DC, September 6–8, 2001.

Garlitz, D. *Canciones de Turista: Cultural Tourism, The Buena Vista Social Club, and Cuban Son*. Master's Thesis, Wesleyan University, 2005. http://davidgarlitz.com/12.

Gibson, C., and J. Connell. 2005. *Music and Tourism. On the Road Again*. Clevedon, UK: Channell View.

Godfried, E. 2000. "Buena Vista Social Club. Critics, Self-Criticism, and the Survival of Cuban Son." *AfrocubaWeb*. http://www.afrocubaweb.com/eugenegodfried/buenavis-tacritics.htm.

Gonzalez, M. 2004. "Music, Dream, and Desire," *Socialist Review*, January. http://www.socialistreview.org.uk/article.php?articlenumber=8730

Henken, T. 2008. *Cuba: A Global Studies Handbook*. Santa Barbara, CA: ABC-CLIO.

Holgado Fernández, I. 2000. *¡No es fácil! Mujeres cubanas y la crisis revolucionaria*. Barcelona: Icaria.

Jiménez, M. R. 2007. "The Political Economy of Leisure." In *A Contemporary Cuba Reader. Reinventing the Revolution*, edited by Philip Brenner, Marguerite Rose Jiménez, John M. Kirk, and William M. LeoGrande, 146–155. Lanham, MD: Rowman & Littlefield.

Kemell, J. 1998. *Interview with the author*. London, UK.

Kempadoo, K. 2004. *Sexing the Caribbean. Gender, Race, and Sexual Labor*. New York: Routledge.

Kirshenblatt-Gimblett, B., and E. Bruner. 1992. "Tourism." In *Folklore, Cultural Performance and Popular Entertainment: A Communications-Centered Handbook*, edited by R. Bauman, 300–306. New York: Oxford University Press.

Levine, A. 1999. "Viva 'Buena Vista Social Club.'" *Salon.com*. March 9. http://www.salon.com/1999/03/09/09feature_html/

McAuslan, F., and M. Norman. 2010. *Cuba. The Rough Guide*. London: Rough Guides.

Molyneaux, M. D. 1996. *State, Gender and Institutional Change in Cuba's "Special Period": The Federación de Mujeres Cubanas*. London: Institute of Latin American Studies (Research Papers 43).

Moore, R. D. 2006. *Music and Revolution. Cultural Change in Socialist Cuba*. Berkeley: University of California Press.

"Now We Make Politics." 2006. *The Economist*. December 15. http://www.economist.com/node/8401940.

O' Connell Davidson, J. 1996. "Sex Tourism in Cuba." *Race and Class* 38(1): 39–48.

Padura Fuentes, L. 2008. "Living and Creating in Cuba. Risks and Challenges." In *A Contemporary Cuba Reader: Reinventing the Revolution*, edited by Philip Brenner, Marguerite Rose Jiménez, John M. Kirk, and William M. LeoGrande, 348–354. Lanham, MD: Rowman & Littlefield.

Pérez, C. M. 1997. "Están matando a la música cubana." *El Caimán Barbudo*, A.30(278): 28–29.

Pérez, L. A., Jr. 1999. *On Becoming Cuban: Identity, Nationality, and Culture*. Chapel Hill: University of North Carolina Press.

Perna, V. A. 2005. *Timba, the Sound of the Cuban Crisis*. Burlington, VT: Ashgate.

Pozo, A. 1993. "Necesario turismo," *Bohemia* 6 (February 5): 37.

Sanchez, P. M., and K. M. Adams. 2008. "The Janus-Faced Character of Tourism in Cuba." *Annals of Tourism Research* 35(1): 27–46.

Schwartz, R. 1997. *Pleasure Island: Tourism and Temptation in Cuba*. Lincoln: University of Nebraska Press.

Sheller, M. 2004. "Natural Hedonism. The Invention of Caribbean Islands as Tropical Playgrounds." In *Tourism in the Caribbean. Trends, Development, Prospects*, edited by D. T. Duval, 23–38. New York: Routledge.

Simoni, V. "Touristic Encounters in Cuba Informality, Ambiguity, and Emerging Relationships." PhD thesis. Leeds Metropolitan University, October 2009.

Stokes, M. 2004. "Music and the Global Order," *Annual Review of Anthropology* 33: 47–72.

Sweig, J. E. 2009. *Cuba. What Everyone Needs to Know*. New York: Oxford University Press.

Taylor, T. D. 1997. *Global Pop: World Music, World Markets*. New York: Routledge.

Thigpen, D. E. 2001. "The Buena Vista Social Club Is Yesterday: The Streets of Cuba's Cities Today are Moving to a Younger Rhythm." *Time* 158(14): 19–21.

Urry, J. 2002. *The Tourist Gaze*. London: Sage.

Voss, M. 2010. "Buena Vista Social Club. Cuban Band or Brand?" *BBC News*, February 25. http://news.bbc.co.uk/2/hi/americas/8528594.stm.

Williamson, N. 1999 "Playing to the Camera." *Songlines* (Summer): 18–20.

DISCOGRAPHY

Buena Vista Social Club. World Circuit/Nonesuch (1997).

La Charanga Habanera, *Pa' que se entere la Habana*. Magic Music (1996).

La Charanga Habanera, *Tremendo delirio*. Magic Music/Universal (1997).

José Luís Cortés y NG La Banda, *La bruja*. Caribe (1994).

Orishas, *A lo cubano*. Cooltempo/Emi France (2000).

Los Van Van, *¡Ay diós, amparame!* Caribe (1995).

PART II

Material and Immaterial Patterns of Circulation and Music Touristics

3

Cruising Cultures

Post-War Tourism and the Circulation of Caribbean
Musical Performances, Recordings, and Representations

MIMI SHELLER ■

The Alcoa Shipping Company promoted its Caribbean cruises with color-ful depictions of Caribbean people, culture, and landscapes in a striking series of print advertisements that ran from 1948 to 1958 in magazines such as *Holiday, Time,* and *The Saturday Evening Post.* In 1954–1955, the accomplished graphic illustrator James R. Bingham created a musically themed series, accompanied by sales of a collection of 45 rpm recordings of Caribbean music. This combination of advertising imagery, music recordings, and tourism promotion by a company that mined bauxite raises interesting questions about the ways in which Caribbean musical cultures circulated in relation to North American tourism and business. This chapter examines the historical entanglement of Caribbean folkloric music production, performance, collection and representation, including its relation to commercial commodification via radio, records, and tourism, and its role in US-Caribbean relations beginning from the period of "pan-Americanism" in the 1930s, through World War II, and into the post-war period, when air travel began and the tourism infrastructure grew.

The Alcoa advertising campaign for its Caribbean cruises can be situated in relation to other forms of Caribbean musical circulation, beginning with the ethnographic collection of traditional musical forms by anthropologists in the 1930s; the recordings of Caribbean folk music made by Alan Lomax in 1937–1938 for the Smithsonian Folkways collection; the ethnological institutionalization of folkloric traditions within various Caribbean countries in the

1940s; the mounting of a National Folk Festival in Washington, DC, which in 1941 included Caribbean and Latin American performers; and the growing use of Caribbean music and dance performance in American popular culture in this period (Broadway theater, Hollywood cinema, advertising jingles, television shows, and the like). How did all of these forms of cultural production shape the meanings and forms of "traditional" folkloric music in the Caribbean region? And how does the modernization of tourism relate to the traditionalization of music?

Through a historical contextualization and close reading of travel articles and Alcoa advertising from *Holiday* magazine, I aim to explore the complex mobilities that informed the production and circulation of Caribbean music cultures in the mid-twentieth century. These mobilities involved constellations of transversal movement of people (musicians, tourists, anthropologists, travel writers, national folk troupes, migrant workers, and so on); the movement of objects and technologies (ships, recording discs, musical instruments, bauxite, magnetic tape, airplanes); and the cultural circulation of images, texts, and other performative material cultures (magazine articles, paintings, novels, advertisements, brochures, costumes). As these hybrid lists suggest, one of the aims of this chapter is to suggest that there is no clear distinction between the "traditional" and the "modern" in the Caribbean, nor between "authentic" culture and "commercial" performance; they are always in touch with each other.[1] In fact, each of these dualities is co-produced and codependent, part of a dynamic relation, and musical mobilities are crucially mixed with human, material, and cultural mobilities of various kinds (including the movement of bauxite, ships, workers, and tourists) that have together generated a distinctive form of Caribbean modernity.

CARIBBEAN MUSICAL CULTURES IN NORTH AMERICA

Kate Ramsey argues that in the 1930s–1940s, "Folklore" was "a crucial commodity in the context of President Franklin D. Roosevelt's Good Neighbor Policy. U.S. efforts to foster a sense of pan-Americanism through cultural means converged with the efforts of Latin American and Caribbean states to construct popular cultures as the repository of national particularity" (Ramsey 2011, 230). With the anthropological recording of traditional music and dance cultures in the 1930s, and the forming of national folkloric troupes in various Caribbean countries in the early 1940s, folkloric traditions became national assets, often "cleaned up" for official consumption by the removal of both their spiritual content (i.e., dances performed in the service of Vodou *lwa* or the *orishas* of Cuban Santería) and at times their sexually explicit bodily choreographies. "Whether packaged as tourist attractions on the national stage or exported abroad for displays of hemispheric unity," Ramsey suggests, "national ballets and folklore groups became a key currency of interhemispheric relations and diplomacy, to be circulated and exchanged much in the same spirit as reciprocal trade" (Ramsey 2011, 230).

Yet at the very same time, popular musical cultures were alive to subaltern mobilities, which grew out of economic survival and fed into alternative modernizing projects. These counter-mobilities supported new transnational fusions of traditional musical forms, new kinds of musical livelihoods through touristic performances, and eventually access to new technologies such as radio and recording. This chapter explores the tensions between these elite and subaltern musical mobilities, as they were implicated in the production of Caribbean musical cultures within tourist markets.

The Haitian Bureau d'Ethnologie, for example, was formed in 1941 under the leadership of Jacques Roumain, and it held events where a group known as Mater Dolorosa performed ritual songs and dances, playing "a key role in the ethnological interpretation and codification of ritual performance as 'folklore' in the early and mid-1940s," according to Ramsey (2011, 224–225). As she notes, it is also important to consider the development of *indigénisme* in Haiti in relation to the concurrent development of *africubanismo* and Latin American *indigenismo*, all of which occurred in the context of Haitian labor migration to Cuba and the Dominican Republic, as well as reactions to the U.S. military presence in the region throughout the 1920s–1930s and during World War II. So traditional Caribbean musical performances were being produced or crystallized as indigenous "folklore" both for modernizing national urban elites and for U.S. visitors, occupiers, and tourists, at the very moment when the "folk" throughout the Caribbean were entering new patterns of labor migration and cultural exchange, often generating new musical fusions.

According to Gage Averill, the U.S. occupation "accelerated the incorporation of Haiti into global commercial and cultural relations, introducing foreign musics such as American jazz and Cuban *son* to Haitian urban audiences," and leading to new hybrid music forms such as Vodou-jazz (Averill 1997, 32). The early to mid-1940s also saw innovation in Cuban *son*, as it modernized in ways that "laid the foundations for salsa" and the invention of mambo, "a fusion of Afro-Cuban rhythms with the big-band format adopted from swing jazz," as Peter Manuel describes it (Manuel 1995, 37–38).[2] This was followed by the craze for mambo and the commercialization of *chachachá* by big band leaders in New York, reaching a peak in the 1950s, when Havana, Cuba, also became a mecca for tourists as "America's bachelor entertainment center, with its glittery world of casinos, cabarets, and over two hundred brothels." Thus the Bingham advertising campaign appears in the wake of ethnological institutionalization of folkloric performance, the popular fusion of traveling musical cultures, and in the midst of Caribbean musical modernization and commercialization.

Where else would North Americans in the 1940s–1950s gain experience of listening to Caribbean and Latin music, besides traveling there? Without the space for a comprehensive history of musical circulation, I just mention a few sites here: the Eighth Annual National Folk Festival, held in Washington, DC, in early May 1941, for the first time brought in "guest groups from Canada, Mexico, one South American Country and some of the Islands," including Haiti (Ramsey 2011, 230–231). It was also in the 1940s that Carmen Miranda became a Hollywood sensation. Born in Portugal, her family migrated to Brazil where she made her career impersonating the exuberant and independent Afro-Brazilian street vendors of Bahia, singing and dancing her way into American popular culture with a Caribbean flair. While big band versions of mambo and *chachachá* were making their way into New York, calypso music from Trinidad and Jamaican mento were being promoted by singers like Harry Belafonte, and Cuban musician Desi Arnaz starred with his wife Lucille Ball in the hit TV series, *I Love Lucy*, premiering in 1951, in which he played a fictitious version of himself, Cuban orchestra leader Enrique "Ricky" Ricardo. In 1951 there were also tours, such as the visits of Haiti's Troupe Folklorique Nationale and the band Jazz des Jeunes to expositions in Canada and Washington, DC, and to New York's Ziegfield Theater (Averill 1997).

Thus it is particularly interesting to consider how a major U.S. aluminum corporation—which mined bauxite in the region as part of a massive wartime industry geared towards the production of US air power—mobilized representations of Caribbean folkloric performances in advertising campaigns for its Caribbean cruises, using these as a crucial form of public relations and tourism promotion. If Caribbean traditional musical and dance cultures were in the process of being consolidated into national repositories of acceptably cleaned up and "respectable" folk culture, they were simultaneously being packaged and sold to tourists, travel writers, and even visiting anthropologists, all of whom also had an interest in their more racy, sexual, and magical aspects.

Besides the tensions and contradictions within various elite projects, both native and foreign, however, there was also a competing popular pull towards modernity, especially in the post-war period, including exposure to new musical influences as well as new modes of disseminating music, such as radio, big bands, and eventually recording studios and sound systems. In the following, then, I explore the Alcoa Shipping Company's specific packaging of folkloric tradition as a constellation of various mobilities and temporalities, while also situating it in relation to the emergence of popular cultures of modernity that were infusing and recreating vibrant "folk" musical and dance cultures across the Caribbean.

THE JOHN R. BINGHAM ILLUSTRATIONS FOR ALCOA

Alcoa played a special role in the Caribbean, not only shipping the vast majority of the bauxite (mined first in Dutch Guiana and later in Jamaica) used to smelt aluminum in the United States, but also carrying cruise ship passengers, commissioning artists to depict Caribbean scenery, selling recordings of Caribbean music, and even sponsoring the Caribbean Arts Prize in the 1950s.[3] In 1946, the company built three "modern, air-conditioned ships," the Alcoa Corsair, Cavalier, and Clipper, as exemplars of what could be done with aluminum, costing about $2,250,000 each. They were in service until 1960, each carrying sixty-five passengers and departing every Saturday from New Orleans on a sixteen-day cruise. The cruise stopped in the ports of Kingston (Jamaica), Curaçao (Netherlands Antilles), three ports in Venezuela (La Guaira, Puerto Cabello, and Guanta), Port of Spain (Trinidad), and Ciudad Trujillo (Dominican Republic), sometimes with varied itineraries. The company also ran several freighters out of New York, Baltimore, Montreal, and New Orleans, which carried twelve passengers and made longer, slower trips; these ships delivered bauxite for Reynolds (which mined bauxite in Haiti) and Kaiser (which mined bauxite in Jamaica), as well as for Alcoa, and cruise ship passengers could also pick up the freighters in Trinidad for a "safari adventure" into the interior of Suriname, where Alcoa's bauxite mines were located.[4]

Here I focus on a particular Alcoa Steamship Company series that ran from 1954–1955, a set of colorful portrayals of folkloric musical performances, parades, and vibrant dances by John R. Bingham, a graphic illustrator known for his extensive body of advertising work as well as pulp fiction paperback covers. Readers are encouraged to write in to purchase 45 rpm recordings of the music that accompanies some of the dances, such as the banda dance of Haiti, the joropo of Venezuela, the merengue of the Dominican Republic, and the beguine of the French West Indies. Other ads represent the Pajaro Guarandol "folk dance of the Venezuelan Indians," the steel pan and "stick dance" of Trinidad, the "Simadon" harvest festival of Curacao, the Seis folk dance of the Jibaros of Puerto Rico, and the John Canoe dancers of Jamaica. In each case, one or two dramatic full-page dancing figures are in the foreground, with smaller figures (including musicians) in the background, and with surrounding text against a white background. What sources do these images draw on? How do they represent the music and dance of the region? And what is their relation both to the production of traditional music and dance performances for tourist consumption and to the circulation of recordings and representations of Caribbean folkloric cultures?

At first glance this series connects touristic consumption of musical performances from across the Caribbean with an almost ethnological project of investigation into traditional cultures and people who seem to persist outside of modernity, a remnant of the past available for modern cruise tourists to visit. The text emphasizes the tourist's access to the diverse musical cultures of the Caribbean. An illustration of a dancing man and woman with musicians—a drummer (playing a single-headed drum, held between the knees), a metal scraper (*güira*), hand-clappers, and singers—in front of white-washed thatched cottages, carries the headline: "Set your spirits dancing on a carefree Alcoa cruise" followed by the text: "Music, dancing, laughter . . . the infectious gaiety of the Caribbean touches all who visit its shores. Perhaps it's the wonderful climate—or the colorful people—or the bounteous natural beauty. In any case the Caribbean is sure to enchant you." Carefree, gay, and colorful, the Caribbean beckons as a simpler world (see Figure 3.1).

Figure. 3.1 Alcoa Steamship Company ad, "Set your spirits Dancing on a carefree Alcoa cruise" by James R. Bingham. (*Holiday* magazine, August 1955)

The text and imagery imply that these dances are not simply to be observed by the tourists, but will also "infect" them with the gaiety and enchantment of the Caribbean. Yet the small print at the bottom somewhat jarringly notes, "Sales-minded executives can profit by examining the Caribbean as a potential market for their products. This thriving area is now America's second largest export customer, and is still growing. To evaluate this market, write on your company letterhead for the 1955 edition of our 'Export Market Opportunities' book." So while the headlines proclaim things like "Be happy—be gay—see the Caribbean the Alcoa cruise way," the subtext is that there are more instrumental reasons for businessmen to combine leisure with business. These textual juxtapositions suggest that beyond the lively folk cultures portrayed in each scene, there are currents of modernity circulating across the Caribbean, along with the opening of new markets and a need for modern products.

Another Alcoa ad features a man holding a cello aloft, played with a bow, and two pairs of dancers with other musicians in the background (see Figure 3.2):

THIS IS THE BEGUINE, a combination of African rhythm and French melody that is indigenous to Martinique and Guadeloupe. You can get an extended play 45 RPM hi-quality recording of the beguine and other French West Indian folk dances, together with descriptive text, by sending $1.00 to Dept. "R" at the New York address below. Ask for Number 6 in our Series of Caribbean Recordings.

Not only can the tourist circulate on a cruise through the Caribbean islands to hear the music of different countries, but the music too can circulate into North America in the form of a record. We can imagine prospective tourists ordering these records to listen to before their trip to get in the mood, or perhaps even as a form of imaginary travel in lieu of the trip itself. Likewise, the records could serve as a souvenir after the trip, bringing back memories of "gay" times. Yet here too the small print notes "If you're not sure [that] domestic sales can keep your plant in full production, consider the billion dollar market in the friendly, nearby Caribbean. The Alcoa-served area is now Uncle Sam's second best export customer." Thus the promotion of Caribbean culture was closely linked to the opening of Caribbean markets to American exports (especially goods made from aluminum); and economic and cultural exchange were envisioned as two-way processes, though not necessarily equal ones. Alcoa had an interest in ensuring the transition of wartime aluminum plants to civilian products, which needed growing markets.

However, the commodification of Caribbean folk culture was not simply a foreign enterprise; it was also carried out by local elites who were promoting

Figure. 3.2 Alcoa Steamship Company ad, "Cruise to the isles where they began the Beguine" by James R. Bingham. (*Holiday* magazine, October 1955)

both local commerce and the growth of tourism. As Krista Thompson observes, Caribbean national elites tried to keep their towns looking quaint and not too modern, their hotels encircled by tropical foliage, and photographers often edited modern infrastructure, such as electricity lines, out of their pictures (Thompson 2007). Yet less well known is that by the 1950s, leading business elites like the Issa family of Jamaica (originally from Bethlehem and Damascus), owned not only historic hotels like the Myrtle Bank, but also the new two-million-dollar modern luxury hotel Tower Isle in Montego Bay, "several hardware concerns; enough real estate to have made necessary the formation of a special company to take care of it; a substantial interest in the Jamaica Telephone Company and the corporation that controls most of the movie houses on the island; and no less than forty-two department stores of varying sizes" (Basso 1951, 134). Thus there were close ties between investments in tourism that encouraged the production of folk culture, and the creation of infrastructure and markets for the circulation of modern commodity cultures.

The point I want to draw from this is that there is a transnational space across which "folk" cultures of the Caribbean were produced and circulated, which is always an already commercial space, tied to tourism and to commerce. In addition to cruise ships, tourists were also beginning to arrive by airplane, such as the Pan-American Clipper, which started flying from Miami to Kingston in the 1940s.[5] More adventurous tourists even sought out music in the nightclubs of Kingston, with one 1946 article in *Holiday* magazine noting: "At night, take your pick of a series of 'punch bowl' bars where the calypsolike ballads of Jamaica are sung by guitar-strumming minstrels with names like Sir Lancelot, the Duke of Middle Age and the Count DeCay" (Rosen 1946, 31). The same writer, Fred Rosen, also refers to staying at the hotels in Montego Bay where "little bands of native musicians drift from bar to bar to play and sing for pennies. Local favorite is 'Porkchops,' a sloe-eyed black youth, master of the Jamaican guitar and an endless series of native ballads, Calypsos and exotic compositions of his own;" not to mention "Broadway Bill" who "will sing for you as he rows across the bay to the coral gardens" in a "gaudily painted rowboat named the Queen Elizabeth." Jamaican musicians and performers were already creating consumable mixtures of "native" traditions, mixed with other regional influences, as well as American radio and perhaps Broadway show tunes.

Perhaps most interesting is Rosen's comment that "if you're extraordinarily lucky and have a good Jamaican friend you might get to a Pocomania. Pocomania is a set of voodoolike rituals performed at night as a wild barefoot dance around lighted candles set in mystical designs on the ground" (Rosen 1946, 32). The Afro-Caribbean religious form known as Pocomania had already been commercialized by the early 1940s, with its dances being performed in floor shows for tourists and depicted in movies such as "The Love Wanga" (1936), a film featuring interracial relationships, "voodoo" and zombies, also known as "Drums of the Jungle."[6] Tourists in the 1940s could apparently gain entrée to many different forms of Jamaican music, which were well integrated with tourism. Finally, Rosen stays at an old plantation house, an hour and a half from Montego Bay, where,

> After dinner, guests sit out on the lawn for entertainment by local bush Negroes. The moon is bright, the palms swish gently and in the air is the strange two-tone melody of the whistling Jamaican frog. Every musical instrument is homemade—the weirdest being the eight-foot *cocolimojo*, made of the branch of a palm tree with a string stretched across its arched

ends like a bow. Two men sit on either end drawing the string taut. One beats the string with drumsticks, the other, facing him, slides back and forth a hollow calabash gourd, changing the pitch. Black backs sweat and ripple as the tom-tom rhythm goes faster and faster until the players are exhausted. This is followed by a soulfull barefoot boy who sings over and over of the 'Hum-hum rancho' where the 'dearsandthecantaloupesplay.' A bush magician swallows fire and dances on broken glass, eight men wrestle at once, and finally everyone stands to God Save the King.[7]

This hybrid production of Bush Negro (Maroon) and American Western (Home on the Range), primitive and commercial, magical and modern, reminds us that the invention of tradition is part of the arrival of modern tourism, even as people held onto and passed down musical practices from a deep tradition.

The Bingham images for Alcoa also emphasize fun, color, and excitement in performances that seem perfectly geared toward tourism. The "processional dance" of the Simadon harvest festival of Curacao is described as "alive with pageantry and color," with lots of smiling dancing boys, women and children in a procession accompanied by drumming and maracas (see Figure 3.3). The main figure is wearing trousers that appear to be made from an export sack marked U.S.A. Another shows a couple "dancing the Joropo (Ho-ro-po), native dance of Venezuela" in which the "flashing steps of this gay Joropo date back to old Spanish dances, for Venezuela's roots lie deep in the history of Spain." In the foreground can be seen colorfully painted maracas, a harp player, and what looks like a bandola llanera; yet, unique to all the ads, there is also inserted a small image of tourists enjoying the swimming pool on the deck of the cruise ship (see Figure 3.4). Thus both the texts and the images suggest a mixture of different kinds of temporality, deep in history yet integrated into modern markets, exotic yet also safely familiar.

While the Alcoa texts emphasize that cruise passengers will move from Spanish influenced ports through French, English, and Dutch, with different musical cultures and dances associated with each, there is also an unspoken eddy of musical performance around the Caribbean and back to North America. The mobility of the tourist is presented as replicating the mobilities of Caribbean history, in which different groups of colonists and settlers moved through and settled on the various islands, many of which changed hands in the course of various sea battles. The music becomes a way to track those mobilities and circulate through them as if on a ride not only through geographical space, but also through historical time presented as folk performances.

In addition to the music itself, images of Caribbean music have also circulated in the form of visual and textual representations, which are also important to the analysis of the Alcoa advertising campaign and of how images of

Figure. 3.3 Alcoa Steamship Company ad, The Simadon Harvest Festival in Curacao, by James R. Bingham. (*Holiday* magazine, June 1955)

the Caribbean circulated in North America. European artists, ethnologists, and philosophers of race have long had an interest in the portrayal of Caribbean music and dance forms, with some of the most famous examples coming from the work of Italian artist Agostino Brunias (1730–1796), who resided primarily in Dominica but also spent time in St. Vincent, Barbados, Grenada, St. Kitts, and Tobago. Brunias's works are some of the earliest depictions of the interactions among various class and color groups in musical settings. Such images are often criticized for romanticizing the conditions of slavery, yet they have also been drawn on in the reconstruction of folk traditions.[8] The re-circulation of similar images in the context of mid-twentieth century tourism thus partakes of the wider history of the relation between circulation of images of Caribbean

Figure. 3.4 Alcoa Steamship Company ad, Joropo dance of Venezuela, by James R. Bingham. (*Holiday* magazine, April 1955)

people, visual representations of musical practices, and cross-cultural travelers who construct taxonomies of difference. In the following sections I examine the historical context for two of the Bingham images more closely, one representing a "John Canoe" dancer from Jamaica, the other the "Banda dance" from Haiti. Both dances have deep historical roots, as well as long representational histories.

The John Canoe Dancer

The dancer in Bingham's John Canoe illustration (see Figure 3.5) has a remarkably similar costume to that found in an 1838 lithograph by the Sephardic

Figure. 3.5 Alcoa Steamship Company ad, John Canoe Dance, by James R. Bingham.
(*Holiday* magazine, May 1955)

Jewish Jamaican artist Isaac Mendes Belisario for his *Sketches of Character,
in Illustration of the Habits, Occupation, and Costume of the Negro Population
in the Island of Jamaica* (1837–1838).[9] In this work the dancer is described as
dressed in a pseudo-military style, with a profusion of large, wild ringlets falling over his face and shoulders, with a house fixed on his head in the same style
as Bingham's illustration:

> The house is usually constructed of pasteboard and colored papers—it is
> also frequently highly ornamented with beads, tinsel, spangles, pieces of
> looking glass, etc. etc. and being firmly fixed on a board, the bearer is
> enabled to balance it whilst going through many strange contortions of
> body and limbs miscalled dancing.[10]

Although the British banned the use of trumpets and drums in Jamaican festivals as early as the seventeenth century, in recognition of their military use in West Africa and their potential to foster rebellion among the enslaved, the so-called John Canoe, sometimes spelled Jankunu or Jonkonnu, dance/parade seems to have persisted by appearing to be an innocuous Christmastime jest.

Kenneth Bilby's extensive research on Jonkunnu traditions—which span not only rural Jamaica, but also the Bahamas (where it has been incorporated in a major national festival) and the Garifuna cultures on the Caribbean coast of Central America—shows that while it is dissimulated as a simple, fun amusement around Christmas and New Year's Day, it has discernible origins in West African and later New World sacred practices relating to departed ancestors (Bilby 2010).[11] Thus we can surmise that "John Canoe"/Jonkunnu is part of a deep-rooted though necessarily evolving masking tradition that has traveled throughout the Atlantic world, taking new shape in diverse settings. Although it includes characters such as "Pitchy Patchy" who appear in Maroon-style "ambush," and involves demands for money from viewers, it has long been amenable to presenting itself as a safe, secular, fun festivity that can be consumed by outsiders.

In the background of Bingham's depiction can be seen a black-masked devil figure, carrying a pitchfork and sword; a skirted dancer with a cow's head; a dancer with feathered "Indian" headdress appearing to ride a horse; and four musicians constituting a fife and drum band (with a fife, drum, and grater visible). The text accompanying it says "You'll find in the Caribbean a colorful, merry-go-round of memories—from these John Canoe dancers in Jamaica to the Calypso singers of Trinidad. You'll find, also, that an Alcoa cruise is the really enjoyable way of seeing the Caribbean's wonderful sights." The historical origins of this creole art form, linked to West African sacred masked dances as well as possibly European military parading and mumming traditions, continue to be handed down in large part because they also mask their own meaning. We see this masking in the way the Alcoa text associates John Canoe with the enjoyment and fun of the tourist, as if on a merry-go-round, a form of child's entertainment at a carnival or fair. It contributes to the image of the Caribbean as a playful, fun place for a vacation, though with the exotic thrill of its apparently primitive musical cultures, festivals, and carnivals.

Carnival and various other parading traditions were an important site for tourist participation and cultural consumption. For example, *Holiday* magazine in 1952 carried a photographic essay "Carnival Isle," describing Trinidad's "bright tropical color and rousing calypso rhythms [that] are alive all the year round, but they come into their uninhibited glory at Carnival time" (Henle 1952, 91). Such masking traditions had historically involved interaction between slaves and masters, working classes and colonial elites, and were part of a pan-Caribbean tradition of cultural contestation through the popular space of the street. In his study of circum-Atlantic performance, Joseph Roach reads the unstable relation between Carnival and the law in New Orleans as suggesting that they "conspire together to craft a contingent margin of behavior that remains easily within the laws' reach, if need be, but hovers provisionally outside their reach" in a liminal and ludic space (Roach 1996, 252). The musical cultures considered here might also hover slightly outside the safe spaces of national institutionalization and tourist consumption crafted by elites; music and dance were always alive to the liminal and ludic practices of popular culture that might exceed the politics of respectability by letting back in the spiritual and the sexual.[12]

A history of John Canoe provided by Kenneth Bilby in the liner notes to the Smithsonian Folkways collection *Jamaica Roots*, Vol. 2 (1975), notes that "John Canoe, or 'masquerade,' as it is often called, is a Jamaican folk dance involving masking, and sometimes singing, which is done during the Christmas holidays up until New Year's Day," and it combines elements from West African ritual yam harvest festivals and possibly British Christmas festivals that had absorbed earlier pagan Spring festivals related to fertility, including Morris dancing and Mumming. Typical characters include what he calls cow-man, devil-man, and wild-Indian, all pictured here, among others. But he also notes that "John Canoe bands often travel fair distances to tourist areas on the north coast, where they can expect to make more money than in the hills." Like colonial white elites, tourists enjoyed this spectacle, even though they might also be somewhat threatened by inscrutable "devils" demanding money (as my own parents were when visiting Jamaica on their first Christmas time trip outside the United States in the early 1960s, and attempting to photograph the John Canoe band that came through Montego Bay).

A recording of John Canoe music can also be heard on George Eaton Simpson's 1954 Smithsonian Folkways Recording "Jamaican Cult Music." Here the liner notes refer to descriptions of John Canoe in Edward Long's *History of Jamaica* (1774) and in Belisario's *Sketches of Character* (1838), which observed that "When these Christmas amusements were more in vogue, sums amounting to ten or twelve pounds per day, were collected by the Actors." So, even a century or more earlier, the "traditional" folk culture involved interaction with outside elites and financial exchanges, which could have been part of the early ritual practices of appeasing inside ancestral spirits with offerings, from which they derived; it is both an element of modern commodification found in touristic performances, yet may also have deep roots in the sacred offerings to the departed ancestors. This traditional Christmas and New Year practice of (m)asking for monetary offerings was therefore easily incorporated into tourism; while the music itself found its way into the earliest Smithsonian recordings, which today have become an ethnological record of the folk music of Jamaica, and have continued to evolve in "living" forms of Jamaican popular music and national festivals.

As Bilby concludes his recent studies of this cultural complex, "Today, in the transformed Jankunu that has survived and is still with us, there is still more than meets the eye, encoded and carried down to us in 'secular' yet sacred sounds to which, 'masked' as ever, the spirit still dances" (Bilby 2010, 217). The connection of masking to the modernizing economy of bauxite and tourism is suggestive of the magical transformations wrought by capitalism, which also hides its labor behind the commodity fetish of bauxite turned to shining aluminum futurity. Alcoa's aluminum-filled ships cruise through Caribbean cultures, proclaiming modernity, even as those cultures ride the sea waves and air waves back into the wider circum-Atlantic cultures traversed by their ancestors.

The Banda Dance of Haiti

The illustration of the banda dance of Haiti is perhaps the most extreme in terms of its graphic portrayal of an exotic scene steeped in darkness and magic (see Figure 3.6). Here we see a costumed man brandishing a cane at a cowering woman, prone on the ground, with a full-moon lit cemetery and snarling black dog in the background. With the title, "The CARIBBEAN . . . where legends are danced to drums," the text describes the scene:

> **This is the BANDA DANCE OF HAITI**, traditionally performed by the leering Baron Samedi, God of the Dead and Guardian of the Graveyard. It is said that one who passes a graveyard at night may provoke the appearance of this fearful apparition. You can get a 45 RPM hi-quality record of this dance, and other Haitian music, together with descriptive text, by sending $1.00 to Dept. "R" at the New York address below. Ask for Number 4 in our series of Caribbean recordings. (emphasis in original)

In this case the image and the text play into commonly circulating imagery of Haiti as a place of "voodoo" and "black magic," of lewd dancing and spooky thrills. Ethnologist Alfred Métraux described the *banda* dance, in his 1959 book *Voodoo in Haiti*, as "a Guédé dance and marvellously indecent. Nevertheless it also has a sacred aspect for it is danced at funerals to dismiss a dead person's spirit to the other world, and it occurs in ceremonies to provide relief in the wake of dire and awful *loa*" (Métraux 1972, 192). North American interest in the "indecent" hip-swaying of the banda dance goes back to travel writing of the nineteenth-century, but was intensified by the best-selling sensational

Figure. 3.6 Alcoa Steamship Company ad, The Banda Dance of Haiti, by James R. Bingham. (*Holiday* magazine, August 1955)

books written during the US occupation of 1915–1934, such as W. B. Seabrook's *The Magic Island* (1929), Faustin Wirkus's *The White King of La Gonave* (1931), and John Houston Craige's *Black Bagdad* (1933).

Kate Ramsey argues that the US occupation played a crucial part in both the emergence of anthropological interest in Haitian spiritual and magic practices and the popular sensationalism of US representations of "voodoo" that also fed into the emerging genre of "zombie" films. The fascination with "voodoo," including especially its drumming and dances, was accompanied by ethnographic collections of Haitian folklore, music, and dance by North American researchers and visitors. Prominent here are, first, Harold Courlander, author of *The Drum and the Hoe*, who first visited in 1932 and used a field recording cylinder to preserve "peasant folk and liturgical music from the 1930s until the 1950s and recorded a series of noncommercial albums for Folkways Records" (Ramsey 2011, 23). Second were the anthropologists Melville and Frances Herskovits, authors of *Life in a Haitian Valley* (1937), who stayed for three months in 1934. And third, Herskovits's student, the dancer Katherine Dunham, who was studying anthropology at University of Chicago and became dedicated to learning and documenting Haitian social and ritual dances during her visits in 1935–1936. In early 1937, as Ramsey points out, there were simultaneous research visits by not only Courlander, but also Alan Lomax who was collecting and recording folk music for the Smithsonian, Zora Neale Hurston who was collecting folklore for what became her book *Tell My Horse*, and the anthropologists Lydia Parrish and George Eaton Simpson, who were also interested in Vodou services. Many of these collectors of folk culture also worked in Jamaica.[13]

This burst of interest was not unrelated to the fact that "superstitious practices" were outlawed during the US occupation, and drums and other sacred objects were being seized and destroyed by the Haitian government, the Catholic church, and the US Marines. Quite a few sacred drums were spirited out of Haiti by both marines and anthropologists, making their way into major museum collections in the United States, such as the Smithsonian, where they remain on display today. Lomax's 1500 recordings of Haitian music (fifty hours of recorded sound) were made in 1936–1937 with the very latest in portable recording technology: "a new 'turntable-cutting unit' from Lincoln Thompson's Sound Specialties Company in Stamford, Connecticut, and a stack of 12" blank aluminum disks."[14] Tellingly, in terms of the complex material, cultural, and commercial circulations of modernity that I am tracking in this chapter, the very aluminum industry that brought Alcoa's ships to the Caribbean (and fed into the buildup of the awesome air power of the US Air Force in the 1940s) also enabled the recording of Caribbean folk music, allowing it to circulate outside of the islands.

As noted above, one of the responses to the US occupation was the championing of the culture and arts of the Haitian peasantry by the emerging black middle class, through movements such as *indigénisme, noirisme,* and *négritude*. In other Caribbean countries, too, there was renewed interest in "indigenous" folk cultures, including so-called witchcraft and sorcery, which fed into best-selling paperbacks, Hollywood cinema, and North American tourism, which promoted the thrill of the primitive and magical. The Alcoa Bingham series has several other portrayals of dances linked to magic or spirituality. An illustration titled "Behold the magic of the Caribbean . . . on a wonderful Alcoa cruise" reads: "A witch doctor's magic brings new life to a fallen bird in the enchanting 'Pájaro Guarandól,' a folk dance of the Venezuelan Indians. But his legendary powers are only a small part of the magic of the Caribbean . . . perhaps most magical of all is the relaxation you enjoy on one of Alcoa's modern, air-conditioned ships." Here the text interestingly leverages the powers of a "witch doctor" to lend magical qualities to its own modern ships. The ships,

Figure. 3.7 Alcoa Steamship Company ad, "Cruise to the throbbing Caribbean where East meets West," by James R. Bingham. (*Holiday* magazine, April 1955)

built to promote new uses of the company's product, also played on the popular notion of aluminum as a "magical metal," due to its unusual strength, lightness, and flexibility. And the cruise is portrayed as a kind of magical experience, carrying passengers back into the kaleidoscope of Caribbean history while surrounding them in modern comforts such as air-conditioning.

Another ceremonial dance is portrayed in an image titled "Cruise to the throbbing Caribbean where East meets West," in which two lavishly jewelry-crowned dancers strike classical Hindi poses, with bells on their ankles and a single musician in the background with a set of four different Indian drums (see Figure 3.7). Here the text reads:

The English and Dutch brought many farmers to the Caribbean, from the East Indies. Today, these people form a large part of the populations of Trinidad and Surinam. Their homes, their customs, their ceremonial dances (one of which is shown here) remain virtually unchanged. The Caribbean is a wonderful blend of more than a dozen nationalities, making it one of the most interesting regions of the world.

Notably, while other examples such as the beguine of the French West Indies and the "stick dance" of Trinidad emphasize the blending and fusion of different cultural traditions, this text notes the "unchanged" nature of East Indian cultural traditions.[15] Indo-Trinidadian music traditions, of course, were as much "in motion" as were others of the Caribbean, as Peter Manuel has explored in his study of "tān-singing" in Trinidad, Guyana, and Suriname (Manuel 2000). The very claims of cultures being "unchanging" versus "blending," "ceremonial" versus secular, traditional versus modern, are part of the political and cultural contestation of who belongs where, in societies that were eminently mobile and dynamic. Musical expression and cultures of dance thus became a means and a ground for contesting cultures, reinventing traditions, and claiming national citizenship and modernity. Their touristic commodification in the Alcoa advertising campaigns, then, is not simply an expression of North American commodification, but also of dynamic processes of Caribbean self-representation and counter-discourse.

CONCLUSION: MUSICAL COUNTER-POWER

Ultimately these various portrayals of Caribbean folkloric dance forms depict a region of great diversity and musical mobility, with multiple cultural streams feeding into a diversity of particular local cultures. What is notable is the way in which this is staged for touristic consumption, yet remains "true" to its own complex cultural dynamics and multiple circulations and re-circulations. Music and dance become not only a way of recounting the history of the Caribbean and discovering its variety of people and cultures, but also a means for engaging the tourist in its "color," its gaiety, its magic, and its excitement. While the texts and images seek to contain each dance form in a kind of national tableau, as did the national elites who were fostering the creation of folk culture institutions, they also hint at the possibilities of overflow and uncontained circulation that were the very matrices of Caribbean cultures.

Labor migration was already leading to transnational musical currents, such as the influence of Cuban music that Averill has noted in the emergence of *twou-badou* music in Haiti in the 1930s, and alternatively the influence of Haitian

music in eastern Cuba, as well as the unclear lines between Dominican merengue and Haitian *mereng*, or the transnational influences on the emergence of
mento in Jamaica (Averill 1997, 39; Manuel 1995; Daniel Neely personal communication). If the potential circuits of traveling music and dance styles linked
cultures across the Caribbean, we also note that the rise of big bands, live radio
broadcasts, and new musical recording technologies (including Alcoa's own
contribution) carried that influence into North America. There were powerful
cultural currents emanating out of these diverse Caribbean popular cultures,
circulating around the Caribbean with labor migrants, and into US urban culture via Caribbean diasporas, their music recordings, and their dance cultures,
as well as the visits of tourists to the ports, brothels, casinos, and music clubs of
the region (Manuel 1995).

While the Bingham illustrations seem to resist these forces of modernization, instead clinging to the colonial past and projecting a kind of innocent
present, they stand on the cusp of an explosion of Caribbean musical export.
Even if the promoters of tourism in the region may have had a vested interest
in preserving and presenting "safe" versions of national folkloric performances
(minus the spirit possession or sexual license that were once associated with
some of these dance forms), Caribbean people were at the same time contesting such images, insisting on their own modernity. Independence movements in the post-war period began to call for self-rule, while return migrants
from London, New York, and other metropoles, along with the radios and
broadcasts by US forces stationed in the region during the war, carried styles
of modern urban cultural consumption back to the Caribbean, along with
the new commodities entering Caribbean markets and promoted by companies like Alcoa and its business partners. In this very period, the influence of
American rhythm and blues entered Jamaica as more radios were purchased
during the war, and American troops broadcast their home sounds, while
magnetic recording tape became available in the early 1950s. Music forms,
tourists, and new technologies were all circulating together, as other chapters
in this volume attest to.

Despite the appearance of frozen tradition in Bingham's portrayal of Caribbean
folk dances in the mid-1950s, the vivid forms of dance and music also attest to
a kind of cultural vitality that could quite literally *move* people in unexpected
(and possibly dangerous) ways. Such struggles over the politics of New World
dance forms have a long circum-Atlantic history that concerns the mobility of
cultural migrations as well as the literal movement of bodies. For example, Jane
Desmond traces how the tango moved "from the dockside neighborhoods of
Buenos Aires to the salons of Paris before returning, newly 'respectable' from
across the Atlantic to the drawing rooms of the upper-class portions of the
Argentine population" (Desmond 1993 and 1997). Tim Cresswell draws on her

work in his discussion of efforts to control the proliferation of a dance known as the shimmy in US dance halls and British ballrooms in the 1930s, as its moves were considered to be overly lascivious and possibly "negro"; thus "movements that originate in working class and subordinate populations and places become 'polished' as they make their way up through the social and spatial hierarchy. An important part of this 'civilizing' process is the abolition or toning down of overtly sexual components" (Creswell 2006, 57).[16] And, we might add, stripping them of their sacred components, culturally forgetting that dance is in service to the spirits, even as the spirits persist in the dance.

Creswell focuses our attention on "the mobility of mobilities—the way, in other words, that these corporeal mobilities resulted from the movement of dance forms across the Atlantic in the first half of the 20th century" (2006, 71). Musicians, musical styles, rhythms, and dances circulated around the Atlantic world, especially through the music venues of the major port cities that became the access points of tourism. Barbara Browning describes the challenges of "infectious rhythm," suggesting the prevalence of discourses conveying how African/Caribbean rhythms literally get into the body, infecting it with danger-ous new forms of movement (Browning 1998). And Carolyn Cooper traces the conflicts over popular Jamaican dance forms that were seen as too raw, too loud, too vulgar, in her works *Noises in the Blood* (1995) and *Sound Clash* (2004). Rhythm and dance carry what Roach calls a "kinaesthetic imagination," and the creation of folkloric traditions is part of these contested mobilities which may include reworking tradition as in the "resistant traditionalism" that Averill notes in Haiti during the US occupation.

To preserve traditions or to change them, to maintain purity or to create new mixtures, are all part of the constant contestation over mobile cultures. Musical genres played a crucial part both in national politics within the Caribbean, and in the international field of representing the modernity of the Caribbean to the wider world.[17] Thus any representation of Caribbean music, particularly for commercial purposes of commodified consumption (such as tourist shows), is always politically enmeshed in the production of meanings around movement and modernity. It is also linked to the political economy of labor, markets, min-ing, and migration, not to mention military incursions and tourist excursions, and visits by anthropologists and ethnomusicologists.

Caribbean writers, musicians, intellectuals, and artists grappled with the meanings of Caribbean modernity, and produced their own visualizations of the Caribbean past, present, and future. In response, the Alcoa Shipping Company also seems to have adjusted its cultural strategy in this period, at least in relation to visual arts, by beginning to sponsor the Caribbean Art Competition in 1954–1955 (see Figure 3.8). This led to a show of 127 paintings by Caribbean artists, selected from "nearly thirteen hundred entered," which

CARIBBEAN ART COMPETITION
1ST GRAND PRIZE—HAITI
In this prize-winning painting Castera Bazile, of Haiti, has caught much of the color and warmth of a Caribbean village on a lazy Sunday afternoon. His use of clear, bright pigments, with cool blues and greens opposing the hot colors of the middleground, give the impression of brilliant sunshine beating down through tropical foliage. And the geometric design of the fence and roof gable contribute a dynamic element that helps convey a feeling of movement and aliveness. The result is a painting rich in realism without being photographic.

ALCOA SAILS THE CARIBBEAN

You'll enjoy the trip of a lifetime journeying through the colorful Caribbean on a de luxe Alcoa cruise ship! She'll have air conditioning in staterooms and public rooms . . . tiled outdoor pool . . . superb cuisine . . . all staterooms outside with private baths . . . and the kind of unobtrusive personal service that Americans like. It's no wonder seasoned travelers write us "Best trip we ever took." These 16-day cruises sail every Saturday from New Orleans to six ports in Venezuela, Jamaica, Trinidad and Curacao or the Dominican Republic. Or you may prefer an Alcoa 12-passenger freighter cruise of 10 to 42 days from New York, New Orleans or Montreal. Write today to Dept. "H" for cruise booklets. Alcoa Steamship Company, Inc., 17 Battery Place, New York 4, N. Y. or One Canal Street, New Orleans 12, La.

Figure. 3.8 Alcoa Sails the Caribbean advertising campaign, Caribbean Arts Prize, painting by Castera Bazile (1958).

toured the region in 1956, with exhibitions in Puerto Rico, the Dominican Republic, Trinidad, Jamaica, Haiti, Venezuela, British Guiana, Surinam, Antigua, Curacao, and Barbados. The exhibition opened at the National Arts Club in New York, where it was judged by a panel of "three eminent New York judges" and cash prizes of $10,000 were awarded. Alcoa also "purchased a number of the paintings, and these are being used in the Company's national colour advertising during the next two years," as well as being reproduced on "travel folders and direct mail brochures for travel agents and the general public throughout North America."[18]

The prize-winning painting by Haitian artist Castera Bazile[19] featured in Figure 3.8 depicts a cockfighting scene, but in the background we see a group of three drummers playing for a circle of male and female dancers under a thatch-roofed open-sided structure. It is a lively and social scene, far more embedded in local culture than the Bingham representations. Bazile's work included both Christian themes and scenes drawn from Vodou practices and local life. Yet the Alcoa sponsorship of the Caribbean Arts Prize reminds us that the evolution of "indigenous" or "primitive" styles of painting, especially in Haiti, paralleled the rise of North American tourism and nationalist appreciation of indigenous music, and both are connected to the circulation of tourists, texts, and cultural artifacts, such as paintings and drums, as well as the travels of artists, musicians, and performers (Averill 1997, 63). Caribbean self-representation was always being negotiated in relation to foreign corporate sponsorship and tourist markets for art and music, with unexpected and sometimes surprising circulations in and around the Caribbean, and between the Caribbean and North America. Musical practices and their representation thus embody complex relations to the secular spaces legislated for entertainment, business, and tourism, even as they kinesthetically encode a terrain for maintaining embodied forms of agency that remain the potential wellsprings for spiritual freedom and social mobilization.

While deeply grounded in the history of traditional performance cultures that were sacred, Caribbean folk cultures have had to mask their origins and present themselves as modern, secular, and safe. This allowed for their codification within dominant colonial regimes and postcolonial national cultures and for their flexible trafficking through international circuits of capitalism and commodification, as well as their central appearance in Caribbean ethnology, anthropology, and cultural history. Yet as Kenneth Bilby argues in regard to Jankunu (especially the Bahamian version of Junkanoo), there is an irony in the fact that forms of national culture that have become the most secularized, commercialized, and closely linked to touristic commodification may still carry the seeds of the spiritual, or the spirits of the ancestors, in ways that transcend the religious/secular dichotomy (Bilby 2010, fn 6, 182). Thus I argue we can read these images from the Alcoa Shipping Company archive not as a mere flattening of Caribbean cultures for tourist consumption and musical commodification, but as one of many vectors by which African-Caribbean and Indo-Caribbean sacred musical cultures reconstituted their own historical continuity, proliferating across aesthetic and kinesthetic fields that were only extended further by modern technologies of transport, recording, and representation, thanks in part to Alcoa.

NOTES

1. This argument regarding the modernity of the Caribbean of course echoes arguments on the modernity of slavery and the sugar plantation, including C.L.R James's, *The Black Jacobins* (1963), as well as anthropological works such as Sidney Mintz's, "Slavery and the Rise of Peasantries" (1979). The fact that James and Mintz were developing their ideas on Caribbean modernity in the late 1950s–1960s may bear some relation to the musical cultures and circulations explored in this chapter.

2. See also Ned Sublette (2007), who points out that Cuba had no recording studio until 1944, so records were cut in New York, while Havana was a hub for US visitors to its casinos and brothels, so there was lots of cross traffic.

3. For a full discussion of the aluminum industry in the Caribbean see Sheller (2014).

4. For other aspects of the Alcoa advertising campaigns, see Sheller (2012a and 2012b).

5. According to *Holiday* magazine, in 1946 the plane fare via Pan American Airways from Miami to Piarco airport just outside of Kingston was $70 one way and $126 roundtrip, plus 15 percent tax; and there were intermittent sailings via United Fruit freighters from New York for around $75 to $100 one way (*Holiday*, October 1946, 155).

6. Thanks to editor Daniel Neely for bringing this to my attention.

7. A similar instrument called a "benta" is still played in St. Mary's Parish, associated with funeral wakes; see Olive Lewin (2000).

8. Another early collector of African musical instruments was Sir Hans Sloane, who in 1689 brought back from Jamaica what he called a "Strum Strum" ("small gourds fitted with necks, strung with horse hairs, or the peeled stalks of climbing plants or withs"), as well as musical notations which are considered the earliest known recorded pieces of African music in the Americas, with three variants identified as "Angola," "Papa" and "Koromanti." He also had an "Akan drum" from Virginia in his collection, now in the British Museum. See Hans Sloane (1707), and images in "Voyage to the Island: Hans Sloane, Slavery, and Scientific Travel in the Caribbean" an exhibit at the John Carter Brown Library. http://www.brown.edu/Facilities/John_Carter_Brown_Library/sloane/pages/culture.html.

9. See also *Art and Emancipation in Jamaica: Isaac Mendes Belisario and His Worlds*, exhib. cat. (New Haven: Yale Center for British Art and Yale University Press, 2007). The exhibition was curated by Gillian Forrester, Associate Curator of Prints and Drawings, Yale Center for British Art; Tim Barringer, Paul Mellon Professor of the History of Art, Yale University; and Barbaro Martinez-Ruiz, Assistant Professor, Department of Art and Art History, Stanford University. The National Gallery of Jamaica also presented "an abridged and amended version of the exhibition" in 2008, "Isaac Mendes Belisario: Art and Emancipation in Jamaica," curated by Dr. David Boxer.

10. Belisario, *Sketches of Character* (1837–1838). The particular image, along with a further collection of images of music and dance during the slavery period in the Caribbean can be seen at the Atlantic Slave Trade and Slave Life in the Americas collection at the University of Virginia: http://hitchcock.itc.virginia.edu/SlaveTrade/collection/large/Belisario05.JPG.

11. On the Bahamian festival, see Timothy Rommen (1999).

12. For a more extended discussion of the spiritual and the sexual in Caribbean popular and political cultures, see Mimi Sheller (2012c).

13. In a 1951 story about a visit to Jamaica in *Holiday* magazine the author writes that on his visit to the Accompong Maroons in the Cockpit country, the Colonel Walter James Robertson told him that "except for a lady named Miss Katherine Dunham, we were the first American visitors that they had had in many, many years" (Basso 1951, 142).

14. However, the poor quality of the recording equipment meant that they were never commercially released until 2009, when "a series of breakthroughs in audio technology" via digital restoration made it possible to transfer the full recordings to a CD box set, *Alan Lomax in Haiti, 1936–1937* (Harte Recordings, LLC, 2009), with liner notes by Gage Averill, Foreword by Anna Lomax Wood.

15. The text about the stick dance, in contrast, notes that it "harks back to the quarter-staff bouts of Robin Hood and his merry crew—blended through generations with the rhythm that is the Caribbean's heritage from Africa."

16. Cresswell notes that the shimmy is thought by dance scholars to be of either Nigerian or Haitian origin (62–63), while the tango craze of 1910–1914 was described as originating in "the drinking shops and bordellos of La Boca and ill famed Barrio de las Ranas [where] seamen and gauchos from the 'camp' competed for the favours of half-Indian habituées. . . . Becoming acquainted with the habanera rhythm [of Cuba] in the Port, as they called the capital city, they immediately adopted it and from it created their insidious tango" (cited by Cresswell, 64). Thus, "Like many other dances of to-day it was brought about by the slave trade and the consequent introduction of negro folk rhythms into Latin America, particularly into Cuba" (ibid.).

17. See, e.g., Browning (1995); Averill (1997); Stolzoff (2000); and Cooper (2004).

18. "Alcoa's Caribbean Find [sic] Art Exhibition," *The Barbados Advocate* (September 29, 1956), 11. Many thanks to Leah Rosenberg for locating and providing this article to me.

19. Castera Bazile was born in Jacmel, Haiti, in 1923. When the Centre d'Art opened in 1944, he was first employed as a general maintenance man, but soon began to paint and was one of the eight "primitive" painters selected in 1947 to paint the landmark murals in the Sainte Trinité (Holy Trinity) Episcopalian cathedral, completed in 1950–1951 in Port-au-Prince. In 1955 he won the grand prize in the international art competition sponsored by Alcoa and in 1957 received $1000 as the winner of an art contest sponsored by *Holiday* magazine. He died in 1966, after contracting tuberculosis. Only three of the fourteen murals in the Holy Trinity Cathedral survived the 2010 earthquake, including Bazile's *The Baptism of Our Lord*, which is undergoing conservation efforts.

REFERENCES

"Alcoa's Caribbean Find [sic] Art Exhibition." 1956. *The Barbados Advocate* (September 29): 11.

Anonymous Advertisement. 1946. *Holiday* 1(8): 155.

Art and Emancipation in Jamaica: Isaac Mendes Belisario and His Worlds. 2007. Exhib. Cat. New Haven: Yale Center for British Art and Yale University Press.

Atlantic Slave Trade and Slave Life in the Americas. Collection at the University of Virginia. http://hitchcock.itc.virginia.edu/SlaveTrade/collection/large/Belisario05. JPG.

Averill, Gage. 1997. *A Day for the Hunter and a Day for the Prey: Popular Music and Power in Haiti*. Chicago: University of Chicago.

——. Liner Notes. *Alan Lomax in Haiti, 1936–1937*. Harte Recordings, LLC, 2009.

Basso, Hamilton. 1951. "Jamaica Journal," *Holiday* 9(3): 134.

Belisario, Isaac Mendes. *1837–1838. Sketches of Character, in Illustration of the Habits, Occupation, and Costume of the Negro Population, in the Island of Jamaica: Drawn after Nature, and in Lithography*. Kingston, Jamaica: published by the artist.

Bilby, Kenneth. 2010. "Surviving Secularization: Masking the Spirit in the Jankunu (John Canoe) Festivals of the Caribbean." *New West Indian Guide* 84(3–4): 179–223.

Browning, Barbara. 1995. *Samba: Resistance in Motion (Arts and Politics of the Everyday)*. Bloomington: Indiana University Press.

——. 1998. *Infectious Rhythm: Metaphors of Contagion and the Spread of African Culture*. New York: Routledge.

Cooper, Carolyn. 1995. *Noises in the Blood: Orality, Gender, and the "Vulgar" Body of Jamaican Popular Culture*. London: Macmillan.

——. 2004. *Sound Clash: Jamaican Dancehall Culture at Large*. New York: Palgrave.

Courlander, Harold. 1960. *The Drum and the Hoe: Life and Lore of the Haitian People*. Berkeley: University of California Press.

Craige, John Houston. 1933. *Black Bagdad*. New York: Minton Balch.

Cresswell, Tim. 2006. " 'You Cannot Shake That Shimmie Here': Producing Mobility on the Dance Floor." *Cultural Geographies* 13: 55–77.

Desmond, Jane. 1993. "Embodying Difference: Issues in Dance and Cultural Studies." *Cultural Critique* (Winter): 33–63.

——. 1997. *Meaning in Motion: New Cultural Studies of Dance*. Durham, NC: Duke University Press.

Henle, Fritz. 1952. "Carnival Isle," *Holiday* 11(2): 91.

Herskovits, Melville. 1937. *Life in a Haitian Valley*. New York: A. A. Knopf.

Hurston, Zora Neale. 1938. *Tell My Horse*. Philadelphia: J. B. Lippincott.

James, C.L.R. 1963. *The Black Jacobins: Toussaint L'Ouverture and the San Domingo Revolution*. New York: Vintage.

Lewin, Olive. 2000. *Rock It Come Over: The Folk Music of Jamaica*. Kingston: University of the West Indies Press.

Manuel Peter. 1995. *Caribbean Currents: Caribbean Music from Rumba to Reggae*. Philadelphia: Temple University Press.

——. 2000. *East Indian Music in the West Indies: Tān-singing, Chutney, and the Making of Indo-Caribbean Culture*. Philadelphia: Temple University Press.

Métraux, Alfred. 1972 [1959]. *Voodoo in Haiti*. New York: Schocken Books.

Mintz, Sidney. 1979. "Slavery and the Rise of Peasantries," *Historical Reflections* 6(1): 213–242.

Ramsey, Kate. 2011. *The Spirits and the Law: Vodou and Power in Haiti*. Chicago: University of Chicago Press.

Roach, Joseph. 1996. *Cities of the Dead: Circum-Atlantic Performance*. New York: Columbia University Press.

Rommen, Timothy. 1999. "Home Sweet Home: Junkanoo as National Discourse in the Bahamas." *Black Music Research Journal* 19(1): 71–92.

Rosen, Fred. 1946. "Jamaica," *Holiday* 1(8): 31.

Seabrook, W. B. 1929. *The Magic Island*. New York: George G. Harrap.

Sheller, Mimi. 2012a. "Metallic Modernities in the Space Age: Visualizing the Caribbean, Materializing the Modern." In *Visuality/Materiality: Images, Objects and Practices*, edited by Gillian Rose and Divya Tolia-Kelly. Burlington, VT: Ashgate.

——. 2012b. "Out of the Ground, Into the Sky: How Aluminum Put the World in Motion." In *Cultures in Motion*, edited by Dan Rodgers, Helmut Reimitz, and Bhavani Raman. Princeton: Princeton University Press.

——. 2012c. *Citizenship from Below: Erotic Agency and Caribbean Freedom*. Durham, NC: Duke University Press.

——. 2014. *Aluminum Dreams: Lightness, Speed, Modernity*. Cambridge: MIT Press.

Sloane, Hans. 1707. *Natural History of Jamaica*. Vol. 1. London: B. M.

Stolzoff, Norman. 2000. *Wake the Town and Tell the People: Dancehall Culture in Jamaica*. Durham, NC: Duke University Press.

Sublette, Ned. 2007. *Cuba and Its Music: From the First Drums to the Mambo*. Chicago: Chicago Review Press.

Thompson, Krista A. 2007. *An Eye for the Tropics: Tourism, Photography, and Framing the Caribbean Picturesque*. Durham, NC: Duke University Press.

Wirkus, Faustin. 1931. *The White King of La Gonave*. Garden City, NY: Doubleday Doran.

4

"Hello, New York City!"

Sonic Tourism in Haitian Rara

MICHAEL LARGEY ■

Until the mid-1980s, Haiti was a popular destination for cruise ships carrying foreign tourists primarily from the United States and Canada. In the spring of 1982, for example, the Royal Caribbean Line's ship, Song of Norway, docked once a week in Port-au-Prince, depositing hundreds of vacationers eager to take in the sights of Haiti's capital and to take advantage of the bargains available at the nearby Mache Fè (Iron Market) as well as the more expensive artworks in the Centre d'Art in downtown Port-au-Prince. At the time, I regularly boarded the Song of Norway with my students from Ecole Sainte Trinité, an Episcopal Church–sponsored school with one of the few classical music programs in Haiti. The students performed arrangements of Haitian folk songs as well as some light classical repertoire suitable for the younger performers. The eager, enthusiastic faces of the children, along with their energetic playing and exuberant behavior, prompted many tourists on board to give generously to our music program as the nuns who ran the school passed the hat through the audience. Employees from the school's gift shop also sold handmade greeting cards decorated with dried banana leaves that depicted typical rural Haitian scenes. The children in the orchestra were given fruit by the cruise ship crew, sharing their orange slices with each other and talking excitedly about which of them would get to perform aboard ship the next week. The money raised on board the Song of Norway was never exorbitant, yet it helped defray some of the school's expenses.

In the late 1980s, however, the Haitian tourism industry declined dramatically, due in part to the political unrest in the aftermath of the Jean-Claude Duvalier regime as well as the mistaken belief that Haitians were carriers of the

AIDS virus. The tourist boats stopped docking in Port-au-Prince and the economic exchanges most closely associated with tourism—souvenir purchases, listening to and watching local entertainment, and buying local rum—slowed as a result. For many Haitians in the 1980s, especially the children who performed Haitian classical music on the cruise ships, tourism ceased to be an effective way to export local goods and culture to foreign audiences.

In many ways, the interactions described above are part of the classic tourism exchange: local vendors prepare and sell items for export to tourists who take their purchases home as mementos of their trip. In addition, foreign tourists listen to local musicians perform and make a good will offering when asked. In this scenario, tourists are inevitably foreigners whose money helps keep the local economy afloat.

Haiti has depended on tourism dollars ever since the tourism industry "discovered" Haiti as a potential destination for foreign visitors after the United States' military occupation of Haiti from 1915 to 1934. As ethnographers like Melville and Frances Herskovits, Zora Neale Hurston, Katherine Dunham, and Harold Courlander began their investigations into Haitian culture during and after the occupation, the Haitian government turned to local practices, especially the Haitian traditional religion known as Vodou, as potential sources of tourism revenue.[1] Kate Ramsey (2011) argues in her recent book on Vodou practice and the Haitian legal system that Vodou traditions were turned into tourist spectacles and repackaged as "folklore," thus stripping the spiritual aspects of the service out so that they would be suitable for tourist consumption at home and festival consumption abroad.

Recent research has challenged the assumption that tourism is primarily concerned with tourists from wealthy countries visiting places that depend on such revenue for their survival. As sociologists Mimi Sheller and John Urry point out (2006, 207–208), physical travel, mobile telephones, computers, and other forms of technology contribute to a "new mobilities paradigm" that forces social scientists to take the movement of people, objects, and information into account when discussing notions of "culture." Such a paradigm calls for what tourism studies specialist Garth Lean claims is a "focus upon mobilities rather than physical travel and tourism" (2012, 169). According to Lean, "Rather than seeing social relations as operating within and between bounded communities, the mobilities paradigm sees humans as inhabiting a mobile world in which we not only travel physically but also virtually, communicatively and imaginatively" (153).

In the case of Haiti, foreign tourists have largely been replaced by diaspora Haitians from the United States and Canada who return to their homeland in search of refreshment, rejuvenation, and reconnection with friends and family. Unlike the foreign tourist who usually spends a short time in the country and who has little understanding or connection to local culture, Haitian diaspora tourists bring a wealth of experience to their visits to Haiti. In the case of Haitian Rara, a Lenten processional music with strong ties to Vodou religious tradition, militarism, and political protest, tourists and locals engage in what tourist studies specialist Maria Månsson calls "consumer-to-consumer networks" (2011, 1639), in which Rara musicians living in Haiti produce media that are intended to promote their cultural performances to Haitian audiences abroad. Haitian tourists purchase recordings of Rara bands directly during their visits to Haiti or indirectly through these networks, bringing recordings to other diaspora Haitians in the United States and Canada.

Sharing cultural artifacts across political boundaries is a common way for Haitians to maintain a sense of connection with their homeland. In the case of Rara recordings from Léogâne, however, it is important to keep in mind that the sound of music not only evokes feelings of "home," but also creates a sense of national connection, what anthropologists Nina Glick-Schiller and Georges Fouron call "long-distance nationalism," that allows diaspora Haitians to participate in Haitian life despite living abroad.

According to Glick-Schiller and Fouron, "Long-distance nationalism is a claim to membership in a political community that stretches beyond the territorial borders of a homeland. It generates an emotional attachment that is strong enough to compel people to political action that ranges from displaying a home country flag to deciding to 'return' to fight and die in a land they may never have seen" (2001, 4). Moreover, long-distance nationalism "binds together immigrants, their descendants, and those who have remained in their homeland into a single *transborder citizenry*" (20; emphasis in original).

Music is a particularly powerful medium for generating "long-distance nationalism" since it has affective powers that allow Haitians to experience personal and collective feelings of belonging; a sense of *Haitianness,* as Glick-Schiller and Fouron call it. Maintaining long-distance nationalism takes more than an imaginative longing for a homeland, however; it requires what Glick-Schiller and Fouron call "specific actions" (20) in order to bring Haitians at home and abroad together as transborder citizens.

One specific action that long-distance nationalists take to enact their connections to their homeland is to bring the sounds of home to those living outside Haiti through what I call *sonic tourism*. Specifically, Haitian Rara bands extend the local performance of Rara to Haitians abroad through the circulation of Rara audio recordings that create an ongoing connection between Haiti and the Haitian diaspora. By participating in this transnational economy, diaspora Haitians are, to quote Glick-Schiller and Fouron, "working to reconstruct Haiti" (2001, 21). Sonic tourism goes beyond establishing a connection between Haitians at home and abroad; it provides a means for the Haitian "transborder citizenry" to engage in political action across national boundaries.

"Long Distance Nationalism"

Rara is an especially effective vehicle for sonic tourism since it is known throughout Haiti as both a mobile Vodou ceremony and a platform for political protest. Elsewhere, I have argued that Rara serves as a public forum for expressing Haitian lower-class concerns, despite elite attempts to subvert Rara's populist messages (Largey 2000). Similarly, Glick-Schiller and Fouron see "long-distance nationalism" not as a "'top-down' fostering of elite beliefs" but as a reflection of "the life experiences of migrants of different classes, whose lives stretch across borders to connect homeland and new land" (2001, 22).

As sonic tourists, diaspora Haitians embody the experience of Léogâne Rara through what cultural geographer Jonas Larsen describes as a "technologically mediated moved body" (2001, 94). Although the term "embodiment" is most often used to characterize what geographer David Crouch (2000, 68) calls a "process of experiencing, making sense, knowing through practice as a sensual human subject in the world," it is possible to extend the notion of embodiment to include sensory experiences through electronic media, especially radio and recordings. Sonic tourism goes beyond what John Urry calls "imaginative mobility" (2000) or what Larsen describes as "armchair travel through books, images and television" (2006, 244). In the case of Rara in Léogâne, recordings are meant both to evoke the memory of the celebration in Haiti, as well as to evoke a shared experience *in the present moment.* As such, recordings combine aspects of nostalgia—or the emotional connection to an imagined past—with the lived, embodied experience of performing Rara. Through their recordings of Rara celebrations, local Haitians transform diaspora "space" into a Haitian "place" by engaging diaspora Haitians with direct references to them and their participation in the celebration (Rakić and Chambers 2012, 1618).

Using technology to transmit the sounds of a street festival to the stereo systems of overseas Rara fans has, however, affected the ways in which performances of Rara are conducted in Léogâne. I will show how both radio and recordings—including "souvenir" recordings made on hand-carried boom boxes, live recordings at kav or Rara feasts, and professionally recorded CDs made in Haiti, the United States and Canada—have influenced the sound of Rara to move away from the boisterous sound of the street procession to a more polished and transportable consumer product. At the same time, Rara recordings evoke the sounds of the procession to pull diaspora audiences into the celebration as they listen to those recordings abroad.

RARA IN LÉOGÂNE

Léogâne, a small city thirty kilometers west of Port-au-Prince, is considered by many Haitians to be the epicenter of Rara, a Lenten processional tradition associated with Vodou religious activity, musical competition, political patronage, and militarism. Every Easter Sunday, bands from as far away as the outskirts of Port-au-Prince converge on Place Anacaona, the gateway to the city of Léogâne, to display their singing and dancing talents, to consummate their religious obligations, and to compete against rival bands. Rara has been popular in Léogâne for over a century; the area's oldest surviving band, Rara Chen Mechan [Bad Dog Rara] was formed in 1884.[2] In the weeks before Easter, bands take to the streets to practice their new repertoire and assert themselves as worthy musical opponents. The largest and most popular bands in the area—Rara Laflè di Woz (Rose Flower Rara, usually called Laflè), Rara Modèl d'Haïti (Model of Haiti Rara, or Modèl), Rara Ti Malis Kache (The Rara of the Clever Children in Hiding, or Ti Malis), and Rara Mande Granmoun (Ask the Elders Rara)—all command enormous crowds that eagerly await new musical compositions for the Rara season. Bands attract participants through the quality of their repertoire and the energy and excitement produced by their processions.

Just as onlookers are moved by the power of the music, they are also swept up physically by the momentum of a large group of dancing revelers moving through the streets. Bands rely on a *kolonèl* or colonel, a whip-wielding, whistle-blowing leader who monitors the forward motion of the group. With a crack of the whip, the colonel encourages the band to lurch forward, unleashing the pent-up energy of the crowd. The colonel also uses the whip to keep the crowd from moving forward too quickly since the band's momentum depends on maintaining close contact between members. Too much space between participants risks a dissipation of energy and a potential threat to the cohesion of the group. Bands that move too quickly through the street may *kraze* or break down, because of too much space between participants, making it impossible for members to work together. Alternatively, bands that have too many members on the road at the same time may be described as *rèd* or hard, stuck in one place and unable to move forward.

Rara's volatile performance practice poses challenges not only to casual listeners, but also to ethnographers, radio reporters, and fans of the bands, all of whom jockey for position to document the processions with recording devices. Making a serviceable recording is a difficult, frustrating, and potentially risky task since Rara bands are known for their occasionally violent clashes. As Elizabeth McAlister notes in *Rara! Vodou, Power, and Performance in Haiti and Its Diaspora* (2002), the spatial arrangement of the Rara band is usually "the drums, banbou, metal horns, and percussion (scrapers, bells, and so on) walk[ing] in battalion-like waves, one group after another, followed by the chorus" (20).[3] Each section produces its own distinctive and very loud music that can obliterate the sounds of the other sections of the band; this is especially true in Léogâne where bands use large brass sections including multiple trumpets, trombones, baritone horns, and sousaphones. In the compact disk that accompanies her book, McAlister (2002, xv) includes a recording she made while walking through a Rara band—a recording that documents the shifting soundscape as she moves from one section of the band to another. To anyone who has walked with a Rara band, McAlister's recording demonstrates both the excitement and the futility of recording inside the ensemble. As the percussionists pound their instruments, the song lyrics float in the distant sonic background, unintelligible to the interested listener. McAlister's close-up recording sounds similar to the dozens of homemade tape cassettes made by Rara band members who hold their portable tape recorders—usually either a Sony Walkman or a boom box—above their heads as the band marches into the night.

A better way to listen to a Rara band, according to McAlister, is "from afar, as it comes closer and passes by, one wave at a time, until it slowly fades into the distance" (21). Her advice works well for the listener who wishes to capture the experience of many Rara onlookers, from those who sit in front of their homes waiting for bands to pass by, to devout Catholics and evangelical Protestants who listen to Rara safely away from the sonic sway of the music. Radio broadcasters also prefer this style since it is easier to mix a balanced recording in which the song lyrics are audible, the percussion is prominent but not overwhelming, and the brass players are energetically present but not dominating the vocal line.

If following McAlister's recommendation to listen to Rara from afar, however, one fails to capture the rush of excitement remembered by those who process with Rara bands. For many Rara participants, part of the attraction of walking with a band is the volatility of the moment; frequent physical squabbles by band personnel signal an energetic, *cho* (hot) performance.[4] In the off-season, Rara participants frequently engage in conversations about the competing qualities of the up-close "hot" recording and the distant recording that sounds more "professional" to some listeners.

Since 1995, recording devices available to Rara participants and spectators have changed from handheld boom boxes to DAT recorders and digital video cameras. In addition, bands have begun recording in different venues, moving from their original location in the street to the confines of the recording studio. As a result, recording producers have sought to capitalize on Léogâne residents' desire for Rara recordings that emulate the studio sound of Haitian popular music groups, as well as the *bann kanaval* or Carnival bands that have released their own recordings. Since 2000, several Léogâne Rara bands have released recordings that were performed live at fixed locations (as opposed to recording the actual Rara procession) or in a studio setting with multiple microphones and multitrack recording equipment.

RARA AND THE HAITIAN DIASPORA

The engineering of Rara performances into commodities helps bring the local activities of the Rara band in contact with the Haitian diaspora populations that fund Rara activity. Several of the large bands in Léogâne, including Rara Laflè di Woz and Rara Ti Malis Kache, have members of their governing committees or *komite* living in the United States. These committee members encourage Rara fans in the Haitian diaspora to maintain their connections with local bands by purchasing recordings of Léogâne Rara performances through a network of diaspora contacts. Rara bands in Léogâne circulate recordings among their *fanatik* (fans) in the diaspora in hopes of stimulating food donations, payments for Rara musicians, rental fees for sound reinforcement equipment, as well as a variety of other expenses incurred during Rara season.

Most band recordings are circulated abroad through these informal economies. Even commercially mastered CDs, like Rara Modèl d'Haïti's *Rasin'n San Bout't (Haitian Roots)*, have not penetrated the US recording market, apart from word-of-mouth sales among Modèl's overseas fans. Still, many band members express interest in participating in the global recording industry, citing the presence of Haitians abroad, the growing interest in foreign festival music in the United States, and what they believe to be the universal appeal of their unique brand of music.

Band members recognize that many other Caribbean genres of music, most notably reggae and dancehall, salsa, zouk, and soca, are already global musics that rely on recording for their enduring successes. Indeed, recordings are an effective medium for the promotion and dissemination of local musical styles, especially for genres like Rara that are not easily transported and that rely on large numbers of participants. While Rara does not yet fit the description of a "mass-mediated music" as Manuel (1988) outlines it, it does have an enthusiastic and committed retinue of practitioners who believe that Rara has the capacity to cross over into a popular music market. In the work that I have done with Rara Ti Malis Kache since 1995, band members have eagerly embraced this idea of Rara music as a potentially profitable, mass-mediated music that could infuse the impoverished local community with much needed revenue.

In the following section, I outline the crucial role of radio in shaping the emergent sound of Rara on recordings. I argue that Rara recordings are a form of transnational communication that is used to send messages to audiences at home and abroad. Rara recordings combine the sounds of radio DJs with culturally encoded messages to engage diaspora Haitians in local affairs. Indeed, DJs play a pivotal role in connecting Haitians at home and abroad through their exhortations to listeners and their energetic engagement with their audiences.

RARA ON THE RADIO IN LÉOGÂNE

In Haiti, radio plays a vital role in the dissemination of information and entertainment. With a literacy rate under 50 percent, Haitians turn to radio rather
than newspapers or television for most of their news. Musical entertainment
is also a staple of most Haitian radio formats, but radio programming is specialized to some degree by audience preference. For example, Port-au-Prince
based Radio Métropole is known as an upper-class station that features some
English-language programming during the weekends. Most stations, however,
play a variety of music, from the 1960s-style *konpa dirèk* to *mizik rasin* or roots
music, Haitian and US rap, Jamaican ragga, and Dominican merengue. In addition, talk radio has become a media staple with interviews and panel discussions as popular formats. Of the five radio stations that operate in Léogâne,
three stations that normally feature music programming and interviews regularly offer special Rara programming throughout the Lenten season including
live broadcasts of Rara performances, interviews with members of different
Rara bands, as well as studio recordings. Radio Anacaona (103.9 FM), Radio
Konpa (102.5 FM), and Force FM (98.1 FM) are privately owned radio stations
that serve the area known as the plain of Léogâne.[5] In addition, Port-au-Prince
station Radio Galaxie features a weekly program on Léogâne Rara during Lent,
hosted by the owner and principal DJ of Léogâne's Radio Anacaona.

Broadcasting Rara on local and national radio stations is a relatively recent
phenomenon. Resistance to programming Rara has come primarily from the
local Catholic hierarchy that has historically been antagonistic towards Rara
performance. Since Rara is associated with Vodou activity and falls during the
Lenten season, it is seen by Catholic officials as antithetical to church teachings
and as a rival procession to the annual *Chemen Kwa* (Stations of the Cross) on
Good Friday. In addition, for many evangelical Protestants, Rara is believed to
be synonymous with Satanism; the mere sound of the procession is considered
to be a threat to worshippers' moral and spiritual fiber. One Haitian I interviewed told me that in the Lenten seasons during his childhood, his devout
Methodist parents gathered the family at home with doors and windows shut,
reciting verses from the Bible as Rara bands circulated in their neighborhoods.[6]
Today, church-sponsored radio stations avoid programming Rara music.

Radio Anacaona was the first station in Léogâne to devote significant airtime
to Rara. In 1995, Radio Anacaona broadcast what are commonly called "souvenir" recordings made by participants in Rara processions.[7] These souvenirs
were made on handheld boom boxes by individuals who were either members
of specific bands interested in documenting their band's repertoire or by visitors who happened to have a recording device. Souvenir recordings featured
not only the sound of Rara bands processing through the streets of Léogâne,

but also the ambient noise of the festival, including boisterous conversations, exclamations from exuberant celebrants, and traffic noise. For most Léogâne residents in the early 1990s, Rara recordings were available only in the souvenir format. Journalists also made their own souvenirs using available technology. Julmane St. Fort, a radio journalist for Radio Haiti Inter in Port-au-Prince, used a handheld microcassette recorder to make his own souvenir recordings of Léogâne Rara, which he shared with Radio Anacaona's director.[8]

Léogâne radio stations also promote Rara celebrations through frequent interviews with Rara organizers. Interview formats range from "shout outs" from Rara organizers who stop in at the station to pay their respects to the DJ on duty to more elaborate panel discussions involving members from different Rara bands. Since 1996, I have participated in several of these informal radio interviews in which members of Rara Ti Malis Kache dropped into the Radio Anacaona studio to praise the band's repertoire, encourage other bands to minimize violent clashes, and wish members of the Léogâne community a joyous Easter season.[9]

Radio is one of the few public venues in which rival bands peacefully coexist in Léogâne. Perhaps the best known rivalry in Léogâne is between Rara Laflè di Woz and Rara Ti Malis Kache. According to Ti Malis participants, Laflè members raided Ti Malis's *lakou* (village compound) during the 1954 Rara season. Ti Malis members have never forgiven Laflè for the attack; they even wrote a Rara song titled "Senkantkat" ['54] in which Ti Malis criticized Laflè for their treachery (Largey 2000, 249). In 1996, despite each band's refusal to appear at the other's Rara celebrations, members of Laflè and Ti Malis sat together for an interview at Radio Anacaona's broadcast studio. Georges Gilles, a senior member of Laflè, took the opportunity to ask revelers to refrain from violence, especially when passing other bands on the street. Reynolds Paraison, a member of rival band Ti Malis, emphasized the need for cooperation between rival bands when he said "tout Rara se sè " (all Rara bands are sisters). Given Laflè and Ti Malis's long-standing enmity, Paraison's comment was especially significant as a public acknowledgement of their mutual responsibility for maintaining civil order during Rara.

As the demand for radio coverage of Rara events has grown, Léogâne radio stations have moved out into the community to bring the sounds of individual Rara celebrations to their radio audiences. Recording Rara processions presents difficult logistical challenges—bands move quickly through the unlighted streets and sometimes fight with rival bands—so radio stations have chosen to broadcast performances from Rara celebrations known as kav rather than on the road. Each Rara band in the Léogâne area has its own kav in which it hosts friendly bands in a patron–client relationship. Host bands erect large reviewing stands, called stang, that feature the host band's leaders. Visiting bands play an ochan or field salute for their hosts who, in turn, raise their straw hats and wave with the beat of the music. Once the ochan is finished, the host band invites the visiting band into their lakou for a meal. This pattern of salutation and commensality continues late into the night as other bands pay their respects to host bands during their kav.

In the mid-1990s, radio stations visited Rara bands on their respective feast days and made recordings that they aired on the radio during the following week. Like the souvenir recordings favored by Léogâne residents, these kav broadcasts featured not only the sounds of the visiting bands, but also the voices of the radio announcers and their fellow revelers. By 2000, Radio Anacaona and Radio Konpa were broadcasting live from kav celebrations with radio correspondents calling in their reports using cell phones.

At the same time that radio brought the sounds of the Rara kav to listeners, the kav celebrants adapted sound reinforcement technology to their feasts. In their 1995 kav, Ti Malis used a battery-operated bullhorn to make announcements to visiting bands, mostly in the form of praise for the visitors' music making. By 1998, the band was using a gasoline-fueled generator to power a sound system with a set of five-foot-tall loudspeakers that played the latest Carnival recordings while Ti Malis members waited for the next band to arrive. When visiting bands came close enough to be heard by attendees on the stang, the Carnival music was turned down and a member of Ti Malis took a dynamic microphone on a fifty-foot cable out to the visiting band. As the visiting band played into the microphone, another announcer on the Ti Malis stang shouted encouragement to the visiting band, using the phrase "woy, woy" (hey, hey), or feigning a swoon at the beauty of the visitors' musical prowess. The loudspeakers not only boomed out the hosts' announcements but also provided a recorded ochan that was blasted back at the visiting bands once they finished their live field salute.

Through recording technology, the host band was able to provide a return salute to their visitors, thereby closing the cycle of public reciprocity expected during the kav. The recorded ochan is, however, a recent addition to the kav celebration. In 1995, host bands did not use ochan in the kav celebrations, but by 2000, most host bands in Léogâne used recordings to salute their visitors in a culturally resonant manner.

The use of sound reinforcement technology by the Rara bands brings the sound of the radio to the celebration of kav, transforming the traditional public display event into a mediated encounter that resembles the souvenir recordings played on the radio. The large loudspeakers, driven by the generator, allow the voice of the commentator to be heard over the sound of visiting bands, much like the "talk over" style favored by Caribbean and African American DJs (Barlow 1999). The kav announcer usually projects a commentary about the quality of the event, much like the radio announcer does back at Radio Anacaona.

Rara celebrations are not the only public events that have been affected by the introduction of sound reinforcement technology. The Catholic church's annual *Chemen Kwa* (Stations of the Cross) has also been transformed by the use of loudspeakers. On Good Friday, Catholics in Léogâne symbolically recreate the journey that Jesus walked on his way to Calvary. The fourteen official stations of the cross recognized by the Catholic church are distributed throughout the city of Léogâne; pilgrims dressed in their church clothes march through the streets, singing hymns, reciting prayers, and, in some cases, walking on their knees as a gesture of solidarity with Christ's suffering.

In 1995, the *Chemen Kwa* featured elaborately decorated stations that graphically depicted Jesus's brutal and arduous final hours. The twelfth station featured an actual worshipper as Jesus on the cross, his clothes torn and dirty, and his forehead smeared with a blood-red substance. Most of the participants walked slowly behind a priest who used a bullhorn to project his prayers over the assembled crowd. By 2000, the priest's bullhorn was replaced with tall loudspeakers and a gasoline generator mounted in the back of a large dump truck. Two singers, carrying dynamic microphones and walking alongside the dump truck, led the congregation in hymns. Upon arriving at a station of the cross, a priest, sitting in the truck's cab, would lead the crowd in prayer. The tableau vivant of the 1995 *Chemen Kwa* was absent in 2000. The booming voice of the Catholic priest asked worshippers to contemplate Jesus's suffering rather than witness the actual mortification of one of their fellow parishioners.

The pervasiveness of a radio broadcast style in the live celebration of Rara, as well as in other facets of public life and ritual, underscores the importance of media for understanding how people consume Rara music today. As radio has come to shape the ways in which Rara is consumed in Léogâne, band members have realized that creating products suitable for airplay is important for getting their musical messages out to the public. In Léogâne, a band's success is measured by the degree to which its seasonal repertoire is favored by the local population. Getting a band's new songs on the radio is an important way to capture the attention of people who are not already associated with the home neighborhood of the band.

In the following section, I outline some of the challenges that Rara bands contend with in order to make recordings that they believe will compete on the local Léogâne market and that will appeal to diaspora audiences. As radio has developed into one of the principal ways in which Léogâne audiences encounter Rara, radio stations have become increasingly influential in determining what types of Rara recordings make it onto the airwaves. Recording engineers have also played an important role in shaping the sonic wave of the Rara procession into a commodity suitable for recording. While bands have not enjoyed consistent success making sales of their recordings profitable, they have nevertheless embraced recording as a vehicle for band promotion and a potential, if risky, source of income.

ECONOMICS OF RARA RECORDING

Turning religious processional music into a recorded performance has extended Rara from a street festival into a transcultural sonic artifact. Each group involved in the production and dissemination of a recording—band members, radio DJs, and recording engineers—has their own agenda in this transformational process.

Band members, especially the *prezidan* (president) of the band, have enormous costs to recoup from the Rara celebration itself. The feasts that each band sponsors in their neighborhoods provide food and drink for hundreds of visiting band members. Rara Ti Malis regularly spends several thousand US dollars on the beef, goat, plantains, rice and beans, salad, and soft drinks that are an expected part of every band's feast. In addition, bands in Léogâne pay three or four musicians from outside the community to act as ringers in the festival. Historically, band members were drawn from the ranks of the local neighborhood and performed on their instruments without payment as part of their service for the band. Today, instrumentalists are drawn from both the surrounding community and from a retinue of professional Rara and Carnival musicians who make large sums of money for their freelance performances with local bands. Petit-Goâve, a small city 15 miles west of Léogâne, is well known for its well-trained trumpet and trombone players who populate many of the larger Rara bands in Léogâne. Brass players from Petit-Goâve and Port-au-Prince often receive large payments for their services—as much as fifty dollars per evening for their work over the Rara season that stretches from just after Mardi Gras to the day after Easter.

In addition, band presidents frequently live in diaspora communities, returning to Haiti for the Rara season. In the case of Rara Ti Malis, several of their presidents have either lived for long periods of time in the US before coming to Haiti or they are based in Miami or New York. Presidents draw upon their overseas constituents for donations, especially to defray the cost of paying musicians and providing food for the band's feast day.

Radio DJs play an important role in determining the cost of participation in Rara as well. As mentioned earlier, in the mid-1990s most radio stations played only homemade "souvenir" cassette recordings of local bands. The souvenir recordings provided the festive ambiance of Rara, but sacrificed sound quality and individual recorded tracks that were more in line with radio formats. Today, DJs act as gatekeepers for Léogâne Rara bands, determining what recordings will be played during the Rara season. Several DJs who I interviewed in 2000 and 2001 expressed exasperation at some of the local Rara bands' refusal to invest in a professionally recorded CD. In one case, a radio DJ refused to play souvenir recordings of Rara at all, demanding instead that bands provide digitally mastered, studio-produced recordings. In addition, some DJs exploit their status as intermediaries with the radio audience, demanding that local Rara bands allow the DJs to produce a CD from a remote recording session set up by the DJ. The power DJs have in connecting Rara bands with potential audiences induces the bands to invest in professional CD recordings and determines how often Rara bands will be broadcast on local radio stations.

Finally, sound engineers and recording studio management have a stake in the recording of Rara for airplay. While local Léogâne studios produce recordings of variable quality, they all charge high prices for their services. As a result, Rara bands find themselves having to raise increasingly large sums to finance their professionally made recordings.

For some band members, such high prices are an indication of the potential economic benefits of producing recordings. Spending money to make money, Rara officials see their expenditures as an investment in a profitable future. Indeed, recordings allow Rara bands in Haiti to connect directly with their diaspora patrons, giving bands the chance to raise awareness of band activities among overseas Haitians and to foment enthusiasm for local Rara activities. Since remittances from diaspora Haitians make up a substantial portion of the Haitian economy, it is understandable that Rara musicians see overseas markets as representing the best chance they have to recoup the investment they make locally in CD recordings.

By making their own CDs that could be distributed and sold in foreign markets, Rara musicians in Léogâne also believe that they may head off what many perceive to be the exploitation of Rara music by Haitian popular musicians, especially practitioners of *mizik rasin* or "roots music." Many *mizik rasin* performers conduct their own form of ethnographic research on so-called traditional Haitian musics, visiting Vodou ceremonies and Rara processions for musical and lyrical ideas. Some Rara bands are concerned that *mizik rasin* groups' use of Rara-inspired music erodes the ability of actual Rara bands to earn money from their music making. For example, many members of Rara Ti Malis complained that the *mizik rasin* group RAM's song "Ambago" borrowed from their own song "Anbago" about the US embargo of Haiti after the ouster of President Jean-Bertrand Aristide in 1991. The fact that RAM's song came out in 1993 and the Ti Malis song was composed for the 1994 Rara season made little difference to the band members I spoke to in 1995; RAM's use of Rara-inspired music and lyrics was perceived as unwelcome competition in the market for topical music.

One of the other challenges that Rara bands wishing to make their own recordings for commercial release contend with is that the Rara festival itself, while costly to the people who sponsor it, has traditionally been free of charge for audiences in Léogâne and elsewhere. Bands are forced to consider how to get people to pay for something they are used to getting at no cost. Most efforts by promoters to raise money for Rara through admission charges and fees have failed. For example, in 1995, some local entrepreneurs in Léogâne organized "Haiti Racines '95," a three-day festival during Holy Week at Ça Ira, a seaside town about three miles from Léogane. Despite the inclusion of nationally known *mizik rasin* groups at the festival, one organizer told me that he doubted that Léogâne residents would be interested in attending the "Haiti Racines" event. The *mizik rasin* performances were aimed at tourists from Port-au-Prince and abroad who wanted to hear their favorite artists during the day and enjoy the ambiance of the Rara festival during the evening hours. The prices for the Haiti Racines festival effectively barred locals from attending. Organizers charged a ten dollar admission fee and demanded hefty prices for cold beers and other concessions; the local brand of beer, Prestige, was available at four times its normal cost from street vendors in Léogâne. I attended the festival and observed only about thirty well-dressed Haitians eat hamburgers and drink beer while listening to the popular music group Kanpech for the better part of an afternoon. The festival was scheduled during daylight hours when most Rara bands were resting, so turnout for Kanpech—a band that normally draws a large crowd—was low. From my perspective as a participant in the event, it appeared that the organizers of Haiti Racines '95 did not recoup the cost of sponsoring the festival that year.

Similarly, most Rara bands do not earn enough income from sales of their studio-produced CDs to cover the cost of production, nor do they have an effective means for distribution for CDs either in Haiti or in the diaspora. Although most Rara bands cannot easily afford to have a commercially mastered CD made each season, band members feel pressure to produce some form of digital recording so that their music is represented on the radio as well as in the Rara procession.

RECORDINGS AS TRANSNATIONAL COMMUNICATION

Recording sales have not brought large revenues to Rara bands, yet band members continue to make them despite the costs involved. The value of a recording, therefore, cannot be measured in economic terms alone, but must also be seen as a type of cultural investment. In his study of Carnival videos made in the Bolivian Andes, ethnomusicologist Henry Stobart observed that little attention "has been paid to the ways in which indigenous people, often with limited technical expertise, have independently grasped the entrepreneurial and creative opportunities offered by cheap audiovisual technologies" (2011, 210). Stobart further proposes that "the demand for these recordings is evidence of a desire among such people to maintain a connection, however nostalgic and imaginary, with the[ir] rural heritage" (216).

Although some Haitians clearly do view Rara as being connected to a rural life, they also see it as an exportable cultural experience, something that can connect distantly located family members with local culture. In her work in Wisconsin with Hmong immigrants who used videotapes to keep in contact with family members back in Laos, anthropologist Jo Ann Koltyk (1993) found that many of her consultants referred to their home videos as their "culture." They used these videos not only to keep family members informed of events "back home," but also to give diaspora residents opportunities to come together and participate in communal video viewing. For Koltyk's ethnographic consultants, videos served as audiovisual backdrops for family life, bringing the sounds and sights of Laos to Hmong people in rural Wisconsin.

Like the Hmong people in Wisconsin, diaspora Haitians have embraced recording technology as a way to communicate with people in the home culture. Before the widespread use of cell phones in Haiti, most working-class Haitians sent what anthropologist Karen Richman calls "cassette-letters" back and forth between Haiti and North America. According to Richman, "Cassette tapes, rather than written letters, are the universal mode of correspondence across this transnational community" (2005, 213).

Not only do cassette-letters offer illiterate Haitians an opportunity to communicate directly with Kreyòl-speaking friends and relatives abroad, they allow people to send encoded messages in the form of *pwen* to compel listeners to support Léogâne Haitians with remittances. Religious studies scholar Karen McCarthy Brown defines *pwen* as "anything that captures the essence or pith of a complex situation" (1987, 151). As encoded messages, *pwen* are frequently used by Haitians to communicate ideas through indirect discourse when direct confrontation would be seen as too aggressive. Richman shows that cassette-letters allow for a more direct and confrontational form of *pwen,* usually directed by Haitians in Léogâne to cassette recipients in the diaspora.

According to Richman, cassette-letters have their own style that encourages individual creativity as well as community appreciation:

Cassette-tape correspondence is thus far more than a means of circumventing illiteracy. Nor is it a mere way of protecting ties that distance threatens to break. The tapes have an aesthetic all their own. They are venues for extending an oral culture that prizes proverbs, figurative, indirect language (epitomized by the art of sending *pwen*) antiphony, and fluid shifting between speech and song, especially verses drawn from the sacred song repertoire. As a means of competitive, public, personal performance, then, the tapes differentiate distant kin as much as unite them. "Persons of words" exploit the medium to maintain and advance their vocal reputations across the vast distances separating communities. (218)

Cassette-letters, then, bring Haitians at home and abroad together through a performance practice that draws upon all of the sender's creative rhetorical resources.

I argue that Rara recordings function as a type of musical cassette-letter, sending messages in the form of *pwen* to band supporters in an effort to convince them of the sender's point of view. In the case of Rara recordings from Léogâne, bands engage in a multilayered discourse that fuses historical, political, and emotional appeals to their supporters in hopes that listener generosity will be stimulated and that the bonds between sender and receiver will be strengthened. In addition, the style of Rara recordings has changed over time, bringing the sound of the radio into the recording studio.

Rara recordings have evolved different ways of expressing their connections with diaspora Haitians since the first commercially produced recording of Léogâne Rara was released by the Association pour la revalorisation des Raras de Leogane (Association for the Revalorization of the Rara [Bands] of Leogane). Titled *Rara Leogane,* this recording featured seven local Léogâne bands each performing one of their Rara songs from the 1999 season.

The recordings on *Rara Leogane* are similar to souvenir recordings in several respects: they contain ambient noise from observers and fans of the band, the instrumental parts dominate the vocal parts (obscuring the lyrics to the songs in several places), and there are no amplified instruments or announcers sounding over the rest of the band. Despite *Rara Leogane's* similarities with earlier souvenir recordings, it is also markedly different from the homemade tapes that Rara participants make on their boom boxes. First, the quality of the recording is much clearer and more defined than any souvenir recording. Although the vocal lines are not the most prominent feature on *Rara Leogane,* they are audible and are performed by singers who know the words and sing on pitch; the yelling that is so characteristic of souvenir recordings is absent in *Rara Leogane.* Also, *Rara Leogane* was produced in Haiti at Studio Valcoui and its CD design—a multicolored background with computer-generated text identifying each band on the CD—was done by Images Creoles, a design company in Port-au-Prince.

Although *Rara Leogane* was successful in that it provided audiences with their first CD of Léogâne Rara music, the fragile collaboration between the seven participating groups did not extend beyond the year 2000. In fact, the appearance of *Rara Leogane* in local markets fueled fierce inter-band competition prompting several groups to pursue the possibility of producing their own CDs. In 2001, many members of Rara Ti Malis expressed their urgent desire to produce a recording that would feature their own music and performers. The idea of collaborating with other bands—especially those bands with whom Ti Malis did not enjoy friendly relations—was out of the question for most people I interviewed.

In 2002, Rara Modèl d'Haïti released the first CD in Léogâne featuring a single Rara band titled *Rasin'n San Bout't (Haitian Roots)*. Whereas *Rara Leogane* was recorded and produced in Haiti, *Rasin'n San Bout't* was recorded in Haiti, but produced in Brooklyn at Haitian Roots Records, a production company set up by Modèl d'Haiti's diaspora patrons to promote Modèl's music in the United States. The CD was released in a jewel case with a two-sided, four-color insert that depicts a young Haitian man playing a *kès* or snare drum. The musicians in Modèl d'Haiti were listed on the back of the jewel case, but their numbers were greatly reduced from the normal forces used to perform during Lent: only two trombones, three trumpets, one baritone horn, one sousaphone, and four percussionists were listed. Since the recording was made in a studio and not at a remote recording session outdoors, several of Modèl's members doubled on instruments and vocals; for example, band member Roody Derameaux played trombone, baritone horn, and sang lead vocal on several numbers.

Rasin'n San Bout't—which translates roughly as "roots without end"—makes explicit connections between Modèl d'Haiti, which is headquartered in the Kafou Difò neighborhood of Léogâne, and its New York diaspora community. The executive producer for the CD is from Brooklyn and is featured in a praise song titled "Franklyn Lambert." The singer hails Lambert for leading the band back to the *demanbre* (ancestral Vodou dwelling) that must be honored before the Rara band takes to the street and to the *bitasyon* (homestead) where workers practice *konbit* or cooperative labor music that also uses the bamboo and drums of the Rara celebration. Unlike the *Rara Leogane* CD, in which the sounds of the bamboo are most prominent, *Rasin'n San Bout't (Haitian Roots)* features an announcer who exhorts the CD audience with his own interpretation of the lyrics of the song. Shouting "Alo, Franklyn Lambert, se pou w/Alo New York City" (Hello Franklyn Lambert, it's for you/Hello New York City), the announcer connects the music directly to Modèl's US fans. The announcer acts as a Rara DJ to mediate the experience of listening to the CD for those expatriates for whom the recording itself may be their only connection to Modèl's Rara celebration.

Once *Rasin'n San Bout't (Haitian Roots)* was available for sale in Léogâne, other bands scrambled to produce their own recordings. In 2005, Rara Ti Malis Kache released their first studio-produced album. Called *Pasyon Malis* (The Passion of Malis), the CD's title refers to the passion that the band generates among its fans as well as the passion associated with Christ's suffering during his procession to Calvary. Like Rara Modèl's *Rasin'n San Bout't (Haitian Roots)* CD, the recording eliminates the ambient street noise of the Rara celebration and features a lead singer who provides spoken and sung commentary over the instrumental music. In several of the songs, the commentator addresses the diaspora audience directly. For example, in "Kiltivate," a song about the hardships facing Haitian farmers, the announcer shouts the following over an instrumental interlude:

> *Anpil armoni, anpil son, djaspora kontan!*
> *Kote moun Miami yo? Moun Canada yo? Moun Gwadloup yo?*
> *Mizik sa se pou nou!*

> Big band, big sound, the diaspora is happy!
> Where are the people of Miami? The people of Canada? The people of
>   Guadeloupe?
> This music is for you!

It is noteworthy that a song about farming addresses diaspora Haitians by name, correlating the big size and sound of the band with the enjoyment of Haitians living abroad. In this example, Haitians unable to attend the celebration physically are included as participants in a global vision of Rara participation. Using culturally resonant concepts like pwen to engage their audiences, Haitian Rara participants send messages to their diaspora relatives that fuse the physicality of Rara, with its emphasis on street processions and exuberant crowd behavior, with the spirit of cooperation of the konbit (cooperative labor group).

In a very different context, Haitian singer Wyclef Jean used the political power of Rara to raise money for earthquake relief in the aftermath of the January 2010 temblor that devastated Port-au-Prince.[10] Starting with a version of the popular reggae tune "By the Rivers of Babylon" in which he likened the suffering of the Jews' exile in Babylon to the current situation in Haiti, Wyclef segued into his popular song "Yele" in which he exorts Haitians to "chache Bondyè " or look for God in troubled times. Finally, Wyclef shouted "Enough of the moping, let's rebuild Haiti, let's show them how we do it where we come from" and turned to the musicians on stage for a rousing performance of Rara complete with snare drum, tanbou (single-headed hand drum), and konè. In the context of a telethon organized to raise money for earthquake relief, the message was for audience members to stand up, engage the music, and dance along with Wyclef's band. Through the medium of television, Wyclef drew upon Haitian audiences' understanding of Rara as an opportunity to physically participate in Rara from where they stood. Playing the part of the colonel (without a whip and a whistle), Wyclef also called upon people to participate by offering financial support, reminding diaspora Haitians that without their contributions, Haitians in Haiti would languish in the aftermath of this recent cataclysm.

Whereas Wyclef Jean could expect to generate a considerable number of monetary donations to Haitian earthquake relief through his internationally broadcast telethon, Rara bands do not harbor any illusions that their sonic products in the form of CD recordings alone will generate income for Léogâne bands. Unlike large-scale, internationally distributed recordings, most Rara recordings are distributed to Haitian diaspora audiences through hand-to-hand exchange; members travel abroad to deliver their sonic messages directly to band patrons.

The worth of Rara recordings thus cannot be measured simply by their exchange value; they have what sociologist Lucy Suchman calls "affiliative powers" that show how "objects are not innocent but fraught with significance for the relations that they materialize" (2005, 379). In the case of Rara recordings, these "affiliative powers" constitute material, cultural, spiritual, and political connections between home and diaspora Haitians through their encoded lyrics, their participatory aesthetic, and their engagement of long-distance nationalist sentiment. As such, Rara recordings give diaspora Haitians ways to perform their identities in ways that go beyond "imagining" them (Anderson 1991).

Sonic tourists in the diaspora embody Rara practice through their consumption of Rara recordings, bringing Haitians at home and abroad closer through their shared experience of listening to the sounds of the celebration. As Angela Impey describes in her study of cassette-letters among the Dinka of South Sudan (2013, 15), the recording itself "has become coopted into the affective dimension of song making . . . replacing persons in performance, yet simultaneously assisting in the mediation and maintenance of those human relationships." Diaspora Haitians need recordings, not only for their personal enjoyment, but also to maintain a sense of being Haitian while living abroad. While Haitians from Léogâne try to exploit a potential media market abroad, they are most concerned with providing diaspora Haitians a means to express their collective identity, bridging the distance between home and host cultures.

NOTES

1. In Haiti, the word Vodou usually is used to refer to a specific religious rite. I use the word Vodou here to refer to spiritual practices in general. See Largey 2006 (243, n. 2) for a detailed explanation of the use of the term Vodou in Haitian studies.

2. Julmane St. Fort, interview with the author, Léogâne, Haiti, April 6, 1996.
3. In Léogâne Rara, the chorus walks in front of the instruments.
4. See Averill 1997 for a similar observation about "heating up" audiences during performances of Haitian popular music.
5. In 2005, Radio Konpa went off the air due to financial problems.
6. Ciceron Desmangles, interview with the author, Port-au-Prince, Haiti, August 1, 1988. As ethnomusicologist Melvin Butler has described in his recent work on Haitian Pentecostals, the tension between Vodou practitioners and evangelical Protestants today ranges from outright hostility to casual indifference (2008, 27).
7. Recordings of Rara performance are more than "souvenirs" in the more commonly used sense of the word in tourism studies. The noun "souvenir" itself comes from the French verb meaning "to remember" or "to miss." If we focus on the action of remembering (instead of the thing remembered), we can see the movement of Rara recordings from Haiti to the diaspora as a vital process that transmits sonic information as a form of cultural action instead of a static transmission of a product from one place to another.
8. Julmane St. Fort, interview with the author, Léogâne, Haiti, April 6, 1996. Although St. Fort no longer works for Radio Anacaona, other journalists and friends of the radio station's director contribute reports from bands on a regular basis.
9. I have participated in interview programs at Radio Konpa and Force FM, but not with members from rival bands.
10. Although Port-au-Prince received most of the news coverage after the earthquake, the epicenter of the quake was closer to Léogâne. Local estimates put the number of damaged buildings in the greater Léogâne area around 80 percent.

REFERENCES

Anderson, Benedict. 1991. *Imagined Communities: Reflections on the Origin and Spread of Nationalism*. London: Verso.

Averill, Gage. 1997. *A Day for the Hunter, a Day for the Prey: Music and Power in Haiti*. Chicago: University of Chicago Press.

Barlow, William. 1999. *Voice Over: The Making of Black Radio*. Philadelphia: Temple University Press.

Brown, Karen McCarthy. 1987. "Alourdes: A Case Study of Moral Leadership in Haitian Vodou." In *Saints and Virtues*, edited by John S. Hawley, 144–167. Berkeley: University of California Press.

Butler, Melvin L. 2008. "The Weapons of Our Warfare: Music, Positionality, and Transcendence Among Haitian Pentecostals." *Caribbean Studies* 36(2): 23–64.

Crouch, David. 2000. "Places Around Us: Embodied Lay Geographies in Leisure and Tourism." *Leisure Studies* 19(2): 63–76.

Glick-Schiller, Nina, and Georges Fouron. 2001. *Georges Woke Up Laughing: Long-Distance Nationalism and the Search for Home*. Durham, NC: Duke University Press.

Impey, Angela. 2013. "Keeping in Touch via Cassette: Tracing Dinka Songs from Cattle Camp to Transnational Audio-Letter." *Journal of African Cultural Studies* 25(2): 197–210.

Koltyk, Jo Ann. 1993. "Telling Narratives through Home Videos: Hmong Refugees and Self-Documentation of Life in the Old and New Country." *Journal of American Folklore* 106(422): 435–449.

Largey, Michael. 2000. "Politics on the Pavement: Haitian Rara as a Traditionalizing Process." *Journal of American Folklore* 113(449): 239–254.

———. 2006. *Vodou Nation: Haitian Art Music and Cultural Nationalism.* Chicago: University of Chicago Press.

Larsen, Jonas. 2001. "Tourism Mobilities and the Travel Glance: Experiences of Being on the Move." *Scandinavian Journal of Hospitality and Tourism* 1(2):80–98.

———. 2006. "Geographies of Tourism Photography: Choreographies and Performances." In *Geographies of Communication: The Spatial Turn in Media Studies*, edited by Jesper Falkheimer and André Jansson, 243–261. Gøteborg, Sweden: NORDICOM.

Lean, Garth L. 2012. "Transformative Travel: A Mobilities Perspective." *Tourist Studies* 12(2): 151–172.

Månsson, Maria. 2011. "Mediatized Tourism." *Annals of Tourism Research* 38(4): 1634–1652.

Manuel, Peter. 1988. *Popular Musics of the Non-Western World.* New York: Oxford University Press.

McAlister, Elizabeth. 2002. *Rara! Vodou, Power and Performance in Haiti and Its Diaspora.* Berkeley: University of California Press.

Rakić, Tijana, and Donna Chambers. 2012. "Rethinking the Consumption of Places." *Annals of Tourism Research* 39(3): 1612–1633.

Ramsey, Kate. 2011. *The Spirits and the Law: Vodou and Power in Haiti.* Chicago: University of Chicago Press.

Richman, Karen E. 2005. *Migration and Vodou.* Gainsville: University Press of Florida.

Sheller, Mimi, and John Urry. 2006. "The New Mobilities Paradigm." *Environment and Planning* 38: 207–226.

Stobart, Henry. 2011. "Constructing Community in the Digital Home Studio: Carnival, Creativity and Indigenous Music Video Production in the Bolivian Andes." *Popular Music* 30(2): 209–226.

Suchman, Lucy. 2005. "Affiliative Objects." *Organization* 12(3): 379–399.

Urry, John. 2000. *Sociology beyond Society: Mobilities for the 21st Century.* London: Routledge.

Discography

Rara Leogane, Association pour la revalorisation des Raras de Leogane. Port-au-Prince: Studio Valcoui (2000).

Rara Modèl d'Haïti, *Rasin'n San Bout't (Haitian Roots)*, HRR001. Brooklyn, NY: Haitian Roots Records (2002).

Rara Ti Malis Kache, *Pasyon Malis.* n.p. (2005).

PART III

Sites and Sounds of Intra-regional, Expatriate, and Insider Tourism

5

Wanderers of Love

Touring and Tourism in the Jamaica-Haiti
Musical Circuit of the 1950s

MATTHEW J. SMITH ■

When tourists go to a resort for a vacation they are looking for and expect high class entertainment. The introduction of first rate concerts and important musical events . . . is something which deserves the greatest support and encouragement; such undertakings will fill the gap which existed for a long time and which we have not been able to bridge before.

—F. H. ROBINSON, *Jamaica Tourist Trade Commissioner*
(Daily Gleaner 1945)

The cultural connections shared between the countries of the northern Caribbean are not apparent at first glance. Indeed it is the contrasts that stand out most: a varied pattern of European colonization, different timetables and processes for independence, two epochal revolutions, and linguistic diversity, with five languages—French, Creole, English, Patois, and Spanish—being spoken across fewer than half a dozen islands.

The proximity of the countries creates a situation of obvious union. Yet their linkages have often been a function of migration and resettlement across the linguistic and political divides. Among the principal islands of the Bahamas, Hispaniola (Haiti and the Dominican Republic), Cuba, and Jamaica, there has been a near constant movement of people and with them a transmission of culture. Haitians and Jamaicans worked together on Cuban cane-fields in the

1920s and 1930s, and histories of political struggles have created a shared experience of exile, immigration, and resettlement.[1]

Like its people, the music of the islands has traveled the length and breadth of the Caribbean region. In the post-war era musicians moved along the familiar route taken by other migrants, visiting, recording, and living in nearby islands. For example, in the 1950s, legendary Haitian singer and multi-instrumentalist Guy Durosier and Jamaican guitarist Ernest Ranglin and saxophonist Harold "Little G" McNair spent time as performers in the Bahamas. At the same time, the music of other islands influenced the styles Haitian and Jamaican musicians adopted in their search to create a unique sound during a period of heightened national consciousness.

This circulation within the region is important in understanding the evolution of seemingly autochthonous musical styles. In his study of Bahamian music, Timothy Rommen (2011) has noted that the Bahamian musical context was shaped by travel, both the physical travel of tourists and people from Haiti, Jamaica, and Trinidad into the Bahamas, and the migration of music around the region. Foreign tourists are generally the most visible category of traveler. They bring with them a tangible representation of North American culture—which for people in the Caribbean regularly exposed to radio and records from abroad has never been far from reach—and they enjoy the cultural products of each island which are custom-packaged for tourists. But as Rommen's typology suggests there are several other "registers of travel" that have their own importance in shaping Caribbean tourism and the development of the region's music (2011, 3).

Musicians form a special category of tourist visitor. Not only are they attracted to the novelty and thrill of the visit, but they are also interested in the culture of the places they encounter. As Caribbean tourism expanded in the 1940s and 1950s to attract large numbers of principally North American visitors, the experiences of (and with) touring musicians in places marketed as tourist destinations contributed significantly to the larger cultural context. Similarly, the music of each island traveled to nearby islands as well as across the sea to North America.

This chapter explores intra-island musical tourism with a discussion of the intersections of Jamaican and Haitian music in the 1940s and 1950s. Whereas the influences of North American styles have been well recognized and studied, comparatively less attention has been paid to musical contact between islands within the region. The years after World War II to the rise of the dictatorship of François "Papa Doc" Duvalier in 1957 were the "golden years" of Haitian tourism (Plummer 1990). Jamaica shared a similar experience in its tourism history. However, its tourist industry continued to expand in the sixties while Haitian tourism contracted significantly. The decade after 1945 is therefore a critical period for the study of inter-Caribbean cultural exchange.

This chapter has three related aims. First, it seeks to de-center North America in its discussion of the evolution of Caribbean tourist markets by highlighting the importance of intra-island tourist networks between Haiti and Jamaica in the post-war period. This is presented as an extension of a longer history of movement between the two countries. Second, it examines the place of music in these cultural exchanges through a focus on the urban musical landscape in Haiti and Jamaica in these years, which was defined largely by big band music. Finally and significantly, the chapter showcases the 1950–1951 tour of Haiti by Jamaica's most popular big band, the Eric Deans Orchestra, and the performances of Haiti's Orchestre Atomique in Kingston in 1953. As argued in this volume's introduction, musicians are quite often treated only as producers of the sound track of a Caribbean that exists in the imagination of the tourist. Rarely are musicians treated as consumers themselves. The focus on the bands and tours of the early 1950s emphasizes the importance of musicians as intra-island tourists and their performances as valuable components of musical tourism in the post-war northern Caribbean.

THE "INVISIBLE EXPORT" OF JAMAICA AND HAITI

The cultural connections that developed between Haiti and Jamaica during the tourist boom years after 1945 were an elaboration of a longer history of musical exchange. From at least the early twentieth century, Haitian and Jamaican music reflected the history of circum-Caribbean migration and, occasionally, key moments in the relationship between the two neighbors. A 1911 Haitian song about ex-president Antoine Simon, for example, featured a verse that referenced Simon's fate as well as the history of political migration of Haitians to Jamaica:

> Antoine Simon said before he left
> That he would leave a bomb in the middle of the palace.
> When it went off he was already in Kingston. (Cited in Courlander
>   1960, 157)

Musicians were among the displaced Haitians who, like Antoine Simon, found a home in Kingston. Some Haitian musicians, like Professor Arthur Bonnefil, became well-known in Jamaica. A classically trained pianist, Bonnefil was born in Aux Cayes in southern Haiti in 1876. He was previously a music teacher in Port-au-Prince and served as director of a leading orchestra in that city before leaving for exile in Kingston in 1908 (Dumerve 1968, 216–217). He was also a composer of reveries, merengues, and waltzes and wrote several pieces for piano and violin including one entitled "Let us Meditate" (*Daily Gleaner*, 1911a and 1915a).

Bonnefil taught piano in Kingston and Spanish Town and performed across the island, from private "at home" shows to larger concerts in Montego Bay and at Theatre Royal and the Ward Theatre in Kingston. Bonnefil's regular performances were in Kingston at the Hotel Cecil, and he was often accompanied by a popular Jamaican singer of the period Madame M. Birch. Together Birch and Bonnefil developed a set that included classical standards, romantic songs, cake walk tunes, and Haitian folk songs.[2] Birch and Bonnefil's audiences in Kingston would have been mixed, ranging from elite Jamaicans and Haitians living in the city to early North American tourists on vacation in Kingston.

In August 1911, under the patronage of a wealthy Haitian exile in Kingston, the duo traveled to Port-au-Prince for a series of performances that made a spectacular impression on elite Haitians. They performed at the Metropolitan Hotel in Port-au-Prince and were invited as the principal entertainers at the inauguration ceremony of Antoine Simon's successor, President Cincinnatus Leconte.[3] The concerts Bonnefil and Birch performed in Haiti attracted excitement in Kingston as well as Port-au-Prince. The Jamaican papers celebrated the shows as a "new venture" for "two well known artistes" from Kingston's "musical sphere" (*Daily Gleaner* 1911b). In addition to the marches and waltzes that featured in their Kingston repertory, the set included Bonnefil's compositions, such as a two-step for piano titled "Allo! Allo!," a song inspired by his years in Jamaica (Dumerve 1968, 217).

The Bonnefil and Birch performances in Kingston and Port-au-Prince were an early example of musical collaboration between the two islands. Even as the political histories of each country kept them separate—especially after the US Occupation of Haiti in 1915—the cultural contacts continued. In April 1925, the Jamaican national football team made a successful tour of occupied Haiti, playing three high-profile games in St. Marc and Port-au-Prince. The matches were not merely exhibition games, but also served as symbols of goodwill between the two neighbors. President Louis Borno and several prominent Jamaicans living in Haiti fêted the Jamaicans with lavish parties and dinners during their one-week stay. Traveling with the footballers were musicians from Jamaica's St. George's Catholic Club, who played at several popular theaters and clubs in Port-au-Prince to wide acclaim. By this time, Haitians and Jamaicans were listening to Cuban music and jazz from the United States (Averill 1997, 45–59). The shows that the St. George's musicians played were, by some reports, wild affairs with Haitian youth surprising their Jamaican guests by dancing feverishly to the music and calling out for more (*Daily Gleaner* 1925).

The tour of the Jamaican national football team and the St. George's band in Haiti came at the dawn of great changes in both countries. An economic downturn in the Caribbean resulting from the Great Depression forced scores of Haitians and Jamaicans to migrate in search of work to the Cuban sugar zones. Both groups shared a similar plight when forced to leave Cuba by the Machado government in the 1930s. The countries they returned to were on the brink of dramatic transformation. In Haiti, a militant reaffirmation of national- ism among Haitian intellectuals and youth in the late 1920s precipitated events that would hasten the ending of marine occupation in 1934. Four years later, Jamaica would explode with a series of labor riots that challenged British colo- nialism and advanced the process toward self-government. During these years Jamaicans and Haitians continued to travel back and forth between the two countries and to Cuba, reporting news of political developments and possibili- ties. Once the dust settled on the political and economic tensions of the 1930s, there emerged an exciting call for a more focused national self-identity.

The search for this national authenticity was always more pronounced in post-occupation Haiti than in Jamaica. The occupation represented a stain on the proud history of independence for Haitian nationalists. When it ended, Haiti was on the verge of a cultural reawakening. Nationalist currents prompted a reevaluation of Haiti's cultural discourse in the 1940s which was manifest in several forms, not the least of which was a conscious integration of folk elements in Haitian popular music. Haitian cultural nationalism proved inspirational for some foreigners who witnessed these changes in the 1940s and 1950s. On a visit to Kingston in 1944, wealthy Jamaican businessman Rickson Fenton— who along with fellow Jamaicans Franck Wilson and O.J. Brandt, amassed great riches in Haiti—commented that one thing that Haitians had that Jamaicans did not was a sense of national consciousness. At an event in his honor at the Myrtle Bank Hotel, he recognized the search for a new order was common to both countries and advocated greater economic and social solidarity between Haiti and Jamaica (*Daily Gleaner* 1944).

The concept of social solidarity between Jamaica and Haiti was more than rhetoric. Middle-class Jamaicans welcomed President Sténio Vincent's (1930– 1941) post-occupation promise of a "second independence" and anticipated great changes in Haiti that would tie both countries closer together.[4] Apart from regular engagements between Jamaican and Haitian football teams, informal gestures of cultural goodwill became more frequent. Haitian coaches traveled to Jamaica to train Jamaican footballers on the skills of the game; the Jamaican Boy Scouts made a much-publicized trip to Haiti in the mid-1940s; an interna- tional Friends of Haiti organization found support in Kingston; elite Kingston women hosted tea parties to raise funds for Haitian causes; many privileged Haitian students traveled to Jamaica for high school education; Haitian writers, musicians, artists, and intellectuals visited Jamaica and were routinely fêted by the local literati; and by the early 1950s, a trip to Haiti became part of the prize package for each winner of the Miss Jamaica contest.[5] Jamaicans who visited the incredible Bicentenary Exposition in Port-au-Prince, 1949/1950, and made annual pilgrimages to the Haitian carnivals throughout the '50s, enhanced this cultural exchange. Perhaps most significant, in the late '40s Haiti's cultural officer to Jamaica, Gerard Pierre-Louis, formed a "Jam-Haiti Link" which, among other things, organized public concerts to commemorate Haitian holidays (*Daily Gleaner* 1949).

This wave of mutual exchange between the two countries was facilitated by the increased attention paid to the Caribbean region in the post-war period. North American tourists with more disposable income flocked to the northern Caribbean in the late 1940s and 1950s. At a three-day conference held in Kingston in 1944 to explore the possibilities of tourism—regarded by the organizers as the "invisible export"—for the future of the island, the point was clearly made: "Tourism is Jamaica's greatest postwar trade potential." The task for the country, it was concluded at the conference, was to figure out "how to house, transport, and entertain deluxe" (*Spotlight* 1944, 8).

The potential of the tourist market in advancing regional economies encouraged each island to consider more seriously than before the culture of its neighbors. This was not always in a spirit of exchange. As tourism expanded, the islands competed with one another in an attempt to offer unique products for the growing tourist market. This was most often in terms of natural attractions but also extended to cultural attractions as well.

For Haiti, Jamaica, and Cuba, this interest in culture and symbolism at times superseded political realities. That Haiti was governed by a military ruler for most of the 1950s mattered little to Jamaicans intent on deepening their ties with Haiti. Indeed, President Magloire's state visit to Jamaica in February 1955 was a spectacle so lavish that it was long regarded as a defining moment for many who witnessed it.[6] Jamaican hotels used the opportunity to attract Haitian visitors to the island. One example was the Mimosa Lodge in Kingston, which took out an advertisement in the *Daily Gleaner* that broadcast their intention: "To His Excellency the President of the Republic of Haiti and Madame Magloire— We extend our Best Wishes for an enjoyable stay in Jamaica. To the people of Haiti—We Say Holiday in Jamaica and stay at Mimosa Lodge Hotel" (1955a).

The opening up of the Caribbean to tourist traffic in the 1940s and 1950s also made the region more accessible to people from nearby islands within the region. Much of this success had to do with the expansion of Pan American Airways (PAA), which not only boasted regular flights to the region but also promoted intra-Caribbean destinations as well. PAA worked with the tourist offices in the islands to organize tours of the region. Haiti was promoted as the "star of the Caribbean" that was only a few hours from Miami. In 1951 PAA financed a film project, *Wings to Haiti*, intended to promote Haiti's attractions and promising industrial development (*Le Nouvelliste* 1951b). In Jamaica's case, PAA organized a series of "Know Jamaica" tours between 1951 and 1953, inviting travel agents and travel editors to the island (Taylor 1993, 157). The effect of these ventures was a significant increase in mass tourism. Where in the years before the war the islands received most visitors by boat, in the years after 1945 the majority came by plane. Not only did this shorten the distance between the Caribbean and North America, but it also shortened the distance between the islands.

By the mid-fifties PAA—operative in Jamaica since 1930—operated daily service between Kingston and Port-au-Prince for seventy-two US dollars round trip. The image of restored political stability with Magloire's presidency and the success of Estimé's Bicentenary Exposition—both occurring in 1950—heightened Haiti's appeal for Jamaicans who could afford a seat on one of PAA's clippers. These flights, combined with the regular visits to Jamaica of Haitian state officials, encouraged middle-class Jamaicans to see Haiti as a popular tourist destination. In 1955 the Inter-Caribbean Goodwill Tours Association, a Jamaican organization that booked and arranged package tours to other islands, began to actively promote Haiti as a tourist location since Haiti was "well worth a visit by Jamaicans" (*Daily Gleaner* 1955b). In April of that year, Basil Rowe, the organizer of the campaign, brought over the first group of Haitian excursionists to Kingston under this new plan. These efforts worked. Jamaican tourists in Haiti reported favorably on their experiences in Haiti in the pages of the local papers. In an article in the *Daily Gleaner*, a Jamaican returning from vacation in Haiti called Haitians the most "delightful people in the world," and waxed sentimental on the effect of leaving the republic to return home in an essay that contained familiar tourist tropes: "All too soon it was time to leave. As we stepped across the place in the dazzling sunshine at Port-au-Prince airport, it seemed as if we were leaving a dear, friendly home to go out into some strange and unfamiliar world . . . As we waved goodbye some nearby radio there floated the strains of 'Choucoune,' surely the most heartbreakingly beautiful of all Haitian folk-songs. The plane rose up in the boundless blue sky; the friendly faces faded, the hills faded and Haiti became only a mist and a memory. Our holiday was over" (*Daily Gleaner* 1956b).[7]

Haiti's physical beauty always received most praise from Jamaican visitors. But the country's culture and especially its folk music excited them as well as evidenced in the above quote. The reference to "Choucoune" (Yellowbird) reflects the important role music played in shaping the holiday experience for intra-Caribbean tourists as well as visitors from outside the region. Haitian music, as we have seen, had long entered the consciousness of Jamaican middle-class listeners. In the post-war years, however, it met an increasingly receptive audience among Jamaican tourists in Haiti and middle-class

Jamaicans at home. Robert A. Hill, historian and son of Jamaica's renowned impresario Stephen O.D. Hill, indicated as much in his reflection on the place of Haitian music among middle class Jamaicans in the 1950s:

> "In the mid- to late-fifties, at parties records of Haitian popular music were much appreciated. I have vivid recollections of how much this music was appreciated, based on how much it inspired dancing among us . . . These records were brought back to Jamaica by my parents from their sojourns in Haiti, where they would often go to present concerts. Personally, I was impressed by the smooth, danceable quality of music. I don't recall that we had anything comparable at the time in Jamaica."[8]

Hill's account vividly conveyed the role that Jamaican visitors to Haiti, like his parents, played in the circulation of music between the islands. It was through the records that they returned with that Haitian music first drew notice from people on other islands. But Hill's recollection of why his parents visited Haiti ("to present concerts") raises a more important issue: that musical performances were a powerful feature in the cultural interchange between Haiti and Jamaica.

"THEY LOVED OUR BRAND OF MUSIC": ERIC DEANS AND THE TOURS OF THE EARLY 1950S

A landmark episode in the Haitian-Jamaican musical exchange was the 1950–1951 tour of Haiti by Jamaica's most popular band of the era, the twelve-piece Eric Deans Orchestra. Often referred to as "Jamaica's greatest big band," the Eric Deans Orchestra was at the top of a list of exceptional orchestras and small bands that dominated the Kingston music scene in the early post-war years when the island's popular music began to take shape. Beginning in 1944, Deans rose to local prominence leading one of the most popular aggregations in Jamaica, the Liberators, and played at the island's leading nightclubs, including Bournemouth Bath, and especially the Colony Club, where Deans held a long residency as bandleader.

The Kingston entertainment scene in the 1940s–1950s included several clubs that provided not only entertainment, but also a space for the island's young talent to perform. In addition to singers there was a host of talented musicians, such as Wilton Gaynair and Baba Brooks, who performed weekly at the clubs; some who would later enjoy international careers.[9]

Although a largely forgotten figure in Jamaican musical history, among his peers Deans was regarded as the leading innovator of popular Jamaican music.

in the decade after World War II. Nicknamed "The Maestro" by musicians and fans, Deans was renowned for having a fine-tuned ear for music. His family was not musical, but he developed an interest in the big band music of the United States that he heard on the radio growing up in Montego Bay. He taught himself to play music and by early adulthood he had become a multi-instrumentalist though his primary instruments were the tenor saxophone and clarinet. In addition to mastering jazz and swing standards with ease, he was also known to have written his own tunes.

Deans began his career as a bandleader and music teacher in the parish of St. James where he worked at the army barracks and the Montego Bay Boys Club. From his early days in Jamaica's western parish, he earned a reputation for demanding discipline and perfectionism from his band; when musicians made a mistake he would note it and reprimand them after the performance. Deans was much like a drill sergeant, pushing his musicians to improve through long hours of daily rehearsals, and insisting that they be able to read music as well as play it.[10] This intense work ethic became ingrained in the band members and would be transmitted to later generations of Jamaican musicians.

Since there was only one major nightclub in Montego Bay, the Jolly Roger, Deans moved to Kingston in the mid-1940s and he immediately began to work the club circuit. The local music scene was expanding rapidly after the war years and Deans quickly found his niche playing popular swing music from the United States. Before long, Deans began to build a following in Kingston, performing regularly at popular clubs. He started out as a band member with several groups before forming the Liberators in 1944. As with other Jamaican big bands of the forties and early fifties—including the Val Bennett Orchestra, the Herman Lewis Orchestra, the Ossie DaCosta Orchestra, the Redver Cooke Orchestra, the Ray Coburn Orchestra, and the Sonny Bradshaw Seven—the group's repertoire was a mix of US jazz (particularly the works of Glen Miller and Duke Ellington), swing, and Broadway numbers, which were staple fare on Caribbean radio. They also played Jamaican folk songs and mentos as well as Cuban standards. Songs such as "War Workers Vanities" and "Honey-Drippers Ball"—standards in the Liberators set list in the late forties—suggest the type of music that was popular in these years. A 1946 advertisement for one of the band's performances at the Bournemouth captured their appeal: "Fresh from their triumph in the swing battle of the times, Eric Deans and his Liberators return to their own bandstand—at Bournemouth tonight to give out with that feeling of confidence of swing. It's hot, they say, these days; but with Eric Deans at one end and the sea at the other, it's both "hot" and cool at Bournemouth to-night!" (*Daily Gleaner* 1946).

Once his reputation spread, Deans actively recruited young musicians from the famous Alpha Boys School in Kingston, a nursery for generations of Jamaican musicians. Winston "Sparrow" Martin, a drummer who entered the school in 1949, recalled that Deans would regularly consult with the school's director, Sister Ignatius, for the list of the top students each year. Selection by Eric Deans often led to the sort of public exposure the young musicians craved.[11] Deans was always keen that the musicians were able to learn quickly, work hard, and sharpen their creativity through regular and rigorous live performances around the island.

One of Deans's motivations for his rigid approach to musicianship was to ensure that the bands he created would come out on top in a competitive musical environment. This competition kept the bands focused on innovation and the adaptation of new styles in their repertoires in order to maintain popularity at a time when Jamaican musicians competed with foreign artists for attention.

After the war, leading recording artists and musicians from the United States including Paul Robeson (1948), Louis Jordan (1951), Cab Calloway (1952), the Nicholas Brothers (1954), Marian Anderson (1947 and 1953), Billy Eckstine (1954), Dave Brubeck (1959), Bill Haley and His Comets (1957), and later Count Basie (1962), Fats Domino (1961), and Duke Ellington (1969) performed in Jamaica and influenced the musical direction of the local big bands.

Many of the foreign artists were invited to the island by impresario Stephen O.D. Hill who began a "Celebrity Concert Series" after the war.[12] The series aimed to bring popular international acts to Jamaica to showcase their talent to a local audience. The concerts served a dual purpose though. They sought to promote Jamaica as a favored tourist destination with a unique "product." In 1945, William Read, a promoter of Jamaican tourism, spoke directly to this:

> The people in Jamaica today realize all the overwhelming importance of tourist trade for the island. However, it is not enough that we offer our beaches and country resorts as the only attractions to the prospective visitor . . . The economic value of these concerts is almost inestimable; the reputation Jamaica will get by the organization of regular celebrity festivals may well be beyond anything we dare hope at this moment, and the influence such concerts will exert on our own musical life is also a factor that by no means should be overlooked. (*Daily Gleaner* 1945)

Critics complained that the focus on foreign acts hindered the development of Jamaica's big band scene because Jamaican audiences preferred foreign performers to local acts. Vere Johns, an eminent promoter, journalist, and commentator on Jamaican music in the 1950s, claimed that the concentration on foreign acts negatively impacted the Kingston music scene and the creative development of the bands. "Tourists on the northside resort[s] can always see Jamaican talent but not those in Kingston" (*The Star* 1953b). Johns argued that visitors appreciated the foreign acts that performed regularly in Kingston, but they also expected to see more local dance bands. The situation was "stifling local talent" (*The Star* 1953c).

On the initiation of female bandleader Ivy Graydon in 1952, some musicians, including Lord Fly, Sonny Bradshaw and, briefly, Eric Deans, organized a Jamaica music union to protect local entertainers from competition from foreign acts.[13] I.C. Redh, a contemporary music critic, sided with the musicians in their protest against the preferential treatment club owners showed foreign artists. Foreign performers were "either on their way in or on their way out . . . [Locals] flock to shows from which the average tourist turns away in disgust" (Redh 1952).[14]

Other local bandleaders welcomed the variety. The radio and celebrity concerts were, for them, encouragement to develop their repertoire and advance their musical skills. Eric Deans wanted to go even further.

Deans, who was stationed as the resident band at the popular Colony Club at Cross Roads, was determined to move beyond the Kingston big band scene and take his Orchestra outside Jamaica. By the mid-fifties, the Eric Deans Orchestra was the only touring orchestra from the island (See Figure 5. 1). He hoped that

Figure 5.1 Eric Deans Orchestra, Colony Club, circa 1950. Included in this photo are Eric Deans (saxophone), Don Drummond, (trombone), Ernest Ranglin, (guitar), "Satch" Dixon (drums).

Figure 5.2 "Deans Orchestra Leaves for Haiti Engagements." *Daily Gleaner*, February 23, 1951. (© The Gleaner Company Limited)

the exposure to new music and regional musicians would strengthen their playing and popularity back home.

On November 10, 1950, Deans and his twelve-piece band boarded a plane at the Palisadoes airport and left Kingston for Haiti (see Figure 5.2). It might well have been the first tour of its kind for Jamaican musicians. The originally scheduled one-month engagement lasted ten days longer because of popular demand (*Daily Gleaner* 1950). René Marini, owner of the famous Haitian nightclub Cabane Choucoune located in Pétionville beside Marini's Hotel Choucoune, promoted the tour. Hoteliers from each island frequently visited neighboring countries to assess their attractions and tourist packages. It is likely that Marini may have heard the Deans Orchestra on a visit to Kingston.[15] The band further impressed Marini when they arrived in Port-au-Prince and insisted on being taken not to their rooms but directly to the club so they could begin rehearsals immediately (*Haiti Sun* 1951).

Hotel Choucoune was popular among tourists in Haiti. Marini recruited the strongest performers to be the house band. A Jamaican orchestra playing at a major venue was unique for Haiti. Certainly few foreign acts were booked for as long as the Deans Orchestra. The tour showcased Haiti as musically diverse, a bonus for the nightclub during the winter season when tourist traffic was highest.

Billed as the "famous Jazz Jamaican" the band débuted at Cabane Choucoune the night after their arrival (*Le Nouvelliste* 1950a). The following week, on November 16th the Deans Orchestra took their show—which featured Broadway hits, Duke Ellington and Count Basie numbers, and Cuban boleros, along with arrangements of Jamaican calypsos and folk songs in the set— to the larger open-air venue Theâtre de Verdure at the site of the Bicentenary Exposition in Port-au-Prince.[16] Word of mouth, cheaper tickets, and positive reviews in the Haitian press helped to raise their profile. A review of their first show appeared in the Haitian daily, *Le Nouvelliste* and concluded that it was "the opinion of all those who have heard" that they are the "best [band] that has visited our Capital" (*Le Nouvelliste* 1950b).[17] The *Haiti Sun* reviewer was even more ecstatic: "They knocked themselves out . . . got in the groove and took off" (*Haiti Sun* 1950b). These favorable reports in the Haitian press suggest the strength of the band's performances and the intensity of Deans's rehearsal for the tour.

Following their major show at Theâtre de Verdure, the band—then called in the local press "Jamaica's Hot Ten"—performed at the Haitian-American Institute and a well-received set at the Bellevue Club (*Haiti Sun* 1950a). Then they returned for regular weekend shows at Cabane Choucoune. They would also continue to perform regular shows at Theâtre de Verdure for locals and tourists.

In early December the band headlined a special ball for President Magloire in honor of his election to the presidency. Magloire was sufficiently impressed with the band to request that they play at an event he hosted at the National Palace. For Ernest Ranglin who was on his first tour outside of Jamaica, this was a high point of their time in Haiti: "That was great man . . . we went to the palace and performed for the president . . . it was quite exciting for all of us."[18]

The Orchestra also became a staple act on Haitian radio, appearing "nearly every day" according to a story in the *Daily Gleaner* (1950). In a review of the band's shows, the English-language Haitian paper *Haiti Sun*, stated that they had been "accepted as Jamaica's finest ambassadors" (*Le Nouvelliste* 1950b). Such adulation likely impressed the younger members of the band, many who came from impoverished neighborhoods in Kingston.[19] By Deans's account, it was the "slower dance melodies" and the calypsos that thrilled the Haitian audiences. Shurland's silky vocals on songs such as "Mona Lisa," which had been a major hit for Nat King Cole that year, were also well-received (Sherman 1951).

On December 18th, after a final soirée held at Cabane Choucoune in their honor, Eric Deans and the band returned to Jamaica. As bandleader, Deans was energized by the experience and by the Haitian hospitality, reporting that the tour was "magnificent . . . they love[d] our brand of music" (*Daily Gleaner* 1950). Deans was eager to showcase the Cuban mambo popular in the sets they heard in Haiti, and to make Jamaica "more mombo [sic] conscious" (ibid.). A reporter who attended a Kingston show shortly after the band's return, commented: "Thrilled by the enthusiastic reception accorded his band in the neighboring Republic, Eric has been swift to pick up all the new tunes and twists of Haitian music so as to maintain his place in the esteem of the public" (Sherman 1951).

The band's Jamaican return would be short-lived; the success of the Haitian engagements prompted Marini to issue a contract for a second tour. The band's new contract, according to reports Deans provided to the Jamaican press, was initially for a year with possible dates in Trinidad and the Dominican Republic. However, the tour would be shortened to four months.

The second tour began on February 22 around the Haitian carnival season. During this busy period, the band was installed at Cabane Choucoune and also returned to Théâtre du Verdure, the site of their successful shows the previous December. As with the first tour, the second also featured Roy Shurland on vocals.[20]

Reports of the activities of the musicians in Haiti are sparse. As guests at Hotel Choucoune, they would have been exposed to the same universe as other tourists. Moreover, their long stay allowed them to visit popular attractions and participate in tourist life in Port-au-Prince. As Ranglin recalled: "We went to a lot of places in Port-au-Prince. We went up in the hills to [Boutilier] and looked at the view, all those places."[21] As visitors, the Jamaican musicians formed personal impressions of the country and its vibrant entertainment scene. Marini and his wife ensured the band had a hospitable reception.

The positive response of Haitian audiences to their music impressed Deans. In an interview in the Jamaican press an ebullient Deans noted: "Haiti is the place for me. I think I'll just remain in Haiti where they treat me and my boys like presidents."[22] This type of openness to Jamaican musicians was reflective of the general embrace of diversity in the Haitian entertainment scene at that time.

Haiti was enthralled with the sounds of jazz coming through phonograph players and tinny speakers of living room radio sets in the parlors of the Port-au-Prince bourgeoisie. The very term jazz had evolved in Haiti to mean any big band collective. Bands such as Jazz des Jeunes, Orchestre Citadel, Orchestre Panamericain, Orchestre Atomique, and Orchestre Saïeh made a mark on the musical scene in Port-au-Prince, playing a range of styles that included Vodou rhythms, French chanson, jazz, and, Cuban styles.

"What emerges in all this," noted ethnomusicologist Gage Averill in a comment on the Haitian music of the period that could also be applied to the

Jamaican scene, "is a portrait of an elite (and, to some extent, middle class) with a strong ethic of cultural participation, and with wide-ranging interests in high-status European art music, contemporary African-American popular and dance music, and nationalist expressions from méringue to Vodou-influenced chamber music" (Averill 1997, 57).

By the early 1950s, Orchestre Saïeh, led by art dealer and musical arranger Issa el Saieh—who like Eric Deans was also referred to as "Maestro"—was a regular at popular nightclubs and proved most adept at bridging Cuban sounds with Haitian Vodou rhythms. Saieh's band often featured Herbie Widmaer as lead singer. In addition to Haitian rhythms and folk lyrics, the band incorporated covers of US big band songs. Saieh went even further, bringing US musicians to Haiti to train his orchestra (Averill 1989, 218). He would later make a series of spectacular recordings in Havana in 1957 with the Bebo Valdés Orchestra.[23]

When the Eric Deans Orchestra returned to Cabane Choucoune they often shared the bill with Orchestre Saïeh. Having two major bands, one local and the other Jamaican, performing a range of musical styles from Europe, North America, and the Caribbean on the same show would have produced thrills for the Haitian music fans and visitors to the island (see Figure 5.3).

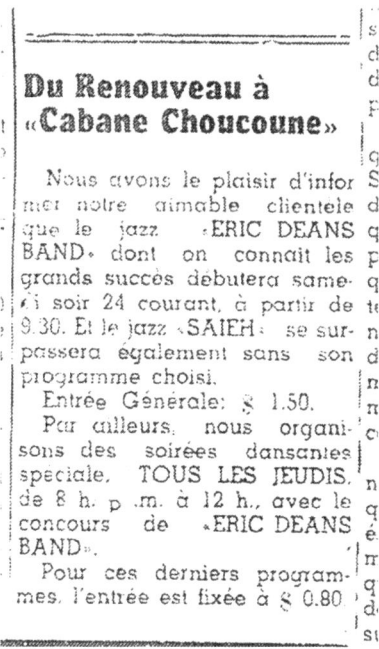

Figure 5.3 Advertisement for Deans Orchestra and Orchestre Saïeh performing at Cabane Choucone, *Le Nouvelliste*, February 23, 1951. (Image courtesy of Le Nouvelliste)

With audiences that were typically elite and middle-class locals, and tourists from North America and Latin America, these nightclub performances represented some of the first forays into commercial music for both Haiti and Jamaica. State support of a burgeoning music scene in Haiti gave musicians the confidence to branch out. Issa El Saïeh had launched his own label, La Belle Creole, which recorded and distributed Haitian records for foreign markets, including the wider Caribbean.

It was the live Haitian performances that had the most powerful effect for the Jamaican musicians during their time in Haiti. Ranglin recalled that the band spent a lot of time with Haitian counterparts watching them rehearse and perform.[24] The busy throb of Vodou drummers such as Ti-Roro and Ti-Marcel, the strident brass sections, and the swirling lead vocals of some of Haiti's premier singers such as Guy Dorosier, were the sounds that reached the ears of the young Jamaicans intent on mastering new sounds. They were as much musical tourists as they were performers. The regular performances of Jazz des Jeunes and the Troupe Folklorique at the Théâtre du Verdure, and the Mardi Gras parades during the carnival season would have drawn their attention. They would have also been fascinated with the performances of other foreign acts in Haiti and their accompanying musical styles. The Spanish-American celebrity bandleader Xavier Cugat and his twenty-eight piece orchestra with their high-energy mambo set in April 1951 no doubt delighted the Jamaican musicians.[25]

In a January 1951 interview in Kingston, Deans emphasized the enormity of the impact of such exposure. He expressed excitement over "Wanderer of Love," a new song he wrote in Haiti, which merged Haitian merengue rhythms with familiar calypso styles. Several decades before, with his composition "Allo, Allo," Arthur Bonnefil, the Haitian pianist in exile in Jamaica had sought to capture in music his impressions as a foreigner in Jamaica. Deans's "Wanderer of Love" reflected his enchantment with what he found in Haiti, shared with perhaps many other tourist visitors of the era.

"Wanderer of Love" was likely a highlight in Deans's new repertory, which was marked by the inclusion of several popular Haitian numbers, including "Colonel Magloire tout les peuple avec vous," a tribute to the Haitian president.[26] Denise Rouzier, a Haitian visitor to Kingston in 1952, noted in an article that appeared in the Haitian press that the Deans Orchestra played Haitian music at the Colony Club "every evening" during her trip (1952).

Jamaican audiences detected a change in the band's performance style after the Haitian tours. In 1953, Vere Johns commented that the musicians came back to Jamaica with new skills and a sound that separated them from their contemporaries, and noted that Deans ". . . evidently picked up a few wrinkles in that country" (The Star 1953c).

Johns's comment on the Deans Orchestra after the Haiti tour was in striking contrast to his verdict on most Jamaican orchestras of the time, which he thought did "not seem to have much individuality about them." A precious few like the Deans band, he argued, were able to transcend from being local dance bands to in-demand show bands that could perform at international standards and in venues outside the island.[27] Ernest Ranglin also noted that the Haiti tour was "a good thing" for Deans, heightening his popularity in Kingston after his return.[28]

Immediately after the Haiti tour, Eric Deans planned other overseas engagements for his orchestra. The band held a residency in Nassau, the Bahamas, playing at the Club Zanzibar for three months (*The Star* 1952e). By the time they returned to full duties on the Kingston nightclub circuit in the mid-fifties, Eric Deans, still excited from his travels and experiences in Haiti and the Bahamas, refashioned himself "The Meringue King," and called the band his "Latin American Band."[29]

The band members who traveled with Deans for these intra-Caribbean tours included several musicians who would shape the direction of Jamaican music later in the decade, such as guitarist Ranglin and trombonist Don Drummond (*Daily Gleaner* 1951).[30] These men were at the beginning of a long and influential career in Jamaican music when Deans recruited them shortly before the tour. Ranglin noted that the band incorporated merengue in their performances in Jamaica. "We were the first band to come back to Jamaica from Haiti and play mambo and meringue."[31] "It [the music scene] got more intense when I worked with Eric Deans . . . I gained much inspiration from musicians from Cuba, Haiti, and the United States" (*Sunday Gleaner* 2001).

Deans's promotion of Haitian music in his performances in local Jamaican nightclubs was coincident with the growing attention to Haitian culture in the Caribbean and North America (Plummer 1992). Harry Belafonte, another musician with Jamaican roots, had made a name for himself singing heavily produced covers of Anglophone Caribbean mento, calypso, and folk songs, all packaged under the generic label of Calypso. He too recorded popular covers of "Haiti Cherie" and "Yellowbird" on his 1957 *Belafonte Sings of the Caribbean* (RCA Victor, LPM 1505, 1957).

The Deans tour found its counterpart in 1953. One of Haiti's leading big bands Orchestre Atomique, led by pianist Robert Camille, played a series of shows in Jamaica during the 1953 Christmas season. Much like its contemporaries, Orchestre Saïeh and Jazz des Jeunes, Orchestre Atomique played several high profile clubs in Port-au-Prince, including the International Casino, a popular spot for visitors to Haiti. The band had also gained experience as a touring band playing South and Central America before their trip to Jamaica.

Robert Camille assembled some of the most promising musicians on the Port-au-Prince scene (see Figure 5.4) into the ten-piece aggregation that arrived with him at the Palisadoes Airport on December 18, 1953.[32] Among them were popular lead singer Joseph Lavaud (also known as Joe Atomik) and the young Haitian saxophonist Wébert Sicot, who along with another member of the Orchestra, Nemours Jean-Baptiste, would later revolutionize Haitian music.[33]

The Orchestra was augmented by a Haitian folk dancer named Constance, and a singer and dancer from Santo Domingo, Maria Theresa. The tour was arranged in Haiti by Joseph "Cobra Man" Clemendor, a Trinidadian contortionist, composer, and calypso singer, already quite well known as a performer in Jamaica and the Bahamas having had several successful tours in both islands in 1953.[34] Just a few weeks before Orchestre Atomique's arrival, Clemendore recorded two of his compositions with George Moxey's band at Motta's recording studio (*The Star* 1953a; Neely 2007, 8).

Camille and the Orchestre Atomique premiered its shows in Jamaica with a midnight floor show at the Colony Club, performing on a bill that included the Colony Club band then under the direction of Roy Coburn. The appeal to an exotic Haitian folk culture, commonly used to market Haiti to visitors inside and outside of the country, was repeated in Jamaican advertisements for the shows (see Figure 5.5). The performance was billed as the "first Voodoo Show in Jamaica" and promised a "spectacular Voodoo Dance" (*Daily Gleaner* 1953e and 1953f).[35]

The band's multilingual performance of mambos, Haitian folk songs, and merengues, along with Dominican and Cuban music, drew interest among

Figure 5.4 The Orchestre Atomique arrives in Kingston. Included in the photo are popular Jamaican entertainer Ranny Williams (back row, first from right) and Haitian music pioneer Webert Sicot (standing next to Williams). Seated from left are lead singer Joseph "Joe Atomik" Lavaud, Robert Camille, Anna Teresa, Reynaud St. Cyr (Haitian Consul in Jamaica), Leonor Clemendore, and her husband Joseph "Cobra Man" Clemendore. *The Star*, December 21, 1953 (© The Gleaner Company Limited)

Figure 5.5 Advertisement for the Orchestre Atomiqe's debut show at *Colony Club.(Daily Gleaner*, December 18, 1953. (© The Gleaner Company Limited)

both Kingstonians and tourists visiting the island during the Christmas season. For the remainder of December, the Haitian Orchestra was booked at several other popular nightclubs in Kingston. Other shows were held at the Queen's Theatre, a Christmas Eve concert at the Blue Jay Club, and the Sugar Hill Club where the band played its final show, a New Year's Eve concert. Immediately after, they returned to Haiti to headline a grand ball at the International Casino in honor of Haiti's 150th anniversary of independence, promising local audiences "music for all tastes: Calypsos, Boleros, Meringues, and Guarchas" (*The Star* 1954; *Le Nouvelliste* 1954a and 1954b).[36]

CONCLUSION

When President Paul Magloire made his highly publicized state visit to Jamaica in February 1955, Eric Deans and his band were in the middle of a long contract on Jamaica's north coast, playing at the Tower Isle Hotel near Ocho Rios. Their musical sets included a range of styles that Deans and the band would have picked up on their tours of the early 1950s, refashioned for an audience of winter tourists at the hotel. The Tower Isle would be the site of another intersection between the bandleader and the Haitian president when the hotel held a special fête in Magloire's honor during his tour of the island. Having played for Magloire in Haiti, Eric Deans knew what type of music he would enjoy. He coaxed the president to loosen up and break from the formality of the evening by leading the band into the Jamaican folk standard "Linstead Market." It did not take long for Magloire to get up from his chair and find his way to the dance floor (*The Star* 1955a). "Linstead Market" would have been included in the sets of the Deans Orchestra's Haiti shows in 1950–1951. It was a song well known to Magloire and the visiting Haitian musicians, consumers of Jamaican music as much as any other tourist visitor to the island.

Haitians in Jamaica, including President Magloire, were familiar with the music they heard in the hotels and at the organized festivals. Similarly, Jamaican middle class men and women who regularly enjoyed holidays in Haiti found themselves in Haitian clubs where they heard firsthand the rhythms that excited them on records at dance parties in Kingston. Much of this music was likely indistinguishable in the sonic awareness of the average North American tourist, who generally regarded all island music as part of a hybrid Latin American-Caribbean sound. Local audiences, on the other hand, might have been more discerning. They knew the different sounds of the northern Caribbean islands and expected to hear them in live performances by standout bands like the Deans Orchestra.

The tours of the Deans Orchestra in Haiti and Orchestre Atomique in Jamaica marked a high point in the history of the big band era in Haiti and Jamaica. By the end of the decade, the music scene on both islands changed dramatically. Sicot and Jean-Baptiste, veterans of the Orchestre Atomique, introduced a new style of music to Haiti, konpa, in the period after 1955. At the same time Haitian tourism began to decline significantly with the coming to power of dictator François Duvalier in September 1957.

The golden age also ended for Eric Deans in the late fifties. After his stint on the north coast, Deans was offered another lucrative long-term contract in 1955 to perform in Haiti (*The Star* 1955b). He chose instead to remain in Jamaica with occasional tours overseas.[37] But his big band sound waned fast in Jamaica. In the late fifties, former members of the orchestra like Drummond and Ranglin branched out and made a name for themselves in the Jamaican jazz scene, overshadowing Deans's popularity. By 1962, the year of Jamaica's independence, Deans and his music were considered passé in an era when younger listeners demanded that fast paced ska music animate their dances. By this time, the Deans Orchestra was gone. Deans himself played briefly with Tommy McCook's band before leaving the island to join thousands of other Jamaicans who migrated to North America and Great Britain. He eventually settled in Manchester, England, where he died in almost total anonymity in the early 1990s.[38]

During its heyday, the big band scene in both Jamaica and Haiti in the 1940s–1950s was intended to provide the "high class entertainment" noted in the epigraph at the beginning of this chapter. The long residency of the Eric Deans Orchestra in Haiti opened up a new musical world for his musicians and likely shaped their performance and musical styles as well. The absence of surviving records of the Eric Deans Orchestra makes it difficult to measure the extent of the band's appropriation of Haitian rhythms or those of any of the other places the band toured. We may find clues, however, in later recordings of some of the musicians. Tommy McCook's "Reggae Merengue," with its distinctive merengue riff over a reggae backbeat, hints at the type of fusion that may have emerged in the 1950s Jamaican scene when the "Maestro" returned to Jamaica from Haiti as the "Merengue King."

A clearer example is Roy Shurland's smooth rendition of "Yellowbird" released years after the Eric Deans tour on an album with Shurland's Big Bamboo Orchestra.[39] The record featured tracks that were by then commonplace on the back of so many similar collections and ingrained in the tourist imagination of the Caribbean. It offered, in song, a constructed and misleading review of life in an impossibly cheerful and nostalgic northern Caribbean where each island's culture melded effortlessly into the others. The song titles bespoke the message: "Kingston Market," "Junkunoo Nassau," "Big Bamboo," "Bahamian Lullaby," "Brown Skin Gal Medley." Among these songs, "Yellowbird" (Choucoune), the ubiquitous melody born in Haiti only later to be placed atop a stack of pan-Caribbean standards, is prominent. With Shurland's gentle bird whistles, plaintive lyrics sung in English and Creole, and improvised guitar (possibly by Ernest Ranglin), the song may have carried for the musicians a fond reminder of their tenure in Haiti. For those in the present, it is an artifact of a distant period of frequent physical and musical travel between the islands.

Notes

 " *Bahamian Rhapsody* "

1. On nineteenth and early twentieth century migration within the northern Caribbean, see Smith (2011); Casey (2011); MacLeod (2001); and Fraser (1990).

2. Bonnefil would later serve as Haitian Consul-General to Jamaica. In 1915, when it appeared likely that the Haitian government would recall him, a petition was taken by over a dozen leading members of Kingston's elite requesting that he remain on the island. It was a mark of his popularity and what the petitioners termed his "artistic and genial personality," which was a "boon" to Jamaica (*Daily Gleaner* 1915b).

3. The shows were the subject of an article in the Kingston paper, the *Daily Telegraph, and Anglo-American Herald*, August 28, 1911.

4. See, for example, the extraordinary comments on Haitian development in the glossy five-page tribute to Vincent on his sixty-sixth birthday (*Daily Gleaner* 1940).

5. For front page coverage of the visit of Miss Jamaica to Port-au-Prince, for example, see *Le Nouvelliste* 1953.

6. There was a high degree of reciprocity in the diplomatic relations between Haiti and Jamaica in the early 1950s. Jamaica's governor, Sir Hugh Foot, made a trip to Haiti the same month; he was the first governor of the colony to pay an official visit to Haiti. Magloire's state visit to Jamaica—which was coincident with the "Jamaica 300" celebrations to commemorate three centuries of British rule in Jamaica—was a major event and given wide press coverage in Haiti and Jamaica. Some witnesses I spoke with still carry vivid recollections of Magloire's arrival. For them, the visit was important on racial grounds since, Magloire, who was also an army general, was the first black head of state they had ever seen in Jamaica.

7. See also comments from Jamaican participants in the 1954 Haitian Carnival, who claimed they loved Haitian merengues as much as they did their own calypsos (Kingston 1954).

8. Robert A. Hill, personal communication with author, November 25, 2012. I also thank musicologist Dermott Hussey for sharing with me comments on the impact of Haitian dance music on young Jamaicans in the 1950s.

9. Winston "Sparrow" Martin, interview with author, Kingston, May 4, 2012. I would also like to thank Herbie Miller of the Jamaica Music Museum for information on the club scene in 1950s Kingston. For further indication of the popular music scene in Jamaica during this period, see Neita (1995).

10. Ernest Ranglin, phone interview with author, January 9, 2013.

11. Winston "Sparrow" Martin, interview with author, May 4, 2012.

12. The other impresario of the period was Dudley MacMillan, owner of the Colony Club.

13. For activities and news about the formation of the Jamaica music union, see *The Star* 1952a; 1952b; 1952c; 1952d; Redh 1952; and Douglas 1952. I thank Daniel Neely for drawing my attention to this point.

14. Places that the band toured after Haiti include Mexico and Costa Rica where, according to band members, they recorded a song in a fire station. I am grateful to Michael Deans, grandson of Eric Deans, for details on the early years of the Eric Deans Orchestra used in this paragraph. Michael Deans, interview with author, Kingston, Jamaica, May 4 and June 16, 2012. Thanks also go to Ernest Ranglin, who was a guitarist with the Orchestra circa 1949–1951. Ernest Ranglin, phone interview with author, January 9, 2013.

15. Jamaican hotelier Abe Issa, for example, visited Haiti in the 1950s to survey the hotels and tourist attractions there.

16. Details on the band's set are taken from Ernest Ranglin interview with author, January 9, 2013.

17. The band was also sometimes billed as the "Eric Deans Band" or, incorrectly, as the "Eric Dike Band" in the Haitian press.

18. Ernest Ranglin, interview with author, January 9, 2013.

19. Ranglin recalled that he had to request special permission for four of the musicians to be absent from school so that they could accompany the orchestra on tour. Ernest Ranglin, interview with author, January 9, 2013.

20. Ernest Ranglin left the band in January 1951 to join a jazz combo and did not return to Haiti. "I was getting out of the big band thing," noted Ranglin. Ernest

Ranglin, phone interview with author, January 9, 2013. Many of the musicians of the first tour, however, returned for the second one. The band included Eric Deans, Don Drummond, Samuel Watson, Linton Thomas, Reuben Alexander, Jocelyn Buchanan, Roy Shurland, Lester Williams, and Gladstone Stirling (*Daily Gleaner* 1951).

21. Ernest Ranglin, phone interview with author, January 9, 2013.

22. Ibid.; see also, *Daily Gleaner* 1951.

23. The recordings were collected and later re-released as El Maestro, Mini Records, MSRD2028. Herby Widmaïer, interview with author, Port-au-Prince, July 1999; and Issah El Saïeh, interview with author, Port-au-Prince, July 13, 1999. See also the obituary for Saïeh (Alter Presse 2005) http://www.alterpresse.org/spip.php?article2209; along with Lundahl and Saint Jean, (2012).

24. Ernest Ranglin, phone interview with author, January 9, 2013.

25. On Cugat's visit to Haiti, see Jolicoeur (1951). Cugat also visited Jamaica as part of that tour.

26. Information here based on the report of a Haitian visitor to Kingston who saw the band perform at the Colony Club (*Haiti Sun* 1952).

27. Johns lamented that the lack of professionalism and willingness to be more creative had significantly impaired many Jamaican orchestras in the early fifties. Among his complaints were late arrivals for shows, an overreliance on playing by ear, limited proficiencies, and a general disinterest in expanding their musical knowledge beyond US popular songs. A hard taskmaster, Eric Deans avoided these pitfalls by insisting on professionalism from his musicians. If musicians made mistakes they would be reprimanded and their pay cut. Michael Deans, interview with author, Kingston, Jamaica, May 4, 2012; and Ernest Ranglin, phone interview with author, January 9, 2013. Other bandleaders, such as Sonny Bradshaw, Val Bennett, and George Moxey, were similarly insistent on high standards from their musicians.

28. Ernest Ranglin, phone interview with author, January 9, 2013.

29. Deans invited singers from the Bahamas to perform with him in Jamaica in the mid-fifties. It is quite likely that he worked closely with Haitian musicians during the months he spent in the republic though Ranglin maintains that Deans never included them in the band.

30. Musicians who later played with Deans included Roland Alphonso and Tommy McCook, both pioneers of Ska along with Ranglin and Drummond. Michael Deans, interview with author, Kingston, Jamaica, May 4 and June 16, 2012. For a partial list of leading Jamaican musicians of the 1950s and 1960s who at one time or another played in the orchestra, see Chen and Chang (1998, 16).

31. Ernie Ranglin, interview with author, January 9, 2013. See also *Daily Gleaner* (2005).

32. For more information on Orchestre Atomique, see Vallon (2007, 7).

33. Both Jean-Baptiste and Sicot performed together in various bands in the forties and early fifties. In the second half of the decade, they both were instrumental in changing the direction of Haitian music with Jean-Baptiste's konpa-direk, a variation of Dominican merengue, and Sicot's similarly popular dance music, kadans ranpa. They popularized their sound through relentless touring across North America, Europe, and the Caribbean in the late fifties and into the sixties. Variations of both styles continue to dominate Haitian dance band music. On this, see Averill (1997,

77–80). Although Sicot was part of the lineup that played in Kingston, Nemours Jean-Baptiste had already left the band by then. However, Nemours's brother, Monfort, was among the musicians who performed in Jamaica.

34. See, for example, comments on his performances in the *Daily Gleaner* (1953a; 1953b; 1953c; and 1953d).

35. On the promotion of Haitian folklore as "exotic" in Haitian promotion campaigns in the 1950s, see Polyné (2010, chapter 4); and Ramsey (2011, chapter 4).

36. In 1955, the year of the 300th anniversary of British colonization of Jamaica, another popular Haitian act, Vodou drummer Ti-Roro, did a short tour of the island as part of Jamaica's anniversary celebrations.

37. Michael Deans, interview with author, Kingston, May 4, 2012; While on a well-received tour of Belize where the band played for Central American tourists, Eric Deans helped with the formation of "The Federation of British Honduran Dance Musicians" (*Daily Gleaner* 1956a).

38. Michael Deans, interview with author, Kingston, May 4, 2012.

39. Roy Shurland and His Big Bamboo Orchestra, The *Big Bamboo*. LP 2015-S.

References

Averill, Gage. 1989. "Haitian Dance Bands, 1915–1970: Class, Race, and Authenticity," *Latin American Music Review*, 10(2): 203–235.

Averill, Gage. 1997. *A Day for the Hunter, a Day for the Prey: Popular Music and Power in Haiti*. Chicago: University of Chicago Press.

Casey, Matthew R. 2011. "Haitians' Labor and Leisure on Cuban Sugar Plantations: The Limits of Company Control." *New West Indian Guide* 82(1–2): 5–30.

Chen, Wayne, and Kevin O'Brien Chang. 1998. *Reggae Routes: The Story of Jamaican Music*. Philadelphia: Temple University Press.

Courlander, Harold. 1960. *The Drum and the Hoe: Life and Lore of the Haitian People*. Berkeley: University of California Press.

Daily Gleaner. 1911a. "Commercial Items." April 20: 14.

Daily Gleaner. 1911b. "Concerts at Hayti." August 30: 3.

Daily Gleaner. 1915a. "Let Us Meditate." February 13: 13.

Daily Gleaner. 1915b. "Petition in Regard to the Haytian Consul General Here." March 27: 10.

Daily Gleaner. 1925. "Recent Tour of Our Footballers in Hayti." April 9: 6.

Daily Gleaner. 1940. "Haitians Are Wonderful." February 22: 19.

Daily Gleaner. 1944. "Jamaican Businessman in Haiti Feted at Mytle Bank Luncheon." October 25: 8.

Daily Gleaner. 1945. "Stress Value to Island of Stephen Hill's Celebrity Concerts." November 16: 9.

Daily Gleaner. 1946. "Bournemouth Tonight." July 26: 15.

Daily Gleaner. 1949. "Haitian Flag Day Celebrations Tonight." May 17: 4.

Daily Gleaner. 1950. "Deans Band Gets One-Year Haiti Contract." December 23: 12.

Daily Gleaner. 1951. "Deans Orchestra Leaves for Haiti Engagements." February 23: 5.

Daily Gleaner. 1953a. " 'CobraMan' for Trench Town Club Centre." July 30: 12.

Daily Gleaner. 1953b. "Special Cobra Man Show at Coke Today." August 12: 12.

Daily Gleaner. 1953c. "'Cobra Man' Returns." October 28: 14.

Daily Gleaner. 1953d. "Cobra Man at Colony." November 6: 16.

Daily Gleaner. 1953e. "Haitian Band at Colony Tonight." December 18: 18.

Daily Gleaner. 1953f. "Tonight at Queen's Theatre." December 22: 4.

Daily Gleaner. 1955a. Advertisement from Mimosa Lodge Hotel. February 14: 14.

Daily Gleaner. 1955b. "Haiti-Jamaica Tours Planned." March 30: 7.

Daily Gleaner. 1956a. "Local Orchestra Well Received." June 7: 15.

Daily Gleaner. 1956b. "You Know What Haitians Are? The Most Delightful People in the World." September 9: 7.

Daily Gleaner. 2005. "Ranglin: Man for All Seasons [interview with Jean Shaw]." February 24: 55.

Daily Telegraph and Anglo-American Herald. 1911. "Going to Hayti." August 28: 1.

Douglas, Wilson. 1952d. Letter to the Editor: "This Can't Work for Musicians." *The Star*, November 11: 4.

Dumerve, Étienne Constantin Eugène Moïse. 1968. *Histoire de la Musique en Haïti*. Port-au-Prince: Imprimerie des Antilles.

Fraser, Peter D. 1990. "British West Indians in Haiti in the Late Nineteenth and Early Twentieth Centuries." In *After the Crossing: Immigrants and Minorities Caribbean Creole Society*, edited by Howard Johnson, 79–84. New York: Routledge.

Haiti Sun. 1950a. "Haiti Beach Comber." December 3: 9.

Haiti Sun. 1950b. "Haiti Beach Comber." December 24: 9.

Haiti Sun. 1951. "Jamaica's Hot Ten." November 19: 5.

Haiti Sun. 1952. "President Magloire's Birthday Celebrated in Jamaica." January 6: 1–2.

Jolicoeur, Aubelin. 1951. "Cugat et son Orchestre à Port-au-Prince." Le Nouvelliste (April 10): 1.

Kingston, Kitty. 1954. "Back from Haiti Mardi Gras." *Daily Gleaner* (March 9): 14.

Le Nouvelliste. 1950a. "Cabane Choucoune." November 11: 4.

Le Nouvelliste. 1950b. "Le Jazz Jamaican au Théâtre de Verdure." November 14: 4.

Le Nouvelliste. 1951a. "Du Renouveau à 'Cabane Choucoune.'" February 23: 4.

Le Nouvelliste. 1951b. "'Wings to Haiti' un Film de Propagande Touristìque." March 7: 1.

Le Nouvelliste. 1953. "Miss Jamaique à Port-au-Prince." December 5: 1.

Le Nouvelliste. 1954a. "Dancing du Casino International d'Haiti." January 5: 6.

Le Nouvelliste. 1954b. "Dancing du Casino International d'Haiti." January 6: 6.

Lundahl, Mats, with Louis Carl Saint Jean. 2012. *Issa El Saieh: Maëstro and Legend. A Portrait of My Pal, His Times, and His Music*. Pompano Beach, FL.: Educavision.

MacLeod, Marc Christian. "Undesirable Aliens: Haitian and British West Indian Immigrant Workers in Cuba, 1898–1940." PhD dissertation, The University of Texas at Austin, 2000.

Neely, Daniel T. 2007. "Calling All Singers, Musicians and Speechmakers: Mento Aesthetics and Jamaica's Early Recording Industry." *Caribbean Quarterly* 53(4): 1–15.

Neita, Hartley. 1995. "Reflections: The Music of Yesterday." *Daily Gleaner*, May 11.

Plummer, Brenda Gayle. 1990. "The Golden Years of Haitian Tourism: U.S. Influence in Haitian Cultural and Economic Affairs, 1934–1971." *Cimarron* 2: 49–63.

Plummer, Gayle. 1992. *Haiti and the United States: The Psychological Moment*. Athens: University of Georgia Press.

Polyné, Millery. 2010. *From Douglass to Duvalier: U.S. African Americans, Haiti, and Pan Americanism, 1870–1964*. Gainesville: University of Florida Press.

Ramsey, Kate. 2011. *The Spirits and the Law: Vodou and Power in Haiti*. Chicago: University of Chicago Press.

Redh, I. C. 1952. "Local Artists." *The Star*, October 31: 4.

Rommen, Timothy. 2011. *Funky Nassau: Roots, Routes, and Representation in Bahamian Popular Music*. Berkeley: University of California Press.

Rouzier, Denise. 1952. "Eight Days in Jamaica." *Haiti Sun*, August 12: 7.

Saïeh, Issah El. 2005. Obituary published in *Un colosse est tombé*, Alter Presse, February 14. http://www.alterpresse.org/spip.php?article2209.

Sheller, Mimi. 2001. *Democracy After Slavery: Black Publics and Peasant Radicalism in Haiti and Jamaica*. Gainesville: University of Florida Press.

Sherman, Gertrude. 1951. "Happy Bandleader." *Daily Gleaner*, January 12: 6.

Smith, Matthew J. 2011. "From the Port of Princes to the City of Kings: Jamaica and the Roots of the Haitian Diaspora." In *Geographies of the Haitian Diaspora*, edited by Regine O. Jackson, 17–33. New York: Routledge.

Spotlight. 1944. "Business, Finance, Industry." Nos. 6 and 7 (June–July): 8.

Sunday Gleaner. 2001. "Ernie Ranglin: One of Jazz's Purest Exponents [interview with Susan Whyte]." August 12: 7.

Taylor, Frank Fonda. *To Hell with Paradise: A History of the Jamaican Tourist Industry*. Pittsburgh: University of Pittsburgh Press.

The Star. 1952a. "Musicians Banding." October 27: 3.

The Star. 1952b. "Musicians Finalize Union Plans." November 3: 3.

The Star. 1952c. "Musicians, Artists Band Up." November 19: 10.

The Star. 1952d. "Performers in Huff Over NLC Stand." November 29: 4.

The Star. 1952e. Entertainment News. December 12: 4.

The Star. 1953a. "With the Stars." November 19: 7.

The Star. 1953b. "Vere Johns Says…" December 15: 5.

The Star. 1953c. "Vere Johns Says…" December 28: 4.

The Star. 1954. Entertainment News. January 2: 7.

The Star. 1955a. Photo and Caption. February 17: 7.

The Star. 1955b. "With the Stars." April 7: 7.

Vallon, Jean Lesly. 2007. *What You Should Know About Haitian Music and the Evolution of Compas Direct, 1955–2005*. Bloomington: AuthorHouse.

DISCOGRAPHY

Belafonte, Harry. 1957. *Belafonte Sings of the Caribbean*. RCA Victor, LPM 1505.

El Saïeh, Issah. 1958. "El Maestro" et son Orchestre avec Guy Durosier. Mini Records, MSRD2028.

Shurland, Roy, and His Big Bamboo Orchestra. 1961. *The Big Bamboo*. Carib Records. LP 2015-S.

6

Outsider, Insider, and Imagined Tourists

Musical and Cultural Tourism in the Dominican Republic

SYDNEY HUTCHINSON ▮

Scholarship on tourism has frequently assumed an external Other in search of an exotic or "authentic" experience. Such a view only partially matches the reality of tourism in the Dominican Republic. There, as elsewhere, tourists hail from diverse origins, and the opportunities for cultural experiences available to them are similarly varied. Nonetheless, the tourism model that has been developed there focuses on all-inclusive resorts that provide mainly European and North American visitors with unlimited quantities of sand, sun, food, and cheap alcohol, but little in the way of culture. The potential to develop Dominican music, dance, or other cultural expressions as sources of tourism revenue has, by and large, not been realized.

This does not mean, however, that no tourists attend cultural events like performances of "roots" musics, including merengue típico, the accordion-based style of the northern Cibao region.[1] Merengue típico ranchos (nostalgic nightclubs where accordion-based "traditional" merengue is played), for instance, attract many visitors to Santiago, the region's largest city. This apparent paradox can be resolved by noting that the tourists who attend such events are themselves overwhelmingly Dominicans, either traveling from other Dominican cities or from outside the country. Thus, while merengue típico groups do occasionally perform at big resorts for foreigners, such occasions remain a minor source of income. In contrast, visiting emigrant Dominicans are some of the most important financial backers of modern-style merengue típico.

In this chapter, I explore the nascent cultural tourism industry in the Dominican Republic, offering examples from my fieldwork in the Cibao. My coverage of the topic is not exhaustive but rather anecdotal, since this research took place tangentially, alongside my project on gender and transnationalism in merengue típico. Since official facts and figures do not yet provide much information about domestic and migrant tourists, my anecdotal approach can serve as an alternative, pointing the way toward unexplored areas in Dominican tourism research. I particularly wish to note the importance of the emigrant tourist, typically left out of industry "insider" tourist categories like "domestic" or "internal." Although migrant tourists are often overlooked as actors in Caribbean tourism, they are significant both economically and culturally. While touring musical practices play an important role in building transnational identities, Dominicans' own vacation practices also contribute to the development of merengue típico music, both as a cultural industry and as a modernizing cultural expression. Local middle and upper classes must also be considered when discussing the impact and import of cultural tourism.

To illustrate these dynamics, I outline three case studies in how culture is used to attract tourists as well as how tourists themselves utilize culture. My first category is the outsider tourist, who, I argue, is generally assumed to be unfamiliar with and uninterested in Dominican culture; thus these tourists are offered only a foggy picture of either an exotic but generic Caribbean locale or a specifically white and middle-class Dominican Republic, and they are given few opportunities to experience Dominican culture outside of the highly controlled, artificial situation of the resort show. Secondly, I suggest the "imagined tourist" as a category to explain the expected presence but actual absence of foreign tourists at commercialized versions of Dominican culture such as merengue festivals. Finally, I explore the attendance of "insider tourists," including both domestic and migrant Dominicans, at heritage-related events like merengue típico shows.[2] While I realize that I am generalizing with these categories, since each individual may have varying degrees of "insiderness" and "outsiderness," these abstractions will help to focus attention on the disconnect between policy and practice. To conclude, I offer suggestions for future research and for tourist policy development projects that offer a broader, more inclusive perspective.

TRAVEL AND TOURISM IN THE DOMINICAN REPUBLIC

Life in the Cibao is marked by constant movement back and forth. Some musicians take the three-hour flight between Santiago and New York so often that it is difficult to determine their place of residence. Even those who cannot afford to make the trip themselves are affected by the journeys of their relatives, neighbors, and friends, and the knowledge, experiences, and material objects they both bring back and take away. Are these travelers tourists? Migrants? Visitors? Residents? It is increasingly hard to tell.

Such travelers are always in evidence when I arrive or depart from the busy Cibao International Airport near Santiago. Yet I have seldom seen the more stereotypical foreign tourists there: those with Bermuda shorts, sunburns, and cameras around their necks. Tourism is the most important source of foreign currency in the Dominican Republic: in 2003, it brought in 3.11 billion US dollars (Valdez 2006, 57) and now provides over a third more revenue even than remittances (Pina 2006). If foreign tourism is the DR's largest industry, where, then, are those legions of foreigners, and what are they up to?

These are not idle questions. The proportional importance of this industry has been growing rapidly in the past two decades, but it began long before, under the leadership of dictator Rafael Trujillo (r. 1930–1961). His efforts to develop tourism ran from construction projects to sponsorship of festivals and staged presentations. In the 1940s, for instance, he created numerous hotels around the country, including the still-popular Hotel Jaragua on Santo Domingo's Malecón, as well as indoor markets called mercados modelos where crafts are still sold today. In 1955, he spent one-third of the national budget on the notorious Feria de la Paz (Peace Fair), intended to showcase his achievements and wealth, both for national and international observers (see Derby 2000, 1122). This same year, the singer Casandra Damirón, already famous for her performances on state radio, began to present stylized representations of "traditional" dances in stage shows said to have been created to satisfy the "sophisticated tastes of the tourists" in the audience (Santiago 1985).[3]

After Trujillo's assassination in 1961, tourism took a nosedive due to political turmoil. But Joaquín Balaguer, a right-wing Trujillo crony who came into power after a coup followed by a US invasion, ousted the democratically elected leftist Juan Bosch, worked hard to rectify the situation. With the help of his Director of Tourism, Ángel Miolán, he created a department to manage tourism, economic incentives for foreign investors, and a financial office for creating tourist infrastructure (Medina 2009; Miolán 1998). Following earlier Trujillo initiatives, Miolán focused touristic development on the colonial zone of Santo Domingo, renovating and reconstructing many of the area's sixteenth- and seventeenth-century buildings. Miolán writes that other touristic initiatives dating to this time include the Merengue Festival (discussed later), early steps in internal tourism, and a Dominican Christmas program geared at "both non-resident Dominicans and international tourism, especially from Puerto Rico and the United States" (Miolán 1996). Since that time, however, the focus of touristic development has shifted from historical monuments to the typical Caribbean sun-and-sand model. The focus on receiving international visitors is part of official policy and has been since the first tourism policy was drafted in 1969 (Váldez 2006, 42–43).

THE OUTSIDER TOURIST

At present, legal foreign tourism in the Dominican Republic revolves around the all-inclusive resort.[4] This tourism model began in 1980 with the establishment of Jack Tar Village at Playa Dorada, a beach near the northern coastal town of Puerto Plata, created by a Dallas-based corporation (Camarena 2009, 31). The concept has since been duplicated by more than a dozen other resorts at the same beach, as well as over thirty in the southeast at Bávaro and Punta Cana, and others in various beach towns around the country. All-inclusives cater to middle- and lower-middle-class foreign tourists, although Dominicans also often take advantage of their inexpensive rates.[5] The resorts spread quickly because they offered a quick-fix solution to the problematic lack of infrastructure such as roads, transportation, security, and basic services—water and electricity being notoriously undependable (Camarena 2009, 29). But their continued domination of the market is problematic for several reasons: the lack of diversification, the segregation of tourists into particular places, and the fact that most resorts are foreign-owned. These factors mean that little money trickles out into surrounding communities, while a great deal of the income generated actually leaves the country.

All-inclusives discourage cultural tourism through their geography, which creates sharp boundaries between resort grounds and neighboring communities. Policies, too, militate against cultural tourism. At some resorts, for instance, employees and posted signs warn tourists of safety and hygiene issues in neighboring towns, and tourism police may even remove foreigners from town bars "for their own safety" (Gregory 2007, 48, 54).

Resorts do, however, program entertainment for their guests. The principal form is the nightly show. According to my observations during visits to resorts in Playa Dorada, near the northern town of Puerto Plata, these shows come in three main varieties. First is the competition for (usually) drunken hotel guests, who generally win a bottle of liquor and the prestigious title of Mr. Name-of-Resort-Here after having to pronounce difficult Dominican phrases, perform feats of strength, dance, or lip-synch in drag. Second are kids' shows featuring clowns singing merengues or conducting group sing-alongs of Latin American favorites. Third and more pertinent to the topic at hand are the shows put on by dancers employed by the hotel specifically for this purpose. These revues run the gamut from pop themes, such as the rather impressive Michael Jackson impersonator I once saw (in whiteface makeup, no less) to more "tropical" ones. For instance, in 2006 I observed a "Dances of the World" program that included difficult-to-decipher interpretive numbers performed in unitards alongside belly dance, "Spanish" dance, a Dominican version of Riverdance, and of course merengue, this last performed in Day-Glo costumes to Juan Luis Guerra's "El Farolito," a kind of higher-class version of merengue típico.

Leiling Chang describes the all-inclusives' entertainment policy as one of "delocalization." She explains that hotel managers deliberately exclude local musics in favor of what they term "international music"—a program of American pop from the 1960s to 1980s with a smattering of Latin American hits, reggaeton, and perhaps a few merengues and bachatas thrown in. This program exists only in recorded form and is played in hotel discos as well as during the nightly shows. It is chosen by the hotel managers, who are employed by multinational chains and often split their time between the Dominican locations and others around the region. The music thus becomes part of the multinational marketing strategy applied similarly to cuisine, stores, and other services with little regard for the hotels' actual locations, creating touristic non-spaces that could be almost anywhere (Chang 2011, 53–57). To borrow a Foucauldian term, we might call these hotels *heterotopias*, spaces of juxtaposition and deviation that may invert or contest the everyday. Like shopping malls and airports, all-inclusives are insulated from the outside world, with clear boundaries and rules for entering and leaving; they are displacing spaces, existing in a curious relationship with their surroundings in that they generally avoid all reference to them (Foucault 2002 [1967]).

As can be seen, Dominican culture, at least traditional Dominican culture, has little place or foothold in resort entertainment. However, on occasions when Dominican food is the hotel restaurant's theme for the day, a merengue típico trio may occasionally play in the lobby. The contrast of this reduced instrumentation with the six-to-nine-member ensemble more common for merengue típico performance at present[6] indicates that such groups are presenting the genre in a self-consciously "folkloric" way, an observation reinforced by the coordinated group outfits that recall performances by the Trujillo-era group Trio Reynoso (see Figure 6.1). Chang mentions that merengue típico trios may also play in airports (2011, 54), showing that the genre is frequently associated with comings and goings and represents, perhaps, the journeys of migrants.

Finally, although I have never witnessed such a performance, some hotels do reportedly hire folk dance troupes. The late folklorist José Castillo described these performances as "incredible disasters."[7]. He claimed that many of the dancers contracted were not even Dominicans but foreigners: they earned 20,000–30,000 pesos per month (about US $600–$900, quite a good living in a country where the private-sector minimum wage is only $81 per month[8]), and

Figure 6.1 Merengue típico group (perico ripiao) plays in the lobby of an all-inclusive resort, Playa Dorada, north coast, 2008. (Photo by Maurice Mengel, used with permission)

management preferred to contract them because of "prejudices." Two decades before Castillo's critique, folklorist Fradique Lizardo had made a similar one, writing:

> It is embarrassing what gets to the foreign public. On the one hand is the folkloric image promoted by [the Ministry of] Tourism, with groups of people chosen to give the idea that in our country there are no blacks, but only a group of white people with straight hair, which is not really the image of our country, and then Tourism has created its own folklore for export. Without a single accredited folklorist who could direct the presentation of our culture, Tourism has created dances that correspond to what they want to sell, but that do not correspond either musically or choreographically to what exists in Dominican reality. (1987; this and all translations mine)

Discriminatory hiring practices in touristic dance companies would not be surprising as to this day all-inclusive resorts will not normally hire dark-skinned Dominicans for front-desk jobs like clerks, waiters, or bartenders, and they bring in higher-level staff and management from elsewhere, such as the capital (Gregory 2007,17–28). In fact, newspaper columnist Juan Lladó wrote that in the 1990s many performing artists were abandoning the city of Santo Domingo for more lucrative work at tourist resorts (2002, 482).

For both Lizardo and Castillo, not only the makeup of the tourist-oriented dance groups but also their artistic quality was suspect. Castillo explained that a part of his own group, the Ballet Folklórico of the UASD (the public Universidad Autónoma de Santo Domingo, oldest university in the New World), performed for six years (1994–2000) under the name of Conjunto Folklórico Dominicano at the Guácara Taína. Frequented primarily by cruise-ship tourists, this famous bar located inside an enormous cave in Santo Domingo has been offering folk dance shows alongside its drinks for decades. Castillo explained, however, that his group eventually left because, "Finally they wanted us to do things we didn't believe in. For example, at one time they demanded that we had to put on 'Indian' dances."[9] Since no "Indian" community has existed in the country for several centuries, any such dance would be a purely creative invention, rather than the work of a dance company whose mission was to present contemporary Dominican folk culture. The same thing had happened to Lizardo, whose group had earlier performed there, Castillo added. Clearly, the tourist industry here as elsewhere favors exoticism over realism, the imagined over the actual.

Cruise ships are a second way in which many tourists experience the Dominican Republic. This type of tourism began in the 1970s with Miami departures to the Caribbean, intended to keep idle ocean liners active. In the 1970s and 1980s, Puerto Plata was a principal stop for cruise ships, with six to eight ships arriving weekly, but this traffic has since stopped since the port has fallen into disrepair (Camarena 2009, 77–78). It appears to have moved east to the peninsula of Samaná: while only ten ships arrived there every year up to 1995, 115 were expected in the 2008–2009 season, bringing about 230,000 visitors (Cepeda 2008).[10]

Since cruise-ship tourism began, it has generated some work for local musicians, but only on a very small scale. For example, merengue típico maestro Rafaelito Román, who grew up in Puerto Plata but now lives in Santiago, reports,

> When the first tourist ships came [in the 1970s] . . . we would play to receive the tourists. They would really applaud for músicatípica. But really, I had to leave Puerto Plata since it did not pay me enough to survive. Santiago is a town . . . that supports músicatípica more than Puerto Plata.[11]

Today, I know local traditional musicians who play on the beachfront walk in the city of Samaná whenever a cruise ship arrives, but they earn only tips and, as in Rafaelito's experience, cannot make a living in this way.

Germán Camarena suggests that cruise-ship tourism has certain advantages: it can generate more interaction between tourists and locals, motivate the reconstruction of port cities, create jobs in diverse areas, and contribute to city pride (2009, 82–83). But it does not necessarily do these things. In conversing with US tourists just stepping off a ship in Samaná, I learned that they had been told expressly not to purchase anything locally because it was not good quality and they would be ripped off. They were also so conditioned to expect all-inclusive treatment that the local musicians who played when they arrived put up a sign pointedly explaining that they were not paid by the cruise ship. Some of the visitors did buy local food or drink and take local boat tours. But if visitors are told not to contribute to the local economy, cruise ships are not a reliable source of income for communities. It is clear that the benefits generated depend to a great extent on the ethics of the ship tour directors. It is equally clear that this tourism model has little to no cultural component, and what does occur is entirely dependent on local musicians' initiative.

Few opportunities thus exist for foreign tourists, except those already extremely knowledgeable about Dominican culture, to experience local music or dance outside of the short-term and necessarily superficial interactions I have described. On Santo Domingo's Malecón (seafront walk) or on public beaches, tourists may be able to purchase a serenade from a wandering típico trio composed of accordion, tambora, and güira, or sometimes a guitar (Figure 6.2; such groups are generally not allowed on resort beaches). They may be able to catch a performance by one of the country's "official" folkloric dance troupes—the Ballet Folklórico Nacional, part of the Ministry of Culture, or the Ballet Folklórico of the Ministry of Tourism, the latter of which opens most festivals and other events the ministry sponsors. Visiting bars, clubs, or restaurants will likely bring them into contact with popular music like bachata, merengue, salsa, or reggaetón.

To my knowledge, none of these encounters are explicitly advertised to tourists: the potential for cultural and musical events to become tourist draws remains unrealized. Nonetheless, similar types of performances are used as promotional tools abroad. For instance in 2008, the Dominican Republic was the featured country at ITB (Internationale Tourismus Börse, or International Tourism Exchange) in Berlin, "The World's Leading Travel Trade Show." Performances by the Ministry of Tourism's Ballet Folklórico supplemented raffle drawings, talks on adventure and ecotourism, and cocktail hours, while pop music star Juan Luis Guerra performed for guests at the opening gala; merengue típico artist El Prodigio also played to entertain attendees at various points. A press release apparently describing the Ballet Folklórico's show explains that the country's representatives will present its musical traditions, "spanning the

Figure 6.2 Wandering quartet led by Fermín Vargas, accordion (here with güira, tambora, and marimba), plays for the author and other tourists on the beach in Sosúa, north coast, 2012. (Photo by author)

ages from the early culture of the Taíno Indians, music from the colonial era and African influences, through to modern works from Europe."

The mention of Taíno dances echoes Castillo's earlier complaints, and also helps to demonstrate that such performances are not intended to entice tourists to experience Dominican culture, but rather to partake of a generalized exotic Caribbean atmosphere. Further support for this notion can be found in the use of a hammock and "palm tree island" to represent the destination at Berlin's Hauptbahnhof, and in the statement in the program that "Dominicans in traditional costumes will greet visitors at the entrances to ITB Berlin."[12] Decades earlier, Fradique Lizardo wrote that the DR had no traditional costume, as there had never been any textile industry there (Lizardo n.d.). Instead, the costumes used by his and all subsequent dance groups appear to be based on those of Amalia Hernández's Ballet Folklórico de México. Moreover, the music chosen for the ITB provides a particularly middle-class vision of Dominican culture: Guerra's versions of merengue and bachata are universally acclaimed by Dominican critics for their sophisticated, jazz-influenced musical arrangements and high-toned lyrics (Guerra trained at the Berklee College of Music in Boston), while El Prodigio is the only merengue típico musician to have had much success in breaking through the class barrier built around that stig-matized style, due in part to his educational background and jazz and rock influences (Hutchinson 2008a, 443–453).[13] In any case, such performances are meant to promote the destination, not its culture or the music.

In sum, the average foreign tourist will most likely not encounter much traditional music on their trip, simply because cultural or heritage tourism has scarcely been considered a possibility by the Dominican tourist industry. I once found myself sitting next to a high-ranking Ministry of Tourism func-tionary at a lunch. When I suggested that this might be an area for growth, as the country has such a great variety of traditional music, dances, and festivals, she responded along the lines of, "But we already have a Ballet Folklórico." And when I had the opportunity, during a talk he gave at New York University in 2005, to ask President Leonel Fernández a question about his cultural policy and how he thought Dominican cultural resources could best be used, the first item he pinpointed as ripe for change was the tourism model, which he felt did not work and was not in the country's best interest. Yet seven years later, that model still remains in force, leading most musicians to simply ignore tourism as a potential source of income.

THE IMAGINED TOURIST

The model of mass-market tourism that focuses on receiving large numbers of short-term visitors via cruise ship or all-inclusive resort precludes much inter-action between foreigners and locals, and explains the absence of foreigners at carnivals and traditional music performances. Music festivals, however, are seen as a promotional tool for tourism in the Dominican Republic, much like the events at the Internationale Tourismus Börse. The Merengue Festival, held yearly in Santo Domingo for over four decades, is the longest running, but only one of many (see Table 6.1). Even though it is conceptualized as an attraction for foreign visitors, its primary audience is in fact local. This is likely also the case for the many other music festivals that have proliferated in recent years. The ideal tourist imagined by festival promoters and organizers continues to exist only in their heads.

It is difficult to trace the history of the Merengue Festival: its program, for-mat, and duration have varied widely due to fluctuations in funding and spon-sorship, and perhaps also to the shifting priorities of the Ministry of Tourism under various administrations (Lladó 2002,473). It is hard even to know if it is the same festival as earlier events with the same name. In 1968, the first merengue festival was reportedly held on Santo Domingo's Malecón, where a carnival-like parade of masquerade groups and floats marked the occasion.

Table 6.1 MUSIC FESTIVALS IN THE DOMINICAN REPUBLIC, 2009

Event	Dates	Location
World Music Festival	January 23–25	Cabarete
Fiesta de la Musica/Fete de la Musique	June 2	Santo Domingo
Festicafé (6th edition)	June 6–7	Polo, Bahoruco
Festival Internacional Palo Sur (19th edition)	July 23–26	Barahona
Festival Brugal del Merengue	July 24–26	Santo Domingo
Festival Brugal del Merengue	September 25–27	Puerto Plata
Dominican Republic Jazz Festival	November 6–8	Cabarete
Festival de Atabales (19th edition)	November 27–29	Sainaguá

Held during the tenure of Miolán (although he credits the previous Tourism Minister under Juan Bosch with the idea), the event was intended to attract tourists but did not appear to succeed in this goal. One anecdote goes that a passerby yelled a question at the stage where officials were seated: "And where are all the tourists?" A chorus of voices gleefully responded, "In Miolán's head!" (Medina 2009) As we shall see, these imaginary tourists continue to hold sway over festival planners even today.

An event held in 1969 was also promoted as the "First Merengue Festival," although it was apparently a rival event, and strikingly different. It was a competition for compositions, held concurrently with the Second Festival of Song and put on by AMUCABA, the Dominican Republic's Association of Musicians, Singers, Dancers, and Announcers. Contemporary reports praised the decision to separate the two competitions because "in this way merengue is given the category it deserves" and noted that most compositions were nationalist in theme (Vásquez 1969, 7), although folklorist Dagoberto Tejeda Ortiz (1969, 37) found that they were overly focused on urban bourgeois points of view rather than a traditional rural outlook. One was even dedicated to tourism!

This vision of the merengue festival did not survive the decade. In the 1970s, attracting foreign tourists became a top priority. Pedro Morales Troncoso, then national director of Tourism and Information, described the merengue as "one of the most intense touristic attractions in the Dominican Republic" (Anon 1978), but once again, the tourists seemed to be only in officials' heads. Thus, by the late 1980s, the Merengue Festival came to be focused around things other than the music, such as a food festival and competitions for waiters and cocktails. Newspaper columnist Lladó complained that the festival needed to be refocused, since its objectives were "recreation through the exaltation of our autochthonous music" and to "show the foreign tourist the best of ourselves"

(2002, 462, 464). In 1993, he still found that, aside from a party/competition titled "Merengue Minifestival" and held in a hotel, "this now-legendary event . . . has everything except music" (471); in 1996, he declared the festival "moribund" due to a lack of organization, funding, and official attention (490).

In recent years, the festival has been refocused on public performances by top groups and staged on the Malecón, Santo Domingo's well-known beachfront avenue. Its goals today are commercial rather than nationalist, as it is now sponsored by the Brugal rum company. Music competitions and traditional music play only a side role, if included at all, although the format of the event and the proportion of different genres involved changes from year to year. In 1999, the festival lasted one week and featured fourteen merengue orquestas and one típico group on two main stages, as well as a one-night-only "Gran Encuentro de Música Típica" (Grand Meeting of Traditional Music) on a side-stage (DR1 1999). The 2001 event lasted eleven days and included an innovative opening-day format in which several "perico ripiao"[14] groups performed in the gardens of the Palacio de Bellas Artes early in the evening, while a "folklore show" in the national theater included performances by a ballet folklórico and the Congos de Villa Mella.[15] Merengues were simultaneously performed on various city plazas by the orquestas of the police, army, navy, and armed forces prior to the usual celebrations on the Malecón (DR1 2001). The two-week 2004 Merengue Festival featured the most diverse program yet, with a smaller "Merengue Village" (Pueblito Merengue) stage featuring ballet folklórico presentations alongside traditional genres like palos, salve, chuines, sarandunga, carnival masquerades, and perico ripiao. On the main stage, a total of forty-seven popular groups played, including five merengue típico acts.

In February 2009, the Cluster Turístico de Santo Domingo pledged to improve touristic development in the city through a refocusing on the touristic element of the Merengue Festival, among other things (Maldonado 2009), but the event that was eventually produced was much smaller than the elaborate 2004 program, with just fifteen groups playing over three nights, two of them típico (El Festival Brugal 2009). Interestingly, in 2012, the Brugal company decided instead to offer a "Festival of Caribbean Rhythms" in order to present reggaeton and other popular "urban" styles besides merengue, with the specific intent of appealing to foreign tourists as well as Dominicans (El Festival de Ritmos 2012).

Uncertain funding and constant change mean that the Merengue Festival's future shape remains as unclear as ever. Nonetheless, imitators have been spawned, including the Puerto Plata Merengue Festival, held since 1984 with the express intention of attracting both internal and external tourists (Ventura 2009), and the Puerto Rican edition of the Festival Brugal del Merengue, held in San Juan in 2009, one week prior to the Santo Domingo event. Twelve merengue orquestas performed, but no merengue típico groups (Más de 10 2009); the event was intended to attract more Puerto Rican visitors to the DR, as they have historically been among those most interested in merengue and the festival (Ministerio 2008).

I have differentiated between orquestas, big bands, mass-market popular merengue groups, and típico groups in my narrative to make an argument about who the festival is actually aimed at. The programs described demonstrate that the Festival del Merengue has focused primarily on presenting orquesta merengue, a style particularly well-known and popular outside the country and among cosmopolitan middle- to upper-class Dominicans. Merengue típico groups, now popular not only in the northern region but among many young Dominicans with transnational experiences, but nonetheless continually iden-tified with local lower classes, have generally appeared only on small stages, neighborhood concerts, or as filler. Other events follow this pattern. In 2002, reporter Susana Veras complained that "in spite of the quality and popular-ity [of their music], the típico musicians and particularly the women [accor-dionists] are excluded from national events where merengue is played," and she offered as an example the fact that no típico groups were included in that year's "Merengazo de Verano" festival (Veras 2002). Although the music is sym-bolically present in most of these events through the musical accompaniment for the Ballet Folklórico of the Tourism Ministry which frequently opens these festivals (e.g. Gilbert 2009), ballet folklóricos use only a perico ripiao trio, a self-consciously folklorized ensemble that does not represent current típico practice. As with the Internationale Tourismus Börse, the Dominican Republic as presented to imagined tourists is basically a middle-class, cosmopolitan one that organizers believe will appeal to middle-class, cosmopolitan potential visitors.

At the same time, those consuming these images are, in the main, likely to be themselves Dominicans (and some neighboring Caribbean nationals, par-ticularly Puerto Ricans). Few tourists are likely to plan their vacations around music festivals, despite the wealth available to them, and the continual variation in the dates of the Merengue Festival causes even interested visitors to give up trying to attend, as evidenced in online discussions on the topic.[16] This is not a new situation. Writing about tourism at carnival, festival, and Christmastime celebrations, Lladó suggested in 1988 that none had become the "magnets of attraction they could be for our foreign visitors," and that the high reported attendance numbers only meant that "the State Ministry of Tourism has been harvesting the fruit of domestic cultural promotion rather than those of the promotion of receptive tourism" (2002, 466). Today, despite official proclama-tions as to their importance, these festivals are primarily marketed not to for-eigners but to Dominicans themselves: domestic tourists and return migrants.

In the following sections, I describe some of these insider tourists' activities, showing that while the tourists in Miolán's head have not materialized, others have.[17]

THE INSIDER TOURIST

While imagined tourists consist of middle-class foreigners who manage to affect tourist policy despite their immateriality, insider tourists are middle-class Dominicans who do not affect policy even though they are real and present. Numbers for insider tourists are hard to come by because tourist organizations categorize them differently: some consider the impact of interregional tourists and some attend to domestic tourists; few record the presence of migrant tourists. Nonetheless, all are important for Caribbean tourism as a whole. Even the Dominican Ministry of Tourism has recognized this, and in 2009 the ministry announced a new initiative called "Dominicana en 80 Caravanas" (The Dominican Republic in Eighty Road Trips), which reportedly will organize inexpensive, mass bus excursions for Dominicans throughout the country (Martínez 2009).[18] Yet more significant for touristic development are Dominicans living abroad, known within the country as dominicanos ausentes (absent Dominicans) or, pejoratively, Dominican yorks; they account for approximately one-fifth of all tourists annually. In 2003, they also provided 12.23 percent of the country's gross national product through remittances of more than 2 billion US dollars, or nearly half of what the country gains in revenue for exports from free trade zones (Pina 2006). So many return to the country at Christmas that one year the Ministry of Tourism sent its folk dancers to the customs area of the national airport to welcome them back—and to underline the passage of a law exempting them from import taxes at Christmastime (Castro 2005). It is clear that this group has enormous economic impact. Yet their interests and habits as tourists have scarcely been considered, at least at an official level. The thinking may be that this group can be treated much the same as any foreign tourist market. However, travel habits of nonresident Dominicans are quite different from those of non-Dominican foreigners.

Air travel statistics begin to suggest this difference: for instance, in 2001, in the country as a whole, nonresident Dominicans accounted for 17 percent of all tourists arriving by air, but they disproportionately made up 43 percent of Cibao Airport traffic (Váldez 2006, 46–48).[19] Many or most of these Dominican visitors to the Cibao Airport are coming to visit family or to conduct business, but many are also coming for vacation, or they are combining the two activities. They and the domestic tourists engage in different activities than do foreign tourists, who form the vast majority of those using other airports like Punta Cana, which caters to the eastern all-inclusive resort area (ibid.). These figures support my experiences at the Cibao Airport, which serves an inland area with few attractions marketed to foreigners.

While the aforementioned 2009 domestic tourism state initiatives have as yet produced no results, independent tour operators are already exploiting this market with weekend bus trips marketed explicitly to domestic tourists. Open-bar bus trips from Santo Domingo to carnival in La Vega are enormously popular,[20] and many Dominican Americans fly back to participate in the carnival as well. Similarly, a 2009 flyer for "Festicafé " advertised two days of lodging and meals, bus transportation, open bar, and entertainment for about seventy US dollars per person. The festival, which promotes conservation, is organized by a committee of local officials and coffee growers and reportedly attracted 12,000 visitors in 2010, making a significant impact on the economy of the village of Polo with its 7,000 inhabitants (Díaz 2009). The combination of folklore with ecotourism is a common one in the Dominican Republic (Troncoso 1999). Such a conjunction is both troubling and hopeful: the first because it seems to equate traditional culture, and thus the people who practice it, with landscapes and nature[21]; the second because it promises a more sustainable tourism model than that of the resort.

Merengue típico events also attract more insider than outsider tourists, and the music is an important motivation for travel to and within the country for its many fans. Paradoxically, although merengue típico receives scant attention in the press, in published histories of merengue, and in the festivals described, it is now more popular than orquesta merengue; sales figures for the music are unavailable, and it is often distributed through unofficial channels, but many more new artists are emerging in the former than the latter.[22] Típico fandom is growing among US Dominicans, for whom it can satisfy nostalgic yearnings as well as a desire to connect with heritage. Trips motivated by típico are thus a type of heritage tourism, and they include those made by Dominican Americans, transnational patrons, and those who work in the music, as well as local fans. Such travel also has real effects on the music, as we will see.

Típico occasions much in-country travel for middle-class supporters. Fans from the capital, like Americo Mejía, travel to Santiago many weekends to enjoy the merengue típico there,[23] while Santiago fans like Juan de León make regular journeys to small towns like Mao, Monción, and Santiago Rodríguez, and to various rural galleras, or cockfight rings, to experience a more traditional atmosphere.[24] Traditional patrons of merengue típico, known as viejetes or seguidores, invest large sums of money through entrance fees, purchasing expensive bottles of liquor, tips to musicians, and the occasional commissioning of a homenaje (praise song).

When such long-term típico supporters move abroad, they often continue their commitment to the music both off and on the island. This behavior may be magnified on return visits, as it enhances the patron's prestige. Fermín Checo, owner of a bodega in Brooklyn, is one such traveler. He explains that it is essential for him to go out and hear típico on his frequent trips to the island: "Merengue típico is like the national anthem for Dominicans; it's what represents us. If you go to Santo Domingo and you didn't hear merengue típico, you have not enjoyed a party. But if you go to a merengue típico gig, you enjoyed yourself."[25]

In the major típico bars and ranchos of Santiago, Dominican visitors from the United States are almost always in evidence. Business owners, many of whom are themselves return migrants, recognize the importance of these visitors as a source of income, and típico shows, particularly in the summer, may be marketed directly and explicitly to this audience. Figure 6.3 shows a flyer for a 2004 típico show geared at attracting dominicanos ausentes. Even the décor at the ranchos is calculated to appeal to this group. DeWitt writes, "Evocations of place are intensified in heritage productions, which employ principles of virtuality to simulate a specific place and time" (1999:76). Merengue típico performance is frequently a heritage production even when taking place on its home turf in the Cibao region. Thus, whether located in New York or in Santiago, the ranchos

Figure 6.3 Flyer advertising a merengue típico show specifically for dominicanos ausentes, or migrant Dominicans returning to the island on holiday.

attempt to evoke a sense of rural life and times past by using items like thatched roofs, clapboard walls, old musical instruments, or straw hats as decorations.

Dominican visitors thus manifest different travel patterns and motivations than do foreigners. And, unlike the men described above, many such travelers were born or raised in the United States. In fact, típico bass player Alejandro Guzmán guesses that most of those who attend típico shows in New York only got interested in the style after moving to the United States (p.c., 2003). For instance, Abelardo Martínez of the Bronx, who moved to the United States on scholarship to study Communication Design at Parsons School of Design, explains that even though he can easily see live merengue típico in New York, whenever he is in the Dominican Republic he considers it essential to go out to hear "classic" merengueros like Fefita La Grande and El Ciego de Nagua in a rancho típico three or four times a week (see Figure 6.4). He elaborates,

> The initial cultural shock pushed me closer to the music I grew up hearing on the radio, what was background music in the past, became the soundtrack of my present life. . . . Merengue típico has been my salvation in the times when I felt I was loosing [sic] my cultural identity. I found Tatico Henríquez [a classic típico accordionist] . . . and I was saved . . . I felt I was at home.[26]

Figure 6.4 A hand-painted merengue típico advertising poster collected as a souvenir by Abelardo Martínez while on vacation in Santiago and displayed in his Bronx apartment. (Photo by Abelardo Martínez, used with permission)

Martínez now maintains an informative blog on Dominican music,[27] owns a farmhouse in the northern Cibao, and travels to the island about four times a year.

José Miguel Marte, Abelardo's brother, similarly reports that he travels to the island from his home in Providence about three times yearly for business and to visit family. When in Santiago, he states,

> I try and go as much as I can to go to Montebar [a popular típico night-club]. . . . [It] is very important to remind myself of w[h]ere I came from, even if I live far away it still connects me in certain way with my roots. When I listen to the very old Típicos (Francisco Ulloa, Tatico Henríquez, El General Larguito, etc.) it all reminds [me] of [small Cibao town] Cotuí and my Dad.[28]

Freddy Peña, also a New Yorker with Dominican roots and a college degree, travels to the Dominican Republic two to four times yearly to visit family and get a típico fix. He emphasizes the heritage aspect of his touring practices, stating, "I have a lot of American friends that can track down their great, great, great grandfather's occupation and all I have is the music my family tree listened to throughout the decades." Peña estimates he spends a quarter of his income on live performances, live CDs, and music-motivated travel (including típico, as well as bachata and popular merengue).[29] Abelardo Martínez places his monetary involvement slightly lower, at $2000–$3000, but it is clear that such travelers are significant in the economic maintenance of this music.[30]

Although these fans may be particularly dedicated, their cases are not atypical. Mark DeWitt found the same in his study of Cajun and Creole migrants in California who had had no interest in Cajun and Creole music prior to migrating, but wanted to hear it once they were away from "home" (1999, 70). And writing about China's Guangdong province, Frederick Lau notes that although Thai-Chinese visitors could also hear Chaozhou opera in Thailand, they found it even more enjoyable and powerful in China, because it had an identity-affirming function tied to place. Furthermore, local musicians felt that visits from overseas Chinese served to sustain the music economically, while also contributing to the maintenance of a traditional style in opposition to the encroachment of foreign pop music and karaoke. Lau writes, "These performances therefore are directed not only toward the tourist 'others/them' but also to the tourist 'us' " (1998, 126).

That tourist "us" is found not only in Santiago's ranchos, but also on the beach. In June 2012, I spoke with a group of wandering musicians on the beach in Sosúa, on the Dominican Republic's north coast. They explained that they played for both foreign and Dominican tourists, but among their various clienteles, Dominicans visiting from abroad were the best customers. "There are many that request, request, request, one by one and name by name for every merengue," accordionist Fermín Vargas reported. "Because, you know, they are over there, in the United States, or in France, in Canada, or in Germany. . . . When they come, they come with a greater desire. They want to take advantage of the time [here]." And among this group, what they most ask for is merengue típico, "because it's catchier. It's traditional. It's better for dancing," according to Fermín. Thus, they ask for many traditional merengues by name. In contrast, foreign tourists prefer guitar trios to accordion music, he stated, and usually request international songs like "Guantanamera" or "La Bamba"; occasionally, they may add "play me a merengue."[31]

If this kind of musical tourism is not statistically significant enough to be recorded in the figures, it is nevertheless extremely important to típico musicians. As the anecdotes above suggest, ausentes bring a good deal of economic support to this musical style, which they back at least in part because of its value as heritage. But these "absent" Dominicans may not stay in this condition: many return to the Dominican Republic to live and work once they have amassed sufficient capital.

Retornados (return migrants) are some of the most important patrons of merengue típico today. For instance, Papote de León of Tamboril, a town just west of Santiago, lived and worked in New York and Providence, Rhode Island, from 1969 until the early 1980s, when he was financially able to move back home; today, he attends three to four merengue típico events weekly. His brother Juan de León lived in New York in the 1990s and now runs a business in Santiago, where he attends two to three gigs per week.[32] Both are well-known figures among típico musicians and fans.

Many of those who run the business end of típico share similar migratory experiences. Travelers who earn a living at least in part through típico, such as impresarios or bar and restaurant owners, are seen so frequently at típico gigs in both Santiago and Brooklyn that it is difficult to determine their residence. Although they are not "typical" tourists, and their travels conflate touristic leisure time with work, they too spend money on attending shows and buying drinks. Aureliano Guzmán, impresario and manager of many of the top típico groups of the past two decades, immigrated from Santiago to New York in 1977, where he began to back típico artists in the mid-1980s; he has since returned to Santiago to manage típico groups and a radio station.[33] José "Peligro" Mateo, a backer of top New York groups, emigrated from La Vega in 1989; since then he has been perhaps the most successful marketer of típico in New York City and his efforts have been influential in the creation of the moderno style (Hutchinson 2011, 2008a, 2006).

Seguidores, whether visiting or returning to live, are a significant source of capital for merengue típico; in addition, the listening and consumption habits of the seguidores may influence the directions that the music itself may take. Fermín Checo explains that while young people who go out on the weekend will pay 200 pesos (six dollars) for an entrance fee and one hundred pesos on beer, "the real seguidor típico begins and ends the party spending money, and this kind of seguidor is useful for the discotheques." He continues,

> If you and I go to a discotheque where El Ciego [de Nagua] is playing and I order a [bottle of] Johnny [Walker], and in a little while it runs out, I am going to want to order another because they are playing a merengue for me that I like. If I go to a party with brincadera [jumping around; a belittling description of recent types of merengue dancing] and I have a bottle, if I don't like the first set I get up and leave.[34]

These seguidores encourage musical conservatism, as they will only pay to hear traditional repertoire they know and love. On the other hand, younger típico tourists visiting from the United States often want to hear the newest groups playing inventive styles, thus encouraging the further development of the moderno style. In the touristics of this genre, musicians cater to the demands of their audiences, and thus típico's travels have split it in two.

Guerrón-Montero has described a case in Bocas del Toro, an island town off the Panamanian Atlantic coast, where live calypso performance was revived for tourists, but it turned out to be more popular among locals (2006, 647). She explains how the calypsonians played all manner of popular songs in calypso style, thereby attracting new listeners and contesting dominant Hispanic/mestizo representations of national culture through the establishment of musical connections with other parts of the Black Atlantic (657). Similarly, although, as we have seen, hegemonic representations of the Dominican Republic focus on middle-class orquesta merengue, típico tourism articulates a different kind of Dominican identity.

Retornados and dominicanos ausentes are typically left out of dominant identity formulations because of their supposedly corrupting influence on national culture (see Torres-Saillant 1999), but típico tourists create transnational networks while promoting a new Dominican identity that draws heavily from international musical and cultural styles (Hutchinson 2006, 2011). By participating directly in merengue típico, migrant Dominicans have contributed to its growth in scope, its visibility, and its economic impact. By wielding economic power, they also have the power to change the shape of Dominican culture, but the form of that impact is not always predictable. Instead of being limiting, it may in fact result in a greater diversity of styles.

CONCLUSIONS: THINKING OUTSIDE THE RESORT

In this chapter I have presented several different images of travel in order to complicate notions of who tourists are and how they relate to local cultures. While I realize that the categories I use are somewhat artificial and limiting, and that many people and practices may in fact cross categories, the distinctions are nonetheless useful as a framework for discussion. Through them, I have shown that the travel habits and interests of Dominicans themselves, including musicians, are important not only economically, but also for the development of cultural expressions considered "heritage," such as merengue típico. Traveling culture thus helps to produce transnational identities, and vice versa.

I have also demonstrated the lack of a guiding policy for cultural tourism in the Dominican Republic, and this neglect has caused the persistence of a tourism model that generally benefits foreign corporations far more than Dominicans. It has also left open a space in which alternative tourist practices have developed among Dominicans themselves.

In putting a name to the category of the imagined tourist, I actually want to suggest that tourism officials have not been imaginative enough. They have failed to recognize that Dominican culture in all its variety and complexity might be attractive or interesting to some visitors. Their lack of attention to the many spectacular cultural expressions in the country is likely due in part to longstanding racism that denies Afro-Dominican and Dominican-Haitian culture any place in national representations. The kinds of "culture" packaged for foreigners demonstrate that Tourism prefers inventing a new—imagined— Dominican history and culture over presenting living Dominican cultures. In imagining an uninterested tourist, they circumvent any possibility of attracting informed travelers, and they force the country to rely on low-budget, all-inclusive tourism with negligible benefits to local communities.[35] In this way, among a certain group of travelers, the Dominican Republic will always be at a disadvantage compared to its nearby competitor, Cuba, with its highly developed cultural offerings.

The fact that Dominican elites continue to deny the African influences in Dominican culture is also significant here: as Pacini Hernández (1998, 113–116) has argued, successful styles of "world music" are those seen as "authentic" by international consumers, and such styles frequently claim authenticity mainly by expressing a black racial consciousness and using African-derived musical features. According to this argument, salsa and merengue have not been successful as "world music" precisely because their practitioners often fail to acknowledge African roots and influences. Cuban music meanwhile became preeminent in the world music market by emphasizing African-derived features and an Afrocentric consciousness, Pacini suggests.

Like world music consumers, Caribbean tourists also often search for a racial-ized authenticity, and in the Dominican Republic, it is most frequently provided not through official channels but by informal workers, like the men who pro-cure customers for beach restaurants, or Haitian hair-braiders and painters (see Gregory 2007, 67–69, 182–190). Again, racist attitudes in the Dominican Republic have economic consequences, as this type of tourist will always find more "authenticity" in revolutionary Cuba, with its "inadvertent" support (Pacini Hernández 1998, 114) for black music and culture. If Dominican offi-cials wish to capture this market, they will need to start paying attention to and valorizing Afro-Dominican culture. They might even want to finally recognize the African heritage present in even the most prominent aspect of "national" culture, the merengue. Although it will be difficult to do this without falling into the exotifying tropes of blackness that characterize tourist promotion in much of the Caribbean, the effort might be helped along with the involvement of actors from outside the tourism industry. For instance, involving respected research and cultural institutions like Santiago's Centro León or UNESCO in planning might help push the industry away from externally-imposed stereotypes and towards representations determined to a greater degree by those represented. In this way, a more just tourism, even a more just country, might be imagined.[36]

The problems inherent in the Dominican tourism industry today are thus both cultural and economic. While the industry does create jobs, most of these are in the service area and offer poor labor conditions; governmental investment in infrastructure is generally restricted to tourist areas, neglecting the provision of basic services to the general population; and overdevelopment of beaches results in environmental degradation. Some Dominicans also worry that overreliance on tourism causes social ills (e.g., Groten 1998, 47–49). The questions that must now be addressed are therefore manifold. First, can we assume that there exists a group of tourists interested in learning more about the world, for whom ballet folklórico, mass market festivals, and an artificial separation from society are not particularly attractive? If we can, what can the Dominican Republic offer such a group? Second, how can the economic benefits of tourism reach communities? And third, how can tourism act to support Dominican music and culture?

Throughout the history of Dominican tourism, officials have catered to imag-ined tourists rather than real ones, even creating imaginary Taínos and folk dance costumes for them. In the quote above, folklorist Lizardo complained that the Tourism Ministry created folk dance that did not corresponded to real-ity, but only to a product they wanted to sell: imagined traditions for imaginary tourists.[37] If policy would make the great shift to attend to Dominican culture as it is, rather than how officials wish it would be, I believe answers to my ques-tions could be found. It is therefore essential that community members and responsible cultural researchers be included in planning.

Scholars, too, have challenges to confront in understanding current tourist practices. Summing up the state of tourism research in 1999, Stokes noted that researchers still had to work to overcome earlier dichotomies between tourist and local, outsider and insider (1999, 142). Although I too use these categories, I also question them by considering membership in the two groups differently, noting that insiders and locals are also often tourists, and by interpolating the imagined tourist between the two. For instance, merengue típico has not played a big role in tourist imaginings of the Dominican Republic, and cultural tourism appears hardly to exist—if we consider tourists to be always foreigners. If we consider Dominicans themselves as tourists, however, the picture changes quite drastically. And while (orquesta) merengue does figure into tourist images of the country, a closer look suggests the insider tourist may be the real consumer of these images, not the imagined one.

The boundaries between insider and outsider tourists are continually blurred. Migrant Dominicans may be cultural insiders with knowledge most foreigners would not have, but they can also be national outsiders whose claims to citizenship are contested. Similarly, the line between "home" and "away," or presence and absence (to evoke Dominican terminology), is not clear when the frequency of travel reaches a certain threshold. Furthermore, just as Dominicans are an important cultural presence in the US, so is there a significant presence of expatriate North Americans and Europeans in the Dominican Republic, who themselves work in the tourist industry (see Gregory 2007, 64). In a sense, then, there is something imagined about all these tourist groups—not just those around which politicians plan their festivals and orient their policies. Nonetheless, examining contrasts between "insider" and "outsider" practices can help here to point out the different aims and interests of different tourists, and thus to refocus tourism research in the Caribbean and rethink policy. We need to picture all the complicated intertwinings of "tourists" and "locals;" to imagine (even create) informed and interested tourists; to envision ways in which tourism can benefit communities and their arts. Until that happens, while travel will continue to be a ubiquitous motif in Caribbean life, it will not do much else for the maintenance of Caribbean lives.

NOTES

1. A detailed musical description is outside the scope of this chapter; see Hutchinson 2006, 2008a, 2008b for more details on merengue típico as music.

2. I plan to write on the similar situation at Dominican carnivals in a future publication. While the Ministry of Tourism regularly touts carnival as an attraction for foreign visitors, few are ever in attendance.

3. Staged versions of traditional music and dance were popular throughout the region in the 1950s. See Rommen, Introduction to this volume, for more on stage shows in the Bahamas, and Neely, chapter 1, for "floor show tourism" in Jamaica.

4. Illicit sex tourism is also common, but falls outside the scope of this article. See Lamen, chapter 10, for a description of the Brazilian case.

5. One would expect that only wealthier Dominicans would be able to afford such a vacation, but this is not entirely the case. On a visit in 2010, my favorite sidewalk pirate CD vendor in Santiago told me he had recently saved up and taken his wife for a weekend at a Bávaro resort.

6. Merengue típico groups today are generally far larger than a trio, adding congas, saxophone, electric bass, and sometimes other instruments to the ensemble. For more on merengue típico as a musical and social practice, see my other articles listed in the references.

7. José Castillo, interview with author, November 4, 2005, Santo Domingo, Dominican Republic.

8. US Department of State. 2008. Human Rights Report: Dominican Republic, accessed June 22, 2010, http://www.state.gov/g/drl/rls/hrrpt/2008/wha/119157. htm.

9. José Castillo, November 4, 2005.

10. See Pattullo 1996 for more on cruise ship tourism in the region.

11. Rafaelito Román, interview with the author, June 25, 2004, Santiago, Dominican Republic.

12. Information obtained from programs provided by ITB Berlin and conversations with El Prodigio, interview with the author, March 1, 2008.

13. It should be noted that in the Dominican Republic jazz and rock are almost exclusively the domain of the middle and upper classes, functioning as strong signifiers of social status.

14. "Perico ripiao" is sometimes used as a synonym for merengue típico, but these days it more often refers only to the music when played in traditional trio format (accordion, güira scraper, and tambora drum). To some professional típico musicians, the term is somewhat disrespectful, deriving, it is said, from a Santiago brothel of yore, and thus they prefer merengue típico.

15. This Afro-Dominican fraternal society, famous for its drumming tradition, has since been accorded UNESCO status as a Masterpiece of the Intangible Heritage of Humanity.

16. See, for example, http://www.dr1.com/forums/santo-domingo/99144-2010-santo-domingo-carnival-2.html, where one participant in the discussion describes the dates and times of Dominican festivals and carnivals as being "shrouded in mystery."

17. Religious tourism would also fall into this category of domestic tourism, and may even be economically significant. For instance, hundreds or thousands of Dominicans travel to attend large pilgrimages like that of the Virgen de Altagracia in Higüey (Tallaj 2008).

18. As of July 2010, I have been unable to find information on any actions resulting from this announcement, even after a visit to a regional office of the Ministry of Tourism.

19. More recent statistics are incomplete, but they do suggest the pattern has continued to hold even after the Cibao Airport expansion (Asociación Nacional de Hoteles y Restaurantes 2010).

20. Again, no figures are available. Dagoberto Tejeda Ortiz (2008, 549) describes figures on La Vega carnival attendance as "state secrets" for the big businesses that sponsor the festival. See also Hutchinson 2009 for more on carnival and cultural policy.
21. Sheller (2003, 104) notes the conflation of local bodies with landscape in other Caribbean contexts.
22. This point of view was expressed, for example, in response to the question "Is merengue waning as a musical interest in society?" on the online forum for merengue fans at Mamboduro.ning.com in 2008.
23. Americo Mejía, interview with author, March 27, 2006, Santiago.
24. Juan de León, interview with author, June 8, 2006, Santiago.
25. Fermín Checo, interview with author, August 7, 2006, Brooklyn, New York.
26. Aberlardo Martínez, electronic communication with author, March 23, 2010.
27. Triculí: http://www.triculi.com.
28. José Miguel Marte, electronic communication with author, February 21, 2010.
29. Freddy Peña, email interview with author, April 7, 2010.
30. Aberlardo Martínez, electronic communication with author, March 23, 2010.
31. Fermín Vargas, interview with author, June 20, 2012.
32. Papote de León, interview with author, May 13, 2006, Tamboril, Dominican Republic; Juan de León, interview with author, interview with author, June 8, 2006, Santiago.
33. Aureliano Guzmán, interview with author, May 25, 2006, Santiago.
34. Fermín Checo, interview with author, August 7, 2006, Brooklyn, New York.
35. Jamaican scholar Stephanie Williams has also contended that Caribbean tourism promoters cater to mediocrity, giving the tourists what they think they want, and assuming that they are mindless, or at least not open to new experiences (17–18). However, she contends, they are missing the point because tourism is in part a teaching tool (19). While tourist experiences certainly can be educational, I would note, however, that education is unlikely ever to be a major motivation for tourism officials and operators whose goals are always primarily economic.
36. Although thus far the official recognition of Afro-Dominican expressions like the Congos and the Guloyas as UNESCO "Masterpieces of the Oral and Intangible Heritage of Humanity" seems to have brought little tangible benefit to the communities in question, the potential is at least there to do more for the communities involved in this UNESCO program.
37. These kinds of performances differ from Hobsbawm's invented traditions in that few Dominicans believe them to correspond to any historical or contemporary reality. Invented traditions have important roles to play in socialization, establishment of identities, and legitimization of institutions; imagined traditions do not.

References

Anon. 1978. "Señalan los objetivos Festival del Merengue." *El Nacional* June 6.
Asociación Nacional de Hoteles y Restaurantes, Republica Dominicana. 2010. Estadísticas turísticas, vol. 91, January, accessed April 3, 2010, http://www.caribbean-hotelassociation.com/source/Members/DataCenter/Destination-DomRep-0110.pdf.

Camarena, Germán. 2009. *Causas de la crisis del turismo en Puerto Plata (1990–2008)*. Santo Domingo: Editora Corripio.

Castro, Rafael. 2005. "Cientos de criollos llegan al país para celebrar navidades." *Listín Diario*, December 8, 15.

Cepeda, Denisse. 2008. "Turismo de cruceros aviva la economía de Samaná." *Listín Diario*, December 10, accessed April 2, 2010, http://www.listindiario.com/app/article.aspx?id=84019.

Chang, Leiling. 2011. "Le paradoxe du milieu touristique dominicain." In *Terrotoires musicaux mis en scène*, edited by Monique Desroches, Marie-Helene Pichette, Claude Dauphin, and Gordon E. Smith. Montreal: Les Presses de l'Universite de Montreal, 41–60.

Derby, Lauren. 2000. "The Dictator's Seduction: Gender and State Spectacle during the Trujillo Regime." *Callaloo* 23(3): 1112–1146.

DeWitt, Mark F. 1999. "Heritage, Tradition, and Travel: Louisiana French Culture Placed on a California Dance Floor." *The World of Music* 41(3): 57–83.

Díaz, Rossy. 2009. "Festicafé, dos días de fiesta en la sierra de Bahoruco." *Blog*, June 9, accessed April 1, 2010, http://rossydiaz.wordpress.com/2009/06/09/festicafe-dos-dias-de-fiesta-en-la-sierra-de-bahoruco/.

DR1. 1999. DR1 Daily News, July 27, accessed March 31, 2010, http://dr1.com/news/1999/dnews072799.shtml.

DR1. 2001. DR1 Daily News, July 10, accessed March 31, 2010, http://dr1.com/news/2001/dnews071001.shtml.

"El Festival Brugal '09 calienta fin de semana." 2009. ListínDiario, 25 July, accessed March 31, 2010, http://www.Listíndiario.com.do/app/article.aspx?id=109225.

"El festival de ritmos Caribeños." 2012. Listín Diario, July 20, accessed August 11, 2012, http://listindiario.com.do/entretenimiento/2012/7/19/240380/El-Festival-de-Ritmos-Caribenos.

Foucault, Michel. 2002 [1967]. "Of Other Spaces." In *The Visual Culture Reader*, 2nd ed., edited by Nicholas Mirzoeff. New York: Routledge, 229–242, accessed January 25, 2010, http://foucault.info/documents/heteroTopia/foucault.heteroTopia.en.html.

Gilbert, Manuel. 2009. "Puerto Plata baila a ritmo de merengue." *Listín Diario.*, September 27, accessed March 31, 2010, http://www.Listindiario.com.do/app/article.aspx?id=116153.

Gregory, Stephen. 2006. *The Devil behind the Mirror: Globalization and Politics in the Dominican Republic*. Berkeley: University of California Press.

Groten, Ursula. 1998. *Elementos de debate acerca de turismo y ecoturismo*. Santo Domingo: Helvetas/PA.

Guerrón-Montero, Carla. 2006. "Can't Beat Me Own Drum in Me Own Native Land: Calypso Music and Tourism in the Panamanian Atlantic Coast." *Anthropological Quarterly* 79(4): 633–665.

Hutchinson, Sydney. 2006. "Merengue Típico: Transnational Regionalism and Class Transformations in a Neotraditional Dominican Music." *Ethnomusicology* 50(1): 37–72.

Hutchinson, Sydney. 2008a. *Merengue Típico in Transnational Dominican Communities: Gender, Geography, Migration, and Memory in a Traditional Music*. PhD dissertation. New York University.

Hutchinson, Sydney. 2008b. Liner notes for the CD, "La India Canela: Merengue Típico of the Dominican Republic." *Smithsonian Folkways Records.*

Hutchinson, Sydney. 2009. *"Cultural Policy from Below: The Making of Music, Dance, and Locality in Dominican Carnival."* Paper given at Society for Ethnomusicology annual conference, Mexico City, Mexico.

Hutchinson, Sydney. 2011. "Merengue Típico in New York City: A History." *Camino Real* 4(5): 104–127.

Lau, Frederick. 1998. "Packaging Identity through Sound: Tourist Performances in Contemporary China." *Journal of Musicological Research* 17(2): 113–134.

Lizardo, F. 1987. *"La música popular dominicana y su contacto con el folklore. Cómo se enriquece la música popular cuando acepta motivos folklóricos."* Typed manuscript, May 18, 1987. Fradique Lizardo Archive, Centro León.

Lizardo, Fradique. n.d. Handwritten notes on all kinds of Dominican folklore held in the Fradique Lizardo Archive, Centro León, Santiago, Dominican Republic. Folder I.3.1.

Lladó, Juan A. 2002. *Turismo y desarrollo: El despegue de la industria sin chimeneas en la República Dominicana,* 2 vols. Santo Domingo: Editora Centenario.

Maldonado, Rainier. 2009. "Santo Domingo unifica su estrategia turística frente a la crisis." *Listín Diario,* February 18, accessed March 31, 2010, http://www.listindiario.com.do/economia-and-negocios/2009/2/17/91546/Santo-Domingo-unifica-su-estrategia-turistica-frente-a-la-crisis.

Martínez, Desiree. 2009. "Turismo en fase de recuperación y con perspectivas 'evidentemente buenas.'" *Hoy Digital,* August 19, accessed March 18, 2010, http://www.sectur.gob.do/Portals/0/docs/Boletin/2009/Agosto/19-8-2009.pdf.

Medina, César. 2009. "En la cabeza de Miolán." *Listín Diario.* March 1, accessed April 5, 2010, http://www.listin.com.do/la-republica/2009/2/28/92797/En-la-cabeza-de-Miolan.

Ministerio de Turismo, República Dominicana. 2008. "Celebración festival aquí y en Puerto Rico contribuye proyección internacional del merengue." July 27, accessed April 1, 2010, http://www.sectur.gob.do/tabid/291/itemid/170/Celebracin-festival-aqu-y-en-Puerto-Rico-contrib.aspx.

Miolán, Angel. [1996.] "Nuestro turismo: Pasado, presente, y futuro." Accessed March 31, 2010, http://www.udel.edu/leipzig/texts2/hid20027.htm.

Miolán, Angel. 1998. *Datos para la historia del turismo de la República Dominicana.* Santo Domingo: Editora de Colores.

Pacini Hernández, Deborah. 1998. "Dancing with the Enemy: Cuban Popular Music, Race, Authenticity, and the World-Music Landscape." *Latin American Perspectives* 25(3): 110–125.

Pattullo, Polly. 1996. *Last Resorts: The Cost of Tourism in the Caribbean.* Kingston, Jamaica: Ian Randle Publishers.

Pina, Diogenes. 2006. "DOMINICAN REPUBLIC: Remittances for Development." *Inter Press Service,* September 18. http://www.ipsnews.net/2007/09/dominican-republic-remittances-for-development/.

Santiago, Germán. 1985. "Después de la Garrido: La soberana se convirtió en la otra reina del merengue." *La Tarde Alegre,* March 5, 6.

Sheller, Mimi. 2003. *Consuming the Caribbean: From Arawaks to Zombies.* New York: Routledge.

Stokes, Martin. 1999. "Music, Travel, and Tourism: An Afterword." *The World of Music* 41(3): 141–155.

Tallaj, Angelina. 2008. "From Bulls to Music: Social, Religious, and Economic Aspects of a Pilgrimage to Nuestra Señora, La Vírgen de Altagracia." *E-misférica* 5.1, accessed April 5, 2010, http://hemi.nyu.edu/journal/5.1/eng/en51_pg_tallaj.html.

Tejeda Ortiz, Juan Dagoberto. 1969. "El festival del merengue y el festival de la canción popular: Música, clases, y alienación." *Ahora!* 319 (December 22): 36–38.

Tejeda Ortiz, Dagoberto. 2008. *El carnaval dominicano: Antecedentes, tendencias y perspectivas. [Santo Domingo]: Instituto Panamericano de Geografía e Historia*, Sección Nacional de Dominicana.

Torres-Saillant, Silvio. 1999. *El retorno de las yolas: Ensayos sobre diáspora, democracia y dominicanidad*. Santo Domingo: Ediciones Librería La Trinitaria/Editora Manatí.

Troncoso, Bolívar. 1999. *"Los impactos socio culturales del turismo y la percepción turística de la sociedad dominicana."* Paper presented at the OMT-SECTUR Touristic Communication Workshop. Reprinted on Kiskeya Destinación Alternativa, accessed April 4, 2010, http://kiskeya-alternative.org/publica/bolivar/socio.htm.

Váldez M., and Clinton A. 2006. *Administración Turística*. Santo Domingo: Editora Universitaria–UASD.

Vásquez, F. 1969. "Festivales del merengue y de la canción: Un rotundo éxito." *Ahora!* 317 (December 8): 7–8, 73–76, 78.

Ventura, Juan. 2009. "El primer festival del merengue de Puerto Plata." *El Faro* 10 (September).

Veras, Susana. 2002. "Mujeres exponen música típica: viven despertar en el Cibao." *El Nacional* [Santo Domingo], June 26.

7

Celebrating Settlement Day in Belize

OLIVER N. GREENE, JR. ◼

GARIFUNA SETTLEMENT DAY IN BELIZE: CELEBRATING RESISTANCE AND SURVIVAL

In Central America, the Garinagu (Amerindian-Africans formerly known as the Black Caribs and commonly called the Garifuna) acclaim the survival of their culture and honor their ancestors through annual reenactments of their arrival to coastal Belize, Guatemala, Honduras, and Nicaragua.[1] The Garinagu (plural for Garifuna) live along the Caribbean coast of Central America and in urban centers in the United States, primarily New York, Los Angeles, and Chicago and number between 300,000 and 400,000.[2] They share a common language, repertoire of music and dance, cuisine, system of beliefs and post-mortem rituals, and history of exile and migrations for continued survival.[3] In Belize, November 19, 1823 is recognized as the date of the arrival of the Garinagu to Dangriga, the largest Garifuna settlement in the country. Every year on November 19, Garinagu commemorate this occasion with music, dance, and various religious rituals. This day, celebrated since 1941 and commonly known as Garifuna Settlement Day (GSD), has since 1977 been a national bank and public holiday in Belize and has developed into a principal moment to showcase the music, dance, and ritual life of the Garinagu.

The growing popularity of GSD in Dangriga, moreover, has served as a catalyst for two other significant events. The Battle of the Drums, inaugurated in 2006 and held in Punta Gorda, Belize, the week before GSD, features drumming ensembles from Belize, Guatemala, and Honduras. The success of this competition sparked the development of the Habinahan Wanaragua Jankunu Festival (a masked dance event) beginning in 2011. It is held annually during the time of the performances of Wanaragua, from Christmas to Epiphany. Because the Battle of the Drums and Habinahan Wanaragua occur in close proximity to the GSD celebrations, a two-month period of heightened cultural expression emerges in the festival calendar—a period that I call Settlement Season. Belizeans of all ethnicities, expatriate Garinagu, Garinagu from Guatemala and Honduras, and tourists from the United States and other countries attend one or more of the events during Settlement Season. Although these distinct Settlement Season activities are sustained on some level by tourists, each is organized and produced by local Garinagu and illustrates the success of a model that Butler and Hinch call indigenous tourism (2007).

This chapter examines how tourism impacts the articulation of identity on Settlement Day in Dangriga, Belize, and during Settlement Season, more generally, by illustrating the complex interplay and dialogue between tourism, music and other forms of cultural expression, and the reenactment of history through collective memory. Of particular importance here is the fact that the Garinagu themselves largely control the means of production, the marketing, and the venues within which GSD and other Settlement Season activities are staged. In contrast to many of the Caribbean contexts explored in this volume—contexts within which the milieu and agenda for tourism is dictated by foreign economic interests—GSD in Dangriga and Settlements Season itself raise two significant questions that frame much of the analysis in this chapter: (1) what is the function of rituals of identity that are orchestrated by emic or native organizations that control the marketing, commoditization, and performance of culture; and (2) during rites that promote culture to tourists, how is music mobilized in both the transmission and preservation of identity and in the simultaneous commoditization of heritage?

I begin these explorations of music and tourism by offering a brief account of Garifuna history through which I identify surviving practices associated with the exile and arrival of the Garinagu to Roatan island off the coast of Honduras. Next, I describe and interpret the commemorations during GSD that include musical activities, specifically the reenactment of the landing, the ancestor veneration ritual, the Garifuna Mass, and the punta rock show. I follow this with a comparative analysis of indigenous and foreign controlled initiatives of Garifuna tourism in Central America, addressing tourism's influence on the performance and preservation of culture and the significance of indigenous tourism in the process. The chapter concludes with an examination of how GSD expresses Garifunaduáü (Garifunaness or the Garifuna way) and how the advent and success of recent music competitions aid in establishing a Garifuna Settlement Season assuring that tourism and the promotion and commoditization of culture remain in the control of Garifuna entities. Before turning to a brief account of Garifuna history, however, I briefly introduce and situate the key concept of indigenous tourism.

INDIGENOUS TOURISM

Tourists and researchers are drawn to Garifuna music, history, and culture in part because they have actively maintained many of the beliefs, customs, and art forms of their ancestors.[4] This is attributed in part to the fact that the Garinagu are perhaps the only people of African descent in the Americas whose ancestors were never enslaved. The current expressions of Garifuna music, dance, and ritual are, as a result, often explored and experienced through the lens of authenticity discourses (academics, research projects) and roots narratives (tourist imaginaries). As Greenblatt et al. point out, "Tourism ... often depends on a commodification of rootedness: cultures that appear to have strikingly unmixed and local forms of behavior become the objects of pilgrimage and are themselves fungible as mobile signifiers" (2009, 5). And because the events during GSD are organized in the form of a festival, tourist access to the "roots" of Garifuna culture and local control over the narratives expressed about those roots are maximized. For, as Hobsbawm notes, "Festivals are, in a sense, constructed around particular performances and rituals that facilitate the diffusion of 'truths' to new audiences of inheriting generations and increasingly interested observers/outsiders. Through performances, traditions ... and rituals ... can be maintained, and histories, whatever their accuracy, can be told and retold" (Hobsbawm 1983, in Robinson and Picard 2006, 12). GSD thus provides a space and structural platform for retelling histories and instilling ideals while simultaneously drawing a wide range of spectators. Interestingly, it is an event primarily for and about Garinagu. As such, the "truths" communicated are meant to be absorbed by both Garinagu and those non-Garifuna who have come to experience the festival's "roots" performances. And it is this dual function of the festival, this dual message, that makes GSD a particularly interesting example of festival tourism in the circum-Caribbean.

Another important facet of GSD (and Settlement Season, more generally) is the fact that local Garinagu organize all activities associated with GSD and therefore reap the financial benefits. This mode of tourism has been called indigenous tourism. Indigenous tourism—that which is controlled and maintained by members of the culture of interest—is based on the premise that such "tourism represents a fair exchange of value for value between indigenous and non-indigenous people" (Butler and Hinch 2007, 3). Value in this context constitutes that portion of cultural expression that is observed by the nonindigenous tourists as well as the financial compensation the observer provides for the opportunity to witness or participate in expressions of identity outside their own. "Based on the centrality of the cultural attraction and increased indigenous ownership, indigenous people can, at least in theory, negotiate their involvement in tourism from a position of strength" (ibid., 4). And GSD serves as a model of this productive approach to creating and maintaining festivals and events that ultimately benefit the indigenous population, not just in terms of revenue, but also in terms of staging. What I mean here will become clear in the comparisons to follow but, just briefly, when the emphasis is placed on productive and accurate cultural practice (and this because Garifuna are performing in order to celebrate and honor Garifuna), these types of performances can become powerful moments of communal solidarity. This is the case with the series of events that unfold during the GSD celebrations. When emphasis is placed on attracting tourists and performing for them, however, it is quite often the case that stereotypes, exoticisms, and other tourist expectations wind up sapping the power of whatever cultural performance is being staged. Indigenous tourism, then, identifies the material benefits of revenue and, perhaps even more importantly, the immaterial benefits of retaining creative control over the proceedings. This paper, then, is ultimately concerned with how indigenous tourism is changing the face of cultural identity in Belize and Central America. In short, it explores the cultural impact of GSD, the commodification of culture as an indigenous method of developing tourism, and GSD as a vehicle for Garifunaduáü (the concept and practice of Garifuna cultural preservation).

THE GARIFUNA DIASPORA: HISTORY AND DISCOURSE

Garifuna history reveals how colonization and travel have shaped the evolution of diaspora. As Greenblatt et al. point out, "We need to understand colonization, exile, emigration, wandering, contamination, and unintended consequences along with the fierce compulsions of greed, longing, and restlessness, for it is these disruptive forces that principally shape the history and diffusion of identity and language, and not a rooted sense of cultural legitimacy" (2009, 2). The disruptive forces that shape history and diffuse identity, including at least dispossession, displacement, adaptation, and dislocation (Clifford 1994, 309) combine to define diasporic condition. Additional pressures include incomplete assimilation in the host country and continued attachments, through collective memory, to the place of cultural origin. All of these forces have combined to influence Garifuna history and to shape the contemporary Garifuna diaspora.

Garifuna cosmology, a product, in part, of a people physically and spiritually dislocated from their place of origin, is rooted in the belief in a recollected utopian past and in the value of migration or radical mobility for survival (Greenblatt et al. 2009, iii). The Garifuna diaspora is, itself, a symbol of this survival—a survival that is, accordingly, celebrated in cosmology and ritual, and which, in turn, impacts directly the tourism sector. It is a diaspora that evolved along a historical continuum marked by life on *Yurumein* (St. Vincent) from 1635 to 1797, exile to Roatan, Honduras, in 1797, migrations to mainland Central America in the early 1800s, and immigration in large numbers to US urban centers in the mid-twentieth century in search of better employment and educational opportunities.

A brief historical overview sheds light on how radical mobility impacted the evolution of a Garifuna diaspora and why resistance is an important symbol of survival. Following the death of the Paramount Garifuna Chief, Joseph Chatoyer, in March 1796, the 5,080 Garinagu that survived were sent to nearby Balliceaux Island, where half perished within six months due to a malignant fever and malnutrition (Kirby and Martin 2004, 49–50). In March 1797, British ships set sail for Roatan, an island under British control off the coast of Honduras, with 2,248 Garinagu. On April 12, 1797, Garinagu numbering 2,026 were set ashore on Roatan, some 222 having died at sea (Cayetano 1997, 16–19). Provisions for twelve months, including seeds, roots, esculent plants, and agricultural tools had been aboard the ships that traveled from Balliceaux to Roatan with the thought that this would be sufficient time to plant and then reap the harvest from fruits and tubers grown on the island (ibid., 18). The Garinagu would replicate this gesture during migrations to mainland Honduras, Belize, Guatemala, and Nicaragua, and it has also become a staple of Garifuna cultural memory and a major component of GSD celebrations. On May 17, 1797, they sailed southwest to the coast of Honduras, where they established Trujillo, the first Garifuna village on mainland Central America (Garifuna.com and Garifuna American Heritage Society, Inc.).

In 1802 the Garinagu made the first in a series of migrations to the Bay of Honduras (British Honduras in 1862 and Belize since 1982). On November 18, 1823, following the massacre of Garinagu after the civil war (1823–1832) in Honduras, Alejo (Elijo) Beni led a contingent of Garinagu from Honduras to Belize. Approximately 500 Garinagu arrived on the 19th with dories packed with staple produce (Ramos 2001).[5] This settlement, known as Carib Town, would be known later as Stann Creek, then Dangriga (Nanci González 1988, 58, quoted in Arrivillaga Cortes, 2005, 65). Today, the transporting of life plants, fruits, and tubers is a twofold symbolic gesture that is traditionally accompanied by drumming and singing in two GSD events. First, it is an integral part of reenacting the landing and represents the sustenance of life and culture.

Second, it is a part of the opening procession for the Garifuna mass and the procession to place offerings at the base of the altar before communion.

Thomas Vincent Ramos (1887–1955), cultural activist, educator, and native of Honduras, spearheaded the efforts to establish a Garifuna holiday in Belize. In 1940, Ramos, accompanied by two Garifuna men, approached and Governor of the Colony requesting that November 19th be established as a national holiday in observance of the arrival of Garinagu to British Honduras. The request was granted and the first official celebration to commemorate the expatriation of Garinagu to Belize was called Carib Disembarkation Day and was held in 1941 in Stann Creek Town (Dangriga) (Ramos 2001). The holiday was extended to the Stann Creek and Toledo districts in 1943 and 1944, respectively, and in 1977 the Government recognized November 19th as a national public and bank holiday (Cayetano 1997, 33–34). It is within the context of this celebration that Garifuna have developed a multiple set of remembrances and celebrations—a collection of events that promote Garinagu solidarity and simultaneously offer non-Garifuna access to music, dance, and ritual, the "truths" of which are not directed at satisfying tourist expectations but are, rather, mobilized by and for Garinagu themselves. It is to this model of indigenous tourism that I now turn.

SETTLEMENT DAY: DESCRIPTIONS AND PERSPECTIVES

Because the impetus for GSD has been, since its inception, a celebration of survival and identity through collective memory, tourism has never served as the primary objective for the organization of settlement day events. GSD has evolved into the primary cultural tourism event in Belize, however, because it is attended by a substantial number of Garifuna expats, as well as non-Garifuna Belizeans and a small but growing number of foreign tourists. The Dangriga chapter of the National Garifuna Council (NGC) with the assistance of local cultural advocates, organizes the various GSD activities: the reenactment of the landing, the Garifuna mass, the thirty-unit parade, and the punta rock show, respectively.[6] Travel books capitalize on the increasing popularity of Belize as a preferred destination for cruises, ecotourism, archeological observations, scuba diving, the favorable exchange rate, and the appeal of Garifuna culture.

> Many Garifuna re-enact their migration in dories loaded with drums, cassava, banana leaves, palm fronds and flags of yellow, white and black. The musical tradition plays an important role in local celebrations . . . packed solid with expatriate Dangrigans returning to their roots. The party begins

the evening before, and the drumming and punta dancing go on all night long. (Eltringham et al. 2007, 243, 10)

The Drums of Our Fathers Monument in the traffic circle south of Dangriga's main bus station underscores the importance of percussion in Garifuna (and Belizean) life, with its large bronze representations of ritual *dügü* drums and *sisira* (maracas) . . . At the other end of town, at the meeting of Commerce and Front Sts. stands a statue of Thomas Vincent Ramos (1887–1955), the early promoter of Garifuna culture who inaugurated Garifuna Settlement Day.[7] (Vorhees and Brown 2008, 85, 222)

It should be obvious from these short passages that, although travel books attempt to promote indigeneity, their descriptions of cultural practices can often border on (or outright promote) exoticism and sensationalism. But it is also important to note the practical effects of fixing GSD on the tourist calendar. By ensuring that GSD occurs at the same time and place each year and adheres to the same basic format from one celebration to the next, organizers emplace the festival in a calendar that can then become a fixed target for tourists. Expatriate Garinagu can thus plan to be present for these performances of cultural memory and cultural reaffirmation, while non-Garinagu are able to read about this indigenous tourism festival in travel books and then plan their participation accordingly.

So, what can participants and spectators, having traveled to Dangriga, expect to experience during GSD? In the following pages, I offer my own ethnographic account of the sequence of festivities on Garifuna Settlement Day 2010 in Dangriga.

Reenacting the Landing

Shortly after dawn on the morning of November 19th, Dangrigans, locals, visiting expats, and tourists converge at the bridge in the center of the town, the arrival point for two doriesthat reenact the commemorative 1823 landing.[8] The bridge overlooks the mouth of North Stann Creek, less than one hundred yards from its intersection with the Caribbean Sea. Between 6:30 and 7:00 a.m., as the drumming and singing ashore increases in volume, two motorized dories slowly enter the mouth of the creek as the first passenger on the lead boat waves the yellow, black, and white Garifuna flag.[9] Women and men aboard the dories typically adorn themselves with straw hats and carry branches from plantain, sugarcane, cassava plants, and other staple foods, and occasionally agricultural tools. Because this act of transporting staple foods draws upon elements of the exile and is, therefore, historically significant, it is replicated in commemorative

Figure 7.1 Hüngü-hüngü ostinato

Figure 7.2 Punta ostinato.

celebrations in Guatemala, Honduras, and Nicaragua. But food is also an essential component of Garifuna spirituality. Ancestor spirits require food to complete their journey to *seiri* (heaven) and to and from earth to participate in ancestor veneration rituals.

Garifuna drummers and song leaders provide a powerful sound track during the reenactment of the landing and the street procession that follows: communal events that are dependent on travel. These represent the first acts of cultural reaffirmation on GSD. The musicians perform indigenous dance-song genres, typically *hüngü-hüngü*, a triple-meter rhythmic ostinato (see Figure 7.1) that accompanies a (usually) circular dance. (Cayetano, E. Roy 2005, 51).[10] *Punta*, the popular dance-song genre of procreation, can also be heard at times. Its name refers to both the duple-meter ostinato rhythm and to song genre itself (see Figure 7.2).[11] A women's social-commentary song, *punta* is the most widely known of the Garifuna dances and the most popular among tourists and non-Garinagu. That said, it is more frequently performed at the public concerts and parties that conclude the day's activities than during the morning's activities.

Spiritual Commemoration I: Ámalihaní, A Ritual of Ancestor Veneration

As the dories dock ashore after the reenactment of the landing, passengers disembark and lead the procession of drummers, singers and dancers, and tourists to an areaon the north bank of the creek, beneath a tent (see Figure 7.3).[12] Drummers begin the characteristic triple meter ostinato of *ámalihaní* (called malí) on the *segunda*, the bass drum that accompanies the responsorial singing. Ámalihaní is the central rite of the two principal Garifuna post-mortem ancestor veneration rituals: *achügürühani*, "feeding the dead" and *adügürühani* (often shortened to *dügü*), "feasting the dead," the longer of the two. Malí is the only part of dügü that is performed on GSD. The repetitive patterns for hüngü-hüngü and dügü songs are almost identical; supporting the belief that hüngü-hüngü is the secular counterpart of *hugulendu*, the characteristic triple-meter shuffle step dance of dügü.

Figure 7.3 Participants gather for Ámalihaní (photo by the author).

In Garifuna cosmology, *ahari* (ancestor spirits) are not considered deities, but they are believed to be overseers of the daily lives of their offspring and liaisons between man and *Bungiu* (God). During a malí, the *buyei* (the Garifuna shaman/herbalists) or the buyei's assistant leads the procession of drummers, singers, and general participants around the center post of the tent in counter-clockwise motion, stopping to shake the *sisira* (two calabash rattles) toward the ground at each of the four cardinal points. When the participants sing *Iyayawü, bamali hounya, iyayawü, a, e* (Grandmother we are quieting you down, Grandmother, a__, e__), the buyei bends toward the earth while shaking his sisira, a gesture believed to venerate and placate restless ancestor spirits. Likewise, the drummers, song leader, and chorus follow suit. This important gesture is repeated at each cardinal point.

Once the circle is complete, the buyei reverses direction, leading the procession of local and expat Garinagu almost twice as fast as the first revolution. The movement of the buyei, drummers, and participants from each of the cardinal points to the center of the tent and back again, while also processing in overall circular formations, results in a pattern of the universal cross (the four cardinal points) within a circle. Tourists often find rituals like malí particularly engaging, with their display of religious indigeneity, responsorial singing, incessant drumming, and the coordinated movements of groups of

Figure 7.4 Ámalihaní, excerpt.

people, and many tourists watch these portions of GSD from the peripheries of the tent.

Though the texts of the malí songs always reference maternal ancestors as shown in the song text that follows, malís are given for specific maternal and paternal ancestors during dügü. This type of gender distinction in song text may reflect the general matrifocality of Garifuna spirituality. In short, women traditionally outnumber men as general practitioners in religious rituals, both indigenous and Christian (see Figure 7.4).

Nagütü, bamali hounya
Iyayawü [also sung as iyawü], bamali hounya, iyayawü, a e.
Iyayawü [iyawü], maniguati, iyayawü.
O mahurei, bamali hounya.

My grandmother, we are quieting you down.
Great-grandmother, we are quieting you down, great-grandmother, a, e
(Great-grandmother, it is silent now, great-grandmother.)
[. . . No translation], we are quieting you down

A nagütü, walagayo, iyayawü
Walagayo, iayaywü.
O maha bahurei, bamali hounya.

Ah, my grandmother, let the cock crow, great-grandmother.
Let the cock crow, great-grandmother.
[. . . No translation], we are quieting you down

Aura buni, amürü nuni, maniguati

I am for you, you are for me, everything is quiet now.

(Greene 1999, 294)

Malí, in dügü and in its recontextualized form on GSD, represents the symbolic, liminal, and communal space where diachronic and synchronic time coexists and where drumming and singing help create an environment where oneness between the souls of the living and spirits of the past coexist. Malí is the space where atonement for the sin of ancestor spiritual neglect is expressed and received, where circular movements represent the continuity of life, and where the universal cross denotes the organization of space (Roy Cayetano, quoted in Flores 2001, 122–123). Conceptually, themes and emblems, such as the atonement for sin, continuity of life, and the cross find further expression in nonindigenous forms of worship and spirituality on GSD.

Lemesi Garifuna (the Garifuna Mass), to which I turn next, takes precedence even over malí in this regard, for most Garinagu are practicing Catholics— including the buyei and they view attendance at the mass as the pinnacle of communal spiritual celebration on GSD. Tourists, for their part, tend to attend Lemesi Garifuna because they recognize it, in part, as an activity familiar to them.

Spiritual Commemoration II: Lemesi Garifuna, Indigeneity and the Mass

As the malí concludes, the drummers and singers lead the entourage of Garinagu and the increasing number of tourists four blocks north to Sacred Heart Church Roman Catholic Church, the performance site of the annual GSD *Lemesi Garifuna* (the Garifuna Mass) (see Figure 7.5). This mass is a translation and a recasting (i.e., a cultural contextualization) of the mass into the linguistic and musical vernacular. Excluding the GSD parade, the Garifuna Mass attracts the largest number of non-Garifuna tourists, many of whom can be seen videotaping portions of the mass. Lemesi Garifuna is traditionally performed in Dangriga every third Sunday of the month at the 6:00 a.m. mass. The mélange of Garifuna spirituality and post-Vatican II Catholicism (1962–1965) that characterizes Lemesi Garifuna includes: (1) traditional Garifuna hymns (those composed in the Garifuna language but utilizing the musical style of western European hymns); (2) newly composed hymns and musical responses using secular and sacred Garifuna rhythmic patterns; and (3) prayers and scriptures in the vernacular.[13]

A portion of Article 119 of Vatican II, the Catholic Church's official response to challenges associated with modernity, states:

In certain parts of the world, especially mission lands, there are peoples who have their own musical traditions, and these play a great part in their religious and social life. For this reason due importance is to be attached to their music, and a suitable place is to be given to it, not only in forming their attitude toward religion, but also in adapting worship to their native genius. (Constitution on Sacred of Liturgy Sacrosanctum Concilium 1963)

Figure 7.5 The procession to the church for the Lemesi Garifuna (photo by the author).

This decree was, in part, the Council's acknowledgment of a state of affairs that had already been accepted on some level, including the various styles of Christian worship popularized in Africa and Latin America (Wilson-Dickson 1992, 224). The hybridization or creolization of the mass—the exchanges between Catholic faith and practice and Garifuna culture and cosmology that this encounter necessitated—have resulted in another example of the approach endorsed in the decree. Put otherwise, Lemesi Garifuna is a local-ized and practical expression of Catholic liturgy at once appealing to and meaningful to Garinagu and immediately recognizable to tourists. Although tourists and non-Garifuna speaking Belizeans lack knowledge of the local language, those who are Catholic immediately realize that they are familiar with this form of the liturgy. Non-Catholic tourists, for their part, usually discover some level of familiarity during the service because the Catholic mass is the basis for many Protestant worship practices as well. To aid under-standing and provide additional points of connection, on GSD, tourists and locals attending the service may purchase a Lemesi Garifuna program for two Belize dollars. Although the program does not typically include the words to individual hymns or the scripture readings, it does include the Garifuna text and English translations for the complete service (the readings and responses).[14]

As the opening procession begins, the sound of triple meter drumming and the unison melody of the popular responsorial hüngü-hüngü song entitled "Nati Maximo" ("My brother Maximo") engulf the church. The entourage, led by Garinagu carrying the Belizean, the Roman Catholic, and Garifuna flags slowly proceeds down the center aisle of the church toward the altar. Two segunda and one sisira player follow the flag bearers. Individuals carrying the same types of staple Garifuna food items used in the earlier reenactment of the landing follow. Garifuna observers sway from right to left to the incessant rhythm of the drums and join in singing as the procession nears the altar. This is all but identical to the sound of the hugulendu drumming that accompanies the singing of "Nati Maximo" during the opening procession of dügü, when participants carry food and supplies into the dabuyaba. Although "Nati Maximo" is performed in both dügü and Lemesi Garifuna and, therefore, performs double duty across ritual genres, it is never performed on GSD with the malí that precedes the Lemesi Garifuna.

> *Nati-Maximo darabei bena*
> *Aye, nati Maximo darabei bubenari nubara*
> *Ayanuhanamuga buma*
>
> My brother Maximo open the door
> Ah, my brother Maximo open the door for me
> So I can talk with you (Ariola[15])

As the procession reaches the altar, the general participants file to their right while drummers and singers move to the benches to the left of the altar (see Figure 7.6). Afterwards a Dangrigan Garifuna proclaims the purpose of the occasion: a mass of thanksgiving for the safe arrival of the Garinagu to Belize (see Figure 7.7).

The first example of indigenous music used in the 2010 GSD mass proper was "Iúnrala Uguchili" ("Lift up the Father"), an unaccompanied, responsorial song that followed the opening procession and readings. As the song leader ascended the podium she extended both arms above her head and sang *Iúnrala, iúnrala, iúnrala, Uguchili*. Immediately the segunda drummer began playing the duple meter rhythm of *paranda* (see Figure 7.8), the male social-commentary song form. The primero drummer improvised rapid rhythmic passages as members of the congregation lifted their hands and swayed gently while singing the response, *Iúnrala tia Liri*, "Lift up His name." This example reveals how the mass is transformed into a communal, participatory, and culturally familiar worship experience for Garinagu. But it also illustrates how, by retaining the liturgical structure of the Roman mass, it enables non-Garifuna tourists to track its form even when language and musical genre become unfamiliar along the way.

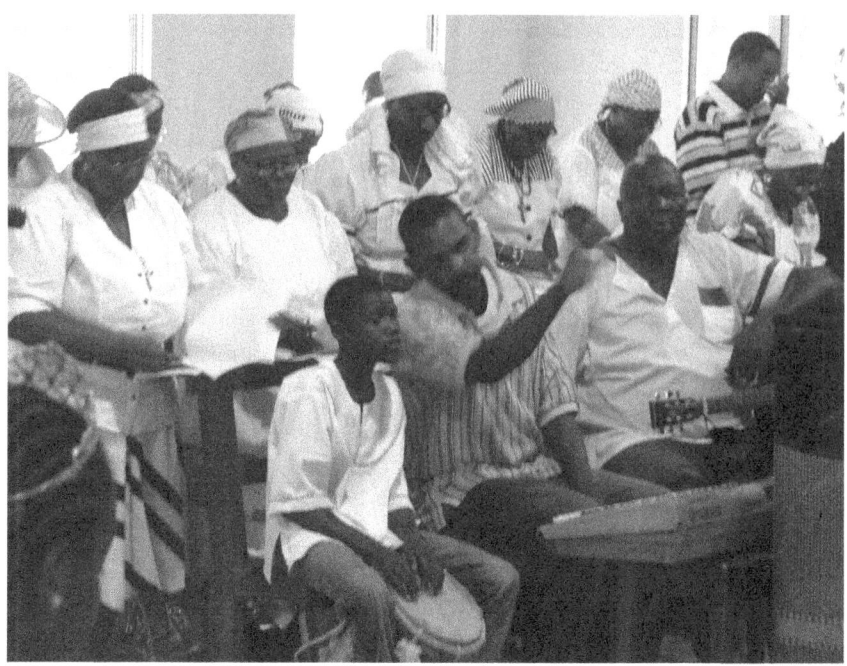

Figure 7.6 The Garifuna choir (photo by the author).

Figure 7.7 Lemesi Garifuna (photo by the author).

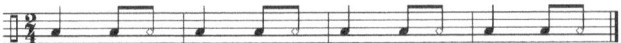

Figure 7.8 Paranda ostinato.

Another example of music unique to the Lemesi Garifuna is "Waguchi Bungiu" ("God Our Father"), a substitute for the Pater Noster (Lord's Prayer). This response and prayer is performed in the manner of *abeimahani*, the women's semi-sacred gestured song form. The slow, folklike melody and simple chord progression played on the guitar supported by the slow repetitive duple-meter paranda rhythm on the segunda is accompanied by the coordinated movements of the participants. Throughout this musical prayer, the clasped hands and forward-and-back arm movements that accompany abeimahani songs are replicated throughout the sanctuary. The congregation (Garinagu and tourists) leans forward on the word *múa* ("earth"), and then upright on the phrase *lidan sun fulasu* ("in all places"), symbolic of the phrase in the Lord's Prayer, "thy will be done in earth, as it is in heaven." This is reminiscent of the buyei's movement toward the earthen floor during malí to honor and appease ancestor spirits. It is also an example of a cultural gesture that performs double duty in the ancestor ritual and in Lemesi Garifuna.

> *Wáguchi Bungiu, lidan sun fulasu*
> *Ñübi la barúeihan woun, adügüwa la le babuserun.*
> *Lidan múa, lidan sun fulasu*
> *Lidan múa, lidan sun fulasu*
>
> Our Father God, in all places.
> We come so that you reign over us, we have done what you want us to do.
> In the earth, in all places.
> In the earth, in all places. (Cayetano 2002, 20)

After the congregation repeats the entire song, they continue to sway while humming the melody softly as a woman delivers a prayer from the podium. The rhythms of the drums and uniform movements by the congregation during musical responses of Lemesi Garifuna, such as "Iúnrala Uguchili" ("Lift up the Father") and "Waguchi Bungiu" ("God Our Father"), create a context in which tourists are encouraged to participate.

At the conclusion of Lemesi Garifuna, members of the National Garifuna Council, public and government officials, and Miss Garifuna (the winners of the junior and senior pageants) travel to Elijo Beni Park, approximately one-half mile south of North Stann Creek, for the official GSD program.[16] The program includes the crowning of the new Miss Garifuna and a presentation of arms by the local regiment of the Belize military, and speeches and remarks by the President of the National Garifuna Council, the mayor of Dangriga, and an ambassador or diplomat from a neighboring country. Visiting expats and tourists and large numbers of locals of all ethnicities line the main thoroughfare for the thirty-five-unit parade. Participants include civic groups representing a variety of ethnicities, local and national businesses, and school marching bands. This display of support shows a broad multiethnic appreciation for the contributions Garifuna Belizeans have made, both nationally and regionally.

Popular Music Culture as Tourism Identity

A few hours after the parade and before sunset, the free, much-anticipated annual public concert of traditional and punta rock music begins.[17] For the past few years, Barbara Norales, founder of Outa Griga Dang Productions, the punta rock association of Belize, has organized a concert featuring local and regional recording artists.[18] The 2010 GSD concert featured guitarist-vocalists Nuru, Lord, Adrian "Doc" Martinez, and Aurelio Martinez, a former Honduran congressman (2005–2009) and the most prominent Garifuna recording artist today. Martinez successfully carries the torch as bard of Garifuna popular music, a position vacated by Andy Palacio, at the time of Palacio's sudden death in 2008.[19] The concert is replete with punta and paranda songs that the musicians transform into punta-rock arrangements. During the concert, young Garifuna women occasionally ascend the stage, turn their backs toward the audience, then rapidly move their buttocks from left to right as they dance punta, the Garifuna version of the cock-and-hen mating dance. Tourists typically absorb the music and observe the dancing from the outer perimeter of the crowd.

The crossover appeal of Adrian "Doc" Martinez's offertory processional hymn "Anihein Baba wama" ("The Father is with Us"), simply called "Baba", propelled him to international prominence.[20] This song found popular commercial success on Andy Palacio's (1960–2008) acclaimed CD *Watina* (2007). "Baba", usually accompanied by drums and a rattle in live performance, is composed in the style of a hüngü-hüngü. The choral refrain that begins and ends the song alternates with Martinez's high tenor voice performing the verses (see Figure 7.9).[21] Baba, a petition for God's intervention during challenging times, is of particular significance to the Garinagu because they are a devout people who believe in a merciful and forgiving heavenly father, "Baba" (Palacio 2007, notes).

Figure 7.9 "Anihein Baba wama," written by Adrian Martinez, published by Stonetree Music (BMI). From the album, *Watina* by Andy Palacio and the Garifuna Collective. (www.stonetreerecords.com; reprinted by kind permission, all rights reserved)

(Refrain)
Anihein Baba wama, furieigiwamá lun Wabügiute
Ideralámugawa lidangien sianti
Anihein Baba wama, furieigiwamá lun Wabügiute
Düsuma lámuga wachara ya ubowagu

The Father is with us. Let us pray to our God
That he may help us out of the impossible
The Father is with us. Let us pray to our God
That our wrongs may be less here on Earth (ibid.)

For non-Garifuna tourists, the attraction of this hymn lies in the plaintive timbre of Martinez's voice and the simple yet effective harmonic and rhythmic accompaniment. The song's appeal within the Garifuna Diaspora is attributed in part to how it navigates and intersects two domains: an original hymn influenced by Christian liturgy framed within the rhythmic context of Garifuna ancestor veneration. Because this hymn, turned popular song, is composed in the style of a hüngü-hüngü, which is all but identical to the rhythmic accompaniment of áma-lihaní and other songs of the dügü, it synthesizes spiritual and sonic realms where the remembrance of ancestors and the veneration of a Christian Father coexist. In short, this song recalls and implores, linguistically and musically, the protection of consanguineal and cultural lineage and Christian heritage. Traditional Garifuna spirituality and worldview are not experienced conceptually as being in opposition to Christianity. Because most Garifuna believe in the coexistence of guardian ancestor spirits and monotheism (viewed as one supreme Christian being, God or Bungiu), they experience no conflict in expressing devotion to Bungiu through the use of rhythms employed to venerate ancestors.

TOURISM AND EXPLOITATION: CONTRASTING EXPRESSIONS OF CULTURAL IDENTITY

Because the festivities for Garifuna Settlement Day in Dangriga are organized and sponsored by the National Garifuna Council, the day's events are ultimately about celebrating the maintenance and control of indigeneity. For expatriate tourists, transnational migration, cultural reclamation, and solidarity are themes that influence Garinagu across generational lines as well as national borders. The question remains: how does tourism, specifically indigenous tourism, impact the preservation and celebration of culture when local communities control the performance of culture and are the primary financial beneficiaries of cost-related activities. When compared to tourism in Punta Gorda, Honduras, where local Garinagu do not control how their culture is presented to tourists, two additional questions present themselves: (1) what happens to rituals of identity that are orchestrated by foreign organizations that control the marketing, commoditization, and performance of culture; and (2) during rites that promote culture to tourists, how is music used in the transmission and preservation of identity and in the commoditization of heritage?

Kirtsoglou and Theodossopoulos, in an article entitled "'They are Taking our Culture Away': Tourism and Culture Commodification in the Garifuna Community of Roatan," state that performances of culture in Punta Gorda, Honduras, the first settlement of Garifuna in Central America, located on Roatan island, are controlled by cruise ships and viewed by bus loads of passengers. They argue that such performances should be "consumed by tourists in a context of mutual exchange as opposed to a hegemonic one," that "cultural ownership relates to the politics of self-representation," that performers desire to promote their own images of their culture, and that such events take place on the performers terms (2004, 135).[22] In short, the Garinagu of Punta Gorda, Honduras, desire to be in control of the organization, expression, and commoditization of their culture. Yet in reality, the expression of Garifuna identity there is heavily dependent on and shaped by the tourist industry and by the exoticizing expectations of tourists. This is, of course, not unique to Punta Gorda, Honduras. Expressions of local culture throughout the circum-Caribbean, more often than not, are constrained or otherwise shaped by a tourist industry seeking to expand its market share through appealing to tourist expectations (and many of the chapters in this volume offer concrete examples of these dynamics). So it should surprise few that this state of affairs exists in Punta Gorda as well.

As described by Kirtsoglou and Theodossopoulos, the scene in Punta Gorda involves the foreign manipulation of the practice of culture for economic gain and a concomitant dismissal of the knowledge of local practitioners. Punta Gorda, one of several barrios on Roatan, is an economically challenged community with dirt roads, seaweed covered beaches, and no apparent tourism infrastructure. Kirtsoglou and Theodossopoulos describe the performer-tourist experience as a daily event that is always held in locations other than the village of Punta Gorda, In these locations (sites that are accessible to vans and buses carrying tourists), entrances, exits, and beverage sales are in spaces controlled by foreign entities, compensation for performers is predetermined, and cruise ship passengers frequently leave one dollar tips. The show, geared toward Western taste, features performances of *punta* and *wanaragua* (a masked and costumed dance of mimicry), and it includes no explanation of the dances and little opportunity for interaction between the audience and performers (Kirtsoglou and Theodossopoulos, 147–148).

Garinagu most likely perform punta and wanaragua for tourists because these dances are among the most well known, visually appealing, and entertaining of the traditional Garifuna dances. The movement of women's buttocks and the sexually suggestive nature with which couples perform punta is particularly entertaining. Tourists are also drawn to the unique costumes and movements of wanaragua dancers: specifically the tall headdresses, the use of wire masks that replicate European faces, the colorful regalia with long paper maché streamers, and the highly acrobatic dances that are characteristics of the Honduran form of the dance. But the context, the meaning of these practices vis-à-vis other practices, and their connection to broader historical and contemporary narratives of Garifuna life are all silenced in favor of a rather one-dimensional spectacle.

Relative to indigenous tourism, it is ironic that the Garinagu of Punta Gorda, the oldest Garifuna settlement in Central America, no longer control the commoditization of their own cultural identity. Yet they reside on an island of plush resorts and culturally diverse beach communities that depend heavily on tourism. Conversely, the Garinagu of Dangriga, a community founded by emigrant ancestors from Roatan, are the controlling agents for tourism during Settlement Season (that is, for GSD, the Battle of the Drums, and Habinahan Wanaragua). For each of these major events, local Garinagu determine all facets of aural and visual representations of themselves, control the venues and access to these locations, and, as such, reap the material and immaterial rewards.

A comparison of tourism in Dangriga to that in Punta Gorda, Honduras, also reveals significant differences concerning ownership, control, performance context, and the distribution of financial resources. Because the Garinagu of Dangriga are much less dependent in their daily lives on remuneration gained from tourism than are those of Punta Gorda, Honduras, tourist-based music events are less influenced by the perceived desires of tourists than similar ones in Punta Gorda. The focus in Dangriga is on the celebration of the cultural-self, and it is indigenous priorities that drive the events calendar (as opposed to cruise ship schedules and multinational resort calendars, as is the case in Punta Gorda).

Some of this dynamic is clearly influenced by matters of scale and structure. The level of participation by non-Garifuna tourists in Dangriga does not come close to rivaling that of Punta Gorda's more developed industry. Until recently, GSD organizers have had the relative luxury of growing this event (and Settlement Season more generally) in gradual, deliberate fashion. They have benefitted, additionally by hosting GSD in a relatively out-of-the-way location (by tourism calculations, that is). As such, Dangriga Garifuna have been afforded a structural opportunity not available to the Punta Gorda community—a community (and location) already more susceptible to encroachment by the tourism industry by virtue of its appeal as the Garinagu's first point of arrival in the region.

But these highly divergent relationships to tourism are also shaped, in part at least, through quite different approaches to the meaning and value of cultural performances. In comparison to Garifuna cultural presentations on the island of Roatan, then, GSD is an event that has been able to shape tourism by privileging local narratives and perceptions of culture. Tourism has been accommodated to this indigenous emphasis in Dangriga, whereas Garifuna cultural practices have been exploited to accommodate the tourism industry in Punta Gorda. As such, the GSD events in Dangriga direct the tourist experience away from the expectation of being *served* cultural entertainment (as is the case on Roatan), and toward the hopeful anticipation of being *accepted* into the proceedings by locals—toward the possibility of being welcomed as onlookers and, even, at several moments (such as during Lemesi Garifuna, the parade, and the Punta rock concert), as participants. GSD, and Settlement Season, then, represent a powerful model for sustainable relationships between indigenous communities and tourism—a model of indigenous tourism.

CONCLUSION: CELEBRATING THE CULTURAL SELF— TOURISM'S EFFECT ON CULTURE

Garifuna Settlement Day is an annual ritualized reconceptualization of Garifuna history and culture. Because GSD includes the reenactment of the landing, ámalihaní, Lemesi Garifuna, and the performance of traditional music and dance, it is arguably the single most impactful and communal gesture towards maintaining Garifunaduáü ("Garifunaness," the Garifuna way). Therefore, it promotes "the idea of a collective consciousness mobilized, enacted and reproduced through the festival space and its diverse festive practices" (Picard and Robinson 2006, 14). Relative to Garifunaduáü, GSD is a festival that encourages Garinagu to promote migration as a concept of cultural survival, to perform an ancestor veneration ritual and a culturally-sanctioned form of the Catholic mass, and to preserve indigenous songs and dances. Garifuna anthropologist Malcolm Servio-Mariano sees its function as the following:

> *Garifunaduáü* . . . and particularly its central tenet of reciprocity *"Aü bu, Amürü Nu"* (roughly translated as "me for you and you for me"), function on multiple levels within the contemporary context of transnational circulation and global power. Garifunaduáü is expressed in rituals, performing arts, and grassroots organizing, where external hegemonic beliefs meet counter-hegemonic practices, and become reconfigured by Garifuna social agents at the local level . . . Garifunaduáü in diaspora provides a way forward, as well as a forum and cultural space for the culture, language, and spirituality to be cultivated. (2010, viii, 3)

In short, Garifunaduáü is a collective affirmation of shared history and a diasporic theory of cultural preservation in the present where the qualities of

self-respect, respect for elders and the environment, reciprocity, and the maintenance of acts that define identity become a way of life.

Through a series of annual community-arts activities, the Garinagu of Belize
have managed to maintain a unique and economically advantageous balance
between tourism and Garifunaduáü. The Garinagu of Punta Gorda, in Toledo
District, Belize, (not to be mistaken for Punta Gorda, Honduras, on the island
of Roatan), have hosted the Battle of Drums, a competition to promote traditional dance-song genres, since 2006. Groups of drummers and singers are
judged on their skill and artistry in playing five categories of Garifuna song
genres. Because the competition, founded by Belizean Garinagu Darius Avila
of Punta Gorda, is held the Saturday before November 19 and has become a
highly anticipated event, it generates substantial revenue for the community
and extends the settlement celebrations by as much as a week. Winners receive
a trophy designed specifically for the occasion and cash prizes, ranging from
$800 to $1800 in Belize dollars, totaling $5000.

The competition includes participants from six Belizean communities in
which Garinagu reside (Dangriga, Punta Gorda, Hopkins, Seine Bight, and
Barranco), including Belize City (home to the largest population of Garinagu
in Belize), and one each from Guatemala and Honduras. Proceeds help fund
local cultural retrieval projects, specifically language preservation, singing,
dance, and drumming in school (Avila n.d., 2–3). An evening of culinary arts
and live music called "Food and Fete" is held the day before the competition.
The immense popularity of the Battle of the Drums has resulted in a competition that is observed by approximately 3,000 people, 75 percent of which are
non-Punta Gorda residents.[23] Observers include locals, Garinagu, and tourists such as non-Garinagu of Toledo and other districts, Garinagu from the
other Belizean Garifuna communities represented in the competition, expatriate Garinagu from the United States, small contingents of Garinagu from
Guatemala and Honduras, and a host of amateur and professional photographers and videographers. Avila states that, in addition to annual sponsorship from local businesses and individuals, the Battle of the Drums receives
approximately $2,000 each in Belize dollars (BZD) from the National Institute
of Culture and History and the Belize Tourism Board. Tickets for the event
range from $15 to $20 BZD, resulting in approximately $50,000 BZD gross,
with an annual net gain of $20,000 BZD, and a total economic impact on the
community of $150,000 BZD.[24] It is remarkable that with such a substantial
profit margin, ongoing cultural preservation remains the primary objective of
the Battle of the Drums.

On January 2, 2011, Dangriga hosted the first annual Habinahan Wanaragua
Jankunu Festival and Competition. In Belize, wanaragua features dancers
whose masks and costumes replicate British militias.[25] Wanaragua is the most

difficult of the Garifuna dance-song genres for both dancers and drummers. It is a dialogue between the movements of the dancer and the rhythms played on the primero (the lead drum) in which the drummer rhythmically interprets the movements of each dancer. Habinahan Wanaragua, like the Battle of the Drums, features ensembles of drummers, dancers, and singers from various Belizean Garifuna communities. Each ensemble is allowed ten minutes to perform and there is much anticipation about the performances of the groups from Seine Bight and Dangriga (belize.com n.d.), the communities most noted for maintaining the wanaragua tradition.

The festival promotes cultural and economic development and its featured attraction is a juried competition for cash prizes. The recent inclusion of a separate junior division competition furthers communal enculturation efforts while promoting wanaragua across generational lines (guardian.bz). The interest among youth and the increase in participation from seven area schools in 2011 to eleven schools from various communities in 2012 is proof of the success of such efforts.[26] Four regional workshops were held prior to the 2012 competition, and prize money ranged from $500 to $1,000 (BZD), totaling approximately $3,000 for both the adult and junior competitions (belize.com n.d.). Although the observers of this competition are typically smaller in number than those who attend Battle of the Drums, they comprise several hundred onlookers and the numbers are increasing each year. Audiences are composed of Dangrigans and tourists from various locations. The latter include Garifuna expatriates, originally from Dangriga, who typically remain in town after Christmas to watch the house-to-house Habinahan Wanaragua processionals, Garinagu from communities represented in the competitions, and a small number of Americans and Europeans. Garifuna linguistic anthropologist Roy Cayetano states that the National Institute of Culture and History increased its support to $4,000 BZD and UNICEF to $19,000 BZD in 2012. The latter amount is to help pay for wanaragua uniforms for school children, most of which cost as average of $175. Proceeds from ticket sales were $2,190.50 BZD for the junior competition and $4,222 BZD for the adult competition.[27] Unfortunately, no studies have been done to date on the economic impact of the GSD or Habinanah Wanaragua on Dangriga.

While the creation of the Battle of the Drums and Habinahan Wanaragua can be attributed to the popularity of the festival that preceded them (GSD), it is the economic impact of the Battle of the Drums and the success of Habinahan Wanaragua as an instrument of cultural maintenance across generational lines that have secured their places as ongoing annual festivals. The success of both events is proof that competition can be mobilized as a self-sustaining tool and model to promote and celebrate identity among Garifuna nationals, expatriates, and tourists. Both competitions encourage community drummers, singers, and dancers to utilize the resources available to them to hone their skills in pursuit of bragging rights and prize money. In Dangriga, perhaps more than in any other of the communities, the GSD Committee has successfully coordinated the efforts of the business and the social sectors to create an itinerary of events that reflect input from these sectors.

Though Punta Gorda continued its GSD festivities, the success of the Battle of the Drums made competition the new model for the maintenance and commoditization of Garifuna culture in that community. This, in turn, served as the impetus and model for Habinahan Wanaragua, with Dangriga again becoming the location of choice because it is home to the largest contingent of annual wanaragua dancers in the country.[28] Because of the success of GSD, Battle of the Drums, and Habinahan Wanaragua, Settlement Season has evolved as a model for sustainable indigenous tourism at multiple levels. First, the success of collaborative cooperation among organizations and businesses in Dangriga for GSD served as a model for community involvement in Punta Gorda, Belize, assuring local involvement in various aspects of tourism. Second, the success of the Battle of the Drums as an economically viable competition served as model for Habinahan Wanaragua assuring that such an approach can work.[29] Third, the success of the Junior Habinahan Wanaragua as a way of promoting enculturation through competition confirms that, even among children, formal competition encourages cultural pride and is a source of interest among Garifuna and non-Garifuna tourists.

Collectively, the three cultural initiatives that make up Settlement Season— Battle of the Drums, GSD, and the Habinahan Wanaragua Jankunu Festival and Competition—extend the period of heightened cultural expression and sensitivity to a span of seven or eight weeks. Settlement Season, because of the highly competitive nature of the two drumming and dance contests, is about enculturating and promoting the highest quality of Garifuna performance arts. Because music and dance, in that order, are the primary performance arts during Settlement Season and are vital elements of each event, they serve as indexes for Garifuna identity. It is not surprising, then, that Garifuna music (both acoustic indigenous and popular syncretic forms), is accessible and aesthetically appealing to Garifuna and non-Garifuna alike, and it is the most commoditized form of Garifuna cultural expression.

The advent of the Battle of the Drums in 2006, and more recently the Habinahan Wanaragua Jankunu Festival in 2011, has resulted in a collective change of consciousness concerning the marketability of Garifuna culture. Although Garifuna expatriates tend to return first to the communities in which they were born and raised during Settlement Season, they usually also travel to Dangriga or Punta Gorda, Belize, for the three major festival events. Non-Garinagu usually visit these cities in substantial numbers for one or more of these Settlement Season endeavors. Therefore, local Garinagu, especially taxi drivers and hotel and restaurant owners, profit significantly from tourism during Settlement Season. Although no quantitative studies have yet been done to measure the impact that tourism has on Dangriga, both Garifuna-, and non-Garifuna-owned hotels and bed-and-breakfast inns are booked months in advance, and Garifuna restaurants are typically near capacity in Dangriga during this time. This information seems to suggest that the impact is immediate and quite substantial.

The economic success of Battle of the Drums and, to a lesser extent, Habinahan Wanaragua, and the appeal of both events to Garinagu and non-Garinagu, warrant their continued existence. The Garinagu in Dangriga and Punta Gorda, Belize, have set in place competitions that reap the economic benefits of cultural commoditization while finding unique methods of maintaining and enculturating identity. In the Battle of the Drums and Habinahan Wanaragua, music and dance are organized and commoditized to be competitive expressions of culture. That said, although both competitions have grown in popularity and attendance, and continue to extend their financial value for local businesses, GSD still remains the primary attraction for tourists during Settlement Season.

In conclusion, this study reveals how Garinagu perceive and promote themselves culturally, the role indigenous tourism plays in the organizational and economic control of cultural events, and how tourism and competition influence the performance of culture. GSD is an interactive cultural festival and performance event where dialogue and discourse across generational lines remembers history and culture, then reenacts these in the contemporary moment—a festival within which the celebration of survival and resistance prevails. Settlement Season, highlighted by GSD and several supporting events, confirm the value of indigenous culture and serves as a model for sustainable indigenous tourism. Because the Garinagu in Belize have been successful in their efforts to promote identity through indigenous tourism and to secure economic validation for the performing arts, they have been able to maintain Garifunaduáü, and in doing so, they have retained control of their cultural and historical narrative.

NOTES

1. In *Labuga* (Livingston), Guatemala, Garinagu celebrate "El Dia Nacional del Garifuna Guatemalteco" on November 26. Alfonso Arrivillaga states that the group of Garinagu that arrived in Livingston from Honduras in 1802 was led by a spiritualist named Marco Sanchez Diaz (2005, 72–73, 65). In Honduras, Garinagu celebrate Garifuna Day on April 12, marking the arrival date of five ships carrying 2026 Garinagu from St. Vincent. In Leguna de Perles, Orinoco, and Bluefields, Nicaragua, Garinagu celebrate November 19 as Garifuna Day. Malcolm Servio-Mariano states

that that date was selected to coincide with that of Belize because the exact date of the establishment of the first settlements, between 1881 and 1912, by Garinagu from Honduras and Belize is unknown (2010, 119–120).

2. Smaller communities of Garinagu live in Miami, New Orleans, Houston, Washington DC, Las Vegas, and Atlanta. Garinagu who reside in New York, Los Angeles, and Chicago as well as in many of these cities, also sponsor GSD celebrations.

3. The Garifuna diaspora evolved along a historical continuum marked by life on *Yurumein* (St. Vincent) from 1635 to 1797, exile to Roatan, Honduras, in 1797, and migrations to mainland Central America in the early 1800s. There are six Garifuna communities in Belize, three in Guatemala, and two in Nicaragua. Belizean Garifuna comprise approximately 6.6 percent of the country's total population of 312, 971 (GeoHive, Belize Census Report). The vast majority, however, resides in Honduras, home to 46 Garifuna communities. Immigration in large numbers to US urban centers starting in the 1950s in search of better employment and educational opportunities, moreover, has contributed to new diasporic itineraries. For additional information on Garifuna diaspora and transnational identities see England (2006) and Johnson (2007).

4. On May 18, 2001, UNESCO proclaimed Garifuna language, dance, and music a Masterpiece of Oral and Intangible Heritage of Humanity. Though the distinction carried no monetary award, it garnered acknowledgement from a prominent global organization that intangible expressions of cultural identity and creativity are worthy of promotion, preservation, and celebration (Cayetano M. and R. Cayetano, 2005, 230, 249).

5. Ramos states that 300 Garinagu settled Stann Creek Town (now Dangriga), 125 in Punta Gorda, 28 in Seine Bight, 24 in Barranco, and smaller numbers in other locations that have not been maintained as Garifuna Settlements: http://www.freewebs.com/adeleramos/garifunahistory.htm.

6. The popular music genre known as punta rock is comprised of faster more contemporary arrangements of traditional song genres, primarily the duple-meter punta and paranda songs. Punta rock songs combine Garifuna instruments (drums, rattles, and, occasionally, struck turtle shells) with electric keyboards, guitars, and a drum machine.

7. This iconic statue of the Garifuna drums, the most recognizable material symbol of Garifuna musical culture, is named after the most celebrated literary work by and about the Garifuna, a poem of the same name by Roy Cayetano, a linguistic anthropologist who served as a former president of the National Garifuna Council.

8. The point of embarkation for the dories is the pier at the Pelican Reef Resort, approximately one mile north of the bridge. Pelican Reef, the most exclusive of the hotel/resort facilities in Dangriga, is the residence of choice for most financially secure tourists. Though it hosts Garifuna drumming and dance shows, it is one of the few hotels in the town that is not Garifuna-owned.

9. For several years the descendants of Pablo Lambey (1932–2003), an esteemed Garifuna activist, have assumed the responsibility of performing the reenactment. They were inspired to do so following an incident of spirit possession during which the spirit of Lambey's mother told her offspring that they were to resume the duty of

leading the reenactment, a responsibility once led by Lambey. See " '92 Convention in L.A.—Tribute to Pablo Lambey," by William Cayetano, http://www.garinet.com/cgi-bin/gksitecontent_ssi.cgi?ACTION=VIEW_ONE_CONTENT&ITEM=4&CATEGORY=19&CONTENT_ID=49&COLOR1=F2A400&COLOR2=FFFFCC.

10. In the notated example, the grace note followed by the eighth note should be played with two hands as a flam, that is, in quick succession. The open-headed note with the diagonal line through the note head is to be played as a mute slap, that is, a note played with a curved palm and clasped finger by pressing down into the drum head when striking the drum. For additional information, see the *Garifuna Drum Method*, DVD, directed by Emery Yost. Belize: Lubaantune Records (2008).

11. In the notated example, the open-headed note is to be played as a rim shot, that is, with three fingers hitting the edge of the drumhead.

12. A tent of approximately fifteen to twenty square feet is used when rain is projected to ensure ritual activity.

13. Mario Gonzalez, guitarist and choir director at Sacred Heart, confirmed my analysis that in Lemesi Garifuna the guitar and drums usually accompany duple and quadruple meter hymns and responses with the simple chord progressions and rhythmic patterns commonly used to perform *parandas*, duple meter male social commentary song form. Similarly the guitarist and drummers accompany triple meter liturgical music with rhythmic patterns associated with *hüngühüngü*, (Mario Gonzalez, interview with the author, November 19, 2010, Dangriga, Belize). Elements of *abeimahani* and *arumahani*, semi-sacred gestured-songs for women and men respectively, which are commonly heard during *dügü*, are also employed during the mass.

14. The book *Bungiu Wabá: Lemesi luma Uremu Garifuna* (God Our Father: The Mass with Garifuna Songs), 2002, compiled by Roy Cayetano, contains a brief summary of the history of Garifuna hymnody, the text in Garifuna for 127 hymns (many composed by Garingu) and musical responses, and a Garifuna translation for the liturgy of the mass and Catholic prayers.

15. Julie Ariola, personal communication with author for translation of "Nati Maximo," July 20, 2008.

16. Miss Garifuna Belize is selected from the winners of pageants held in the various Garifuna communities throughout Belize in the weeks preceding the November 19th celebration. Each of the high schools in Dangriga—public and state-run institutions as well as church affiliated schools—conducts its own Miss Garifuna pageant.

17. It is ironic that punta rock—Garifuna contemporary popular music and the most popular style of music among many locals, expats, and tourists—was born out of acts of rebellion and resistance by Garifuna youth toward the performance of traditional dance-song genres by elders during the 1978 GSD celebrations. This inspired Pen Cayetano, a local visual artist, to study punta, paranda, and other genres of Garifuna music and reconstruct traditional acoustic versions of Garifuna staple songs into amalgamated arrangements using indigenous instruments and the electric guitar.

18. Norales states that the concept for Outa Griga Dang Productions evolved following efforts to sponsor a GSD concert in 1995 by the Garifuna Kids, a New York–based

band composed of young first generation Garifuna Americans (Barbara Norales, interview with author, November 20, 2010).

19. Aurelio's last album *Laru Beya* (2011) is a tribute to the late Andy Palacio who Martinez met in 2000. Ivan Duran produced *Laru Beya* as a musical and stylistic continuation of Palacio's *Watina* (2007). It represents Aurelio's venture into West African (Senegalese) and Afro-Caribbean influenced compositions and arrangements of Garifuna songs. It followed Martinez's residency in 2008/2009 in Dakar, Senegal, as a participant in the Rolex Mentor and Protégé Arts Initiative with pop music icon Youssou Ndour. See Rolex Mentor and Protégé Arts Initiative, Mentor and Protégé Journal, Aurelio Martinez Laru Beya. http://www.rolexmentorprotege.com/journal/6340.

20. The decision to analyze Anihein Baba Wama, as opposed to a punta rock song, is based on the fact that it holds a unique position as a celebrated song among Garinagu of Central America and the US that successfully coexist in two realms: first in the domain of sacred liturgical music and second in popular commercial music. Dangrigan Adrian Martinez toured with the Palacio and the Garifuna Collective and performs regularly in Garifuna music shows.

21. On Watina, *Adrian Martinez*, with the assistance of Andy Palacio and Ivan Duran (bass player and producer on the CD), reframed this hymn by adding acoustic rhythm guitar, lead electric guitar, *guitarron*, dobro, sisira rattle, segunda and primero. See "Baba" in *Watina* (2007) by Andy Palacio and the The Garifuna Collection, Cumbancha Records, CMB CD-3. On the Watina CD, an ensemble of vocalists perform the refrain in harmonic intervals of thirds and sixths, breaking the Garifuna tradition of responses being sung in unison.

22. Kirtsoglou and Theodossopoulos's article is a case study that continued the 1990s trend of anthropological research on indigenous rights, sparked by particular interest in indigenous "exploitable knowledge" (Strathern et al. 1998) and intel-lectual property (Benthall 1999; 2001); (Harrison 1991; 1995) (Kirtsoglou and Theodossopoulos,136).

23. Darius Avila, interview with the author, March 10, 2013.

24. Avila, interview.

25. Popular Christmastide music and dance processionals in other circum-Caribbean locations that share the same generic name include Jonkonnu in Jamaica and Jankunoo in The Bahamas.

26. Roy Cayetano, email and phone interview with author, March 11, 2013.

27. R. Cayetano, interview, March 11, 2013.

28. The idea for wanaragua festival predated the Battle of the Drums. The NGC received funds from UNESCO following the 2001 Declaration as a part of a project entitled Safeguarding Garifuna Language, Dance, and Culture with the thought that GSD would serve as a national festival with a wanaragua festival to be added later (R. Cayetano, interview, March 11, 2013).

29. R. Cayetano, interview, March 11, 2013.

REFERENCES

Arrivillaga Cortés, Alfonso, 2005. "Marcos Sánchez Díaz: From Hero to *Híuraha*—Two Hundred Years of Garifuna Settlement in Central America." In *The Garifuna: A Nation across Borders*, edited by Joseph O. Palacio, 64–84. Benque Viejo del Carmen, Belize: Cubola Productions.

Avila, Darius. n.d. "Battle of the Drums: An Initiative to Promote Garifuna Culture and Cultural Tourism" (unpublished prospectus).

Belize.com. "The John Canoe Festival." Accessed December 26, 2013. http://www.belize.com/the-john-canoe-festival.

Benthall, J. 1999. "A Critique of Intellectual Property." *Anthropology Today* 15(6).

Benthall, J. 2001. "Indigenous and Intellectual Property Rights." *Anthropology News* (April): 5.

Butler, Richard, and Tom Hinch. eds. 2007. *Tourism and Indigenous Peoples: Issues and Implications*. Boston: Elsevier Ltd.

Cayetano, E. Roy, comp. 2002. *Bungiu Wabá: Lemesi luma Uremu Garifuna*. Dangriga: Belize. National Garifuna Council of Belize.

——, ed. 2005. *The People's Garifuna Dictionary*. Dangriga, Belize: National Garifuna Council of Belize.

Cayetano, Marion, and Roy Cayetano. 2005. "Garifuna Language, Dance, and Music: A Masterpiece of the Oral and Intangible Heritage of Humanity. How Did It Happen?" In *The Garifuna: A Nation across Borders*, edited by Joseph O. Palacio, 230–252. Benque Viejo del Carmen, Belize: Cubola Productions.

Cayetano, Sebastian, and Fabian Cayetano. 1997. *Garifuna History, Language & Culture of Belize, Central America, and the Caribbean*, Bicentennial Edition, April 12th 1797—April 12th 1997.

Cayetano, William R. 2003. " '92 Convention in L.A.—Tribute to Pablo Lambey." Accessed December 18, 2012, http://www.garinet.com/cgi-bin/gksitecontent_ssi.cgi?ACTION=VIEW_ONE_CONTENT&ITEM=4&CATEGORY=19&CONTENT_ID=49&COLOR1=F2A400&COLOR2=FFFFCC.

Clifford, James. 1992. "Travelling Cultures." In *Cultural Studies*, edited by L. Grossberg, C. Nelson, and P. Treichler, 96–116. New York: Routledge.

——. 1994. "Diaporas." *Cultural Anthropology 9(3): Further Inflections: Toward Ethnographies of the Future* (August): 302–338.

Constitution on the Sacred Liturgy Sacrosanctum Concilium, 1963. Accessed August 10, 2012, http://www.vatican.va/archive/hist_councils/ii_vatican_council/documents/vat-ii_const_19631204_sacrosanctum-concilium_en.html.

Dangriga, Belize. Wolfram Alpha, accessed December 17, 2012, http://www.wolframalpha.com/input/?i=dangriga,+belize.

Eltringham, Peter, with Daniel C. Chang, Nadine Pedoe, and AnneLise Sorensen. 2007. *The Rough Guide to Belize*, 4th Ed. New York: Rough Guides.

England, Sarah. 2006. *Afro Central Americans in New York City: Garifuna Tales of Transnational Movement in Racialized Space*. Gainesville: University of Florida Press.

Flores, Barbara Anne Therese. *Religious Education and Theological Praxis in a Context of Colonization: Garifuna Spirituality as a Means of Resistance*. Dissertation in Religious and Theological Studies. Evanston, Illinois, Northwestern University, 2001.

Garifuna.com. "Garifuna Society Today." Accessed June 20, 2012. http://www.garifuna.com/.

GeoHive, Belize. "Census Report 2010." Accessed June 10, 2012. http://www.geohive.com/cntry/belize.aspx.

GeoNames Geographical Database. "Population of Dangriga, Belize." Accessed December 16, 2012. http://population.mongabay.com/population/belize/3582228/dangriga.

González, Nancie. 1988. *Sojourners of the Caribbean.* Chicago: University of the Illinois Press.

Greenblatt, Stephen, with Ines G. Zupanov, Reinhard Meyer-Kalkus, Heike Paul, Pal Nyiri, and Friederike Pannewick. 2009. *Cultural Mobility: A Manifesto.* Cambridge, UK: Cambridge University Press.

Greene, Oliver N. 1999. *"Aura Buni, Amürü Nuni," "I Am for You, You Are for Me": Reinforcing Garifuna Cultural Values through Music and Ancestor Spirit Possession.* Dissertation in Musicology. Tallahassee: The Florida State University.

Guardian.bz. "2nd Habinahan Wanaragua/dance Jankunu." Accessed December 23, 2013. http://www.guardian.bz/index.php?option=com_content&id=4084%3A2nd-habinahan-wanaraguadance-jankunu.

Harrison, S. 1991. "Ritual as Intellectual Property." *Man (n.s.)* 27: 225–244.

Harrison, S. 1995. "Anthropological Perspectives on the Management of Knowledge." *Anthropology Today* 11(5): 10–14.

Hobsbawm, E. (1983) "Introduction: Inventing Traditions." In *The Invention of Tradition*, edited by E. Hobsbawm and T. Ranger, 1–14. Cambridge, UK: Cambridge University Press.

Johnson, Paul Christopher. 2007. *Diaspora Conversions: Black Carib Religion and the Recovery of Africa.* Berkeley: University of California Press.

Kirby I.E. and Ci. Martin. 2004. *The Rise and Fall of the Black Caribs (Garifuna)*, 4th ed. Toronto: Cybercom Publishing.

Kirtsoglou, Elisabeth, and Dimitrios Theodossopoulos. 2004. "'They Are Taking Our Culture Away': Tourism and Culture Commodification in the Garifuna Community of Roatan." *Critique of Anthropology* 24(2): 135–157.

Martinez, Adrian "Doc." 2007. "Baba" on Watina by Andy Palacio and the Garifuna Collective. Cumbancha Records, CMB-CD3.

Mentor and Protégé Journal. 2011. "Aurelio Martinez Laru Beya." Rolex Mentor and Protégé Arts Initiative. Accessed September 12, 2012. http://www.rolexmentorprotege.com/journal/6340.

National Garifuna Council of Belize. "Garifuna Settlement Day." Accessed July 20, 2012. http://ngcbelize.org/content/view/16/142/.

Palacio, Andy, and the Garifuna Collective. 2007. *Watina.* Cumbancha Records, CMB-CD3.

Picard, David, and Mike Robinson. 2006. "Remaking Worlds: Festivals, Tourism, and Change." In *Festivals, Tourism and Social Change: Remaking Worlds*, edited by David Picard and Mike Robinson, 1–31. Buffalo, NY: Channel View Publications.

Ramos, Adele. 2001. "Changing Portraits of Garinagu." November 20. Accessed November 9, 2012. http://www.freewebs.com/adeleramos/garifunahistory.htm.

Report on Habinahan Wanaragua. 2012. *Dangriga*, Belize: Habinahan Wanaragua Steering Committee.

Servio-Mariano, Boyd Malcolm. 2010. *GARIFUNADUÁÜ: Cultural Continuity, Change and Resistance in the Garifuna Diaspora.* Dissertation in Anthropology. Albany: University at Albany, State University of New York.

Strathern, M., M. Carneiro Da Cunha, P. Descola, C. Alberto Afonso, and P. Harvey. 1998. "Exploitable Knowledge Belongs to the Creators of It: A Debate." In *Social Anthropology* 6(1): 109–126.

Vorhees, Mara, and Joshua Samuel Brown. 2008. *Lonely Planet—Belize*. Oakland, CA: Lonely Planet Publications.

Wilson-Dickson, Andrew. 1992. *The Story of Christian Music: From Gregorian Chant to Black Gospel and Authoritative Illustrated Guide to all the Major Traditions of Music for Worship*. Minneapolis, MN: Fortress Press.

Yost, Emery, dir. 2008. *Garifuna Drum Method*. DVD. 100 mins. Belize: Lubaantune Records.

Recordings Cited

Andy Palacio and the Garifuna Collective. *Watina.* Cumbancha, CMB 3 (2007).

Aurelio Martinez. *Laru Beya*. Real World (2011).

Aurelio Martinez. *Garifuna Soul*. Stonetree Records (2004).

Paranda: Africa in Central America. Stonetree Records (1998).

PART IV

Festivalizing Music Touristics

8

DestiNation

The Festival Gwoka, Tourism, and Anticolonialism

JEROME CAMAL ■

In July 2012, I was in Guadeloupe to conduct fieldwork and attend the Festival Gwoka (FGK),[1] the longest-running festival on the small French Caribbean archipelago. For the past twenty-five years, the Comité d'Actions Sportives et Culturelles de Sainte Anne (CASC) has worked closely with Rèpriz, the center for popular music and dance of Guadeloupe, to organize the annual event in the scenic coastal community of Sainte Anne, one of Guadeloupe's most popular tourist destinations.

The opening of the twenty-fifth gwoka festival outlined the two principal issues facing cultural tourism in postcolonial zones: an unresolved tension between the desire for economic development and the struggle to maintain control over the dignified representation of local culture. In his opening remarks, Blaise Aldo, the mayor of Sainte Anne, expressed a thinly veiled criticism: after twenty-five years, the FGK seemed to be losing steam, continually struggling to find financing. Underlying this criticism was the recognition that the festival has so far failed to become a major touristic event. In contrast to Aldo's criticism, French economist Jean-Michel Lucas's keynote address served as a reminder of the festival's primary goal. Basing his argument on the UNESCO's convention for Intangible Cultural Heritage and the Agenda 21 for Culture, Lucas advocated for an approach to sustainable cultural development that, instead of focusing on economic growth, serves to preserve individual dignity in cultural production.

In this chapter, I demonstrate how the stage of the FGK provides a space where nationalism, tourism, and neocolonialism collide to put the nation "in play" (Sheller and Urry 2004). Analyzing the festival's history in the context of

Guadeloupean's anticolonialist efforts, I build on Susan Pitchford's model (2008) to consider its role as a "medium" that reaches both local and international audiences. I examine the FGK's ongoing role as a venue for the performance of diverging visions of Guadeloupean identity that, in often contradictory ways, seek alternatives to both exoticist tropes and Eurocentric aesthetics. This analysis allows me to propose a possible answer to Anthony Carrigan's question (2011, 2): "Could a situation be envisaged in which tourism in regions with histories of western domination is not interpreted as neocolonial?"

TOURISM, NATIONALISM, AND POSTCOLONIALISM

Anticolonial Nationalism and Identity Tourism

To answer Carrigan's question, we must consider how centrifugal and centripetal forces shape both anticolonial nationalism and tourism. By using the phrase "anticolonial nationalism," I mean to combine two aspects of nationalism. First, following Thomas Turino's model, I understand nationalism as a political movement aimed at establishing a sovereign state coterminous with a "nation," however it may be imagined (2000, 13). As such, in the case of Guadeloupe, nationalism can be equated with separatism. I take issue, however, with what I see as Turino's artificial separation between nationalism as political movement and what he terms "national sentiment" or patriotism. Indeed, the success of any nationalist, or separatist, movement depends both on seeking international recognition for the budding state but also on intensifying support from that state's future citizens. In other words, to paraphrase Rex Nettleford (1993), nationalism requires both an "outward reach" and an "inward stretch." Anticolonial nationalism differs from its European counterparts for the very reason that it is a product of the system it aims to challenge. As Partha Chatterjee has demonstrated, nationalism in colonial zones is itself an ideology disseminated by colonial institutions, making ideological liberation potentially more challenging than political independence (1986). As I'll discuss below, tourism development further complicates this process.

To create either a nation or a destination, the centripetal and centrifugal forces associated with nationalism and tourism provoke a reinterpretation of place. Indeed, both tourism and nationalism rely on establishing a dialectic relation with a putative Other. As a consequence, they demand a careful balance between the need to affirm difference on one hand and to display some level of cosmopolitan fluency on the other. In the Caribbean, "the classic 'place to play' in tourism economy" (Sheller 2004, 12), nationalist efforts to define the nation for those who belong to it can intersect with touristic efforts to represent

a destination to those who are foreign to it.[2] These intersections require striking a difficult equilibrium between often contradictory sets of demands and
expectations.[3] Thus, the intersection of anticolonial nationalism and tourism
has profound implications for the articulation of what Timothy Rommen calls
the "ethics of style," a discursive field within which "political agendas, doctri-
nal imperatives, personal aesthetics, and communal identities intersect with
one another and find musical expression" (2002, 39). Two questions arise from
these considerations: Can anticolonial activists mobilize the tools of tourism,
such as a festival, towards nation building? Conversely, can an event created
primarily to shore up national sentiment also serve as an engine of tourism
development?

Sheller and Urry write that "the identity of places depends upon their location
within, and upon, [a] global stage" (2004, 9). This is as true of nations—which
cannot exist without being recognized by other nations (Turino 2000)—as it is
of destinations. Indeed, the success of various destinations increasingly hinges
on their abilities to distinguish themselves from one another, lest they run
the risk of seeing their "somewhere" become an "anywhere" (Sharpley 2004).
Increasingly, the growth of niche tourism is forcing places to "demobilize"
certain aspects of their culture, society, or history, and "re-mobilize" others in
order to entice new visitors (Sheller 2004). Various locations have thus tried
to capitalize on their environment (Duffy 2004) as well as on their tangible
and intangible heritage. As the case of the FGK will demonstrate, it is in these
situations that various forms of nationalism and tourism most clearly intersect. These encounters, in which "culture for us" becomes "culture for them,"
often result in conflicts over who and what gets represented (Sarkissian 1998).
The commoditization of culture in these situations also generates much anxiety
around issues of exoticization, authenticity, and preservation (for example, see
Bruner 2004; Desmond 1999; Harnish 2005; Rees 1998; Titon 1999). However,
the interaction of nationalism and tourism can also actually generate a synergy.

Susan Pitchford's study of "identity tourism" (2008) remains one of the
most helpful analyses of this synergy to date. Exploring the role of tourism as
a medium through which nationalist activists can reach their own constituency
and sympathizers along with outsider groups (ibid., 3–4, 83–84), she explains
that "identity tourism" combines attractions that focus on "history and cultural
distinctiveness, both traditional and contemporary, of marginalized groups
in both periphery and core." Thus identity tourism enables Pitchford to focus
on those sites and situations in which identities are contested, especially those
where a subaltern group challenges the national narrative presented by the state
(2008, 2–3).

Considering identity tourism as a medium disturbs the conventional distinction between hosts and guests that has been central to tourism studies in the

past (Urry and Larsen 2011 illustrates this approach) but has recently come under criticism. For example, Stokes rightly suggests that "boundaries separating incomers from residents operate as any other ethnic boundary, establishing semantic categories between which people still might move with great fluidity" (Stokes 1999, 142). Indeed, most Caribbean nations also encompass a sizable and mobile diaspora, therefore blurring the distinctions between residents and visitors. Consequently, we must investigate the difference between international and domestic tourisms, two categories that have too often been conflated (Bruner 2004). In addition, recognizing the fluid boundaries between visitors and residents allows us to think about difference beyond ethnicity. Indeed, identity tourism recognizes that some tourists do not seek to come face to face with an exoticized ethnic Other; rather, some may wish to overcome their own exoticization and experience a different vision of the Self. This, I believe, is the central function served by the FGK.

Tourism and Exoticism in Postcolonial Zones

Within postcolonial zones, identity tourism enables us to deal with the issue of exoticism from different and complementary angles: from the perspective of Western travelers seeking exotic thrills; from that of the tour operators, event organizers, and artists who are responsible for satisfying these tourists' demands, even if it means exoticizing their own culture; and from the perspective of those who attempt to resist such touristic co-optation. Turning our attention to these various positions allows us to further explore postcolonial contributions to tourism studies.

As Hall and Tucker remark, "tourism both reinforces and is embedded in postcolonial relationships" (2004, 2). Indeed, because metropolitan capitalist structures dominate the tourism industry, because they tend to reap the benefits of work performed abroad, and because tourism tends to reinforce economic relations between the core and its periphery that are defined by exploitation and dependence, many authors have argued that tourism is a form of "leisure imperialism" or "the hedonistic face of neocolonialism" (Hall and Tucker 2004, 5; see also Hollinshead 2004). It is precisely these hegemonic tendencies that lead Carrigan to wonder if tourism in postcolonial zones could ever escape the forces of neocolonialism.

Carrigan's question underscores that tourism in postcolonial zones creates problems beyond economic exploitation. Indeed, "issues of identity, contestation and representation," issues that have been the central focus of postcolonial studies, "are increasingly recognized as central to the nature of tourism studies" (Hall and Tucker 2004, 2). As Hall and Tucker have argued, many tourists seek to experience a specific type of difference, one predicated on a distinction between the West and an exotic Other. This creates a dialectic in which, on one hand, tourists' expectations are shaped by exoticism and, on the other, destinations adapt to certain exoticist tropes to satisfy these expectations (ibid., 8). Thus the flow of tourism capital from metropolitan centers through peripheral destinations (and back into metropolitan coffers) is intimately tied to the circulation of the ideology of exoticism along with its attendant hierarchies and tropes, reinforcing dependence and subjugation in the process. Unsurprisingly, Caribbean destinations have historically been mired in this dialectic. Indeed, Sheller writes that "the real Caribbean is always a performance of the vivid Caribbean of the imagination" (2004, 12). There, the circulation of exoticism has not only led to the development of hedonistic forms of tourism, it has also contributed to the naturalization of social and economic inequalities in the eyes of foreign visitors (ibid., 17–18).

Jane Desmond rightly underscores the centrality of bodily displays in the experience of difference in touristic situations. She argues that tourist experiences are greatly shaped by what she terms "physical foundationalism," an epistemological phenomena in which "bodies function as the material signs for categories of social difference, including divisions of gender, race, cultural identity, and species." Following this logic, gazing at the bodies of performers in touristic shows not only naturalizes the difference between Western visitors and exotic locals, it also creates a temporary bond of community among the spectators (Desmond 1999, xiv–xvi). Through physical foundationalism, the hierarchies of place identified by Stokes (1994, 4) as well as Hall and Tucker (2004) become hierarchies of communities. Thus, we need to pay particular attention to song and dance spectacles as strategically important sites where difference and community are constructed, broadcasted, and experienced. The case of the FGK, though, presents an interesting contrast to the situations analyzed in Desmond's book. Whereas Desmond's case studies are based on the experience of foreign tourists, the FGK mainly serves a local audience. Given the FGK's nationalist agenda and its focus on domestic audiences, the question arises: can a nationalist movement harness physical foundationalism in order to naturalize a different conception of the national community? Can this serve to transcend the forces of neocolonialism?

Keith Hollinshead would like to think so. For him, tourism in postcolonial zones "should prove to be a vital field through which revered or targeted 'strategic essentialisms' can be clarified and codified for internal consumption and otherwise announced and articulated for external digestion" (2004, 31–32).But once postcolonial nations learn to master tourism's potential to communicate the "suppressed and stifled being" of their societies, what message are they going to want to broadcast?

Studies of tourism and nationalism, such as Pretes (2003), rely heavily on Benedict Anderson's "imagined community," a model in which a sense of national unity emerges through the development of certain technologies like the circulation of printed materials or the metropolitan administrative pilgrimages of provincial officials (Anderson 2006). While Anderson's theory did much to expose the historical and social construction of nationalism, his imagined communities left very little space for internal debates and contestation. Yet, as Katherine Verdery has demonstrated, nationalism is best understood as an "ideological process. . . in which alternative conceptions of the world enter into conflict and, through their encounter, acceptance of or resistance to the existing order of domination is furthered" (1991, 9; see also Askew 2002). Thus Verdery argues that national sentiment, even in its hegemonic manifestation, cannot be prescribed; rather its construction is necessarily discursive (1991, 10).

The political status of Guadeloupe—a territory for which independence appears as if stuck at the end of one of those ever-lengthening Hitchcockian hallways—highlights this discursive ideological process. As I will explain in a moment, forty years or so of cultural nationalism have had mixed results. The FGK may be one of its greatest successes, or at least one of its most enduring tools. Nonetheless, its stage hosts the performance of various, competing, and sometimes contradictory, visions of Guadeloupeanness. The Guadeloupean nation is still very much in play.

GUADELOUPE: A CARIBBEAN ANOMALY

Decolonization through Assimilation

Understanding the role of the FGK today requires a longer historical perspective. I don't feel the need to address here the colonization of the French Antilles and their incorporation within the capitalist "machine" (Benitez-Rojo 1996). From a regional perspective, this story is unremarkable. However, since the mid-1940s, the French Antilles have followed a political path that has established them as "anomalies" in the Caribbean basin (Burton 1995, 1). Indeed, in 1946, as the European colonial world was starting to crumble, the so-called "old colonies" of France in the Caribbean and Indian Ocean campaigned for their full integration within the French political system. Perhaps paradoxically, I see this move for greater political integration as the "point of departure" (Chatterjee 1986) for Martinican and Guadeloupean nationalisms.

The quest for political assimilation was led by Martinican *homme de lettres* and communist mayor of Fort-de-France, Aimé Césaire (Adélaïde-Merlande 2002, 79–82). By seeking decolonization through assimilation rather than emancipation, Césaire and his allies were holding France up to its Jacobinical promises of radical egalitarianism (Hintjens 1995).[4] Practically, at a time when the local sugar industry was collapsing, Antillean politicians hoped that political integration would force France to extend its social protection policies to its overseas territories (Adélaïde-Merlande 2002, 79–82; William 1997, 317–325). Their campaign was successful. In 1946, the assemblée nationale voted unanimously to transform Martinique, Guadeloupe, French Guiana, and Réunion into départements d'outre mer (DOM), administrative units with (almost) the same rights and benefits as those in the metropole.

Unfortunately, departmentalization failed to mitigate the economic decline of the French Antilles. The islands saw no real reform: economic and social structures inherited from the nineteenth century were essentially kept in place (Adélaïde-Merlande 2002, 83). If anything, the collapse of the sugar industry accelerated and unemployment continued to rise. As it soared to nearly 25 percent by the early 1960s and social unrest became increasingly frequent, the French government responded in two ways. First, between 1958 and 1981, it sponsored the massive migration of Antillean workers to metropolitan France (Anselin 1995). Second, it artificially propped up the Martinican and Guadeloupean economies through subsidies. As political scientist Justin Daniel (2001) explains, most of these subsidies have served to fund social programs rather than agricultural or industrial development, thus helping to inflate the departments' GDP while precluding actual economic development. These mobilities of people and capital have helped not only maintain the political status quo, they have also reinforced the DOM's subordinated status. Indeed Daniel explains that any discontent with the political situation of the DOM gets "transmuted into economic and social claims," rather than claims for greater autonomy or even independence from France. Conversely, "fearing nationalist reactions in the periphery, French politicians make concessions in exchange for loyalty. The cost to the peripheral population is the perpetuation of dependency" (Daniel 2001, 66). However, as economic dependency increases so does the intensity of cultural and identity movements (ibid., 72). It is exactly within this logic that the FGK, from its creation to its latest developments, must be understood.

The DOM's Anomalous Touristic Patterns

Because of their special relation to France, and unlike most nations around the Caribbean basin, the DOM escape the direct economic domination of the United States.[5] This applies to the tourist sector as well. Whereas most Caribbean territories attract mainly US tourists, about 70 percent of people visiting Martinique and

Guadeloupe each year come from metropolitan France. Unfortunately the French government does not track how many of the estimated 623,000 passengers who traveled to Guadeloupe in 2010 were in fact part of the over 100,000 Guadeloupeans living in the metropole and vacationing "home" (Marie and Qualité 2002, 16).

Whether staying for a week or two months, these special tourists who travel to the Antilles to reconnect with their native culture blur the line between domestic and international tourism. They also magnify one of the consequences of centuries of cultural assimilation under French colonialism. Indeed, in his seminal Discours antillais, Edouard Glissant argues that colonialism and the lack of true economic development since departmentalization have resulted in a situation where original expressions of creole culture—such as the Creole language or biguine—are now completely divorced from the social and economic environments that saw their creation and sustained their relevance. According to Glissant, this reduces Antillean culture to a "broken" or even "delirious" discourse, a discourse that he ultimately sees as "tragic" (1997, 283–297; my translation). Going one step further, Burton concludes: "Modern French West Indians do not so much live the creole culture as observe it, tourists in their own countries, from outside" (1995, 13). This assessment may have rung true in the early 1990s, but I would argue that, based on my own observations over the past five years, it fails to fully recognize the achievements of the Guadeloupean nationalist movement.

THE GUADELOUPEAN NATIONALIST MOVEMENT

The AGEG

It took a little over a decade for the resentment against departmentalization to produce full-fledged demands for a change of political status. The emergence of autonomist and, later, separatist movements in France's overseas departments was closely tied to the broader geopolitical context: the wars of independence in Algeria and Indochina, the Cuban revolution, the Bandung conference, the emergence of Black Power in the US, and, finally, within the communist block, increasing tensions between the USSR and China. Indeed, according to my conversations with several separatist activists, it was in metropolitan France that Guadeloupean students met with students from other French colonies in the 1950s. These encounters and discussions prompted the Association Générale des Etudiants Guadeloupéens (AGEG) to transform itself from a purely social to a political organization, advocating first for autonomy, and then, as its political outlook hardened, for outright independence from France (Camal 2011, 123–126; see also Schnepel 2004, 47–54).

By the late 1960s, the AGEG had become the principal training ground for separatist activists operating in both Guadeloupe and France. In 1970, it proposed a program of cultural reforms aimed at bolstering Guadeloupean national identity. This platform was rooted in Marxist-Maoist ideology and centered on an effort to promote the Creole language and to modernize gwoka, a local African-derived music and dance tradition (AGEG 1970).

Gwoka: Musical Qualities and Political Significance

The exact definition of gwoka is still the subject of much debate in Guadeloupe. Both musical and ontological elements recur in most definitions. Among the musical elements are instrumentation, structure, and the location of performances. Most commonly, gwoka describes the music and dance performed during outdoor events known as swaré léwòz. Generally, a gwoka ensemble comprises three barrel-shaped, single-headed drums. Two boula, the lowest of the drums, play a rhythmic ostinato chosen from a limited stock of available rhythms to match the characteristics of the song.[6] A single, higher-pitched drum called makè improvises in coordination with the movements of the dancer in front of him, or more rarely, her. Singing involves a call and response pattern between a lead singer (Creole, chantè) and members of the audience (Creole, répondè).

Beyond these structural aspects, many gwoka musicians insist on gwoka as a musical representation of Guadeloupeanness. For example, percussionist Christian Dahomay writes that gwoka is "what is left when you have forgotten everything" (Dahomay 1997, 18; my translation). Radio personality Alain Jean explains: "There isn't one bit of culture in Guadeloupe that escapes gwoka" (my translation).[7]

The fact that so many people see gwoka as an essential expression of their identity speaks volumes about the impact of the synergy between what Thomas Turino (2000) calls "participatory ethics"—which govern the interaction of musicians, dancers, and audience members at the léwòz—and nationalist politics. In his landmark study of music and nationalism in Zimbabwe, Turino argues for the power of participatory musics in constructing national consciousness. One of four ideal types of music, participatory music is primarily designed to ensure the maximum engagement of those in attendance. There is ideally no distinction between musicians and their audience: everyone contributes to the performance, either through clapping, singing, dancing, or playing an instrument (Turino 2000, 47–48). The combination of nationalist discourse and participatory music is particularly effective because it allows "people to begin not only to imagine the nation, but to have the experience of being part of it" (ibid., 174). Thus, gwoka songs, with their responsorial structure, helped diffuse nationalist and separatist ideologies through recordings and, more effectively, through their performance during léwòz (Camal 2011; Laumuno 2011).

However, musical elements alone cannot explain the AGEG's desire to turn gwoka into a national symbol nor the relative success of this strategy. After all, by the 1960s, gwoka had been reduced to a marginal place in the Guadeloupean soundscape, its practice limited to communities at the bottom of the social ladder, such as agricultural workers and those toiling in the few remaining sugar factories. Indeed, gwoka was far less popular than biguine and quadrille, the other two forms of creole music found on the island. This can partially be explained by the fact that, of the three, gwoka is the most African sounding. European settlers' disdain for African-derived musics has been well documented as have been the many laws passed to try to restrict their performance. In addition, like many practices associated with slavery, gwoka had been consistently stigmatized since emancipation in 1848 (Cyrille 2011).[8] Yet, precisely for these reasons, the AGEG was able to present gwoka as deeply rooted in the experience of the proletariat, as a symbol of resistance against French colonialism and, therefore, as the only genuine musical expression of Guadeloupe's national identity.

My interviews with Guadeloupean nationalist activists revealed that most of them had little to no initial knowledge of Guadeloupean traditional music on which to base their reformist project. Their thinking in this domain was greatly influenced by a guitar player named Gérard Lockel. Lockel was born in Guadeloupe but, like many Antilleans, moved to France in the 1950s in search of better job opportunities. In France, Lockel made a living playing in jazz and biguine orchestras but also met with members of the GONG (Groupe d'Organisation Nationale de la Guadeloupe), an early separatist organization. In 1969, he returned to Guadeloupe, got in touch with the underground separatist leadership, and started to promote a new music that he called gwoka modènn (modern gwoka) (Lockel 2011). Lockel's ideas had a profound influence on the AGEG's cultural platform (Camal 2011, 141–144).

Gwoka modènn illustrates the process of modernist reform described by Turino in which a local participatory music is adapted to conform to cosmopolitan aesthetics and modes of presentation (2000; see also Dudley 2007). Strictly speaking, gwoka modènn is an instrumental music mixing instruments commonly found in jazz combos (electric guitar, piano, trumpet, saxophone, drum set) with the gwoka drums. Compositions are based on traditional rhythmic ostinati while typical performances follow a well-trodden jazz model: a statement of the original melody, a series of improvisations by individual soloists, and a recapitulation of the original theme. More peculiarly, Lockel's system dictates that soloists rely on an atonal scale based on a succession of whole steps and minor thirds (Lockel 1981), a quality aimed at distancing gwoka modènn from European models.

Perhaps due to its complexity, few musicians fully adopted Lockel's model. Nevertheless, in the 1980s, when Haitian konpa dominated the Guadeloupean soundscape, the call by Lockel and the AGEG to develop a national music based on gwoka resonated with many. Calling their music "gwoka moderne," "gwoka progressif," or simply "gwoka instrumental," numerous groups have since taken on the gwoka mantle. One of the common gwoka ostinati even served as the rhythmic foundation of zouk, the popular music style that came to dominate Antillean music in the 1980s and '90s (Guilbault 1993). The gwoka festival was created first and foremost to provide a forum for these emerging new styles, and to broadcast their attendant nationalist message.

THE FESTIVAL GWOKA

Over its twenty-plus years of existence, the FGK has arguably grown to become the most important institution in Guadeloupe for the promotion of gwoka, both in its traditional and contemporary forms. Yet it would be a mistake to view the festival strictly as a cultural event. Indeed, the FGK has played an important role in not only broadcasting but also shaping Guadeloupe's shifting anticolonialist efforts.

The festival grew out of Félix Cotellon's efforts, starting around 1978, to organize cultural activities in conjunction with a youth soccer tournament held in Sainte Anne every July. Cotellon is himself the son of a local communist leader. He studied law in Bordeaux where he became deeply involved in the AGEG's political activities. Upon his return to Guadeloupe, he joined the UPLG (Union Populaire pour la Libération de la Guadeloupe), the main political outgrowth of the AGEG. Like other outreach events organized by the AGEG and the UPLG, the tournament was an effort to diffuse these organizations' political message and, potentially, to recruit new activists. Cotellon's organizing efforts initially encountered a lot of resistance. Sainte Anne was a communist holdout and tensions ran high between the communist old guard, closely linked to the Soviet Union, and the new nationalist Maoist organizations.[9]

Almost from its inception, music was associated with the tournament: each year, the closing night featured concerts by emerging local artists such as the zouk singer Tanya Saint-Val or the newly created gwoka ensemble Kimbol. In 1987, the informal group of activists that had organized the tournament created the not-for-profit CASC, with Cotellon at the helm. One of their first actions was to organize a concert of gwoka modènn alongside the tournament. The

year 1987 is regarded as the FGK's birth year. Four years later, the soccer tournament ended and the festival grew from a single-night to a weeklong event.[10]

As it stands now, the festival proposes five to ten evenings of music and
dance, depending on each year's budget. Every night, four or five groups follow each other on the outdoor stage set up on the plage des Galbas, a short
walk away from Guadeloupe's only all-inclusive resort. The program blends
traditional and contemporary forms of gwoka with occasional concerts by
quadrille ensembles, carnival groups, and foreign musicians. Besides the concerts, the festival always includes daily pre-concert presentations and debates
related to each year's theme, a large léwòz on Saturday night, and a special
heritage day held on an estate in les Grands Fonds, the scenic hills north of
Sainte Anne. In a blatant act of political resistance, the final concert is generally scheduled on the evening of July 14 so as to disrupt Bastille Day celebrations in Sainte Anne.

The Community Festival as Medium

The Festival Gwoka perfectly illustrates what Michelle Duffy calls a "community festival." Echoing Martin Stokes's classic work on the musical construction of place (1994), Duffy sees music festivals as "centers of intensity where
the creation of place is concentrated [through musical performance] and spills
out onto surrounding space" (2000, 59). She further proposes that community
music festivals "can be seen as a means of promoting a community's identity,
or at least how that community would like others to see it" (51). I would now
like to examine the festival's function as a medium that attempts to inflect the
way Guadeloupeans think of themselves, to transform how visitors experience
Guadeloupean culture, and, eventually, to alter the power dynamic between
France and its overseas department.

Since its emergence as a tool of political and cultural activism, the festival
gwoka has first and foremost addressed local audiences. Didier Berald-Catelo,
the current president of the CASC, explained to me that through the festival the
CASC hoped to reach mainly Guadeloupeans living in the archipelago and those
living in metropolitan France.[11] Through local audiences, the festival mainly
strives to have an impact on local cultural life. Cotellon made this clear: "The
festival aims to contribute to the cultural development of Guadeloupe. We
want to see if we can encourage political awareness about traditional music and
dance."[12] Berald-Catelo has slightly less ambitious goals. In his view, even after
thirty years of cultural activism, gwoka still does not have an adequate representation in local media. In this climate, the festival ensures that the music has
at least a yearly spot on the local cultural calendar.[13]

Most of the activities organized in conjunction with the nightly concerts participate in the process of defining Guadeloupeanness through the presentation of what Raymond Williams calls "selective traditions" (1977, 115–116). The FGK's program, its debates, and its announcements in Creole all offer a specific vision of Guadeloupean identity that strongly privileges African-derived traditions. This feature is consistent with Stuart Hall's observation that 1970s Caribbean nationalisms have been marked by a desire to reclaim an Afro-Caribbean identity in response to centuries of hegemonic Eurocentrism (Hall 1990, 231–233).

For Cotellon, the most important of these activities is undoubtedly the kozé-bokantaj addressing each year's theme. It follows that picking a theme year after year is more consequential for him than putting together the concert program.[14] Past themes have served to highlight the cultural heritage of slavery (1998); the cultural links between Guadeloupe, Europe, India, and Africa (2001, 2002, 2003); the exchanges between gwoka musicians living in France and Guadeloupe (2006); and, recently, educating the public about UNESCO's list of Intangible Cultural Heritage (2011, 2012). The kozé-bokantaj usually attract between twenty and thirty people, a fairly good turnout considering their often very dry titles. "Le droit à la culture: droit interne et droit international" (The Right to Culture: National and International Law) stands as a particularly austere example. On occasion, these debates can turn confrontational, as they did in 2009 when they raised questions of ethnicity and national belonging following the general strike that paralyzed the island for forty-four days earlier that year.[15]

Perhaps the role the festival plays in presenting a restrictive vision of Guadeloupeaness shaped by the nationalist discourse of the 1970s is nowhere more evident than during what has recently been billed as a "heritage day," a daylong gathering organized every year on the estate of the Geoffroys in the Grands-Fonds. The Geoffroy brothers, René and Zagalo, are the sons of a family of farmers. Even though they now run a successful body shop in Pointe-à-Pitre, the Geoffroys are also well-known gwoka musicians and lead one of the island's most successful traditional groups, Kan'nida. Once a year, they open their estate to festival attendees. The event starts with a traditional breakfast, consisting of fresh coconut water and a shot of rum, known as dékolaj (take-off). Throughout the day, guests are treated to traditional music and traditional food: soups, grilled fish and chicken, rice, and kassav. Overall, the event acts as a performance of the sort of traditional lifeways that Guadeloupean nationalists have argued are at the center of their national identity. The day is also peppered with speeches from Cotellon and members of Rèpriz presenting their work, offerings details about traditional musics, or honoring various musicians and dancers. As a result, the event serves to promote that organization's activities, to raise support for traditional music in general, and, by extension, to boost national consciousness.

In addition to these heritage day gatherings, the political function of the festival is also on display during each year's swaré léwòz. The FGK's léwòz are among the most attended such events in Guadeloupe. The political efficacy of participatory ethics are clearly in evidence during the léwòz as those in attendance join in the performance of songs. Many of these songs were composed at the height of the separatist movement and their lyrics refer to specific events in the anticolonialist movement, like union-sponsored strikes, while others express a general discontent with Guadeloupe's political and economic status. Even more emphatically than during staged performances, the festival functions here as a media promoting national consciousness. And because these performances are exclusively in Creole, filled with specific local references, and require some familiarity with the codes of the léwòz, they exclude foreign visitors.

In keeping with its original focus on local audiences, the first efforts at touristic development around the FGK were aimed specifically at local tourists. Given Sainte Anne's popularity as a destination for foreign tourists, this put the festival on a collision course with local resort operators. Around 1992, as the festival became a weeklong event, the CASC joined a wider tourism development program called "July in Sainte Anne." Working with restaurant and hotel owners, as well as public transportation companies, the CASC and the city of Sainte Anne sought to encourage Guadeloupeans to vacation in the beachside community for the duration of the festival, which takes place during a lull in the influx of foreign visitors. According to Cotellon, everyone was asked to work towards maximizing the economic and cultural impact. The DRAC (Direction Regionale des Affaires Culturelles), the local cultural arm of the French government, subsidized gwoka performances in restaurants. In exchange for the free entertainment, chefs were expected to prepare traditional food and special dishes named after the different gwoka song types. The rest of the population was encouraged to participate by crafting and selling small souvenirs. Unfortunately, "July in Sainte Anne" failed to gain much traction. Cotellon cites several reasons. For one, the tourism sector in Guadeloupe was still too disorganized to sustain a common development plan. More importantly, the festival quickly ran into opposition from some resort operators who, in order to attract more foreign visitors, would have liked for the FGK to make its shows more accessible by using French on stage and by programming more popular music. The CASC is fundamentally opposed to the idea. As Cotellon explained:

> This festival is meant for Guadeloupeans and tourists are welcome to participate alongside us.... They have to make an effort and learn Creole.... It

isn't desirable to change the image of the festival to accommodate tourists. They may come and they will discover what Guadeloupean culture is all about. Otherwise, we will fall into "folklorization."[16]

The issue of folklorization is key. As noted earlier, tourism in postcolonial zones, especially on tropical islands, has generally carried exoticist tropes. As the CASC attempted to work with local resorts, it was subjected to the same kind of pressures. Cotellon described the following scenario:

We tell them: "Bring tourists to our event." They reply: "No, you have to bring the show to our hotel." You try to organize a léwòz, it won't do, they ask for a staged show. There's plenty of stuff like that, just to sell. You are forced to push aside a number of beliefs.. . . And every time you make a concession, it's like you're undressing. And at the end, you're left naked. (my translation)[17]

Gwoka has a long association with this kind of exoticization. In the 1950s, Man Adeline[18] was the first person to adapt gwoka dancing for stage performance when her group La Briscante began offering what Guadeloupeans call "ballets" to tourists. Although she played an important role in transforming gwoka dancing from a succession of improvised solos to group choreographies, her shows delivered the kind of exoticist performance foreign tourists expected. Her choreographies painted life in Guadeloupe, including life on the plantation, as carefree. They reinforced stereotypes of Guadeloupe as a tropical paradise, an aesthetic that French West Indians describe as doudouiste. Needless to say, the cultural activists who came out of the AGEG in the 1970s reacted strongly against these tropes, whether in literature, music, or dance. Since its creation, the gwoka festival has struggled to escape this kind of exoticization and instead offer a dignified representation of Guadeloupean culture, even at the cost of limiting its potential as a major touristic attraction.

The festival's relative failure to develop a comprehensive strategy to attract tourists has become particularly evident in the past four or five years. The effects of the 2008 global economic recession were amplified in Guadeloupe by the 2009 general strike. Tourism was greatly affected and is just, as of this writing, starting to recover. In this climate, the FGK has struggled to secure enough revenue and has gradually grown smaller. Berald-Catelo explained to me that, like other festivals in France, the FGK depends on three sources of revenue: government subsidies, private donations, and proceeds from the sale of tickets and merchandise. Whereas most French festivals balance all three sources of revenue, this is not the case for the FGK. The largest share of revenue comes from local and national subsidies with donations from patrons and corporations coming in second. Unfortunately, those have been the most affected by the economic crisis. Conversely, the festival generates very little direct revenue.[19] In keeping with its Marxist roots, the FGK is free and therefore cannot depend on ticket sales. And while the buvette does a brisk job during the shows, it must compete with the numerous food trucks that descend on Sainte Anne every evening and set up shop near the festival's entrance. In an effort to generate more revenue, audience members are constantly reminded to purchase commemorative T-shirts or posters. Yet these revenues are not sufficient to sustain the festival, let alone build a realistic development plan. It is clear that for the FGK to grow, it must reconsider both its Marxist foundations and its domestic focus. Unless major changes are enacted, changes that could potentially threaten the festival's mission, the FGK is left replicating the condition of dependency that characterizes Guadeloupean society at large.

Although Berald-Catelo admits the need to develop the FGK as an international tourist destination, he admits that the CASC has done next to nothing to make that a reality. There is no media campaign targeting foreign visitors, the advertising is very limited, and it is entirely in Creole, as are each night's announcements by the MC. The CASC does not maintain an online presence, not even a Facebook page. For someone wishing to travel to Guadeloupe to attend the festival, it is nearly impossible to learn its exact dates. The festival is a celebration of Guadeloupe's heritage, but it is a media event aimed at an insider audience. In spite of a genuine desire to reach out to French and international visitors, in its present organization, the FGK cannot function as an introduction to Guadeloupean culture for those who do not already belong to it.

However, the festival's outward reach is not limited to attracting foreign visitors. Indeed the FGK also serves as a launching platform for exporting Guadeloupean culture. As he outlined the FGK's mission, Berald-Catelo explained to me that the festival plays an important role in helping to professionalize gwoka musicians. Although all léwòz depend on the presence of professional (that is to say, paid) musicians with the necessary skills to ensure audience participation, the FGK goes a step further. By asking gwoka musicians to perform on stage where they have to work with a stage manager and sound engineer, the festival provides them with an important experience that prepares them for an eventual career outside the archipelago.

In the past few years, the festival has also served as a platform for the international promotion of gwoka through a campaign, organized by Cotellon and Rèpriz, to add the musical tradition to UNESCO's Representative List of the Intangible Cultural Heritage of Humanity. This project is Cotellon's brainchild, an initiative he has been slowly building since 2004, a year after UNESCO drafted the Convention for the Safeguarding of the Intangible Cultural Heritage (henceforth ICH) and two years before France even ratified it. Since then, the festival has served as the principal media through which Cotellon and members of Rèpriz could reach Guadeloupean audiences and gwoka musicians in order to enlist their support for the project. In 2011, the festival was fully mobilized to this effect with kozé-bokantaj about various aspects of the convention before each evening's concerts; onstage announcements from members of Rèpriz throughout the night; a campaign to collect signatures from audience members in support of the inscription; and an effort to recruit musicians, dancers, and educators to join the committees that would write the actual application over the course of the following year. In July 2012, the FGK was again mobilized to present the fruit of that labor and, quite literally, drum up support for the project.

The complete political implications of the ICH project are too complex to detail here. For our purposes, suffice it to say that sustainable and dignified tourism development lay at the center of Cotellon's argument for the inscription of gwoka on the ICH list, a fact underscored by the invitation extended Jean-Michel Lucas to open the 2012 edition of the FGK. During the festival, Rèpriz circulated a booklet that contained the text of the Guadeloupean application and outlined potential benefits for the gwoka community and for Guadeloupe in general. Foremost among them, it contends that having gwoka recognized by UNESCO will "boost the presence of Guadeloupe in the world and contribute to a better promotion of Guadeloupe as a destination; gwoka will thus contribute to cultural tourism" (Rèpriz 2012, 12; my translation). Moreover, in addition to increasing gwoka's role in tourism development, the application booklet insists that the project will allow Guadeloupeans to look at their musical heritage differently and take pride in it. This renewed pride, it is argued, will encourage new artistic creations and new pedagogical models. In short, the ICH list offers a forum for the dignified representation of Guadeloupean culture and its promotion both at home and abroad.

Thus the project is not only consistent with the goals of the FGK, it also resonates with the long-term cultural policies of Guadeloupean separatist organizations. Indeed, when the UPLG outlined its vision for a transitional, if ambiguous, "new associated collectivity" in the early 1990s, the group insisted on the need to "preserve our heritage and affirm the Guadeloupean personality responsibly inscribed in modernity" (7, my translation). This included broadcasting Guadeloupean culture both internally and internationally. The ICH project therefore highlights the role of the FGK as a medium through which a selective tradition is "clarified and codified for internal consumption and otherwise announced and articulated for external digestion," to reprise Hollinshead's words.

Negotiating the Ethics of Style in the DestiNation

If the FGK functions as a medium with the potential of reaching local audiences, Guadeloupeans in the diaspora, and foreign visitors simultaneously, the message being communicated is far from circumscribed. Rather, just as the kozé-bokantaj often lead to heated arguments, the festival's musical stage also offers a space where the performance of Guadeloupeanness is conflicted, caught "in the process of the articulation of elements: where... the image of cultural authority may be ambivalent because it is caught, uncertainly, in the act of 'composing' its powerful image" (Bhabha 1994, 308).

Although the festival started as a platform for gwoka modènn artists, it has since expanded its coverage. Now, both contemporary and traditional expressions share the stage with occasional biguine or quadrille groups, as well as artists from other Caribbean islands. The juxtaposition is striking because aesthetic differences reveal competing definitions of gwoka, disputed visions of its place in Guadeloupean culture, and profound disagreement about how best to react to the sonic and financial pressures of globalization. Thus the various performances on the FGK's stage highlight the challenge of articulating "ethics of style" that simultaneously address a desire to preserve the gwoka tradition, to cultivate standards of artistic representation worthy of a modern nation, and to develop gwoka as a commodity which can both be exported and help sell Guadeloupe as a tourist destination.

This complex balancing act is most obviously visible when one considers dance and movement. Both the léwòz and the staged presentations at the FGK benefit from what Desmond describes as physical foundationalism, although here the performance does not serve primarily to establish boundaries between foreign visitors and local hosts; rather, through clothing and movements, artists have an opportunity to transcend the exoticist tropes that marred gwoka performances for tourists in the 1950s and '60s. Conversely, audiences can witness different visions of Guadeloupean identity. While these visions are, at least in principle, united in their rejections of colonialist and exoticist tropes, they are nonetheless discrepant.

Let me contrast three examples. As mentioned earlier, the mobilization of elements evocative of an Afro-diasporic past—a certain Afrocentric aesthetic—has been a hallmark of Caribbean counter-hegemonic discourse. This continues to be true of many performances at the FGK. For example, MC Patrick Solvet generally sports a dashiki and kufi hat on stage. Likewise, the all-female group Fanm Ki Ka commonly performs with their face painted, their hair wrapped in scarves, and wearing African-style dresses. Certainly, Guadeloupean imaginings of Africa often betray a certain exoticist essentialism. Yet I would argue that these tropes function very differently from the exoticism on display at

Hawaii lu'aus. The specter of sexual availability that haunts common touristic representations of the tropical female body is totally absent from the concerts of Fanm Ki Ka. In this mise-en-scène, physical foundationalism serves to perform a vision of the self that departs both from Euro-normative styles of dress and from exoticist touristic expectations.

Not all Guadeloupean performers subscribe to this Afrocentric aesthetic. For example, choreographer Lena Blou has embraced the logic of modernist reform and developed a modern dance technique based on traditional gwoka that she calls techni'ka. At the center of Blou's techni'ka lays the concept of the bigidi, a state of permanent imbalance that characterizes the movements of many léwòz dancers. Blou explored this idea as she performed on the FGK stage with her own Compagnie Trilogie in July 2011. Clad in white button-down shirts and bare legged, Blou and three of her students performed an original choreography that emphasized losing and regaining balance, often coming to an uneasy rest on an unusual part of their feet, such as the heel. The choreography was set to a pre-recorded track of electronic music and accompanied by a live gwoka percussionist. Through these aesthetics, Blou distances herself from the norms of European ballet in which dancers balance on their pointe, and from most traditional forms of Afro-diasporic dance in which performers rest on the sole of their feet. Thus Blou presents a vision of Guadeloupean identity that is resolutely modern and cosmopolitan, that implicitly avoids a nostalgic look at a lost African past, and that, while rooted in a local tradition, celebrates its own instability.

In contrast to Blou's unapologetic embrace of modernist reform, most gwoka dance schools in Guadeloupe follow the ballet model first developed by Man Adeline and updated to suit the new nationalist sensitivity by Jacqueline Cachemire-Thole in the 1980s. Every year, young dancers under the leadership of Cachemire-Thole, Mario Coco, or Raymonde Torin take to the stage of the gwoka festival. Their group choreographies, while based on traditional moves, abandon the ring of the léwòz and leave very little room for individual improvisation.

The difficulty for these groups is to find a way to celebrate gwoka's origins on the plantation while avoiding the kind of doudouiste imagery that plagued folkloric groups like La Briscante. I asked Cotellon if he thought that there was a danger that these groups may revive old exoticist tropes. He expressed his confidence that the discourse of cultural reappropriation that has accompanied the Guadeloupean nationalist movement since the 1970s has been effective enough that groups like Cachemire-Thole's Akadémie du Ka can borrow from Man Adeline's choreographic model without reproducing her ideology.[20] Similarly, at the end of my interview with Raymonde Torin in July 2012, she pointed to an engraving of the mulatresse Solitude, the legendary pregnant slave who fought the reinstatement of slavery in Guadeloupe in 1802.[21] Torin explained that Solitude is a source of inspiration for her work. In a veiled jab at Blou, she praised the former slave for standing firm on her two feet and for fighting. Yet her own choreographies, like that of her colleague Mario Coco, seem haunted by the specter of doudoudisme. For example, in July 2011, when students of Torin's took to the stage of the FGK, they were dressed in traditional costumes, twirling wicker baskets, and smiling to the sound of a fast-paced traditional gwoka accompaniment. The boundary between exoticism and dignified self-representation in this case is, at best, blurry.

Thus, on the stage of the FGK, the Guadeloupean nation is literally "in play." Different styles of dress and body movements are mobilized to help naturalize competing visions of Guadeloupeanness, to test and stretch the limits of how Guadeloupeans represent and see themselves. It is more difficult, however, to assess their capacity to also reach out, to create not only a nation, but also a destination. Whether stretching inward or reaching out, the success of their endeavor depends on the reaction of those gazing at them from the audience, reactions that are likely to be conflicted and relative to each audience member's subject position. Guadeloupeans' celebration of their African heritage can be seen as an expression of anticolonial resistance or it can betray a kind of diasporic exoticism. Blou's techni'ka garners the admiration of some but baffles others who struggle to find the connection between her modern aesthetics and the traditional music with which they are familiar. In each case, a nationalist desire to distance artistic creations from Eurocentric norms or to embrace modernist abstraction stands at odd with the expectations of metropolitan tourists in search of sea, surf, and exotic sounds. While more accessible, the ballets of Torin and Coco flirt perhaps dangerously with common exoticist tropes, especially for these tourists who are unfamiliar with Guadeloupean culture and its history of anticolonial resistance.

CONCLUSION: THE DESTINATION AS VORTEX

In its twenty-five years of existence, the Festival Gwo Ka has gone from a tool of political recruitment to a medium of cultural activism to a platform from which artists and activists could work to increase both the prospects to export Guadeloupean music abroad and to attract visitors to the island. Through its focus on attracting and addressing local audiences, the FGK has provided a stage from which the national community can be imagined, performed, witnessed, and even contested. The traffic jams that clog the entrance to Sainte Anne for a week to ten days every July attest to the festival's relative success in enhancing the beachside town's appeal as a cultural destination. However, the festival's outward reach does not yet match its inward political, cultural, and touristic achievements. So far, it has only served as a launching pad for one group of Guadeloupean musicians, Kan'nida, who have recorded an album for the French record company Label Bleu and who represented Guadeloupe at the World Music Expo (WOMEX) in 2011. It could be argued that the recordings of musicians who have had no involvement with the festival, such as those by jazz saxophonist Jacques Schwarz-Bart, have done far more to increase Guadeloupe's visibility on the global stage. Added to the fact that the festival still struggles to attract international visitors, it seems that Rèpriz's and the CASC's efforts to use the FGK to create a destiNation have only had partial success. Moreover, the festival's incapacity to put in place a long-term plan to ensure its financial viability has meant that it continues to perpetuate the dynamic of economic dependency typical of neocolonial zones.

Overall, it could be that the combined centrifugal and centripetal forces that converge at the intersection of tourism and anticolonialist nationalism cannot be fully reconciled. To answer Carrigan's question, it may be impossible to imagine a form of tourism development that escapes neocolonialist pressures. Indeed, the FGK's efforts in this direction seem to have inhibited its development as a major touristic attraction. Yet, it is also possible that the CASC's and Rèpriz's increased attention to international mobilities and resources will be sufficient to overturn the FGK's recent decline and help bring its economic impact in line with its cultural achievements. It is also possible that the FGK's greatest impact on securing Guadeloupe as a destiNation will actually result from its support for gwoka's addition to the UNESCO's list of intangible cultural heritage and will come to fruition not on an outdoor stage but in governmental offices in Paris and New York.

NOTES

1. There is no standard spelling for gwoka. Banners for the festival sometimes use the spelling "gwo ka" even though the single word "gwoka" has become more common. The spelling "gro ka" is still found occasionally.
2. Besides the FGK, the month-long celebration of heritage leading to the crowning of the winners of the national music competition on National Day in Dominica offers a similar opportunity to observe this intersection of tourism and nationalism.
3. Timothy Rommen (2011) explores a similar situation in the Bahamas.
4. They also undoubtedly realized that the same Jacobinical tradition, especially the notion that the republic is indivisible, would doom any demand for outright independence to failure.
5. For discussions of US economic and political involvement in the Caribbean, see Knight and Palmer (1989); Maingot (1989).
6. It is commonly claimed in Guadeloupe that there are seven different boula (ostinatos played by the drums of the same name) in gwoka: toumblak, graj, léwòz, woulé, kaladja, pajanbèl, and menndé. In practice, some of these rhythms are performed

much more frequently than others. In addition, Guadeloupean musicians continue to create new ostinatos, making for a greater rhythmic variety than generally acknowledged.

7. Alain Jean, interview with author, July 22, 2009.
8. Dominique Cyrille explains how the socio-racial hierarchy of Antillean colonial societies led to the social stratification of Creole musical practices in which the European-derived quadrille served as a tool of social ascendency while African-derived dances, painful reminders of slavery, became markers of lower social status.
9. Félix Cotellon, interviews with author, July 29, 2008, and July 15, 2012.
10. This chronology was put together based on my interviews with Cotellon, July 29, 2008 and July 15, 2012.
11. Didier Berald-Catelo, interview with author, July 14, 2012.
12. Cotellon, July 15, 2012.
13. Berald-Catelo, July 14, 2012.
14. Cotellon, July 15, 2012.
15. Starting in January 2009, Guadeloupe was paralyzed for forty-four days by a general strike as the Lyannaj Kont Pwofitasyon (Alliance against Profiteering) demanded greater consumer price parity between the metropole and its overseas department. For detailed discussions and analysis of the movement, see *Les Temps Modernes* 66(662–663), January–April 2011.
16. Cotellon, July 15, 2012.
17. Cotellon, July 15, 2012.
18. "Man" is the Creole equivalent of the French "Madame."
19. Berald-Catelo, July 14, 2012.
20. Cotellon, July 15, 2012.
21. Slavery was first abolished in Guadeloupe during the French Revolution, but Napoleon moved to reinstate it upon seizing power in 1802. It was finally permanently abolished in 1848.

REFERENCES

Adélaïde-Merlande, Jacques. 2002. *Histoire contemporaine de la Caraïbe et des Guyanes, de 1945 à nos jours*. Paris: Karthala.

AGEG. 1970. Rapport Culturel, 9ème Congrès.

Anderson, Benedict. 2006. *Imagined Communities: Reflections on the Origin and Spread of Nationalism*. London: Verso.

Anselin, Daniel. 1995. "West Indians in France." In *French and West Indian: Martinique, Guadeloupe, and Guiana Today*, edited by Richard D. E. Burton and Fred Reno. London: Macmillan.

Askew, Kelly. 2002. *Performing the Nation: Swahili Music and Cultural Politics in Tanzania*. Chicago: University of Chicago Press.

Benitez-Rojo, Antonio. 1996. *The Repeating Island: The Caribbean and the Postmodern Perspective*, 2nd ed. Durham, NC: Duke University Press.

Bhabha, Homi K. 1994. "Narrating the Nation." In *Nationalism*, edited by John Hutchinson and Anthony D. Smith. Oxford, UK: Oxford University Press.

Bruner, Edward M. (2001) 2004. "The Maasai and the Lion King: Authenticity, Nationalism, and Globalization in African Tourism." In *Tourists and Tourism: A Reader*, edited by Sharon Bohn Gmelch. Long Grove, IL: Waveland Press.

Burton, Richard D. E. 1995. "The French West Indies à l'heure de l'Europe: An Overview." In *French and West Indian: Martinique, Guadeloupe, and Guiana Today*, edited by Richard D. E. Burton and Fred Reno. London: Macmillan.

Camal, Jerome. "From Gwoka Modènn to Jazz Ka: Music, Nationalism, and Creolization in Guadeloupe." PhD dissertation in Music. Washington University in Saint Louis, Saint Louis, 2011.

Carrigan, Anthony. 2011. *Postcolonial Tourism: Literature, Culture, and Environment*. London: Routledge.

Chatterjee, Partha. 1986. *Nationalist Thought and the Colonial World: A Derivative Discourse?* London: Zed Books for the United Nations University.

Cyrille, Dominique. 2011. "Creole Quadrilles of Guadeloupe, Dominica, Martinique, and Saint Lucia." In *Creolizing Contradance in the Caribbean*, edited by Peter Manuel. Philadelphia: Temple University Press.

Dahomay, Christian. 1997. *Métòd Ka*. Guadeloupe: n.p.

Daniel, Justin. 2001. "The Construction of Dependency: Economy and Politics in the French Antilles." In *Islands at the Crossroads: Politics in the Non-Independent Caribbean*, edited by Aarón Gamaliele Ramos and Angel Israel Rivera. Kingston, Jamaica: Ian Randle Press.

Desmond, Jane C. 1999. *Staging Tourism: Bodies on Display from Waikiki to Sea World*. Chicago: University of Chicago Press.

Dudley, Shannon. 2007. *Music from Behind the Bridge: Steelband Aesthetics and Politics in Trinidad and Tobago*. New York: Oxford University Press.

Duffy, Michelle. 2000. "Lines of Drift: Festival Participation and Performing a Sense of Place." *Popular Music* 19(1): 51–64.

Duffy, Rosaleen. 2004. "Ecotourists on the Beach." In *Tourism Mobilities: Places to Play, Places in Play*, edited by Mimi Sheller and John Urry. London: Routledge.

Glissant, Edouard. (1981) 1997. *Discours Antillais*. Paris: Gallimard. Guilbault, Jocelyne. 1993. *Zouk: World Music in the West Indies*. Chicago: University of Chicago Press.

Hall, C. Michael, and Hazel Tucker. 2004. "Tourism and Postcolonialism: An Introduction." In *Tourism and Postcolonialism: Contested Discourses, Identities, and Representations*, edited by C. Michael Hall and Hazel Tucker. London: Routledge.

Hall, Stuart. 1990. "Cultural Identity and Diaspora." *In Identity: Community, Culture, Difference*, edited by Jonathan Rutherford. London: Lawrence and Wishart.

Harnish, David. 2005. "New Lines, Shifting Identities: Interpreting Change at the Lingsar Festival in Lombok, Indonesia." *Ethnomusicology: Journal of the Society for Ethnomusicology* 49(1): 1–24.

Hintjens, Helen. 1995. "Constitutional and Political Change in the French Caribbean." In *French and West Indian: Martinique, Guadeloupe, and Guiana Today*, edited by Richard D.E. Burton, and Fred Reno. London: Macmillan.

Hollinshead, Keith. 2004. "Tourism and New Sense: World Making and the Enunciative Value of Tourism." In *Tourism and Postcolonialism*, edited by C. Michael Hall and Hazel Tucker. London: Routledge.

Knight, Franklin W., and Colin A. Palmer. 1989. "The Caribbean: A Regional Overview." In *The Modern Caribbean*, edited by Franklin W. Knight, and Colin A. Palmer. Chapel Hill: University of North Carolina Press.

Laumuno, Marie-Helena. 2011. *Gwoka et politique en Guadeloupe: 1960–2003: 40 ans de construction du "pays."* Paris: L'Harmattan.

Lockel, Gerard. 1981. *Traité de gro ka modên.* Baie Mahault: n.p.

——. 2011. *Gwo-Ka Modèn.* Baie Mahault: ADGKM.

Maingot, Anthony P. 1989. "Caribbean International Relations." In *The Modern Caribbean*, edited by Franklin W. Knight and Colin A. Palmer. Chapel Hill: University of North Carolina Press.

Marie, Claude-Valentin, and Lionel Qualité. 2002. "Un quart des personnes nées aux Antilles vit dans l'hexagone." *Antiane* (52): 15–18.

Nettleford, Rex. 1993. *Inward Stretch, Outward Reach: A Voice from the Caribbean.* London: Macmillan Caribbean.

Pitchford, Susan. 2008. *Identity Tourism: Imaging and Imagining the Nation.* Bingley, UK: Emerald Group Publishing.

Pretes, M. 2003. "Tourism and Nationalism." *Annals of Tourism Research* 30(1): 125–142.

Rees, Helen. 1998. "'Authenticity' and the Foreign Audience for Traditional Music in Southwest China." *Journal of Musicological Research* 17(2): 135–161.

Rèpriz. 2012. *Lyannaj pou gwoka: Le dossier de candidature.* Pointe-à-Pitre: Rèpriz.

Rommen, Timothy. 2002. "Nationalism and the Soul: Gospelypso as Independence." *Black Music Research Journal* 22(1): 37–63.

——. 2011. *Funky Nassau: Roots, Routes, and Representation in Bahamian Popular Music.* Berkeley: University of California Press.

Sarkissian, Margaret. 1998. "Tradition, Tourism, and the Cultural Show: Malaysia's Diversity on Display." *Journal of Musicological Research* 17(2): 87–112.

Schnepel, Ellen M. 2004. *In Search of a National Identity: Creole and Politics in Guadeloupe.* Hamburg: Helmut Buske.

Sharpley, Richard. 2004. "Island in the Sun: Cyprus." In *Tourism Mobilities*, edited by Mimi Sheller and John Urry. London: Routledge.

Sheller, Mimi. 2004. "Demobilizing and Remobilizing Caribbean Paradise." In *Tourism Mobilities*, edited by Mimi Sheller and John Urry. London: Routledge.

Sheller, Mimi, and John Urry eds. 2004. *Tourism Mobilities: Places to Play, Places in Play.* London: Routledge.

Stokes, Martin. ed. 1994. *Ethnicity, Identity, and Music: The Musical Construction of Place.* Oxford, UK: Berg.

Stokes, Martin. 1999. "Music, Travel, and Tourism: An Afterword." *The World of Music. Journal of the Department of Ethnomusicology, Otto-Friedrich University of Bamberg* 41(3): 141–155.

Titon, Jeff Todd. 1999. "'The Real Thing': Tourism, Authenticity, and Pilgrimage among the Old Regular Baptists at the 1997 Smithsonian Folklife Festival. The World of Music: Journal of the Department of Ethnomusicology, Otto-Friedrich University of Bamberg* 41(3): 115–139.

Turino, Thomas. 2000. *Nationalists, Cosmopolitans, and Popular Music in Zimbabwe.* Chicago: University Of Chicago Press.

Urry, John, and Jonas Larsen. 2011. *The Tourist Gaze 3.0.* Los Angeles: Sage.

Verdery, Katherine. 1991. *National Ideology Under Socialism: Identity and Cultural Politics in Ceauşescu's Romania*. Berkeley: University of California Press.

William, Jean-Claude. 1997. "Aimé Césaire: les contrariétés de la conscience nationale." In 1946-1996: *Cinquante ans de départementalisation outre-mer*, edited by Fred Constant and Justin Daniel. Paris: L'Harmattan.

Williams, Raymond. 1977. *Marxism and Literature*. Oxford: Oxford University Press.

9

"*Jockomo Fee Na Nay!*"

Afro-Caribbean and Afro-Creole Sensorialities and the Festivalization of New Orleans's Musical Tourism

RUTHIE MEADOWS ■

As the sun set on the second day of the New Orleans Jazz and Heritage Festival in late April, 2012, my sister, a friend, and I—along with thousands of other festival-goers—bottle-necked out of the festival entrance at Sauvage and Fortin streets, following the masses through the oak-lined streets and past the worn, wooden homes of Mid-City toward Esplanade Avenue. On the first street corner, a young, ten-piece brass band caught the exiting crowds before they reached their taxis, hotel shuttles, parked cars, and bicycles, exhorting concert-goers to keep on dancing while taking advantage of the opportunity to self-advertise and pass out CDs. Wearing T-shirts emblazoned with the logo "TBC," the To Be Continued . . . Brass Band intoned an aurally characteristic and decidedly New Orleanian blend of second line "street" playing, with high-tuned, rolling snares, rapid-fire and shuffled bass drum hits, and wailing, interlocking harmonies on their trumpets, trombones, tuba, and saxophones. As many hundreds of tourists merely walked on, a few dozen festival-goers and a handful of local residents stalled around the band to dance to the upbeat, tuba-driven bass hooks and major-keyed, unison-call verses. Together, tourists, a spattering of locals, and the band danced in the street, animated by a celebratory sound that nevertheless belied the dark underbelly of the lyrics:

> I'm in the right now
> Tryin' to get to the not yet . . .
> We all been through somethin'

> We'd rather forget
> All the tears I done seen,
> Coulda made a flood itself . . .
> But the music was always there to help . . . [1]

Localized on the immediate boundary outside the designated spaces of the New Orleans Jazz and Heritage Festival, this performance by the TBC Brass Band wed the musical aesthetics of Afro-Caribbean–derived "street" playing and topical references to the recent traumas of Hurricane Katrina with the complex dynamics of presentational intent within the contexts of musical tourism. Indeed, TBC's "street" sound indexes two complexly interrelated spheres of New Orleans brass band performance: the extensive vernacular networks of Social Aid and Pleasure Clubs, or African American benevolent societies, who have hired brass bands for their processional anniversary parades, funerals, and other social events since the late nineteenth century (Burns 2006; Collins 1996; Schaefer 1977); and, the network of uptown, Mid City, French Quarter, and Central Business District clubs, music venues, convention centers, festival grounds, and other touristic spaces in which the New Orleans brass band sound—and the racialized visuality of the "second line" traditions out of which it is born—serve as symbolically potent aural and visual icons for the city itself (Regis 1999; 2001).[2] As evidence of this iconicity, the logo for the New Orleans Jazz and Heritage Festival (Jazz Fest) employs a silhouetted, touristic image of a second line procession as its backdrop. The logo's iconic sun umbrella and brass trumpet visually ground the festival's authority as a purveyor of New Orleans's unique second line traditions and musical heritage and were, in this case, displayed just a few blocks from the intersection where the TBC performed its own, "street" style of second line music (see Figure 9.1). In this way, the performance of the TBC on the very periphery of Jazz Fest—only, as I later discovered, one week before their scheduled performance *inside* the official festival itself—serves as a potent metaphor for the complex and fraught juncture of vernacular practice, black heritage production, and musical tourism in New Orleans.

The processes by which specific aspects of processional practices in New Orleans—with their important historical and sensorial links to the Afro-Caribbean—have been entextualized (Bauman and Briggs, 2003; Ochoa, 2006) for presentational intent (Hagedorn, 2001) within a music-driven and tourism-oriented New Orleans economy form the basis of this chapter."[3] Specifically, I examine how select sensorial aspects of three Afro-Caribbean-derived New Orleanian vernacular phenomena—(1) the second line parades associated with Social Aid and Pleasure Clubs; (2) second line brass bands; and (3) the Mardi Gras Indians—have been elevated as central aural and visual symbols of New Orleans's own "uniqueness" and sense of authenticity

Figure 9.1 The Stooges Brass Band play for the VIP Ladies and Kids Social Aid and Pleasure Club "Second Line" Parade, March 2013. (Photo by author)

since the 1960s. All three phenomena concretized in the late nineteenth century with strong aesthetic, linguistic, and spiritual ties to Cuba and colonial Saint Domingue, and their sonically and visually rich practices, have been inextricably bound with the emergence of a music-centered tourism industry in New Orleans since the decline of the manufacturing and port-based industries in the 1960s.

The catalyst for an increasingly music-centered tourist economy occurred with the development of the Preservation Hall Jazz Band (est. 1961) and the New Orleans Jazz and Heritage Festival (est. 1970), which now outstrips even the world-famous Mardi Gras as the city's largest source of annual tourist revenue (Regis and Walton 2008), followed by the WWOZ New Orleans Jazz and Heritage Radio Station (est. 1980) and other music-oriented print magazines, touristic media, and festivals since the 1980s. I argue here that the emergence of increasingly music-centered tourist and heritage industries in New Orleans since the 1960s has contributed to the consolidation of what sociologist Kevin Fox Gotham terms a "touristic culture" in New Orleans, or one in which local understandings and assertions of heritage, culture, memory, and authenticity are increasingly implicated in and framed by touristic logics, discourses, and practices (Gotham 2007, 121). Crucially, shifts in the mediations of specific sensorial aspects of these three Afro-Caribbean–derived phenomena for presentational intent have been central to the formation of an increasingly "touristic culture" in New Orleans.

I refer to these specific sensorial aspects here as *sensorialities*. The term builds upon select studies within sensorial anthropology which posit a central, if discretely elaborated, claim that the senses and the human sensorium are foundationally "cultural," historically constituted entities whose "materiality and sociality" differentially mediate human experience (see Classen 1993; 2005; Feld 1990; 1996; Howes 1991; 2003; 2005; Porcello et al. 2010, 52; Seremetakis 1994; Stoller 1989; 1997). Following this assertion, *sensorialities* refer at once to any given sensorial phenomenon (i.e., the sonic), as well as to its inherent interrelatedness to intelligibility within and across given historically constituted and culturally constituted sensorial orders. This notion places the aural, for example, in direct relationship to intelligibility within other realms of sensorial experience—for example, the visual, the haptic, the olfactory, and so on—while also explicitly connecting the embodied experience of the aural and the senses to knowledge-formation (Feld 1996) and the intelligible. The notion of intelligibility inherent to the term *sensorialities* furthermore recognizes heterogeneity in the valences and meanings accorded to any given sensorial phenomenon by discrete historical actors, as is particularly evident in the mediations of Afro-Creole and Afro-Caribbean–inspired sensorialities within New Orleans's increasingly tourism-driven economy.

This chapter examines how the consolidation of Afro-Caribbean and Afro-Creole sensorialities as a central component of touristic—as well as local—notions of authenticity and heritage points at once to the inextricability of music from tourism in New Orleans as well as to the embeddedness of music in powerful "ideologies of aurality" (Ochoa 2005) in which the specifically musical is linked to extra-aural notions of black heritage and Afro-Caribbean or Afro-Creole uniqueness. The interpenetration of touristic logics of heritage production and manufactured authenticity (Kirshenblatt-Gimblett 1998) with local understandings of Afro-Caribbean heritage and Afro-Creole uniqueness raises questions about the specificities of the relationship between "music touristics" and vernacular practice in New Orleans (see Introduction, this volume): to what extent do vernacular practices lie "outside" of the tourist industry itself (i.e., to be commodified), and to what extent do "music touristics" influence vernacular practices themselves, defining notions of musical heritage for tourists and residents alike?

NINETEENTH-CENTURY NEW ORLEANS: INCIPIENT TOURISTICS AMID AFRO-CARIBBEAN AND AFRO-CREOLE SENSORIALITIES

By the late nineteenth century, when New Orleans was forcibly integrated into the Anglo-Saxon United States in the wake of the Civil War, New Orleans already held—and was beginning to actively nurture—a unique place in the national imagination as a site of sensorial and spiritual Afro-Caribbean and Afro-Creole alterity. The alternate history of Louisiana's French (circa 1699–1766) and Spanish (circa 1766–1803) colonial periods formed the bedrock of this sense of alterity by enveloping New Orleans legally, economically, and spiritually within Franco-Caribbean and Hispano-Caribbean colonial spheres. This Franco-Caribbean and Hispano-Caribbean colonial orientation contributed to a history of slaving that was highly divergent from that of the formerly British United States and to alternate legal and racial policies toward New Orleanians of color (Manuel 2009, 41; Midlo Hall 1992; Roberts 1974; Sublette 2008). The extension of Louis XIV's *Code Noir* to Louisiana in 1724, for example, "incorporated people of African descent in St. Domingue and New Orleans into a common French Catholic colonial culture" (Turner 2009, 19), granting legal permission to African slaves and free New Orleans "Creoles" of color to rest on Sundays and holy days, follow Catholic customs in baptisms and burials, and, crucially, incorporate the sensorial poetics of Afro-religious drumming, song, and spiritual dance into their Sunday festivities (Evans 2011; Turner 2009). This allowance stood in marked contrast to the intentional banning of drums within the Ango-Saxon plantation and slave environments of the British, and later American, South—a difference cited by innumerable scholars and musicians alike as impacting the alternate trajectory of New Orleans's rich musical and Afro-sensorial traditions (Berry et al. 2009; Evans 2011; Sublette 2008; Turner 2009).

After the ceding of Louisiana to the United States in 1803, the demography of the nascent city of New Orleans continued to lean substantially toward a Franco-Caribbean make-up, particularly following an influx of Franco-Haitian planters, slaves, and free people of color to the city in 1809. In that year, a racially diverse group of Franco-Haitian whites, their enslaved Africans, and free Haitians of color who had fled Saint Domingue in the wake of the Haitian revolution were expelled from colonial Cuba, and many of them headed to Louisiana (Fiehrer 1979; LaChance 1992). This influx increased New Orleans's population alone from 17,001 in 1806 to 24,552 in 1810 (LaChance 1992, 247). These Franco-Haitian immigrants integrated into and solidified a relatively fluid, three-tiered racial system in antebellum New Orleans consisting of enslaved blacks, free "Creoles" of color, and whites—a tertiary racial system that differed substantially from the binary dynamics of the slave-based economy of the Southern United States (Charters 2008; Long 2006; Turner 2009).

Additionally, these Franco-Haitian slaves and free "Creoles" of color—the majority of whom had direct or familial ties to colonial Saint Domingue—substantiated the Afro-religious sensorial poetics of Haitian *vodou* as mainstays in New Orleans and, particularly, in the legalized Sunday festivities of peoples of African descent that occurred throughout the city following the extension of the *Code Noir* almost a century earlier (Evans 2011). In 1817, a city ordinance restricted the Sunday gatherings that occurred at various sites throughout New Orleans to Congo Square, likely in an attempt to control the feared revolutionary potential of *vodou* in the wake of the Haitian Revolution (Evans 2011; Turner 2009, 21). In Congo Square, the Afro-religious sensorial poetics of Haitian *vodou* met with an array of diverse Afro-religious and, increasingly, Afro-Creole practices, including dances, percussion and stringed instruments, and songs of Kongo-Angolan and Senegambian derivation, as well as earlier iterations of *vodou* brought directly from West Africa by Fon and Yoruba slaves (Evans 2011; Thompson 2005; Sublette 2008, Turner 2009).

These rich, Afro-religious sensorial displays of up to several thousand enslaved and free peoples of African descent in Congo Square shocked numerous white observers who came to New Orleans as visitors in the early 1810s and 1820s. The British-born architect Benjamin Henry Latrobe, for example, who witnessed and wrote of the gathering at Congo Square on Sunday, February 21, 1819, left the most vivid description extant of the ring shouts, drums, stringed instruments, and dances at Congo Square, including drawings of the Kongo-Senegambian *banza,* a stringed instrumental precursor to the banjo, along with sketches of drums that he witnessed there (Latrobe 1980; Evans 2011; Sublette 2008; Thompson 2011). Between 1817 and the 1840s, when the gatherings in Congo Square reportedly ceased, Congo Square emerged as a meeting ground not only for enslaved Africans and some Creoles of color but also for white observers and voyeurs, who "reportedly came by the hundreds, even thousands" to witness the displays of Afro-religious aural and sensorial alterity at the gatherings (Evans 2011, 51). During this period, Congo Square became a "tourist attraction—no doubt one of the first in the city," and caricatured versions of the bodily gestures, dances, instruments, and aural texts witnessed at Congo Square entered the national minstrel circuit through appropriations by white observers (ibid.).

Afro-Caribbean-derived rhythmic cells present at the displays of Congo Square also entered into popular and art compositions by New Orleans bandleaders and composers during the mid-nineteenth century. New Orleans–born composer Louis Moreau Gottschalk, for example, whose mother had escaped from colonial Saint Domingue along with her Afro-Haitian nurse, based his composition "La Bamboula: Danse des Négres" (circa 1844–1845) on a dance he had witnessed in Congo Square during frequent childhood visits (Evans 2011; Sublette 2004). As Sublette notes, "La Bamboula: Danse des Négres" begins with a right-handed *habanera* rhythmic figure, which, along with the Afro-Caribbean rhythmic cells known as the *tresillo* and *cinquillo,* aurally connected nineteenth-century Congo Square—and the larger city of New Orleans—to the Afro-Caribbean spaces of

Havana and Saint Domingue (Floyd 1999; Sublette 2004; Evans 2011; Manuel 2009). As various scholars and musicians have argued, these Caribbean-derived rhythmic cells later transformed into the rhythmic bedrock of several of the most important New Orleans vernacular styles, including the second line or "street" beat of New Orleans brass bands, the Mardi Gras Indians' percussive tambourine rhythms and chants, and the "clave" or "Spanish tinge" of early jazz compositions (Berry et al. 2009; Evans 2011, 117; Sublette 2004; 2008; Washburne 1997). Several of these foundational, Afro-Caribbean-derived, and yet decidedly Creole New Orleanian practices—the "second line" brass bands, the Social Aid and Pleasure Clubs who sponsored their "second line" funeral, anniversary, or celebratory processions, and the Mardi Gras Indians—all appear to have concretized in the 1870s and 1880s a few decades after the banning of the gatherings in Congo Square (Burns 2006; Charters 2008; Regis 1999; 2001; Mitchell 1995; Schaefer 1977).

Significantly, the rise of these vernacular practices between the 1860s and 1890s occurred within a context of forced integration of the city's unique, three-tiered racial system into the binary racial logics and legal restrictions of the Southern United States. Additionally, the emergence of these vernacular practices coincided with the rise of an incipient tourism industry in New Orleans as local elites began making conscious and concerted efforts to promote specific signifiers of the city's unique cultural alterity to draw visitors (Gotham 2007). Both the Mardi Gras carnival celebrations and New Orleans voodoo—a derivate of Haitian *vodou* popularized among New Orleanians of all races and classes in the nineteenth century (Long 2001; 2006)—witnessed commodification as symbolic markers of New Orleans's unique cultural alterity on a national scale (Evans 2011; Gotham 2007). Local elites began promoting Mardi Gras themes in national railroad company advertisements in the 1870s and 1880s and made efforts to "rationalize Carnival" by transforming the previously ad hoc, unorganized carnival celebrations into organized balls and spectator processions (Gotham 2007, 35). The rationalization of Carnival included the founding of such elite, "old-line" Mardi Gras carnival krewes as the Krewe of Rex (1872), the Krewe of Momus (1872), and the Krewe of Proteus (1882) (Gotham 2007; Mitchell 1995). The elite rationalization and commodification of Carnival marked part of a larger process of touristic place promotion that "aimed to aestheticize space and culture and to make both residents and visitors 'New Orleans conscious'" (Gotham 2007, 70). Crucially, this self-conscious promotion of local signifiers of cultural alterity and the "[transformation of] markers of New Orleans authenticity into consumable objects and consumption-based entertainment experiences" (ibid.) marked an effort to raise—and produce—both local and national awareness of New Orleans's nineteenth-century cultural uniqueness and heritage.

Through concerted efforts at touristic place promotion by local merchants, steamboat agents, lawyers, accountants, bankers, and other professional elites (Roach 1996), by the end of the nineteenth century New Orleans already held a special place in the national—and local—imagination as a site of unique, cultural alterity and, accordingly, of touristic consumption and pleasure. During this time, voodoo witnessed commercialization on a national scale as its practices transcended boundaries of race and class locally, with ceremonies advertised in local newspapers and the founding of a firm that "manufactured, advertised, and sold charms along with powders" nationally (Evans 2011, 5). The 1897 creation of Storyville as a designated red light district by the city government marked the additional incorporation of sexual exploitation into the processes of touristic commodification, where it served as a significant tourist attraction until its closing in 1917 (Collins 1996). The emergence of the incipient music that would later be known as "jazz" out of the brass band and second line traditions of the 1890s marked the further incorporation of Afro-Caribbean–derived aural phenomena into the touristic spaces of New Orleans, and, particularly, Storyville, into the early twentieth century (Burns 2006; Collins 1996).

Although the Afro-sensorial gatherings at Congo Square had been among the first touristic sites in mid-century New Orleans, the late-nineteenth century touristic, and particularly elite, place promotion of New Orleans's was decidedly "whitened," with the national advertising of Mardi Gras specifically touting Carnival as a white phenomenon (Gotham 2007; Mitchell 1995; Stanonis 2006). This "whitening" of Mardi Gras reflected the increasingly segregated nature of the officially organized balls and "old-line" krewe parades themselves since the mid-nineteenth century. Despite this, an array of black informal and formal processional organizations flourished on the periphery of the official parades, ranging from what would later consolidate into the city-condoned Zulu Social Aid and Pleasure Club parade to the rogue, peripheral processional practices of the Mardi Gras Indians (LaBorde 2007; Mitchell 1995).

At the end of the nineteenth century and into the twentieth, a rich array of Afro-Caribbean–derived and Afro-Creole practices, including the Mardi Gras Indians, the Social Aid and Pleasure Clubs, and the second line brass bands, emerged alongside—and to an extent, within—a broader context of touristic commodification and corporate development founded upon increasingly consolidated—if contradictory—notions of New Orleans's unique cultural authenticity and heritage. The Afro-Creole sensorialities of these three specific practices, however, and the specificities of their aural alterity formed the backdrop to an incipient tourist industry emerging within a context of heightened racial segregation, and they were not yet that industry's promotional centerpiece. The consolidation of these processional practices as symbolically and sensorially central to a more specifically music-centered tourist economy would begin to emerge in New Orleans only in the mid-twentieth century in tandem with a heightened turn toward tourism as the basis of the city's economy more generally.

MID-CENTURY NEW ORLEANS: JAZZ FEST, PRESERVATION HALL, AND THE SHIFT TOWARD AN AFRO-CREOLE AND AURALLY CENTERED TOURIST ECONOMY

By the 1950s, the tourist industry in New Orleans had consolidated into approximately one-third of an overall three-part urban economy balanced by the petroleum industries and the port industries of military shipbuilding and manufacturing (Pierce 2005; Gotham 2007). With the post-industrial decline of the manufacturing and port industries in the 1960s, along with increased suburbanization, decreasing urban populations, and the threat of economic stagnation, city officials turned to tourism as a primary means to encourage economic growth and urban prosperity, initiating private–public partnerships and forging institutional ties aimed at revitalizing the urban landscape (Gotham 2007). The 1960s also witnessed a burgeoning, white countercultural movement on a national level that would have profound consequences on the development of musical tourism locally, as "roots" authenticity and folk reverence were sought—often through music—as antidotes to a seemingly overly manufactured, lifeless modernity (Regis and Walton 2008, 408; Souther 2006). In New Orleans, the emphatic turn to tourism by city officials during the 1960s and 1970s matched a grassroots organizational effort aimed at historic preservation, heritage production, and the raising of local and extra-local awareness of New Orleans's unique historical and cultural authenticity. This included the founding of Save Our Cemeteries, the Arts Council of New Orleans, the Preservation Resource Center, the Community Arts Center, and, in the realm of the aural, the Jazz and Heritage Foundation and the Preservation Hall Jazz Band (Gotham 2007, 19–20; Souther 2006).

It was during these decades that key figures in the promotion of New Orleans's unique musical heritage were drawn to New Orleans from other U.S. cities, many of them seeking and heralding jazz as an aural and visual emblem of New Orleans's—and, by extension, America's—roots and folk authenticity (Regis and Walton 2008; Souther 2006). Importantly, these music and festival promoters and their heritage-oriented musical ventures collectively initiated a turn toward a more specifically music-centered tourist economy in

New Orleans. The establishment of Preservation Hall in 1961 by Milwaukee native Lorenz "Larry" Borenstein and its takeover by Pennsylvania couple Allan and Sandra Jaffe in 1962, for example, reflected an effort to "protect and honor New Orleans Jazz" in the face of its "[declining] popularity to modern jazz and rock n roll" (Hall History 2010; Souther 2006). The preservationist and folk-roots impetus to honor the "living legends" of authentic and traditional New Orleans-style jazz inspired New York-based music producer George Wein, who began developing the New Orleans Jazz and Heritage Festival in the late 1960s. Wein's partners Allison Miner and Quint Davis, who he met as students through jazz archivist and historian Dick Allen of the Hogan Jazz Archive at Tulane University, developed the "Louisiana Heritage Fair" component of the festival to pay homage to New Orleans and Louisiana's unique culinary, crafts, and "folk" heritage (Miner and Smith 1997; Regis and Walton 2008; Smith 1991; McCaffrey 2005). Significantly, Miner and Davis turned to New Orleans's processional second line traditions, brass bands, and Mardi Gras Indians as aural and visual emblems of New Orleans's unique "folk" heritage (Miner and Smith 1997; Regis and Walton 2008; Smith 1991). This initiated a process that, with the increasing economic success of the festival over the next four decades, contributed to consolidating Afro-Caribbean and Afro-Creole sensorialities as central components of touristic—as well as local—notions of New Orleans's unique authenticity and black, "roots" heritage.

The appearance of Mardi Gras Indian tribes in the first New Orleans Jazz and Heritage Festival in 1970 contributed greatly to a newfound audibility and visibility of this highly secretive, spatially segregated, and hierarchical Afro-Caribbean and Afro-Creole "masking" practice (Berry 1988; Draper 1973; McCaffrey 2005; Mitchell 1995; Turner 2009). The Mardi Gras Indians appear to have emerged as a processional phenomenon by, at the latest, 1883, when Chief Becate Batiste, who was allegedly of mixed African and Native American descent, founded the original Creole Wild West Mardi Gras Indian Tribe. The Creole Wild West served as an organizational, aesthetic, and spiritual model for other predominantly African American tribes in the late nineteenth and twentieth centuries (Berry 1988; Turner 2009). The Mardi Gras Indian phenomenon, then, emerged within late-nineteenth century contexts of increased binary racial segregation and elite commercialization of the decades-old, informal practices of Mardi Gras itself (see Figure 9.2). Additionally, this period witnessed the persecution and criminalization of Haitian *vodou*/New Orleans voodoo, and select aspects of the sensorial and Afro-religious poetics of *vodou*/voodoo were clandestinely incorporated into the sequin arts, religious and symbolic weaponry, and Haitian Kreyol-influenced linguistic chants of the late-nineteenth and early-twentieth century Mardi Gras Indian tribes (Turner 2009).

Figure 9.2 The Creole Wild West Mardi Gras Indians perform at The New Orleans Jazz and Heritage Festival, April 2012. (Photo courtesy of Leah Meadows)

By the opening of the Jazz and Heritage Festival in 1970, Mardi Gras Indian tribes comprised of largely lower-class, African American males had been "masking" for almost a century, spending a full year sewing intricate, feathered and beaded costumes and practicing chants and percussive rhythms in preparation for the competitive aesthetic and aural battles of Mardi Gras day (Berry 1998; Draper 1973; Mitchell 1995; Turner 2009). At the time, however, the Mardi Gras Indian phenomenon was largely unknown outside of the racially segregated neighborhoods in which it occurred—though the Krèyol-influenced language of Mardi Gras Indian chants had bubbled up into well-known New Orleans rhythm and blues singles such as Sugarboy Crawford's 1954 hit "Jockomo" and the Dixie Cups 1965 "Iko Iko" (Lipsitz 1990). The incorporation of the aural and visual display of the Mardi Gras Indians in full "masking" costume at the original Jazz Fest reflected an effort on the part of festival organizers Miner and Davis to display the Afro-Caribbean-derived sensorialities of the Indians as evidence of New Orleans's authentic "folk" and roots "heritage";

at the same time, however, the public display of the Mardi Gras Indians at Jazz Fest also formed part of a gradual process of increased audibility and visibility of the Mardi Gras Indians within the New Orleans musical mainstream during the early- and mid-1970s (Draper 1973). Bo Dollis's release of the 45 rpm single "Handa Wanda" as chief of the Wild Magnolias in 1970, for example, marked the first recording by a Mardi Gras Indian Tribe. This release was followed by the recording of The Meters hit "Hey Pocky Way" in 1974, which took its chorus from a Mardi Gras Indian chant, as well as the Neville Brothers and The Meters' recording of a full, funk-inflected album with Mardi Gras Indian chief George Landry, of the Wild Tchoupitoulas tribe, in 1976 (Berry 1998; Wild Tchoupitoulas 1976).

Significantly, the inclusion of second line brass bands in the first years of the New Orleans Jazz and Heritage Festival occurred during a period when the Social Aid and Pleasure Club and brass band processions were in serious decline. This decline followed the economic waning of the manufacturing and port industries in the 1960s and the social climate of the post–Civil Rights movement, when older, "traditional" brass band players associated with the revivalist impetus of the Preservation Hall Jazz Band held "Uncle Tom" connotations for black youth (Burns 2006, 5; Souther 2006). New Orleans jazz veteran Danny Barker is generally credited with reviving the ailing brass band and second line movements during the 1970s by organizing and leading youth brass bands in conjunction with local churches. His Fairvew Baptist Church Brass Band performed at Jazz Fest throughout the 1970s, spurning offshoots of other youth bands, including the Hurricane Brass Band, the Roots of Jazz Brass Band, and the Tambourine and Fan Youth Center (Burns 2006; Miner and Smith 1997). The Hurricane Brass Band and other youth brass band offshoots were encouraged by these performance opportunities and worked to make brass band music more "hip" and danceable for young people (Burns 2006; Miner and Smith 1997; Souther 2006). To do so, they inserted rhythm and blues and funk themes such as Ray Charles's "I Got a Woman" or The Meters' Mardi Gras Indian-inspired hit "Hey Pocky Way" into the brass band repertoire, also eliminating the 32-bar AABA jazz structure and chord changes of the traditional brass band repertoire in favor of static, non-teleological riffs and tuba-driven bass ostinatos. This new "street" style of brass band playing came to fruition with the creation of the highly successful Dirty Dozen Brass Band, an offshoot of the Hurricane Brass Band, in the late 1970s, followed by the Rebirth Brass Band in the 1980s (Burns 2006).

Importantly, the revitalization of brass band playing among New Orleanian youth, which also accompanied an increase in the activities of the Social Aid and Pleasure Clubs, was linked to a larger context of musical revitalization and music-centered heritage and touristic production in New Orleans in the

1970s and 1980s. In addition to the increasing prestige of the New Orleans Jazz and Heritage Festival throughout the 1970s, the uptown club Tipitina's opened in 1977 as a venue dedicated to preserving New Orleans's unique vernacular musics—and particularly the Caribbean-inflected New Orleans "rhumba"-blues piano playing of club icon Professor Longhair (History in the Music 2013; Keyes 2008). Additionally, the WWOZ Jazz and Heritage Station (90.7 FM), developed by Texas-based community radio producer Jerry Brock, opened in 1980 as a community-based radio station dedicated to New Orleans's unique vernacular musics and heritage (Burns 2006; McCaffrey 2005). With the establishment of WWOZ in 1980, Brock partnered with music activist and jazz veteran Danny Barker to bring both "traditional" New Orleans jazz musicians and younger "street"-style brass bands on air (Burns 2006). Both Brock and Allison Miner, of the New Orleans Jazz and Heritage Festival Foundation, were instrumental in jumpstarting the local, national, and international recording and touring careers of the Dirty Dozen Brass Band, whom Brock first introduced to uptown audiences at Tipitina's in 1982, and Rebirth Brass Band, whom Miner managed for five years in the 1980s (Burns 2006; McCaffrey 2005). In 1987, WWOZ transferred its license to a corporation established by the New Orleans Jazz and Heritage Festival Foundation, partnering with the foundation to become the WWOZ New Orleans Jazz and Heritage Station (McCaffrey 2005; History of WWOZ 2013).

The establishment of the New Orleans Jazz and Heritage Festival (1970), Tipitina's music venue (1977), the WWOZ New Orleans Jazz and Heritage Station (1980), and other music-centered print media such as *Offbeat* (1988) in the 1970s and 1980s marked a shift within the New Orleans's tourist economy toward a more specifically music-centered and aurally led industry. Through the festivalization and musicalization of New Orleans tourism, these institutions contributed to consolidating Afro-Caribbean and Afro-Creole sensorialities as central components of both local and extra-local notions of New Orleans's authenticity and black heritage. The emergence of Afro-Caribbean–derived and Afro-Creole sensorialities as validating emblems of Jazz Fest and of a larger, increasingly music-centered tourist industry furthermore complemented the revitalization of the vernacular processional practices themselves, with the Social Aid and Pleasure Clubs and second line parades that employed "street"-style, young brass bands flourishing through the 1980s, 1990s, and 2000s (Burns 2006; Regis 1999; 2001; Sakakeeny 2008). However, these Afro-Creole processional practices were mediated within the festival spaces, aural and print media, and performance venues of New Orleans's music-centered tourist economy in complicated—and often paradoxical—ways, leading to the development of wide sensorial gaps between the New Orleans "second line" in festivalized/touristic versus street-based contexts.

FESTIVALIZED MUSIC TOURISTICS: PARADOXES OF VISIBILITY AND ERASURE, AUDIBILITY AND ABSENCE IN THE NEW ORLEANS'S "SECOND LINE"

The New Orleans Jazz and Heritage Festival emerged as a roots-oriented commercial, racial, and social project aimed at celebrating, defining, and preserving the "folk"—that is, the "authentic, native, and real" in New Orleans (Regis and Walton 2008, 400). Since the festival's inception within the preservationist and roots-oriented environment of the 1960s, Jazz Fest has grown into "an economic powerhouse" in New Orleans, one "that wields corporate-like power within the New Orleans economy and is even a recognizable power in the national and global music marketplaces" (ibid.). Jazz Fest brings in more tourist dollars to the city than any other annual event—including the world-famous Mardi Gras—with over $300 million tourist dollars generated annually by hundreds of thousands of visitors (Plaisance 2012b; Regis and Walton 2008).

Since its inception in 1970, Jazz Fest has also been instrumental in consolidating music as not supplemental to but constitutive of an increasingly festivalized New Orleans economy, which now depends upon an annual calendar of over a dozen music-centered festivals for its five-billion-dollar-a-year tourist industry (Plaisance 2012b; Schultz and Day 2010). These annual festivals include French Quarter Fest (est. 1984), the Essence Music Festival (est. 1995), Satchmo Summer Fest (est. 2001), the Voodoo Music Experience (est. 1999), the New Orleans Cajun-Zydeco Festival (est. 2007), and many others. A 2007 study demonstrated that of the top ten highest-grossing tourist events held annually in New Orleans, fully four of them are music festivals, including, in order of economic importance, Jazz Fest, the Essence Music Festival, French Quarter Fest, and the Voodoo Music Experience (Webster 2007a–d). Jazz Fest, then, as the earliest-founded and largest-grossing annual music festival, spearheaded the festivalization of New Orleans's musical tourism and continues to have a "proportional year-round economic impact on musicians, craftspeople, and the city as a whole" (Regis and Walton 2008, 402).

Intimately associated with Jazz Fest's image and brand—and its ideological production of the "folk"—are the Afro-Creole and Afro-Caribbean-derived sensorial poetics of the cities' unique second line processions, including the Social Aid and Pleasure Clubs, the second line brass bands, and the Mardi Gras Indians. The Jazz Fest logo, which employs a silhouette of second liners holding iconic sun umbrellas and a brass trumpet, serves as an emblem of New Orleans's unique, Afro-Creole visual and aural authenticity, while also grounding the festival's authority as a site in which festival-goers can directly experience New Orleans's unique vernacular practices and musical traditions. Inside the festival grounds themselves, Jazz Fest hires Social Aid and Pleasure Clubs led by second line brass bands as well as Mardi Gras Indian tribes to parade through the Fairgrounds for the benefit of festival-goers, a practice that dates to the festival's inception in the early 1970s when the Young Men Olympian, the Jolly Bunch, the Buckjumpers, and the Gentlemen of Leisure Social Aid & Pleasure Clubs paraded with the Olympia Brass Band or the Majestic Brass Band (Miner and Smith 1997; Smith 1991). Jazz Fest attendees continue to join in these second lines as they proceed annually through the festival grounds in imitation of the "joiners" who give name to the actual Social Aid and Pleasure Club parades themselves (Regis 1999; 2001). Alternatively, festival-goers catch performances of the same brass bands and Mardi Gras Indian tribes on festival stages or admire the beading techniques of the Mardi Gras Indians' costumes (see Figure 9.3) on display at the festival's varied heritage- and folk-centered "marketplaces" and "villages" (McCaffrey 2005).

The Afro-Creole and Afro-Caribbean-derived sensorial poetics of the Social Aid and Pleasure Clubs, the second line brass bands, and the Mardi Gras Indians have entered into New Orleans's festival and touristic spaces in

Figure 9.3 The Furious Five Social Aid and Pleasure Club parade in a "second line" through the Fairgrounds Race Track at Jazz Fest, April 2012. (Photo by author)

complex—and often paradoxical—ways. The proliferation of staged Social Aid and Pleasure Club parades within the festival spaces of Jazz Fast did not, for example, contribute to an increased awareness of the street-based anniversary parades and funeral processions occurring contemporaneously in New Orleans's spatially segregated neighborhoods. Rather, as anthropologist Helen Regis argues, these touristic re-presentations paradoxically served to "conceal the popular, street-based tradition" behind "a minstrel-like show" that framed the jazz funeral as an antiquated and "dying" tradition (Regis 1999, 473; 2001). By the 1970s and 1980s, staged second lines abounded within the city's touristic French Quarter and convention centers, which multiplied in number along with downtown and French Quarter hotels since the touristic turn of the 1960s (Gotham 2007, 168; Souther 2006). This contributed to the transformation of the second line into an aural and visual emblem of New Orleans within Jazz Fest as well as in other touristic spaces. As Regis argues, this process coincided with a photographic turn toward black-and-white depictions of the second-line "jazz" funeral as a timeless—and antiquated—tradition, a process that denied the coevalness of the contemporary, street-based parades and contributed to the "continued invisibility of the organic, street-based tradition to the mainstream cultural life of the city" (Regis 1999; Fabian 1983; Regis 2001, 767).

The actual, street-based Social Aid and Pleasure Club and second-line brass band parades had flourished in New Orleans since at least the early 1980s, when youth, "street"-style playing brass bands such as the Hurricane Brass Band, the Dirty Dozen Brass Band, and the Rebirth Brass Band revived the ailing processional idiom in "back of town" club performances and Social Aid and Pleasure Club parades (Burns 2006). Between the 1980s and early 2000s, over fifty Social Aid and Pleasure Clubs organized annual anniversary second line parades on Sundays between August and April, easily attracting several thousand neighborhood "joiners" along with the Social Club and brass band participants. These anniversary parades furthermore accompanied a vibrant yearly calendar of dances, fundraisers, birthday celebrations, funerals, and other events put on by the Social Aid and Pleasure Clubs or other neighborhood residents (Burns 2006; Regis 1999; 2001, 755). The entextualization of the "jazz funeral" as a dying tradition within touristic, black-and-white photography and the staging of "minstrel-like show[s]" of the second line as a timeless tradition within Jazz Fest and New Orleans's convention centers belied the flourishing—and yet spatially segregated—practices of the actual Social Aid and Pleasure Clubs themselves (Regis 1999, 473).

The paradoxical wedding of increased visibility and simultaneous erasure in the iconicity of the New Orleans second line relied upon mediating select sensorial aspects of these processional traditions, such as the "bead-bedecked parasol" with its Afro-sensorial links to the sun umbrellas of colonial Benin

(Berry 1988, 7) or, within the realm of the aural, "traditional" and "street"-styles of brass band playing as markers of New Orleans's Afro-Caribbean-derived alterity, while excluding other, crucial aspects that gave meaning to the contemporary parades. Within the realm of the visual, commemorative banners, ribbons, pins, and memorial T-shirts with large, colored photographs of the recently deceased—both old and young—were increasingly important within the second line parades of the 1990s and early 2000s but visibly absent from the staged, mimetic second lines of New Orleans's touristic spaces (Regis 2001, 764). As Regis argues, these visual memorializations grounded the aural and spatial take-over of thousands of black, second line "joiners" and Social Club members in New Orleans's streets as, at once, mass laments to the loss of young life to gang violence and police brutality within contexts of extreme economic decline and citywide corruption and, simultaneously, mass celebrations honoring those who had led lives of "respect and dignity" in the face of urban plagues (770). In the realm of the aural, the sonic mingling of "street"-style brass band music with car stereos and PA systems blasting New Orleans's bounce and hip hop along parade routes (Sakakeeny 2008, 202), the shouts of hundreds or even thousands of second liners following the bands' verses and choruses, the stomping of feet against pavement—or on top of cars—while dancing the "second line" steps, and the hitting of stop signs and other material emblems of legal and civic order in New Orleans's streets with sticks or found objects (Regis 2001) combined to enact a sensorial experience with highly discrete social, racial, and ideological implications from those found in the staged second lines of New Orleans's festivalized and touristic spaces (see Figure 9.4).

These paradoxes of visibility and erasure and audibility and absence within the festivalized second line speak, on the one hand, to an experience of Jazz Fest predicated upon an "imaginary leveling of difference," or one in which overwhelmingly white festival-goers can share the same spaces and enjoy the same musics with performers "who in everyday life are widely separated from each other" by race and class (Regis and Walton 2008, 427). Within the festival grounds, Jazz Fest attendees can enjoy seemingly unmediated experiences of blackness while ignoring the structural inequalities that plague the neighborhoods and extra-festival spaces in which actual Social Aid and Pleasure Club and second line funeral processions occur. As numerous scholars have theorized, this "erasure of uncomfortable references to poverty, inequality . . . [and] structured privilege" is often inherent to the processes of heritage production and tourist marketing in general (Kirshenblatt-Gimblett 1998; Regis and Walton 2008, 427). However, as Regis and Walton note, this imaginary leveling of difference can alternately be read as forming part of a utopian social and racial project in which "radically different racial and social relations are imagined" within the spaces of the festival even as "entrenched structural inequalities are

Figure 9.4 VIP King Dion "Spiff" Walker presides over the Ladies and Kids Social Aid and Pleasure Club annual anniversary parade, March 2013. (Photo by author)

ignored" (Regis and Walton 2008, 400). Importantly, this utopian claim to music as an aural embodiment of cross-racial and cross-class transcendence grounds the appeal of the Jazz Fest experience while also extending to New Orleans's music-centered touristic marketing in general—a phenomenon that reached particular poignancy in the media coverage following Hurricane Katrina, when music was framed as emblematic of New Orleans's purported "will to carry on" (Berry et al. 2009; Spera 2011; Swenson 2011).

On the other hand, these paradoxes of visibility/erasure and audibility/absence in mediations of the second line speak to the complexities of shifting modes of presentational intent within New Orleans's diverse performance contexts. The notion of presentational intent here draws upon Katherine Hagedorn's formulation of "sacred intent" as a means of examining the complex, shifting, and ambiguous place of the sacred in Afro-Cuban religious and folkloric performance (Hagedorn 2001, 6). In her study, Hagedorn theorizes sacred and secular performances as informing each other in the invocation of the sacred, and she examines the presence or absence of the sacred within discrete performance contexts from the perspective of performers' and religious adherents' own "intent." New Orleans's second line processions hold overtly secular as well as sacred dimensions;[4] however, the importance of intent in the mediation and enactment of Afro-Caribbean-derived, Afro-Creole, and other aural, tactile, and visual sensorialities that give second line processions their meaning and performative weight is crucial in examining the complexities that lie at the crux of second line performance in both street-based and overtly touristic contexts.

For brass band musicians in particular, the performative multiplicity inherent to shifting modes of presentational intent is not entirely new. In the late nineteenth century, the black-edited newspaper *The Weekly Pelican* documented brass bands as performing second line musics within highly diverse performative contexts—and often on the same day—in functions that included debutante and Carnival balls, "fish fries," "ball games," church events, private parties, Social Aid and Pleasure Club parades, and second line funerals (Schaefer 1977, 28; Raeburn 1998). Following the push toward the commodification of Carnival for touristic purposes in the late nineteenth-century (Gotham 2007; Stanonis 2006), the aesthetics of New Orleans's wailing brass bands also entered the aural spaces of white neighborhoods during the weeks preceding Mardi Gras (Raeburn 1998). By the 1910s and 1920s, the popularity of jazz, which was born from and wedded to the highly idiosyncratic aesthetics of New Orleans's brass band music (Schaefer 1977; Burns 2006), further enabled the entrance of brass band musicians and music into upper-class, white, high-society dancehalls (Raeburn 1998). In ways, the shifting modes of presentational intent inherent to brass band performances in the late-nineteenth and early-twentieth centuries mirror that of contemporary brass band performance today, in which groups such as Rebirth Brass Band or the Hot 8 might play three or four different events—a Social Aid and Pleasure Club parade, a Tulane University fraternity party, and two or three stacked, night-time club shows—all within the same twenty-four-hour period (Sakakeeny 2008; Burns 2006).

What is new about musicians' and artists' presentational intent over the last five decades is the emplacement of brass band performances and Mardi Gras Indian "masking" practices within what Gotham, Reed, and others argue as the consolidation of a more specifically "touristic culture" in New Orleans since the 1960s—or one in which local understandings and assertions of heritage, culture, memory, and authenticity are increasingly implicated in and framed by touristic logics, discourses, and practices (Gotham, 2007, 121; Reed 2011). If Afro-Creole and Afro-Caribbean–derived aural and other sensorial phenomena formed the backdrop to—if not the explicit centerpiece of—a nascent tourist industry in New Orleans in the late-nineteenth and early-twentieth centuries, they became explicitly central, symbolically and sensorially, to the emergence of a music-driven and festivalized tourist industry in New Orleans since the 1960s. This process implicates second line and Mardi Gras Indian performances within increasingly overlapping logics of touristic as well as local assertions of black heritage, collective memory, and Afro-Creole authenticity—even as wide gaps continue to separate the sensorialities of these street-based processions from club-based, festivalized, and touristic performances.

"SHALLOW WATER OH MAMA": HURRICANE KATRINA AND AFRO-CARIBBEAN AND AFRO-CREOLE SENSORIALITIES

In the wake of Hurricane Katrina, the entextualizations of second line and Mardi Gras Indian practices within festivalized performances and touristic media shifted further as the actual street-based processions of Social Aid and Pleasure Clubs, second line brass bands, and Mardi Gras Indians came under the media lens both locally and nationally. Amid the threat of perceived cultural loss, street-based second line processions—and not only the mimetic, antiquated representations of the "jazz funeral" as a dying tradition—entered mainstream consciousness as symbolic emblems of New Orleans's unique cultural heritage via locally and nationally based aural, visual, filmic, and digital media.

When Regis conducted her extensive fieldwork on second line and Social Aid and Pleasure Club processions in the 1990s and early 2000s, she noted a gap between the rich, sensorial displays of second line processions within largely black, "back of town" neighborhoods and those put on for tourists and middle and upper-class New Orleans locals in uptown clubs, touristic spaces, and festivals. Even as second line and brass band musics became iconic visual and aural emblems of the "festive state" of the city (Guss 2000), the massive, weekly second lines of several thousands of Black New Orleanians through New Orleans's streets remained largely unknown to a significant, and particularly, white portion of New Orleans's residents (Regis 1999; 2001; Regis and Walton 2008, 432). Regis stated the following in 2001:

> Most white residents of the city have never been to such a second-line parade and have little or no awareness of the significance of this black tradition, an astonishing pattern I gradually came to recognize through numerous conversations with friends, neighbors, coworkers, classmates, and students in New Orleans over a period of ten years. (2001, 456)

As an undergraduate at Tulane University between 2001 and 2005, I can attest to this, as my regular attendance at brass band and Mardi Gras Indian shows in uptown clubs, in the CBD neighborhood, in the French Quarter, and in Mid City—the Rebirth Brass Band on Tuesdays at the Maple Leaf, the Soul Rebels on Thursdays at Les Bon Temps Roulé, the Dirty Dozen and Hot 8 at Tipitina's or the Howlin' Wolf, the Mardi Gras Indians at the Maple Leaf, French Quarter Fest, and Jazz Fest—did not signify any corresponding awareness on my part of the massiveness of the contemporary second line processions in other neighborhoods or the significance of brass band music to these processions. As a student—a liminal designation placing me somewhere between uptown resident and extended-stay tourist—brass band and Mardi Gras Indian musics were consistently aurally present and yet this presence did not correspond to increased visibility or audibility of the street-based processional practices via extensive local or national media coverage.

In the wake of Hurricane Katrina, however, a powerful and dual narrative of New Orleans emerged that led to shifts in the entextualizations of these processional practices within New Orleans's mainstream media and within the city's touristic and festivalized performance spaces. National media coverage following the disaster simultaneously framed New Orleans as, on the one hand, a "Third World backwater" plagued by economic stagnation, endemic political corruption, and national indifference and, on the other, as a cultural mecca of Afro-Creole authenticity and musical flourishing on the verge of loss (Berry et al. 2009, xii; Reed 2011; Spera 2011; Swenson 2011). Although already selectively elevated as emblematic of New Orleans's unique Afro-Creole authenticity, the processional and musical practices of the Mardi Gras Indians and the street-based second line processions witnessed novel forms of visibility and audibility within this post-Katrina context of national media scrutiny.

David Simon's HBO Series *Tremé,* which premiered in April 2010, was particularly influential in mediating the Mardi Gras Indians, brass band musicians, and street-based second line processions for a national viewing audience, also influencing shifts in their subsequent presences within New Orleans's festivalized and touristic spaces. Thematically, *Tremé* weds the dual Katrina narrative of New Orleans's political corruption, economic stagnation, and black abandonment with touristic—and, increasingly, local—assertions of New Orleans's Afro-Creole and Caribbean-derived authenticity (Lynell 2005; Reed 2011). Mardi Gras Indians and New Orleans's second line and brass band musicians serve as principal protagonists within the highly music-inflected narrative drama. Following the success of *Tremé,* the Mardi Gras Indians in particular witnessed increased visibility and audibility on a national scale, influencing their elevated aural and visual presences within the New Orleans Jazz and Heritage Festival as well as other local print and digital media. In 2012, the Mardi Gras Indians were featured at Jazz Fest's Cultural Exchange Pavilion, a folk-heritage display usually reserved for countries such as Haiti, Martinique, and Brazil, whose cultures "resonate" with that of New Orleans (Dunn 2012; MacCash 2012). The explicit featuring of the Mardi Gras Indians in the Pavilion—along with their chants, costumes, and Haitian-derived beading techniques (Turner

2009)—responded directly to increased local and national interest following their incorporation into the *Tremé* series (Plaisance 2012a).

In 2010, the WWOZ Jazz and Heritage Radio Station incorporated the "Takin' It to the Streets" program into their station programming and web site, advertising and publishing detailed parade routes for the street-based Social Aid and Pleasure Club anniversary parades, with block-to-block schedules for bar stops and turns, along with practice locations and parade schedules for the Mardi Gras Indians. The incorporation of pictures, parade routes, and practice times of the actual, street-based processions and second lines into the city's heritage-centered aural and digital media marked a shift in the entextualizations of the city's street-based processions within New Orleans's mediated sphere. The relative erasure of the street-based processions that accompanied the icon-ization of the "second line" as a touristic and festivalized emblem between the 1970s and early 2000s moved toward a desire to showcase the actual, contem-porary street-based processions in the wake of the perceived cultural losses of Hurricane Katrina. WWOZ's interest in and advertising of the street-based second line within New Orleans's varied neighborhoods following Hurricane Katrina furthermore accompanied the increased visibility and audibility of these processions in other local and extra-local mediations, including the City of New Orleans's Official Tourism web site, *Gambit Weekly, Offbeat* magazine, and other local digital and print publications (Cotton 2012; Offbeat 2011; Super Sunday 2013).

CONCLUSION

When the young, ten-piece To Be Continued . . . Brass Band performed for exiting festival-goers outside of the New Orleans Jazz and Heritage Festival in April, 2012, their street-corner performance aurally and sensorially enacted a long history of performative multiplicity and shifting presentational intent within diverse nineteenth-, twentieth-, and twenty-first-century contexts of New Orleans second line brass band performance. At the same time, their into-nation of a "street" style of brass band playing on the periphery of the official festival grounds placed their performance at the fraught juncture of "music touristics" and vernacular practice in New Orleans (see Introduction, this vol-ume). Since the 1960s, the Afro-Caribbean-derived and Afro-Creole sensorial poetics of New Orleans's diverse processional practices—including "second line" brass bands—have been elevated as central symbolic emblems of New Orleans's unique culture and heritage within an increasingly festivalized and music-centered tourist industry. This process implicates second line proces-sions, brass band musics, and Mardi Gras Indian "masking" practices within increasingly overlapping logics of touristic promotion with local assertions of black heritage and Afro-Creole authenticity. In the wake of the perceived cultural losses of Hurricane Katrina, New Orleans's unique second line practices came under further scrutiny as the actual, street-based processions and Mardi Gras Indian performances received national—and heightened local—media coverage. This preservationist impetus further consolidated Afro-Caribbean-derived and Afro-Creole sensorialities as central symbolic emblems of New Orleans's unique cultural authenticity and black heritage within post-Katrina contexts of musically centered and festivalized tourism.

NOTES

1. To Be Continued . . . Brass Band. "ToBeContinued." *To Be Continued Brass Band.* Independent label (2013).
2. As Helen Regis describes, the term "second line" is an ambiguous term that refers to "multiple dimensions of the same phenomenological reality" in New Orleans (Regis 2001, 755). The term may refer to, at once, the funeral or anniversary processions sponsored by Social Aid and Pleasure Clubs, the dance steps associated with these processions, the "joiners" or followers who follow the "first line," consisting of the Social Aid and Pleasure Club members and the hired brass band, or the "second line" beat or syncopated rhythm associated with brass band musics. See Regis 1999; 2001; and Evans, 2011.
3. In her theorization of the "aural public sphere" in Latin America (Ochoa, 2006), Ana María Ochoa reframes Bauman and Briggs's (2003) term "entextualization" within the realm of the aural by proposing it as a means to refer to the "cultural construction of a bounded, sonorous item" from an overall "circulation of sound" (Ochoa, 2006: 805). Ochoa's emphasis on acts of capturing, framing, bounding, and (re-)bounding within processes of "entextualization" speak here to the complex processes of mediation of New Orleans's processional practices within an increasingly tourism-driven economy.
4. See Turner (2009) for an argument on the explicitly sacred dimensions of "jazz religion" within the second line and in Mardi Gras Indian processions.

REFERENCES

Bauman, Richard, and Charles L. Briggs. 2003. *Voices of Modernity Language Ideologies and the Politics of Inequality.* Cambridge, UK: Cambridge University Press.

Berry, Jason. 1988. "African Cultural Memory in New Orleans Music." *Black Music Research Journal* 8(1): 3–12.

Berry, Jason, Johnathan Foose, and Tad Jones. 2009. *Up From the Cradle of Jazz: New Orleans Music Since World War II.* Lafayette: University of Louisiana at Lafayette Press.

Burns, Mick. 2006. *Keeping the Beat on the Street: The New Orleans Brass Band Renaissance.* Baton Rouge: Louisiana State University Press.

Charters, Samuel Barclay. 2008. *A Trumpet Around the Corner: The Story of New Orleans Jazz.* Jackson: University Press of Mississippi.

Classen C. 1993. *Worlds of Sense: Exploring the Senses in History and Across Cultures.* London: Routledge.

——. 2005. *The Book of Touch.* New York: Berg.

Collins, R. 1996. *New Orleans Jazz: A Revised History: The Development of American Music from the Origin to the Big Bands.* New York: Vantage Press.

Cotton, Red. 2012. "Sunday: Sudan Second Line Parade." *Gambit: The Best of New Orleans.* November 9. Accessed March 9, 2013. http://www.bestofneworleans.com/blogofneworleans/archives/2012/11/09/sunday-sudan-second-line-parade.

Draper, David Elliott. 1973. *The Mardi Gras Indians: The Ethnomusicology of Black Associations in New Orleans.* Ann Arbor, MI: University Microfilms.

Dunn, Sydni. 2012. "Cultural Exchange Pavilion Spotlights Mardi Gras Indians." *The Times Picayune*, April 28.

Evans, Freddi Williams. 2011. *Congo Square: African Roots in New Orleans.* Lafayette: University of Louisiana at Lafayette Press.

Fabian, Johannes. 1983. *Time and the Other: How Anthropology Makes Its Object.* New York: Columbia University Press.

Feld S. 1990 [1982]. *Sound and Sentiment: Birds, Weeping, Poetics, and Song in Kaluli Expression.* Philadelphia: University of Pennsylvania Press.

——. 1996. "Waterfalls of Song: An Acoustemology of Place Resounding in Bosavi, Papua New Guinea." In *Senses of Place*, edited by Steven Feld and Keith H. Basso, 91–135. Santa Fe, NM: School of American Research Press.

Fiehrer, Thomas M. 1979. "The African Presence in Colonial Louisiana: An Essay on the Continuity of Caribbean Culture." In *Louisiana's Black Heritage*, edited by Robert MacDonald et al. New Orleans: Louisiana State Museum.

Floyd, Samuel A., Jr. 1999. "Black Music in the Circum-Caribbean." *American Music* 17(1): 1–38.

Gotham, Kevin Fox. 2007. *Authentic New Orleans: Tourism, Culture, and Race in the Big Easy.* New York: New York University Press.

Guss, Davis. 2000. *The Festive State: Race, Ethnicity, and Nationalism as Cultural Performance.* Berkeley: University of California Press.

Hagedorn, Katherine J. 2001. *Divine Utterances: The Performance of Afro-Cuban Santeria.* Washington, DC: Smithsonian Institution Press.

"Hall History." 2010. *Preservation Hall History.* Preservation Hall. Accessed March 9, 2013. http://www.preservationhall.com/hall/hall_history/index.aspx.

"History of WWOZ." 2013. *New Orleans WWOZ 90.7 FM.* New Orleans WWOZ 90.7 FM. Accessed March 9, 2013. http://www.wwoz.org/about/history.

"History in the Music." 2013. *Tipitina's.* Tipitina's Foundation. Accessed March 9, 2013. http://www.tipitinas.com/history-music.

Howes D. ed. 1991. *Varieties of Sensory Experience: A Sourcebook in the Anthropology of the Senses.* Toronto: University of Toronto Press.

Howes D. 2003. *Sensual Relations: Engaging the Senses in Culture and Social Theory.* Ann Arbor: University of Michigan Press.

——. 2005. *Empire of the Senses: The Sensual Culture Reader.* Oxford, UK: Berg.

Keyes, Cheryl. 2008. "Funkin' with Bach: The Impact of Professor Longhair on Rock'n'Roll." In *The Funk Era and Beyond: New Perspectives on Black Popular Culture*, edited by Tony Bolden. New York: Palgrave Macmillan.

Kirshenblatt-Gimblett, Barbara. 1998. *Destination Culture: Tourism, Museums, and Heritage*. Berkeley: University of California Press.

Laborde, Errol. 2007. *Krewe: The Early New Orleans Carnival: Comus to Zulu*. Metairie, LA: Carnival Press.

LaChance, Paul. 1992. "The 1809 Immigration of Saint-Domingue Refugees." In *The Road to Louisiana: The Saint-Domingue Refugee, 1792–1809*, edited by Carl A. Brasseaux and Glenn R. Conrad. Lafayette: Center for Louisiana Studies.

Latrobe, Benjamin Henry. 1980. *The Journals of Benjamin Henry Latrobe 1799–1820 from Philadelphia to New Orleans*, Vol. 3. *The Star*. New Haven: Yale University Press.

Lipsitz, George. 1990. "Mardi Gras Indians: Carnival and Counter-Narrative in Black New Orleans." In *Time Passages: Collective Memory and American Popular Culture*. Minneapolis: University of Minnesota Press.

Long, Carolyn Morrow. 2001. *Spiritual Merchants: Religion, Magic, and Commerce*. Knoxville: University of Tennessee Press.

——. 2006. *A New Orleans Voudou Priestess: The Legend and Reality of Marie Laveau*. Gainesville: University Press of Florida.

Lynell, Thomas. *Race and Erasure in New Orleans Tourism*. Unpublished PhD Dissertation, Emory University, Atlanta, Georgia, 2005.

MacCash, Doug. 2012. "New Orleans Jazz Fest Focuses on Mardi Gras Indian Culture." *The Times-Picayune*, May 2.

Manuel, Peter, ed. 2009. "Introduction: Contradance and Quadrille Culture in the Caribbean." In *Creolizing Contradance in the Caribbean*. Philadelphia: Temple University Press.

McCaffrey, Kevin. 2005. *The Incomplete, Year-By-Year, Selectively Quirky, Prime Faces Edition of the History of the New Orleans Jazz and Heritage Festival*. New Orleans, LA: e/Prime Publications.

Midlo Hall, Gwendolyn. 1992. *Africans in Colonial Louisiana*. Baton Rouge: Louisiana State University Press.

Miner, Allison, and Michael P. Smith. 1997. *Jazz Fest Memories*. Gretna, LA: Pelican Publishing Company.

Mitchell, Reid. 1995. *All on a Mardi Gras Day: Episodes in the History of New Orleans Carnival*. Cambridge, MA: Harvard University Press.

Ochoa, Ana María. 2005. "García Márquez, Macondismo, and the Soundscapes of Vallenato." *Popular Music* 24 (May) Literature and Music: 207–222.

——. 2006. "Sonic Transculturation, Epistemologies of Purification and the Aural Public Sphere in Latin America." *Social Identities* 12(6): 803–825.

Offbeat Staff. 2011. "New Orleans Ladybuck Jumpers 2011 Second Line Parade Route and Map." *Offbeat Magazine*. November 25. Accessed March 9, 2013. http://www.offbeat.com/2011/11/25/new-orleans-lady-buckjumpers-2011-second-line-parade-route-and-map/.

Pierce F. Lewis, 2005. *New Orleans: The Making of an Urban Landscape*, 2nd ed. Charlottesville: University of Virginia Press.

Plaisance, Stacey. 2012a. "Mardi Gras Indians on Display at Jazz Fest." *Associated Press*, May 4.

——. 2012b. "New Orleans Music Festivals Booming as Jazz Fest Starts." *Associated Press*, April 24.

Porcello, Thomas, Louise Meintjes, Ana Maria Ochoa, and David W. Samuels. 2010. "The Reorganization of the Sensory World." *Annual Review of Anthropology* 39: 51–66.

Raeburn, Bruce. "The Atlantic New Orleans Jazz Sessions." Liner notes booklet for boxed set. Atlantic Recording Corp., Mosaic MD4-179 (1998).

Reed, Adolph, Jr. 2011. "Three Tremés." Editorials. Nonsite.org. Accessed February 13, 2013. http://nonsite.org/editorial/three-tremes.

Regis, Helen A. 1999. "Second Lines, Minstrelsy, and the Contested Landscapes of New Orleans Afro-Creole Festivals." *Cultural Anthropology* 14(4): 472–504.

——. 2001. "Blackness and the Politics of Memory in the New Orleans Second Line." *American Ethnologist* 28(4): 752–777.

Regis, Helen A., and Shana Walton. 2008. "Producing the Folk at the New Orleans Jazz and Heritage Festival." *Journal of American Folklore* 121 (Fall): 400–440.

Roach, Joseph. 1996. *Cities of the Dead: Circum-Atlantic Performance.* New York: Columbia University Press.

Roberts, John Storm. 1974. *Black Music of Two Worlds.* New York: Paperback Editions.

Sakakeeny, Matt. "Instruments of Power: New Orleans Brass Bands and the Politics of Performance." Unpublished PhD Dissertation. Columbia University, 2008.

Schaefer, William. 1977. *Brass Bands and New Orleans Jazz.* Baton Rouge: Louisiana State University Press.

Schultz, Kelly, and Jennifer Day. 2010. "Tourism, Hospitality, and Cultural Economy Fact Sheet: Five-Year Anniversary of Hurricane Katrina." New Orleans Metropolitan Convention and Visitors Bureau, Inc.

Seremetakis, N. C. 1994. *Perception and Memory as Material Culture in Modernity.* Boulder, CO: Westview.

Smith, Michael P. 1991. *New Orleans Jazz Fest: A Pictorial History.* Gretna, LA: Pelican Publishing Company.

Souther, Mark J. 2006. "Making the Birthplace of Jazz." In *New Orleans on Parade: Tourism and the Transformation of the Crescent City.* Baton Rouge: Louisiana State University Press.

Spera, Keith. 2011. *Groove Interrupted: Loss, Renewal, and the Music of New Orleans.* New York: St. Martin's Press.

Stanonis, Anthony J. 2006. *Creating the Big Easy: New Orleans and the Emergence of Modern Tourism, 1918–1945.* Athens: University of Georgia Press.

Stoller P. 1989. *Taste of Ethnographic Things: The Senses in Anthropology.* Philadelphia: University of Pennsylvania Press.

——. 1997. *Fusion of the Worlds: An Ethnography of Possession among the Songhay of Niger.* Chicago: University of Chicago Press.

Sublette, Ned. 2004. *Cuba and Its Music: From the First Drums to the Mambo.* Chicago: Chicago Review.

——. 2008. *The World That Made New Orleans: From Spanish Silver to Congo Square.* Chicago: Lawrence Hill Books.

"Super Sunday." 2013. *NewOrleansOnline.com: The Official Tourism Site of the City of New Orleans.* New Orleans Tourism Marketing Corporation.

Swenson, John. 2011. *New Atlantis: Musicians Battle for the Survival of New Orleans.* Oxford, UK: Oxford University Press.

Thompson, Robert Farris. 2005. "When the Saints Go Marching In: Kongo Louisiana, Kongo New Orleans." In *Resonance from the Past: African Sculpture from the New Orleans Museum of Art*, edited by Frank Herreman. New York: Museum of African Art.

——. 2011. *Aesthetic of the Cool: Afro-Atlantic Art and Music*. Pittsburgh, PA: Periscope Publishing.

Turner, Richard Brent. 2009. "The Haiti–New Orleans Vodou Connection: Zora Neale Hurston as Initiate Observer." In *Jazz Religion, the Second Line, and Black New Orleans*. Bloomington: Indiana University Press.

Washburne, Christopher. 1997. "The Clave of Jazz: A Caribbean Contribution to the Rhythmic Foundation of an African-American Music." *Black Music Research Journal* 17 (Spring): 59–80.

Webster, Richard. 2007a. "N.O.'s Top 10 Tourism Events Based on Economic Impact: #7—French Quarter Festival." *New Orleans CityBusiness*, September 24.

——. 2007b. "N.O.'s Top 10 Tourism Events Based on Economic Impact: #10—Voodoo Music Experience." *New Orleans CityBusiness*, September 24.

——. 2007c. "Top 10 Tourist Events in New Orleans; No. 2: New Orleans Jazz & Heritage Festival." *New Orleans CityBusiness*, Oct 5.

——. 2007d. "Top 10 Tourist Events in New Orleans: No. 4: Essence Music Festival (tie)." *New Orleans CityBusiness*. October 1.

Wild Tchoupitoulas. *Wild Tchoupitoulas*. [Vinyl LP]. New York: Antilles (1976).

PART V

On the Music Touristics of Sex and Spirituality

10

Sound Tracks of a Tropical Sexscape

Tropicalizing Northeastern Brazil, Channeling Transnational Desires

DARIEN LAMEN ■

September 8th, 2008. It's a Monday night, nearly 10:30 p.m. It's been only a few days since I moved to the sprawling coastal city of Fortaleza in Northeastern Brazil to study forró, the accordion music traditionally associated with the arid interior. I'm on my way to a restaurant in the Iracema neighborhood to meet with an accordionist who I hope might take me on as a private student. Although Wanderson (a pseudonym) is only in his mid-thirties, self-proclaimed defenders of local culture have cast him as a sort of savior of traditional forró music. Yet, as I would learn, he is also a consummate trickster. We speak for a while as he sizes me up and assesses my motives. After some time, he suggests we see whether there is any "forró de qualidade" playing in Iracema tonight. Although the clubs that usually offer live music are no more than a ten-minute walk away, Wanderson instinctively springs for a taxi, since the wide and abandoned avenue that leads from the restaurant down to the beachside clubs has in recent years developed a fearsome reputation for armed muggings.

We follow a slowly moving line of cars toward the heart of Iracema's night-life district. The cab's radio is tuned to one of the many local FM stations that play the ubiquitous pop style known as forró eletrônico *or* forró estilizado, *a "shameful excuse for Northeastern music," Wanderson states, apparently for my benefit. I catch snatches of lyrics from a song I will hear again and again during my time here:*

I'm the king of slackness [putaria]
The stallion of the midnight hours . . .
I'm good-looking, single, and loaded
And when I go out to party
It's with four women by my side . . .
I sit down at the table, I don't think about the cost
If you want pretty women you've got to spend

We approach two of the largest nightclubs in Iracema, but Wanderson instructs the driver to continue on. Evidently, he has something else up his sleeve; another test, perhaps. Some hundred yards later, pedestrians dressed in clubbing attire spill into the street, bringing traffic to a standstill. We open the door to get out, and I am surprised to hear not more of the ubiquitous forró estilizado, but throbbing electronic dance music. On the sidewalk, several local women in their twenties reach out to gently grab the hands of the men cruising past in groups of four, five, six, or more.

"Look—there's more French, Italian, and English spoken here than Portuguese," Wanderson says in mock admiration for this most "cosmopolitan" corner of the city. The concentration of foreign men between the ages of thirty and fifty is certainly striking for a Monday night in the off-season. There are small groups of them milling around outside the discotheques—discotheques with names like "Africa" and "Europa" that lay bare the racial-geographical contours of the fantasies in play.

When two young women come to speak with us, Wanderson casts me in the role of the loaded blue-eyed sex tourist, cheio de dólar. *He takes great delight in orchestrating a scene that is re-enacted hundreds of times a night on this same street corner, but I am unable to find the humor in the situation or change the script in any meaningful way. The joke quickly gets old, and after a time we turn to hail one of the recently vacated taxis rumbling up the cobblestone street. They form a seemingly unending caravan, an infernal conveyor belt delivering carload after carload of men eager to play the role of intrepid "sexplorer" in tropical paradise. As we climb into a cab, Wanderson turns with an impish look: "Bem-vindo ao paraíso," he says. Welcome to paradise.*

This chapter examines some of the audible entanglements between musical, tourist, and sexual economies in Iracema, a seaside neighborhood in the Northeastern Brazilian city of Fortaleza, Ceará. Iracema's population is roughly 3,150, making it one of the smallest neighborhoods in this city of over 2.5 million people. Yet despite its size, it has long held a privileged place in the hearts and minds of Fortalezenses. Since the 1920s, Iracema has been a coveted space of leisure for the local bourgeoisie; with the growth of national and international tourism in the 1980s and 1990s, it also came to serve as the main showcase for urban development and modernization initiatives; and as I discovered early on during my fieldwork during the late 2000s, it is one of the city's most vibrant nightlife districts, with dozens of clubs, bars, discotheques, and community cultural spaces within a few blocks of one another. As the sonic and social terrain sketched in the opening narrative suggests, Iracema is one of Fortaleza's most socially heterogeneous neighborhoods, one in which musical, tourist, and sexual economies overlap and intertwine.

Over the course of conducting fieldwork in Iracema, I paid close attention to the ways music served to mediate contact between locals and foreigners, between men and women, and between the local bourgeoisie and the racialized lower and lower-middle classes. I found that, in Iracema, music often served less as a commodity in itself, than as a medium through which libidinal forces are stimulated and directed, and by which economic value is created. The question that remained in my mind was, value for whom, and at whose expense?

This chapter considers the role that music plays in the valorization of the tourist product, in the hypersexualization of local women, as well as in the strategies locals employ toward the fulfillment of their own desires. In the first half of this chapter, I provide a macro-level analysis of Northeastern Brazil's touristification during the late 1980s and early 1990s, attending to the ways in which the region has been constructed as a staging ground for colonial fantasies and hedonistic indulgence. I argue that music—and in particular music that signifies as in some way "tropical" or Afro-Caribbean—played an important role in rendering the Northeast legible within an eroticized tropical tourist imaginary. In the second half of the chapter, I turn to a more micro-level analysis of the practices local women and music professionals have employed in the hopes of capitalizing on touristification from their marginal yet integral positions relative to the formal tourist economy. If we attend to the physical spaces in which erotic encounters occur, we find that music and musicians mediating contact between local women and foreign men in a variety of ways. Although the terms of these encounters are often overdetermined, their outcomes are never predetermined.[1]

This chapter is grounded in a number of ethnographic studies of Fortaleza's sexual economies (e.g., Sousa 1998; Bezerra 2006; 2010; Piscitelli 2001; 2006), as well as seven months of ethnographic research I conducted among music professionals, local women, and foreign tourists in Iracema between 2008 and 2009. It is important to note that this study is limited to heterosexual encounters between local women and foreign men in the Praia de Iracema neighborhood. What differentiates Iracema's sexual economies from those found elsewhere in Fortaleza is the higher concentration of foreigners and the practice of what Adriana Piscitelli terms "middle class" or "elegant prostitution"—i.e., a highly flexible form of sexual-affective labor characterized by quid pro quo arrangements that are often indistinguishable from heteronormative courtship.

TOURISTIFICATION AND TROPICALIZATION IN FORTALEZA, BRAZIL

"Sex" and "sensuality" are perhaps as pervasive and naturalized as tropes of the Caribbean as "sun," "sea," or "sand." Kamala Kempadoo (1999; 2004), Mimi Sheller (2003; 2004), and others have shown how the racialized and gendered power relations that historically undergirded European colonialism in the Americas continue to shape both representations of the circum-Caribbean and the material realities of its inhabitants. The Caribbean today serves as a staging ground for Western colonial fantasies in which tourists from the Global North seek erotic encounters with the "authentic" racialized Other. The fact that the neighborhood serving as focal point for international sex tourism in Fortaleza is named "Iracema" therefore seems especially poignant. During the 1920s, this former fishing village was renamed from "Praia do Peixe" (Fish Beach) to "Praia de Iracema" after the tragic Amerindian heroine of José de Alencar's eponymous nineteenth century novel. An anagram for America, Iracema is the racialized object of European colonial desire personified.[2]

Even though Fortaleza and the Brazilian Northeast are located outside the Caribbean proper, they are nonetheless caught up in what I, drawing on Denise Brennan's work, refer to as a "tropical sexscape," and one that encompasses parts of the circum-Caribbean. Adapted from Appadurai's well-known notion of "scapes"—"the multiple worlds which are constituted by the historically situated imaginations of persons and groups spread around the globe"—the term sexscape refers to an eroticized geographical imaginary comprised of discreet sites of desire. The notion of sexscapes encourages us to think more broadly of the "libidinization" of the globe wherein Western capitalist states "use their 'masculine' power to 'penetrate' local economies," namely, those "opened up" to global capital under neoliberalism, "turning the dominated nations into 'sites of desire' and 'economies of pleasure'" (Brennan 1999, 24). In this sense, domination is not only symbolic but economic, with the eroticization of postcolonial geographies also serving as a means of turning a profit. We might ask who, then, is in a position to collect on the surplus value thus created from the sexual surplus—the erotic capital—projected onto the bodies of local women?

The Government of Changes and Touristification as the Path to Development

Throughout the late twentieth century, the Brazilian Northeast possessed some of the highest poverty rates in all of Brazil. A study published in 1996 found that 47 percent of the Northeastern population survived on the equivalent of less than two minimum wages per household (compared to a national average of 27 percent), with women among the lowest earners. Poverty has become especially pronounced in rapidly growing urban centers such as Fortaleza, where the population, now over 2.4 million, has nearly doubled since 1980. Another study from 1996 found that 40 percent of Fortaleza's population lived below the poverty line, making it the second poorest in the nation behind Recife, the capital of the Northeastern state of Pernambuco.

In the face of such systemic issues, the administrations of Governor Tasso Jereissati (1987–1990, 1995–2002) and Governor Ciro Gomes (1990–1994) set in motion an ambitious regional development plan that they hoped would transform the regional economy. Harnessing the spirit of *abertura* ("opening") that characterized the period of Brazilian re-democratization during the 1980s and 1990s, Jereissati's administration dubbed itself the "governo das mudanças" (the government of change) and forged an alliance with members of an economically ascendant class of regional industrialists and entrepreneurs. Together they sought to wrest political power from what remained of a recalcitrant regional oligarchy of *coronéis* who maintained large concentrations of cattle ranching land in the interior. Opening up the regional economy to investment came to be framed as part of a larger imperative of democratization and development.

The *governo das mudanças* and its successors embraced "touristification" as one strategy among others for invigorating and diversifying the regional economy. Statistics suggest that efforts to grow tourism quickly began to bear fruit. According to Ceará's State Secretariat of Tourism, the tourist economy has been responsible for a 5 percent increase in income per capita since the 1980s. Between 1995 and 2009, visits by Brazilian tourists increased by 323.8 percent, while visits by foreign tourists increased by 550.4 percent. Where once Fortaleza did not figure into tourists' geographical imaginaries of Brazil and the circum-Caribbean, today it is a prominent destination within transnational tourism circuits. In 2009 it hosted over 2.4 million tourists, about 200,000 of which were foreigners.[3]

Fortaleza's incorporation into tourism circuits (both licit and illicit) has depended on the creation of investment incentives and on place marketing that takes advantage of Fortaleza's "tropical" attributes. During the late 1980s and early 1990s, state and municipal governments initiated a process of rapid urban transformation that some residents have pejoratively dubbed the *miamização*—the "Miami-ization"—of Iracema. By rezoning the neighborhood and allowing for relatively unimpeded real estate speculation, local government opened the way for the construction of seasonal apartments, condominiums, and hotel high-rises, as well as for the proliferation of new bars, nightclubs, and beach stands. Taxpayer money was also used to develop and renovate tourist infrastructure, including the restoration of landmarks like the scenic *Ponte dos Ingleses* pier and the construction of a *calçadão*—a broad beach sidewalk resembling the one for which Copacabana is famous.

Fortaleza's touristification has also depended on constructing an image of the city that is immediately intelligible to tourists and investors. Within what critical geographer Milton Santos has referred to as "the war of places" to attract capital (1996, 197), the local approach to place marketing has involved projecting an image of Fortaleza and surrounding areas as a coastal paradise with abundant sunshine, palm trees, and friendly natives. Administrators have cast Fortaleza as the "city of sun," and, in one short-lived marketing gimmick, even promised monetary compensation to tourists for any days that it rained during their visit. José Nelson Bessa Maia, an economist associated with the Jereissati administration, coined the slogan "Fortaleza: capital of the Brazilian Caribbean,"[4] while local bars have also made use of tropical or "Caribbean" themes, perhaps none to so great effect as the renowned "Bar Pirata" (Pirate Bar), which in 2008 even maintained a prominent informational stand in the international airport. Renovated in the early 1990s, Pirata has the feel of a theme park. Overhanging the stage-left side of the venue is a brightly painted, colonial-style façade that houses the establishment's administrative offices. In the rear of the club, parallel to the beach, is a raised wooden patio resembling the deck of a pirate ship. The space is playfully constructed to invite patrons to explore fantasies of tropical paradise.

By all accounts, the architects of Fortaleza's tropical touristification got more than they bargained for. In a frequently quoted sound bite from 2008, for example, Ciro Gomes, champion of the aggressive 1990s tourism expansion policies and then federal representative of Ceará state, indelicately stated, "We were once the primary tourist destination of Brazil and today we've become an open-air whorehouse. Nothing against prostitutes. I'm talking about the deterioration of the urban fabric." As Roselane Gomes Bezerra explains, the construction of large hotels and the proliferation of all manner of commercial establishments in Iracema were accompanied by great economic and social volatility (2006, 9; 2010, 2). Property owners' desires for quick returns on risky investments led some of them to court a growing contingent of international sex tourists with a higher power of consumption than Brazilian tourists. Although I uncovered no evidence that the state ever encouraged sex tourism as a matter of policy, a number of local tourist agencies customize packages for such a clientele, brokering special deals with hotels, restaurants, and bars in and around Iracema for men arriving from Europe. Given this incipient transnational[5] sexual economy, many young women, especially single mothers, began to seek in foreign tourists a means of subsistence, if not longer-term relationships and social mobility. By the late 1990s, Fortaleza had developed a reputation inside and outside Brazil as one of the country's top sex tourism destinations, a dubious honor that it still holds, as evidenced by a 2010 Playboy article published in Portugal that names it the "paraíso do turismo sexual."

Music and the Tropicalization of the Brazilian Northeast

It is particularly striking that the touristification of Fortaleza and other coastal cities in the Brazilian Northeast coincided so closely with the internationalization of select styles of what might be called "tropical" Northeastern Brazilian music.[6] Beginning around 1990, the consolidation of the international market for "world beat" music had created the conditions for hybrid forms of dance music from the African diaspora to circulate widely. Northeastern Brazilian music that audibly drew from circum-Caribbean and specifically Afro-diasporic styles gained considerable traction within transnational musical economies.[7] These included, for example, the samba-reggae of Olodum, one of Salvador's *blocos afro* that fused Brazilian percussion with reggae, salsa, and merengue; the Afro-Bahian *axé music* movement represented by Daniela Mercury, Carlinhos Brown and Timbalada; and the amalgam of Colombian *música tropical*, Antillean zouk, Jamaican reggae, and Brazilian forró known as lambada. These self-consciously circum-Caribbean styles helped to put the coastal Northeast (above all Bahia state) on the world music map and shore up its place in tropical tourist imaginaries where it had only figured peripherally before.[8]

The international notoriety of the lambada, perhaps more than any other style, contributed directly to troping the Brazilian Northeast as a space of tropical abundance and sensuality.[9] Although an in-depth analysis of the tropical tropes comprising the lambada phenomenon is outside the scope of this chapter, I wish to mention a few of them here to suggest the inherent connection of tropicalization and eroticization in emergent musical and tourist economies. The 1989 video for Kaoma's famous single "Chorando se foi," features two pre-pubescent children—"Chico," a twelve-year-old boy of mixed race from Porto Seguro, and "Roberta," a blonde ten-year-old girl from Brasília—in an amorous pursuit that culminates with the two dancing lambada on the beach in the company of scantily clad couples of dancing adults. While the story-line reads superficially as an allegory for interracial harmony, the orgiastic eroticism running throughout infuses the video with an even more obvious subtext: the lambada is the privileged medium through which erotic heterosexual encounters are realized, and coastal Brazil is the privileged place in which taboos against interracial intimacy are routinely transgressed.[10]

The circulation of the lambada cemented the association of tropical sensuality and Northeastern Brazil, with Salvador da Bahia as its epicenter. Some of the club owners and musicians active in Iracema during the early 1990s explained how they had sought to tap into tourist expectations and thereby cash in on the "libidinization" of the Northeast. One foreign-born club owner reasoned that Fortaleza's most distinctive local music—*forró*—was not "palatable" or "recognizable" to foreign tourists, and could therefore not easily be used to promote the local musical economy without being first fused with lambada and other "recognizably Brazilian" styles. Traditional forró (also referred to as *forró pé-de-serra*) is characterized by a more rustic "country" aesthetic, typically featuring fiddle, accordion, triangle, and lyrics about the rural *sertão* interior.[11] He explained:

> Forró is a genre that doesn't neatly correspond to the image foreigners have of Brazil. When they discover forró, they become sad because they . . . were expecting something tropical, equatorial, something that grooves and what not. . . . "Hold on, this here isn't Brazil, is it?" *They don't recognize Brazil.* (emphasis added)

Beginning in the 1990s, his venue underwent a transformation, deviated from the predominantly bourgeoisie-oriented programming he had maintained throughout the 1980s, and the house dance bands began to perform a repertory of forró mixed with other more "recognizably Brazilian" styles in an attempt to make Fortaleza more sonically intelligible to the growing foreign clientele. Significantly, the musical styles coded as "recognizably Brazilian" were ones like the lambada—styles deeply indebted to a circum-Caribbean, Afro-diasporic aesthetic, rather than nationally hegemonic styles such as samba, pagode, and the like.

Although a deracinated style of pop forró has since replaced the lambada as the foundational dance band idiom throughout Fortaleza, in 2008 most of the tourist-oriented venues also included sets featuring the Afro-Bahian styles known as "axé " and "pagode baiano." While axé is a high energy, up-tempo style associated with carnival, pagode baiano (also known as "swingueira") is characterized by its down-tempo groove and highly sensual form of dancing[12] reminiscent of Caribbean "wining." At two different venues in Iracema, members of the audience, both men and women, were invited up on stage during slow "swingueira" numbers to show off their dance moves. It is remarkable that, even after the development of a fiercely territorial music industry in Fortaleza, Bahia continues to mediate the sonic representations of tropical paradise that circulate as a sort of common currency throughout regional tourist-oriented musical economies.

For many gigging musicians with whom I spoke, performing lambada, forró estilizado, swingueira, or whatever the market demanded, represented a strategic calculation. Although several musicians admitted quite candidly that they'd rather be playing other styles, they did not seem to be hung up on issues of artistic purity or authenticity, since stylistic flexibility is the skill in most demand for dance band musicians.[13] Most musicians who play in Fortaleza's dance band circuit depend on this source of income. Many are of modest means, many are recent migrants from the rural interior, and few have formal musical training. Several musicians rationalized their complicity with the local "mafias" of producers and club owners as temporary strategies that they hoped would at least ensure a dependable income, if not lead to opportunities in more lucrative musical economies in Bahia, São Paulo, or abroad.

One such opportunity recalled by former house musicians of Pirata was a 1990 tour of Italy that took place in conjunction with the World Cup. With the support of the State Secretariat of Culture and the Italian Ministry of Tourism and Sports, Pirata's house band Alta Tensão performed over thirty shows of lambada mixed with forró, imprinting the names of Pirata and Fortaleza onto the consciousness of their international audiences. The following decade would see a sharp rise in the number of Italian visitors to Fortaleza, a trend that continues to this day with Italian tourists accounting for nearly 25 percent of foreign visits to Fortaleza in 2011. This is an especially emblematic example of synergy between musical and tourist economies, and one in which the success of the cultural envoy depended on the implicit commodification of the Brazilian woman.

Emergent transnational tourist and musical economies in the Brazilian Northeast implicitly traded on the erotic, symbolic capital of the Brazilian woman, above all the mixed-race *mulata* of African and European descent. In Fortaleza, this has made for some confusion as visitors are confronted with the incongruities between realities on the ground and tropical images of the Brazilian Northeast circulated in the ether. In contrast to the demographic makeup of Salvador da Bahia, for example, the physical features of Fortaleza's population evidence more of an indigenous ethnic inheritance than an African one. While vacationing in Fortaleza, one woman from Rio de Janeiro commented with some degree of horror that local women seemed to be putting on airs and ineptly attempting to perform a sensuality that was not proper to them:

The sensuality here, it is not natural, it is copied, produced, brought by the media. It is something that has happened in the last 8 years. It comes from Bahia, it comes from Rio. I think that even the foreigners might feel deceived. [Here] you do not find that *natural sensuality* of dark, long haired women. What you see here is . . . *unnatural sensuality*. (Piscitelli 2006, 13; emphasis added)

This visitor surmises correctly that foreign sex tourists are often disappointed at not encountering the Other—specifically, the voluptuous *mulata*—they imagined. On one user-maintained web site that maps the known sexscape for the benefit of future sex tourists, posters describe in language that is at once crass and pseudoscientific the "flat asses," "round bellies," and overly "short" height of many local women. At the same time, some sex tourists suggest that what Fortaleza lacks in stereotypical tropical sensuality, its women make up for by being "far more pleasant, laid-back and into more of a 'girlfriend' mode"[14] than the "down-to-business" sex workers in more traveled destinations like Rio de Janeiro. In this sense, the highly flexible character of sexual-affective labor in Iracema—for example, women's willingness to forego direct payment and to provide services *in addition to* sex, such as affection and company—constitutes one of the signal differences that distinguishes Fortaleza favorably from other sites in the larger tropical sexscape.

As I have examined in this section, the international currency of tropical musical styles associated with the coastal Northeast (such as the lambada, pagode baiano, and forró estilizado) have helped to inscribe Northeastern coastal cities like Fortaleza within an existing tropical sexscape, making them legible as sites of desire. I also suggested that musical and tourist economies have traded on the erotic capital ascribed to Brazilian women in the process of consolidating profitable "economies of pleasure." In the next section I consider prevalent discourses which construct contemporary pop forró as a sexually charged medium of contact within Iracema's sexual economies. While such views of forró often serve to pathologize local women as hypersexual and irrational, they also suggest that forró functions as a "dense transfer point of power" in which women may exercise some degree of erotic agency.

FORRÓ ESTILIZADO AS MEDIUM OF CONTACT IN IRACEMA'S SEXUAL ECONOMIES

I walked to the taxi stand at around 10:15 p.m. in order to arrive at the forró estilizado *dance by the time doors opened at 10:30. One of the first questions the driver asked when I said I was going to a forró was:* pé-de-serra? *It seemed like a simple question, but I was well aware that the answer could implicate me in particular moral and sexual economies. I stated truthfully that I loved the "roots" pé-de-serra style, but that I was actually going to a forró estilizado dance to conduct some research. He promptly seized the opening left by my evident ambivalence and launched a full verbal assault on the contemporary forró scene. He said he detested the "pornographic" lyrics of many recent radio hits that described things best left "entre quatro paredes" (behind closed doors). He proceeded to lament the fact that Cearense women no longer* "dão valor ao homen cearense" *(recognize the value of Cearense men). Even though they talk about* "todo o carinho que o gringo faz" *(how affectionate the gringo is), he said that in the end they all end up* "arrasadas," *devastated, when their foreign paramours leave. Evidently, he saw* forró estilizado *as not only the audible symptom of a sort of moral deterioration, but also as the medium through which the victimization of local women occurs.*

Although a wide variety of styles were played in Iracema and throughout Fortaleza in 2008, most of the citywide dance band circuit was built around a cosmopolitan pop variant of *forró* known as *forró estilizado*. Elsewhere I have suggested that the historical emergence of this style in the early 1990s can be understood as a re-localization of the lambada, in the sense that the first wave of *estilizado* bands simply added iconic markers of Northeastern ruralness (e.g., the accordion) onto the lambada dance band format that had become the standard within the local musical economy during the late 1980s (Lamen 2011). Although the style is more commonly referred to as *forró eletrônico* in the scholarly literature, I prefer the term *forró estilizado* for the way it captures this music culture's emphasis on style, glamour, and materialism.

In its celebration of hedonism and ostentatious consumption, contemporary *forró* breaks sharply with the genre's older associations with poverty, humility, and the moral economy of the rural interior that propped up the power of the *coroneis*. For many fans, any trappings that remain of traditional *forró* stand as quaint folkloric remnants, reminders of just how far the Northeast has evolved.[15] The space of the *forró* dance holds out the possibility of actualizing desires for regional development and "First World" power of consumption. For most of Fortaleza's lower and lower-middle classes, however, the *forró* dance is merely a tiny oasis of hedonistic consumption within a regional desert devoid of opportunities for stable employment and social mobility.

Within *forró estilizado* culture, "transactional" hookups and more assertive forms of female sexuality are becoming increasingly naturalized. Monalisa Dias Siqueira writes, for example, that, "Forró is the stage for a particular type of encounter . . . marked by its ephemerality and hedonistic character. The encounters promote the immediate satisfaction of partners, seeing as how their durability is limited to a night, or rather, the relationship is governed by the time of the *festa*" (2009, 16). *Forró estilizado* would thus seem to provide a natural context for encounters between local women and foreign men. Moreover, the *forró* dance serves as an ideal space in which the foreign sex tourist may indulge what I call the "will-to-excess." Denise Brennan, Amalia Cabezas, and others have suggested that the sex tourist who is willing to travel halfway across the world does so not to buy sex *per se*, nor even to buy sex with racialized Others, since the red light districts of the metropoles of the Global North can themselves accommodate such demands. Rather, the sex tourist goes in search of something more, namely, an "experience" in which the pleasure and power of "feeling rich" and being able to consume without worrying about the cost (as in the forró lyrics cited in the opening narrative of this chapter) mingle with the feeling of virility and male dominance. By paying cover charges or buying food and drinks for a female companion, foreign men may seek to recuperate a sense of gender dominance, particularly in an age when many complained about traditional gender hierarchies back home being undermined by women's entrance into the labor economy. One particularly prominent example of foreigners' indulgence of the will-to-excess is the practice of ordering imported whiskey—which in Iracema's upscale clubs is conspicuously brought to the table in the bottle and sold by number of centimeters consumed—before inviting local women to join.

In their roles as both witnesses to and enablers for Iracema's transnational sexual economy, gigging dance band musicians are well-positioned to comment on the role of music in mediating encounters between local women and foreign men. One musician mused that it was the dance, more than any sonic element, that accounted for the centrality of *forró* within Iracema's sexual economies. "Gringos like *forró* because of the *dança colada*," literally, the "glued-on" or close partner dancing. "In this respect," he said, "*forró* is like all *música latina*. It helps facilitate the hookup."[16] In Fortaleza's *forró estilizado* scene, the dance is much more reminiscent of the lambada—the notorious "forbidden dance"— than of "traditional" forms of *forró* dancing which involve shuffling of the feet (*arrastar o pé*). In *forró estilizado*, the partners' legs are typically intercalated, and sinuous hip movements accompany a side-to-side step. The comparison between *forró* and "all *música latina*" points to forró's inclusion within a larger repertory associated with tropical sensuality.

The characterization of forró as a sort of technology of seduction was widespread among both local and foreign men. One local university student stated, "people who go to forrós go because dancing close with your partner provokes sexual stimulation. . . . Men who are really men win their woman with words [*lábio*], intelligence, and wisdom. I do not respect those that use forró to seduce women."[17] A middle-aged French man I met at a local dance academy in Iracema explained that he was taking *forró* lessons to please his "much younger" and "very jealous" local girlfriend, since "getting dressed up and going out to dance is the thing she most likes to do."[18] By developing proficiency in the *forró* dance, he sought to position himself between his girlfriend and what he took to be the principal object of her desire—dancing and consumption—imagining himself to thus stand a chance of mastering her hypersexuality.

The notion that local women are highly vulnerable to seduction through dancing, wining, and dining pathologizes them as irrational and at the mercy of their bodily desires. As one sixty-year-old Italian resident interviewed by Adriana Piscitelli said of local women, "They just think of making love and dancing *forró*" (Piscitelli 2001,15). Posts on sex tourism web sites similarly suggest that local women in Fortaleza, "pro" and "non-pro" alike, are sexually available and open to having sexual encounters with foreigners. Hypersexualized in this way, local women are subject to harassment and unwanted advances from foreigners whether they participate actively in transnational sexual economies or not. Moreover, local women who go unaccompanied or accompanied by foreigners to certain spaces in Iracema are presumed to be "prostitutes" and may suffer discrimination at the hands of locals. In this way, the social roles and physical spaces open to local women are often restricted.

While the hypersexualization of local women functions as a form of social control, it may also create opportunities for them to resist existing social hierarchies. Due to the juxtaposition of various social and physical spaces in Iracema, a "climate of uncertainty" surrounds the intentions of local women and foreign men. Adriana Piscitelli suggests that the ambiguity of social roles and identities "shades international encounters, propagating 'romances' and opening ways for the eventual departure for a foreign country even for the girls who go on *programas*," for example, the local euphemism for money-for-sex transactions (2001, 23–24). Thus, as Mimi Sheller writes, "Every embodied encounter is a moment of improvisation, role-playing, and interaction in which a re-scripting of power is always risked" (2012, 212).

Along these lines, local women have suggested that foreign men are also susceptible to getting caught up and swept away in the space of a *forró*. The libidinal forces that *forró* mobilizes make it a field of instability, a "dense transfer point for relations of power," particularly in cases where the man is not accustomed to receiving so much attention. One woman who cultivated on-and-off relationships with foreign men stated, "The first thing a man does when he arrives in Fortaleza is to find a woman and go to a *forró*, because what they really want to is to cut loose [*se soltar*]. Many of them come from very uptight countries, and here they can go crazy. They're not used to so much attention. Especially the ones who come for the first time."[19] As I discuss in the next and final section, the possibilities for converting erotic capital into financial benefits in the transnational sexual economy depend on intimate forms of sexual-affective labor, some of which take place within the space of the club.

EROTIC AGENCY AND TRANSACTIONAL COUPLING

One Saturday night I invited local friend to keep me company during one of my fieldwork outings to Iracema's live music venue Nick Bar (a pseudonym). After

paying the $20 in Brazilian Real (BRL) cover charge (approximately $10 in US
dollars) we head inside as the headlining band's bus pulls up, its sides decaled
with the faces of the band's lead singers. Inside is an air of glamour—the walls
are bathed in soft, colored lights projected from the floor; to one side of the stage
a waterfall is built into the wall. Later that night, my friend spots a colleague,
a well-dressed twenty-something-year-old woman, with whom she attends pri-
vate university. I introduce myself; she asks where I'm from. "New York." "Ah,
I have a French boyfriend," she offers, "we actually met here last year. He's so
sweet . . . the love of my life! He's coming for a visit in July." My friend is obviously
skeptical of her colleague's "performance of love" and explains how Nick Bar is a
"dating service" for many local women in search of a foreign príncipe encantado,
or prince charming, "one who can carry them away to a better life abroad."[20] The
cover charge means that not just anyone can afford to go cruising here, although
sometimes having a sympathetic bouncer for a friend can lessen the financial
burden. I gather that my friend's discomfort over what she interprets as her col-
league's shallow utilitarianization of sexuality may be related to the fact that she
has herself suffered mistreatment and public humiliation after being taken for a
sex worker. Ultimately the ontological question—whether one "is" or "is not" a sex
worker—seems to distract from the more fundamental political issue, namely, the
gendered relations of power that maintain local women in precarious or depen-
dent positions in society.

Sex tourism is a favorite focus of Fortaleza's sensationalist crime reportage programs and a perennial talking point among local political candidates. Among
the different types of legal and illegal sexual-economic exchanges that take place
in Fortaleza, tourist-oriented sex work—even of the legal, freelance variety[21]—
is among the most vociferously condemned. While local elites have historically
been content to condone other forms of sexual economic exchange when those
sexual economies preserve class power or generate profit,[22] the striking public
presence of couples of "white" foreigners and "brown" locals *a ceu aberto*—on
the boardwalks, in restaurants, and in clubs frequented by the local bourgeoisie,
for example—is decried as an unprecedented collapse in the moral order. This
suggests that the quarrel is not actually with the sexist regime of prostitution as
such, but with the way in which "freelance" sex work, together with the transna-
tionalization of Iracema's sexual economies, undermines heteropatriarchy and
the local system of racialized social segregation.

    In Iracema in 2008, the highest concentration of women offering *pro-*
gramas—sexual-economic transactions with pre-agreed-on terms—was found
in the modest *boates* located a block from the waterfront. Here, electronic
dance music rather than *forró* was played throughout the night, delineating
a sound space in which foreign tourists—the majority of whom hailed from

Europe—might presumably feel at home. After midnight, according to convention, one *boate* served as clearinghouse for women who had not yet attracted a client at other venues on their circuits. Women used the dance floor to display themselves by dancing alone or in small homosocial groups until the approach of a potential client. Private tables or a quieter corner of the club could then serve as spaces for the couple to define the terms of the *programa*. Online sex tourism forums stated that the going rate for a "short overnight" in Iracema in the mid-2000s ranged between $60 and $100 (BRL)[23] plus the cost of an hourly motel or a nightly hotel room, since *boates* were not in the business of providing rooms. *Boates* typically offered free admission for women, but charged men the equivalent of two drinks to enter. In this way, club owners attempted to expropriate the erotic labor of local women and turn a profit from male patrons. Owners in turn provided the conditions of possibility—a secure space, alcohol, and a lively soundtrack—for women to meet foreign men.

For women seeking to meet foreigners in more socially mixed venues, more discretion was required, since making advances that exceeded the norms of propriety—especially if they were women of color—might get them ejected. Adriana Piscitelli writes that women who frequented Iracema's upscale nightclubs often "deploy practices through which . . . they obtain financial benefits from their foreign partners [while] distancing themselves in behaviour from sex tourists' pre-conceived notions of sex work" (2006, 12). These practices included allowing the man to make the initial "approach" and invitation to dance;[24] substituting direct and immediate payments for sex with more or less explicitly stated expectations of compensation in the form of gifts, nights out on the town, and the like; as well as engaging in displays of affection, passion, or love in which "tears and the intensity of contacts after [the tourist's] departure acquire value as indicators of the amount of love involved" (Piscitelli 2001, 8). This allows us to see the taxi driver's assessment of local women's emotional "devastation" at their foreign boyfriends' departure in a potentially different light. Rather than tears necessarily signifying victimhood and lack of agency, they may be understood as a form of affective labor that serves to convert a relationship delimited by the length of the tourist's visit into a more lasting bond, perhaps one with the possibility for sustained financial support, greater consumptive power, social and geographical mobility, as well as romance.[25]

Of course, foreign men also have a vested interest in maintaining the semblance of a "conventional" heteronormative relationship. The type of quid pro quo agreement characteristic of what one sex tourist referred to as "girlfriend mode" is more conducive to maintaining the fantasy of a consensual, non-exploitative relationship; it shields them from being associated with human trafficking and more predatory forms of sex tourism; and it helps them differentiate themselves from local men, who are represented as hypermasculine, chauvinistic, and frequently cuckolded. As was already mentioned, maintaining a local girlfriend also offers foreign men the opportunity to play the role of powerful provider. Thus, the fact that relationships between local women and foreign men often develop in the ambiguous space between "romance" and "sex work" helps women resist capture within the stigmatized category of "prostitute" while also providing ideological cover for both parties.

Women engaging in practices that Piscitelli somewhat problematically defined as "elegant" or "middle class prostitution" drew a sharp distinction between their own instrumentalization of sexuality and that of streetwalkers and "garotas de programa." Whereas these women associated programas and sex work with precarity, lack of agency, and victimhood, their own involvement in the transnational sexual economy did not preclude pleasure and "genuine" romance, even if it did entail an acknowledged element of necessity. Interestingly, this view of erotic agency resonates strongly with articulations of female sexuality that have emerged in the context of *forró estilizado* hookup culture. Monalisa Dias Siqueira describes the advent of a new Northeastern woman who

> exercises her power of sexual attraction and shares her body with whomever she is interested in. She claims entertainment, leisure, and diversion for herself. She refuses definition for her gender: she is neither a housewife nor a prostitute. With this, she produces another place for the feminine in which she makes use of her body and her time [by] seeking pleasure. (2009, 16)

Although such uses of erotic agency within local sexual economies have earned women derogatory labels—such as "piriguete," from the word "perigosa" for dangerous, or "gato véi" (old cat), a typically lower class woman who is perpetually "on the prowl"—*forró* lyrics bear witness to the anxiety such assertions of female sexual agency have provoked in men.[26] However, any suggestion that the exercise of sexual agency in these contexts is genuinely emancipatory seems dubious since it represents, at best, a form of what Siqueira calls "dependent independence" (2009, 17).

CONCLUSION

Fortaleza's insertion into both licit and illicit tourist economies in the late 1980s and early 1990s depended on remaking the city—culturally, socially, and even physically—in the image of other, already established, beach destinations. Music of a "tropical" nature has helped to construct the region as a welcoming playground for international tourists. In the process of rendering the neighborhood of Iracema, the city of Fortaleza, and the northeastern region of Brazil legible as sites of desire within a transnational sexscape, the presumed tropical sensuality of local women, together with the presumed sensuality of tropical music, has become a source of value that individuals and businesses alike trade on. It is the sexual-affective labor of women woven together with the labor of dance-band musicians that effectively animates the incipient transnational economies of pleasure that emerged in Fortaleza during the 1990s and early 2000s. In this sense, music not only serves as the pretense for sexual-economic exchange between foreign men and local women; it is also the very medium that structures libidinal forces in ways that are more or less amenable to (though never entirely predetermined by) capital.

The eroticization of local women within Fortaleza's economies of pleasure entails relations of domination and control reminiscent of those operative under colonialism. Yet for some women eroticization also presents openings for the exercise of agency.[27] For some women, engaging in intimate forms of sexual-affective labor at the edges of the formal tourist economy has represented one strategy among others for resisting the local social order, one which has historically excluded them from more reliable work in the formal sector and from the fruits of neoliberal development promised by the "Government of Changes." Within the emergent and illicit economies of pleasure, music and the space of the forró dance serve as "dense transfer points for relations of power" in which existing social roles may be contested and subverted.

NOTES

1. Much recent scholarship on sex and romance tourism in the circum-Caribbean has focused on questions of local agency in the face of seemingly intractable structural inequality (Alexander 1997, Fairley 2004, Fernandes 2006, Sheller 2012). Ethnographic studies in particular have foregrounded the active strategies some women use to capitalize on eroticized differences of race, gender, and nationality in pursuit of a wide range of short- and long-term objectives (Babb 2010, 2012; Brennan 2004; Curtis 2009; Piscitelli 2001, 2006). In some cases—as for example in the so-called "middle class prostitution" (Piscitelli 2001) that predominates in many of Iracema's nightclubs—these strategies include "the performance of love" (Brennan 2004, 17), the emulation of heterosexual courtship rituals, and the adoption of more flexible forms of compensation (Piscitelli 2001, 12). The present chapter is informed by these studies and the intellectual politics that animate them, yet it does not focus on the question of individual agency.

2. In Alencar's work, Iracema, an Amerindian woman from the Northeastern interior, falls in love with and is impregnated by Martin, a Portuguese captain at war with a different Amerindian tribe inhabiting the coast. Having forsaken her vow of chastity, Iracema is forced to leave her own tribe. She is then effectively abandoned by Martin as well, and so dies after giving birth to what would become "the first Cearense."

3. It has been suggested that the financial crisis of 2008 disproportionately affected the national economies of the Global North, so these numbers may be somewhat atypical.

4. Fortaleza is not the only place in Brazil to deploy "Caribbeanness" as a synonym for natural beauty and leisure within an official tourism campaign. The river beach "Alter do Chão" in the Amazonian state of Pará, voted the "most beautiful in the world" by the British newspaper *The Guardian* in 2009, has also been dubbed the "Caribe Brasileiro," as has "Porto de Galinhas" in Pernambuco state, among others.

5. It is important to note that Iracema has long been the site of a local sexual economy. Sex work had been conveniently condoned by local elites, but the emergence of a transnational economy posed a more serious threat to local patriarchal control and has consequently been vociferously attacked in the local media, and in a manner disproportionate to the scale of sex tourism when considered in relation to other, even more exploitative kinds of sexual economies.

6. At the same time that the *governo das mudanças* was developing Iracema as a tourist destination, several other coastal Northeastern Brazilian cities—such as Salvador da Bahia and, somewhat later, Recife and São Luiz—were undergoing similar transformations.

7. Particularly emblematic were the high-profile collaborations between Olodum and Paul Simon for the album *Rhythm of the Saints* (1990) and, later, between Olodum and Michael Jackson for "They Don't Care About Us" (1995).

8. This is remarkable, since from the hegemonic national perspective, quite the opposite has been true throughout the twentieth century. The arid Northeastern interior—associated with drought, messianism, poverty, and indigenous cultural and ethnic heritage—came to stand for the region as a whole within the national political economy (see Albuquerque).

9. Though perhaps apocryphal, the genesis story of the lambada band Kaoma was brought up on a number of occasions as a sort of allegory for the possibilities and limits of local complicity with transnational capital/tropicalizat. The story begins with a French producer, Olivier Lorsac, vacationing in Porto Seguro, Bahiam during the late 1980s. While sunbathing on the beach, Lorsac is said to have overheard a lambada song by Beto Barbosa (one of Fortaleza's adopted hometown heroes) playing from a radio. Captivated by the "hot" tropical rhythm, he decided to assemble a group of Brazilian and non-Brazilian musicians to record an album of the style. Kaoma's hit record *Worldbeat* was produced in a state-of-the-art studio in Paris and distributed with carefully orchestrated international promotion, reaching double gold status in France, and peaking at number forty on the US Billboard 200 chart. The band toured Europe for a number of years, an experience about which the Brazilian participants recently waxed nostalgic during a retrospective documentary. The story represents a sort of "opportunity myth" that parallels those told by local women hoping to meet a foreigner and move abroad, but it was also trotted out as a cautionary tale. Fortaleza's local musical economy is fiercely hierarchical and paternalistic, so, for many musicians, the internationalization of the lambada represented the possibility of social and physical mobility. However, the fact that the lambada fizzled so quickly after its international debut means that the

story is also invoked as a morality tale, a critique of the ephemeral forms of value attributed to certain types of music within capitalist musical economies.

10. Similar tropes were deployed in the 1990 feature length movie *The Forbidden Dance (Is Lambada)*. A theatrical release poster for the film shows the lead actors dancing, legs intertwined, against a background of palm trees and a city skyline silhouetted at dusk. The tagline of the poster reads, "LAMBADA . . . If it got any hotter, it wouldn't be dancing!" The movie's plot involves a Brazilian woman who travels to Los Angeles to save her home in the Amazon from devastation at the hands of a transnational corporation. There, after unsuccessfully seeking work in a brothel/exotic dance club, she falls in love with an American man and the two compete in a dance competition to save the rainforest.

11. Júlio Trindade, interview with author, January 15, 2009.

12. See Ari Lima's "Modernity, Agency, and Sexuality in the Pagode Baiano."

13. The politics of work and the virtue of "flexibility" within dance band economies are issues that have recently been discussed by Jeff Packman in "Signifying Salvador: Professional Musicians and the Sound of Flexibility in Bahia, Brazil's Popular Music Scenes and Bob White in *Rumba Rules: The Politics of Dance Music in Mobutu's Zaire*.

14. See Dexter Horn's Worldwide Discussion. 2003. Accessed March 31, 2013, http://www.dexterhorn.com/discus/messages/75/108542.html.

15. In a personal interview in December of 2008, Carlos Aristides, young co-founder of the wildly successful *forró estilizado* production company A3, showed palpable disdain for those who harbor sentimental feelings for the old style of *forró*, "restricted to a class of poor little Northeasterners," asserting that "it's because contemporary *forró* distanced itself from roots forró that it's come so far." For more on regionalist evolutionist discourse within the Northeastern music industry see Maria Érica de Oliveira Lima's 2005 doctoral thesis, "Somzoom Sat: do Local ao Global."

16. Luis Zalém, interview with author, October 6, 2008.

17. "Júlio," personal communication with author via Orkut (social networking site), December 4–10, 2007.

18. "Philippe," personal communication with author, September 1, 2008.

19. "Fátima," personal communication with author, December 11, 2008.

20. This is not to suggest that all women are "dupes" of "opportunity myths." I recognize that my subject position may well make it difficult or undesirable for local women to reveal their "true" intentions regarding their dating practices, yet this is a problem that other ethnographers have encountered as well. Denise Brennan, for example, while working in Sosua, Dominican Republic, noted that local women there seemed to have a vested interest in performing their savvy and cynicism about romance tourism while in front of other women since to admit a "genuine" romantic interest is to make oneself vulnerable to exploitation.

21. Although prostitution involving individuals over eighteen years old does not constitute a crime in Brazil, third-party exploitation of prostitution (*lenocínio*) is illegal, and is covered by articles 227, 228, 229, and 230 of the National Penal Code.

22. Institutionalized forms of sex work have a long history in Fortaleza and Northeastern Brazilian society. According to Francisca Ilnar de Sousa, the *cabaré* or brothel has traditionally played a complementary role to the institution of

marriage, performing the function of "male sexual initiation while preserving *moças de família* [daughters of well-to-do families] who had to remain virgins until marriage" (1998, 41). In this sense, the *cabaré* as an institution has served to buttress the virgin–whore dichotomy of female sexuality necessary to the maintenance of heteropatriarchy while also reinscribing sex work "into the circuits of profit, if not . . . of production" (Sousa 1998, 61). On the other hand, the growth of new forms of sex work—including sex, companion, and romance tourism—that does not confine itself to the *zona de tolerância* (red-light district) but spills onto seaside restaurants and boardwalks frequented by well-to-do families represents a grave threat to the moral order that necessitates immediate state attention.

23. Approximately $20–$30 (USD), significantly cheaper than the rate in Copacabana at roughly the same time, which, according to Da Silva and Blanchette was roughly $100 (USD) and up.

24. For more on gender dynamics in the context of Fortaleza's contemporary forró scene, see Felipe Trotta's (2008) "O Forró de Aviões: a circulação cultural de um fenômeno da indústria do entretenimento."; and Monalisa Dias Siqueira's (2008) "Os gato véi e o estilo de vida forrózeiro em Fortaleza."

25. Denise Brennan's ethnographic research (2006) suggests that such "opportunity myths" should be viewed warily, and that permanent social mobility represents more of an exception than the norm.

26. The lyrics of the song "Pegou piriguete pensando que é patricinha" are especially indicative:

See? I told you not to get carried away
You saw a pretty face and fell in love right away
In less than a week, you already wanted to get married
And everyone on your street said:
See stupid? See wiseguy?
You got hold of a *piriguete* thinking she's a lady [*patricinha*]

27. For an overview of theorizations of sexual agency in the circum-Caribbean in relation to music, dance, and "work" (see Sheller 2008).

REFERENCES

Albuquerque Júnior, Durval Muniz de. 1999. *A Invenção do Nordeste e Outras Artes.* Recife: Massangana.

Alencar, José Martiniano de. 2000. *Iracema*. Translated by Clifford Landers. Oxford: Oxford University Press.

Alexander, M. Jacqui. 1997. "Erotic Autonomy as a Politics of Decolonization: An Anatomy of Feminist and State Practice in the Bahamas Tourist Economy." *Feminist Genealogies, Colonial Legacies, Democratic Futures*, edited by M. Jacqui Alexander and Chandra Talpade Mohanty, 63–100. New York: Routledge.

Babb, Florence E. 2010. "Sex and Sentiment in Cuban Tourism." *Caribbean Studies* 38(2): 93–115.

——. 2012. "Theorizing Gender, Race, and Cultural Tourism in Latin America: A View from Peru and Mexico." *Latin American Perspectives* 39(6): 36–50.

Bezerra, Roselane Gomes. 2006. "Praia de Iracema como cenário de encontros de alcova." In III *Reunião da Associaç ão Portuguesa de Antropologia. Digital conference proceedings*. Lisboa: Associaç ão Portuguesa de Antropologia.

——. 2010. "'Gringos e nativas': representaç ões do turista estrangeiro e suas acompanhantes no bairro Praia de Iracema na cidade de Fortaleza-Ce." In *Mulheres da vida: Mulheres com vida: Prostituiç ão, Estado e Políticas*, edited by Manuel Carlos Silva. Ribeirão Preto, Brazil: Húmus.

Brennan, Denise. 2004. *What's Love Got to Do With It? Transnational Desires and Sex Tourism in the Dominican Republic*. Durham, NC: Duke University Press.

Curtis, Debra. 2009. *Pleasures and Perils: Girls' Sexuality in a Caribbean Consumer Culture*. New Brunswick: Rutgers University Press.

Fairley, Jan. 2004. "'Ay Díos, Ampárame' (O God, Protect Me): Music in Cuba during the 1990s, the 'Special Period.'" In *Island Musics*, edited by Kevin Dawe, 77–97. UK: Berg.

Fernandes, Sujatha. 2006. "Fear of a Black Nation: Local Rappers, Transnational Crossings, and State Power." In *Cuba Represent! Cuban Arts, State Power, and the Making of New Revolutionary Cultures*, 85–117. Durham: Duke University Press.

Jackson, Michael. 1995. "They Don't Care About Us." In *HIStory: Past, Present and Future, Book 1*. Epic Records EK59004.

Kempadoo, Kamala. 1999. "Continuities and Change: Five centuries of prostitution in the Caribbean." In *Sun, Sex and Gold: Tourism and Sex Work in the Caribbean*, edited by Kamala Kempadoo. Lanham, MD: Rowman and Littlefield.

——. 2004. *Sexing the Caribbean: Gender, Race, and Sexual Labor*. New York: Routledge.

Lima, Ari. 2011. "Modernity, Agency, and Sexuality in the Pagode Baiano." In *Brazilian Popular Music and Citizenship*, edited by Idelber Avelar and Christopher Dunn, 267–277. Durham, NC: Duke University Press.

Lima, Maria Érica de Oliveira "Somzoom Sat: do Local ao Global." PhD dissertation. Universidade Metodista de São Paulo, 2005.

Packman, Jeff. 2009. "Signifying Salvador: Professional Musicians and the Sound of Flexibility in Bahia, Brazil's Popular Music Scenes." *Black Music Research Journal* 29(1): 83–126.

Piscitelli, Adriana. "On 'Gringos' and 'Natives': Gender and Sexuality in the Context of International Sex Tourism in Fortaleza, Brazil." Presented at Latin American Studies Association, Washington, DC, 2001.

——. 2006 "Transnational Sex Travels: Negotiating Identities in a Brazilian 'Tropical Paradise.'" In *Translocalities/Translocalidades: Feminist Politics of Translation in Latin America*. Amherst, MA: Amherst.

Santos, Milton. 1996. *A Natureza do Espaço: Técnica e Tempo, Razão e Emoç ão. São Paulo*: Editora Hucitec.

Sheller, Mimi. 2003. *Consuming the Caribbean: From Arawaks to Zombies*. Oxford, UK: Routledge.

——. 2004 "Natural Hedonism: The Invention of Caribbean Islands as Tropical Playgrounds." In *Beyond the Blood the Beach and the Banana*, edited by Sandra Courtman, 170–185. Kingston, Jamaica: Ian Randle Publishers.

——. 2008. "Work that Body: Sexual Citizenship and Embodied Freedom." In *Constructing Vernacular Culture in the Trans-Caribbean*, edited by Holger Henke and Karl-Heinz Magister, 345–376. Lanham, MD: Lexington Books.

——. 2012. *Citizenship from Below: Erotic Agency and Caribbean Freedom.* Durham, NC: Duke University Press.

Simon, Paul. 1990. *Rhythm of the Saints.* Warner Bros 9 26098-2.

Siqueira, Monalisa Dias de. "Quem convida é a mulher: experiências femininas e subversão nos bailes de dança de salão," Master's thesis. Fortaleza, Brazil: Universidade Federal do Ceara, 2009.

Siqueira, Monalisa Dias. 2008. "Os gato véi e o estilo de vida forrózeiro em Fortaleza" in *Experiências Musicais*, edited by F. J. G. Damasceno. Fortaleza, Brazil: EdUECE.

Sousa, Francisca Ilnar de. 1998 *O cliente: o outro lado da prostituiç ão.* São Paulo: Annablume.

Trotta, Felipe. "O Forró de Aviões: a circulaç ão cultural de um fenômeno da indústria do entretenimento." Paper presented at XVII Encontro da Compós, UNIP, São Paulo, 2008.

White, Bob. 2008. *Rumba Rules: The Politics of Dance Music in Mobutu's Zaire.* Durham, NC: Duke University Press.

11

Resorting to Spiritual Tourism

Sacred Spectacle in Afro-Cuban Regla de Ocha

KATHERINE J. HAGEDORN ■

TOURISM IN CUBA: BACKGROUND

Since the 1970s, revolution-era Cuban intellectuals and bureaucrats have debated the merits of foreign tourism on the island. Major steps toward making Cuba a viable tourist destination—such as refurbishing some of the island's once-grand hotels and restaurants—occurred during the 1980s, but the main impetus for making foreign tourism the centerpiece of the Cuban economy occurred during the 1990s, when Cuba experienced the economic tailspin caused by the collapse of the former Soviet Union, which deprived Cuba of the subsidized oil and the inflated sugar prices on which it had come to depend (see chapter 2). From 1990 to 1993, the Cuban gross domestic product declined by about 30 percent (Ritter 2003, 6), and Cuba's economy struggled mightily to recover during the rest of the decade. This period of economic scarcity, which lasted officially through the 1990s but which appears to have continued through the first decade of the 2000s, was known as "the special economic period in time of peace," and resulted in widespread shortages of food and other basic necessities. Alberto Pozo Fernández (1926–2012), a respected and long-standing Cuban journalist and editor[1] who specialized in the economy, wrote a slim volume entitled *Cuba y el Turismo*, published in 1993, during the trough of Cuba's special economic period. In it, he urged Cuba to invest its resources in foreign tourism, which, in his estimation, would yield several times the profit of Cuba's traditional crops of sugar, coffee, and tobacco, and would have the added benefit of raising the socioeconomic level of Cuban citizens.

After stating that Cuba in the 1950s was "an underdeveloped nation that could be divided into three parts: one-third of the population was living, one-third of the population was surviving, and the last third of the population was dying" (1993, 23), Pozo Fernández goes on to recount the triumphs of the 1959 revolution in terms of education, health care, employment, and homes, emphasizing that the post-revolutionary economy needed to focus on the infrastructure of the nation before it could plan seriously for foreign tourism.[2] As a result, Pozo Fernández argues, the pillars of Cuba's pre-revolutionary tourist trade—such as hotels, bars, and restaurants—fell into disrepair. In the mid-1970s, he writes, Cuba initiated *"la reconquista del turismo"* (the reconquering of tourism), with the creation of INTUR (Instituto Nacional de Turismo). INTUR incorporated and broadened the mandate of INIT (Instituto Nacional de la Industria Turística), which had been founded in the early months of the Revolution (1993, 26, 93). During the 1976–1980 development plan, twenty-five new hotels were opened for foreign tourism. In 1987 Cubanacán S.A. was created for the purpose of facilitating joint ventures with foreign companies. One year later, Grupo Gaviota was founded, whose primary mission was to look after important foreign visitors, as well as attracting upper middle-class foreign tourists "of high rank" (1993, 94–95).[3]

According to Pozo Fernández, the primary focus of foreign tourism was to be the beaches of Varadero, in the western province of Matanzas. The full plan for foreign tourism, however, would include 67 localities throughout the island (mostly beach-adjacent), with approximately 200,000 hotel rooms (30,000 of these in Varadero). Pozo Fernández estimated that each hotel room could bring in $20,000–$40,000 per year, depending on the quality of the hotel. With 200,000 hotel rooms, the yield would be more than 4 billion dollars annually. This figure is roughly 3 times the amount that sugar brings in annually. He described jobs in the tourist industry as "fine, clean work," the demanding nature of which would contribute to a higher level of education and awareness for the Cuban people (1993, 118).

Toward the end of the book, Pozo Fernández outlines further areas for touristic development—including family and health tourism, health spas and mineral baths, convention hosting, hunting and fishing, and culture. With regard to culture, he gives particular mention to the Conjunto Folklórico Nacional, as well as the Instituto Superior del Arte, and the Centro de Conservación y Restauración Museológicas. 1993, 127–136). He notes that "the great star of Cuban tourism" in the future will be ecotourism, and cites Cuba's many pristine habitats and nature preserves. He also points out the untapped potential of "multi-destination" tourism, focusing on the Bahamas, the Dominican Republic, Jamaica, and Mexico as likely partners in multi-destination tourism (1993, 142).

In 1995, the goal was to attract 1.5 million visitors; in 1999, Cuba welcomed 1.6 million. In 2000, the goal was to attract 2 million visitors, thus placing Cuba squarely in the midst of the competitive Caribbean tourist market (Pozo Fernández 1992, 141), though actual figures for 2000 were more like 1.74 million, bringing in approximately 1.9 billion dollars in revenues (Ritter 2003, 10). According to World Bank figures, from 2008 to 2011 the number of foreign tourists arriving in Cuba has been increasing steadily from approximately 2.3 million in 2008 to approximately 2.7 million in 2011.[4] The goal for 2012 was 2.9 million foreign visitors.

Echoing Pozo Fernández's recommendations, in 2011, Cuba's 31st International Tourism Fair had as its featured product multi-destination tourism, and its guest country was Mexico (Bianchi Ross 2011, 9). In 2012, the International Tourism Fair featured family tourism, with Argentina as its guest country. Priorities in the Cuban tourist industry remain the rehabilitation and the revitalization of hotels in Varadero, Havana, the keys north of Villa Clara, Jardines del Rey, Cayo Largo, Santiago de Cuba, and Santa Lucia (Montserrat 2012, 23), as well as the development of ecotourism, especially birdwatching and marine observation ("Cuba: The Accidental Eden" 2010).[5]

Pozo Fernández emphasized that tourism would need to be internationally focused and that internal tourism would not be a priority for Cuba's infrastructure. It is through foreign dollars that Cuba's tourist industry will be rebuilt, and for that to happen, hotels and restaurants need to be renovated and made ready for steadily increasing numbers of foreign visitors. He pointed to the reconstruction and renovation of such landmark hotels as the Hotel Inglaterra and the Hotel Plaza, as well as the famous Hotel Nacional. He also noted that most Cubans will not be able to patronize the hotels and restaurants in which they work because their salaries will be too low—a necessary cost of bolstering the centralized state economy.

These words were prophetic, and they took on an unexpected poignancy during the decades of the 1990s and the 2000s in Cuba. As tourists from Canada, Western Europe, and Latin America arrived in Cuba's major cities with seemingly limitless cash, Cubans were encountering increasing deprivations—from sharply reduced food rations to shortages of all household goods. The enormous difference between tourist standards of living and Cuban standards of living was thrown into sharp relief in tourist hotels, as Cuban hotel workers suffering through the special economic period confronted the comparatively wealthy tourists from Canada, western Europe, and Latin America courted by INTUR.[6] The average salary for a Cuban professional (a doctor, for example) remains about $17 to $20 per month, yet all the Cuban facilities dedicated to foreign tourism are pegged at North American and Western European rates, ranging from $50 to $250 per night for a hotel room, and from $15 to $50 for a dinner. Clearly, a Cuban professional would not be able to enjoy a weekend away at one of these facilities. Even those Cubans who work in the tourist industry and earn extra money in tips could not afford these prices.

Peter Sanchez and Kathleen Adams (2010) explore what they call the "Janus-faced" character of Cuban tourism—which has provided a much needed influx of hard currency that helped Cuba "weather the economic storm" of the 1990s and 2000s but has also undermined the support of the Cuban people for socialist ideology (2010, 420). They note several other ways in which the increase in foreign tourism has disrupted Cuban society: (1) by deepening the racial divide (lighter-skinned Cubans are more likely to get jobs in the tourist industry)[7]; (2) by creating a two-class system, whereby Cubans involved in tourism have access to hard currency and thus are able to live better than those Cubans who do not; and (3) by creating a two-class system between Cubans and foreign tourists, whereby Cubans are forced to confront their material shortages in comparison to the apparent abundance of material goods possessed by foreign tourists (2010, 423–426).

TRAVELING TO CUBA: A US SCHOLAR'S PERSPECTIVE

Cuba represents a special case within the context of Caribbean tourism because of its long-standing opposition to the United States, and because of the concurrent US embargo against Cuba. As a result, traveling to Cuba for US citizens (not of Cuban descent) takes on a countercultural patina.[8] In addition, travel to Cuba from the United States is tightly controlled by the US government, so getting to Cuba as a US citizen is more of a challenge than getting to other Caribbean countries. Even from the point of planning a trip, the idea of "leisure tourism" for US citizens in Cuba becomes unlikely, simply because the logistics are so complicated, and they typically require more specialized knowledge and preparation than most Caribbean vacations. For example, there are only certain categories of US citizens who can travel to Cuba legally: those who wish to visit close relatives living in Cuba (immediate family); freelance journalists/photojournalists; professional researchers or conference attendees; those participating in an educational activity or educational exchange; those who are sponsoring or cosponsoring an academic seminar, conference, or workshop; those who are engaging in religious activities; those who are engaging in a public performance, clinic, or workshop; those who wish to show their support for the Cuban people (but not the Cuban government); those who are participating in humanitarian projects; those who are members of private research foundations or educational institutes; those who are engaging in the export, import, or transmission of educational materials; and those who are involved in exporting US products via foreign firms.[9]

Ironically, though holiday makers and casual tourists are expressly *not* included in these categories, "tourist" visas are the most common visas issued by the Cuban government to US travelers to Cuba. There are limited flights that go to Cuba from the United States, and even those charter flights that do travel to Cuba occasionally get cancelled last-minute, making planned travel to Cuba unreliable. In addition, there is a weight limit on baggage to Cuba (mainly because US travelers of Cuban descent want to bring supplies to their Cuban families), but this weight limit and the accompanying overage fees seem to change with each charter flight. Additionally, there is a currency limit for US travelers to Cuba, which seems to fluctuate depending on current US policy. And, on the way back, there are restrictions on what can be brought back from Cuba (currently, no rum or cigars are permitted, though these restrictions change frequently). All of these reasons discourage casual, spontaneous US tourism to Cuba. In short, a US citizen cannot spontaneously go to Cuba for spring break.

Despite these challenges—and perhaps because of them—there remains considerable interest among US citizens in traveling to Cuba. US citizens who do manage to travel to Cuba often do so in support of Cuba's recent history, in particular the Cuban Revolution. These same tourists do not have an equivalent interest in traveling to other islands in the Caribbean, precisely because other Caribbean islands have not been able to challenge US domination in the region so successfully. Other US travelers are interested in Cuban architecture, Cuban ecology, Cuban music, Cuban art, Cuba's African heritage, Cuban medicine—all the areas of tourism outlined by Pozo Fernández in his 1993 book. Most US travelers who wish to visit Cuba are "forced" to travel under these study group categories because of the tight travel restrictions imposed by the US government. In effect, this creates a self-selecting group—people who by definition are interested in what they would consider to be "authentic" Cuba—that is, the medical system, the ecosystem, history, music and dance, architecture, art, and so on. These are not people looking for a resort vacation.

My first trip to Cuba was in 1989, with the Manhattan-based Center for Cuban Studies, founded in 1972 by Sandra Levinson, who serves as the center's executive director and curator of its gallery, Cuban Art Space. At that time, the Center for Cuban Studies ran about a dozen study trips per year, aimed at academics who were researching various aspects of Cuban culture but were not able to travel there easily because of US-imposed restrictions on travel to Cuba, and because of Cuban-imposed restrictions on visa types. In a nutshell, the US government prohibited US citizens from traveling to Cuba with a tourist visa, while the Cuban government permitted mostly tourist visas to be given to US citizens traveling to Cuba. The study-trip model has long been an elegant and legal way to bypass the conflict-ridden relationship between the United States and Cuba, allowing scholars to travel to the island for a few weeks to learn more about their topic. Center for Cuban Studies, Global Exchange, Smithsonian Institution, Pastors for Peace, and Insight Programs Cuba are a few of the organizations that are currently licensed by the US Department of Treasury, Office of Foreign Assets Control, to sponsor trips to Cuba.[10] It is worth noting that it is the Office of Foreign Assets Control within the US Department of Treasury, and not the US Department of State, that is responsible for controlling the travel of US citizens to Cuba.[11] What is at issue here is the restriction of potential revenues from US tourism to Cuba.

On that first three-week trip, the theme of which was Afro-Cuban Culture, I found myself in a group of about fifteen people, including a recent PhD from Yale (American Studies), two literature professors from NYU, a scholar from the University of Houston working on *cabildos*, a literature professor from Wake Forest University, a New York-based author, a visual artist from Manhattan, and a former Venceremos brigadista[12] from UT Austin. All were working on Cuba-related projects, some of which were to be published in the early 1990s, but most of which came to fruition in the first decade of the twenty-first century. I make this note because for most of these scholars that 1989 trip to Cuba was their first trip to the island but not their last. Some of these people traveled to Cuba again in the 1990s with the Center for Cuban Studies, and some made arrangements with other travel organizations, but most of them likely entered Cuba with tourist visas.

Of particular interest to me was the recent PhD from Yale University because his research topic was directly related to my own. This scholar was Dr. David H. Brown, and his book, *Santería Enthroned: Art, Ritual, and Innovation in an Afro-Cuban Religion* (2003), was to become a highly regarded text in Afro-Cuban studies. What I noticed about Dr. Brown's itinerary while he was in Havana was that he met with religious practitioners of Regla de Ocha (more commonly known as Santería) almost every day, and participated in a number of Ocha ceremonies. I accompanied him to some of these ceremonies, but remained more focused on my topic of Afro-Cuban folkloric performance within the Conjunto Folklórico Nacional de Cuba. During the next ten years, I returned to Cuba roughly once every year, and during the first decade of 2000, I made three additional trips. With each successive trip, I became more interested in Afro-Cuban religious music, particularly the music and dance traditions associated with Regla de Ocha. Soon I was attending *tambores* (a *tambor* is a central religious drumming ceremony in Ocha) with each field trip.

To my surprise, in addition to the Canadians and Europeans I expected to see, I met quite a few other US citizens who were attending these *tambores*, too. Some were interested primarily in the music, others were interested in the dance, and still others had an anthropological interest in the ceremony itself. Whatever the reason, these US citizens were repeat travelers to Cuba, and came back year after year to the same *casa templos*, interacted with the same musicians, dancers, and ritual specialists, and usually stayed in the same small hotels or rented apartments. These travelers formed relationships with Cubans outside of the Cuban government's controlled relationship category of "tourist: tourist industry worker," and the main vehicle for these relationships was Afro-Cuban religious performance.

AFRO-CUBAN RELIGIOUS MUSIC AND THE SPIRITUAL SEEKER

MacCannell (1976), Graburn (1989), and others have suggested that, in this era of postmodern secularism, tourism is a "sacred journey," replacing religious reverence with a reverence for nature, or music, or food, or travel itself. I would argue that, at least in the case of Cuba—and likely in the case of other places that connect music and spiritual experience in deeply affective ways—tourism replaces religious reverence with a reverence for, well, religious performance.

Afro-Cuban music has long been a tourist attraction in Cuba, from the *danzón* of the nineteenth century to the *son, rumba, mambo,* and other popular dance genres of the twentieth century. These genres have their roots in Afro-Cuban religious music, with its polyrhythmic drumming patterns and its repeated melodic refrains. Similarly, Cuban dance, and especially sacred Afro-Cuban dance, has contributed to the Cuban national project of attracting foreign tourism while maintaining its roots in sacred performance.[13] Afro-Cuban religious performance offers an added bonus to travelers who seek the potential of spiritual enlightenment. The *tambor* provides a number of sensorial entry-ways for religious congregants and for tourists. For some tourists, engaging in Afro-Cuban religious performance helps define not only their goals as travelers but their spiritual identities. Expanding on Cohen's (1979) phenomenological typology of tourist experiences, one can consider these travelers "experimental" and "existential" tourists, who seek an alternate, often permanently changed, mode of existence; what Cohen calls an "elective center." The drumming and singing at *tambores* function as a "spirituality highway" for the existential tourist, offering multiple possibilities for engagement and self-exploration. For the musicians and many of the congregants, the *tambor* is a form of religious work—an obligation and a responsibility. For those attendees who are neither congregants nor musicians, the sung liturgy and drummed rhythms of the *tambor* provide a comfortable cognitive distance as well as a compelling musical and visual spectacle.

Through the sights and sounds of the *tambor*, tourists can test out another way of being, projecting themselves temporarily into a vibrant spiritual community. Although the Cuban state has long subsidized folkloric and touristic performances of Afro-Cuban sacred performances, there is a growing number of independent *casa templos*, especially in urban areas. The two types of performances—touristic/folkloric and independent sacred—are in some senses interdependent; indeed, some folkloric performances draw on performers who are also independent religious practitioners. Compelled by the search for the "authentic" (MacCannell 1976), existential tourists shy away from the state-sponsored folkloric performances staged in the lobbies of resort hotels, and they are instead drawn toward small *casa templos*. For existential tourists, these independent Afro-Cuban religious practitioners offer social and spiritual networks that exist far outside the reaches of the state tourism economy, thus making possible a local, personal, sustainable, and enduring model of tourism.

TOURISM AND "AUTHENTICITY"

As of this writing, almost twenty-five years have passed since I began my fieldwork in Cuba, and many people have written about tourism in Cuba. Friends and colleagues have written eloquently about the commodification of religious practice, objects, and performance in Cuba, especially as a result of special economic period, which marked the beginning of the near-collapse of Cuba's centralized, planned economy. (See Delgado 2009, Knauer 2009, Cabezas 2006 and 2009, Routon 2011, Hernandez-Reguant 2009, and Carter 2008, among others.) What the work of these scholars has in common is the assumption that the Cuban government commodifies its citizens for foreign consumption in an attempt to gain badly needed hard currency, and that tourism—including sex tourism, ecotourism, sports tourism, heritage tourism, performance tourism—is the most efficient and lucrative means of doing so (Cabezas 2006). Many of these scholars also note that Cuban citizens are forced to be complicit in the commodification of their bodies and their expressive and material culture because they have no other way of making ends meet (see chapter 2). A familiar Cuban adage about the dysfunctional relationship between labor and state compensation is: "We pretend to work and they [the government] pretend to pay us." All Cubans, it seems, are trying to get some *fula* (hard currency) on the side, by whatever means necessary. At its worst, according to these scholars, the commodification of Cuban culture for foreign consumption evacuates the value from the few activities and experiences from which Cubans derive pleasure, relief, and meaning. The assumption here is that the "dumbing down" of these experiences for foreigners makes the experiences less profound, less deep, less meaningful, less "authentic." Within the Afro-Cuban cultural milieu, examples of the types of objects and performances proffered to tourists include material culture (such as Afro-Cuban religious artwork, artifacts, clothing) and expressive culture (such as Afro-Cuban religious drumming, singing, and ceremonial practices).

On the flip side, "authenticity" is exactly what tourists are seeking, according to MacCannell, Cohen, and other prominent sociologists of tourism. "Touristic consciousness is motivated by its desire for authentic experience," writes MacCannell (1976, 101)—MacCannell uses no quotation marks around "authenticity." According to MacCannell's argument, people from industrialized, prosperous communities suffer from such intense alienation that they must look elsewhere for "reality and authenticity" (1976, 3). Later scholars consider the search for "authenticity" through tourism doomed: "Tourism is an inevitably commodifying process, and the very search itself ruins the authenticity of the object: 'the moment that culture is defined as an object of tourism, or segmented and detached from its indigenous sphere, its aura of authenticity is reduced'" (Taylor 2001, 15; and Kim and Jamal 2007, 183).[14]

Writing about tourism in Cuba (and especially in Havana), Thomas Carter focuses on the original and enduring alienation of the foreign tourist (which causes the tourist to seek a Cuban experience) and the reification of colonial structures enabled by state-run tourism in Cuba. Carter suggests that foreign tourists to Cuba "do not experience everyday life in socialist Cuba but instead travel through a hyper-real (Eco 1986) version of Havana. . . . [consuming] spectacles built upon imperialist nostalgias that create illusionary social worlds in which Cubans do all the labour, [in which] living is easy and one can engage in a myriad of excesses in sensuous abandon by indulging in eating, drinking, fucking and smoking until satiation is reached. Such transgressions only serve to reconfirm the boundaries of historical domination and difference." (Carter 2008, 243, 245). Carter goes on to note that "The structuring of space for tourist consumption and the removal of citizens by state authorities are attempts to maintain the illusion of Cuban socialism 'as it really is/was.' As a consequence of these spatial practices, most Cubans remain somewhat distanced from foreign tourists—a social distance reinforced by the state through physical and moralistic means" (Carter 2008, 245).

While these observations may be accurate for European and Canadian tourists, they do not hold true for tourists from the United States. Because of the difficulty in traveling between the United States and Cuba, the main type of tourist from the United States is a "study tourist"—that is, someone who travels to Cuba to find out more about environmental practices, medical training, cultural performance, architectural history, and the like. These tourists seem puritanical in comparison to the hedonistic pleasure-seekers to which Carter refers. These US study tourists typically have a deep interest in the field(s) represented by the study tour, and if they engage in excessive behavior, it is usually a form of naïvete. For US tourists, Cuba is "framed" not as a haven for pleasure-seekers, but as a socialist hold-out, standing in counterbalance to the United States. Its tropical climate, beautiful beaches, and vibrant performance—so compelling for tourists from other countries—are often overshadowed for US tourists by other more "authentic" considerations.

Enter what I call "the spiritual seeker"—who is poised to problematize this dynamic. The spiritual seeker tends to help close the social, physical, and moral gap imposed by the exploitative structure of large-scale tourism by showing up at non-tourist religious ceremonies, and, more to the point, by participating. My idea of a "spiritual seeker" is based on Erik Cohen's "experiential and existential tourists"—from Cohen's phenomenological typology of tourists: briefly, the "recreational" tourist, who is attached to rather than alienated from the societal center, and who may replicate societal structures even while on vacation; the "diversionary" tourist, for whom tourism provides nothing more than an alternative to daily monotonous routine; the "experiential" tourist, who is alienated from the societal center and actively seeks authenticity in the lives of others; the "experimental" tourist, who does not adhere to the center of any society, and who looks for alternatives in many different forms; and the "existential" tourist, who is completely alienated from society to the point of embracing another society as an "elective center." According to Cohen, the existential tourist is deeply concerned with "authenticity" of experience.[15] I locate the spiritual seeker in between Cohen's experiential tourist and the existential tourist. In my experience, the spiritual seeker in Cuba has a deep interest in music, and shares with Cuban musicians the philosophy that music, especially drumming, is a powerful means to a spiritual end.

AFRO-CUBA

In March 2013, highly regarded Cuban editor and writer Roberto Zurbano wrote an article for the *New York Times* entitled "For Blacks in Cuba, the Revolution is Not Yet Finished." *The New York Times* altered the title to "For Blacks in Cuba, the Revolution Hasn't Begun," setting off a firestorm of accusations and recriminations about mistranslations and race issues in Cuba, and resulting in the removal of Zurbano from his post as editor at Casa de las Americas.[16] Though the context of this article and the responses to it can be interpreted in a number of different ways, one thing is clear: the disparities in goods and services experienced by Cubans of different skin colors is a subject of open debate among Cubans, largely because of the economic reforms enacted in the wake of the special economic period. Zurbano writes, "Over the last decade, scores of ridiculous prohibitions for Cubans living on the island have been eliminated, among them sleeping at a hotel, buying a cellphone, selling a house or car and traveling abroad . . . [T]he reality is that in Cuba, your experience of these changes depends on your skin color" (Zurbano 2013). Zurbano writes of "two contrasting realities" in Cuba today: that of the white Cubans, who have "leveraged their resources to enter the new market-driven economy," mainly through remittances from abroad (which are estimated to total between $700 million and one billion annually [Ritter 2003, 10]), and that of the black plurality, which "witnessed the demise of the socialist utopia from the island's least comfortable quarters." Black Cubans, according to Zurbano, have to contend with "pervasive racism," manifesting itself in such potentially lucrative industries as tourism, in which hotel managers "hire only white staff members, so as not to offend the supposed sensibilities of their European clientele." These statements would seem to leave Cuba's population of African heritage out of the tourism industry altogether—except for one important aspect: Afro-Cuban music and dance. It is in Afro-Cuban performance, particularly in tourist venues, that black Cubans participate fully and can reap some of the benefits of Cuba's commitment to foreign tourism.

Through their expert training in the performance traditions of Afro-Cuban religious and folkloric traditions, and through their networks of scholars and performers in the United States, Cuban performers such as Carlos Aldama, Susana Arenas Pedroso, Yesenia Fernández, Kati Hernandez, Cusito Peñalver Lombira, and many others have been able to relocate to major metropolitan areas in the United States and create new lives. These performers have all been trained both in religious and folkloric performance, and when they relocate to the United States, they begin giving folkloric classes in music and dance, and performing at religious ceremonies. I include this group of people because it is my belief that their landing in the United States is directly connected to the visit of a few US spiritual tourists years prior to when they relocated to the United States. The people I cite above came to the United States during the last fifteen years (since the late 1990s), but one can trace the phenomenon back farther. Each of these performers can be connected to at least one spiritual tourist, usually a musician, and sometimes someone who becomes initiated into Ocha. That person becomes a sponsor or provides informal support for the performer to come to the United States. And the Cuban folkloric/religious performers find an enthusiastic home base in places like San Francisco, Los Angeles, New York City, and Miami, precisely because there are spiritual tourists in waiting in these places. Consider the following scenario from December 2000:

Fifty people crowd into a tiny whitewashed room with a low ceiling. It is midday in December 2000, and although the temperature outside is pleasant, the heat in this urban Havana apartment is stultifying. The tangy fragrance of ripe mangos and guavas, arranged in groups of five on the multi-tiered altar in the next room, meanders through acrid cigarette smoke. The lead singer and three drummers push their way into the small room, past friends, relatives, neighbors, and a handful of strangers. Lugging folding chairs and *batá* drums, each has a cigarette dangling from his mouth. They are dressed in white; two sport red kerchiefs around their necks and white knit caps, another wears a yellow cap, and the singer has a red-and-white gingham cap, which he places on his head just as the drummers sit down to play. The four musicians finish their cigarettes and each takes a swig of potent-smelling clear liquid from a white plastic cup. Some of the congregants watch these preparatory gestures with interest; others salute the porcelain-housed deities in front of the altar with customary gestures—prostration on the rush mat in front of the altar, and shaking a rattle, maraca, or metal bell. The strangers and some of the neighbors mill about the adjoining room, admiring the altar. When the singer intones "I barago moyuba," everyone tries to squeeze into the small room where the musicians are. The *tambor* has begun.

But how do we categorize the attendees at this *tambor*—a religious drumming ceremony central to Regla de Ocha? As strangers and neighbors? As congregants and tourists? As musicians and dancers? At most of the *tambores* I have attended, people play multiple roles. Someone who may be an excellent *orisha* dancer may also have no interest or background in Regla de Ocha. This person, a Cuban of African heritage, may "look" like a native to the *tambor* but may be just as new to the experience as a Canadian percussionist whose closest Cuban experience is hearing a few recordings of *batá* drumming. Similarly, many of the most respectful and observant attendees at a *tambor* may be foreigners. They may have a musical or spiritual affinity that leads them to attend *tambores* and listen quietly, not taking pictures, not speaking loudly, not getting drunk—not "engaging in a myriad of excesses until satiation is reached" (paraphrasing Carter 2008, 245). These tourists tend to establish enduring relationships with their hosts (collapsing the distance so often imposed by the Cuban government), and may come back year after year, simply to do the same things: go to religious ceremonies, hear religious music, and learn more about what it all means. Not all of them are ethnographers, though some of them are engaged in the type of scholarship we practice. There is a persistence and a discipline in their behavior that diverges greatly from the hedonistic models of tourism characterized in recent literature. Rather than embracing a postmodern secularism, these tourists seem to be creating a new spirituality—if not religiosity—with the essential help of Cuban hosts. And Cuban socialism has an important role to play in this. Ironically, by creating conditions that spiritual seekers find consonant with their own preferences—a de-emphasis on material goods, a struggle for necessities, a satisfaction with basic food, shelter, and clothing—Cuban socialism helps emphasize spiritual rather than material considerations.

In this way, Cuban "hosts" and foreign "guests" tend to complement each other. I am not arguing that there is no difference in material circumstances—clearly, the global economy that allows one group of people to be "tourists" on a regular basis is also complicit in the systematic impoverishment of the hosts. As Sheller puts it, "The movements of some things and people require the immobility of others, and movement can often become a means by which boundaries are enforced rather than undone" (2003, 201). But I am arguing that there may be more common ground between the spiritual seeker tourist and the Cuban host than has previously been assumed. Because of the many sensorial avenues of entry into the experience, each person attending a *tambor* can engage with the ceremony in a different way, allowing a continuum of engagement between practitioners of religious performance and those who witness these performances but do not comprehend the religious intention conveyed by the performers. For the musicians and many of the congregants, the *tambor* is indeed a form of religious labor, for which they are compensated primarily in spiritual terms. For those attendees who are neither congregants nor musicians, the ceremony is potentially a leisure activity—a compelling and colorful spectacle to observe and absorb at will. The spiritual seeker is somewhere in between—wishing to comprehend religious intent, searching for that elusive "elective center," and hoping that repeated exposure to the performance will open the road.

POSTSCRIPT

Ironically, it is precisely beach tourism—the first resort of almost all other Caribbean islands who have decided that tourism should play a large role in their economies—that will serve the Cubans least well. The model of the hard-working European or Canadian or American who wants to go to a Caribbean island just to lie on the beach and drink mojitos is not a sustainable model for tourism in Cuba because the double standard of life for Cubans and for tourists is too extreme. It is very difficult to imagine a successful program of beach tourism in which a *mojito* sold to a European tourist costs the equivalent of a Cuban doctor's salary for one week. With a population as savvy and as independent as Cubans are, such disparities are infuriating and humiliating, as well as out of step with revolutionary rhetoric. It is not that Cuba's beautiful beaches should play no part in tourism; rather, they should be part of an independent, new model of foreign tourism, which showcases the many unique facets of the island.

In response to Polly Pattullo's dire prediction regarding sustainable tourism in the Caribbean (2005), I would argue that Cuba enjoys an exceptionalist position both in its relationship to the United States, and in its status as a leader in the Caribbean. As long as Cuba remains a socialist country, and as long as it continues to work with tour groups that emphasize its unique architecture, expressive arts, ecology, religious traditions, and medical training, Cuba will be able to create a sustainable model of tourism for many decades to come.

NOTES

1. Pozo Fernández worked on the weekly news magazine *Bohemia* as a writer and editor from 1968 until his retirement more than two decades later.
2. See Schwartz 1997 for a vivid account of Cuba's courting of foreign tourism during the twentieth century. Although Castro made a valiant attempt to continue Cuba's booming tourist trade during the first years of the revolution by committing $200 million dollars to a four-year tourism development plan, tourism to Cuba largely stopped by October 1960, when Castro began nationalizing private property (Schwartz 1997, 200–203), and did not pick up again until the 1980s.
3. Gaviota operates under the control of the Cuban Ministry of Armed Forces (MINFAR), which may explain the emphasis on taking care of high-ranking visitors.
4. Data from World Bank web site: http://data.worldbank.org/indicator/ST.INT. ARVL.
5. Cuba has many live coral reefs boasting tremendous biodiversity for its small size.
6. The great majority of tourists come to Cuba from Canada (800,000 in 2011), with other significant tourist populations coming from the United Kingdom, Italy, Spain, France, Germany, Argentina, Mexico, Russia, and Venezuela, in decreasing order of number of tourists (Guzman 2012, 24).
7. See also Cabezas 2006 and 2009, in which she asserts that hiring light-skinned Cubans to work in the tourist industry is a policy adopted by the Cuban government to attract white-skinned tourists from Canada and Europe.
8. For the purposes of this article, I am referring to US citizens not of Cuban ancestry. Cuban émigrés or descendants of Cuban émigrés in the United States are excepted from this characterization. The politics of family and nation loom large in the travel equation for US citizens of Cuban descent, and often outweigh considerations of US foreign policy.
9. See the US Department of Treasury's web site for an overview of US sanctions against Cuba and for a more detailed description of the categories of US citizens who may apply for a license to travel to Cuba: http://www.treasury.gov/resource-center/sanctions/Programs/pages/cuba.aspx.
10. See the Fund for Reconciliation and Development web site: http://www.ffrd.org/cuba/travel.html.

11. Other travel organizations licensed by the US Department of Treasury, Office of Foreign Assets Control, to take tour groups to Cuba include Marazul Tours, Witness for Peace, Common Ground Travel, Insight Programs Cuba, Cuba Travel Service, Cuba Travel USA, and Island Travel Tours, among others. For a full list of travel providers authorized by the Office of Foreign Assets Control, see the US Department of Treasury web site: http://www.treasury.gov/resource-center/sanctions/Programs/Documents/cuba_tsp.pdf.

12. The Venceremos (We Shall Overcome) Brigade was founded in 1969 by members of Students for a Democratic Society as well as other young people interested in challenging the US embargo against Cuba by traveling to the island and working alongside Cuban agricultural workers for a couple of weeks each summer. The Venceremos Brigade trips have continued for more than forty years, and participants are called "brigadistas."

13. See Hagedorn (2001); Yvonne Daniel's article "Economic Vitamins of Cuba: Sacred and Other Dance Performance" (2010).

14. This version of the "authenticity" argument reminds me of Walter Benjamin's (1969) idea of the "aura" of the original, missing from the copy.

15. Cohen's analysis is informed by a critical reading of Boorstin 1964, Turner 1973, and MacCannell 1976 (see McCabe 2005, 88–89).

16. See Archibold 2013 for the response of the *New York Times* to Zurbano's plight.

REFERENCES

Archibold, Randal C. 2013. "Editor Who Wrote of Racism in Cuba Loses His Post, Colleagues Say." *New York Times, Americas Section*. April 6.

Benjamin, Walter. 1969 [1936]. "The Work of Art in the Age of Mechanical Reproduction." In *Illuminations*. New York: Schocken Books.

Bianchi Ross, Ciro. 2011. "A Tour of Havana." *Cuba Plus* 18: 8–12.

Boorstin, Daniel. 1964. *The Image: A Guide to Pseudo Events in American Society*. New York: Harper.

Brown, David H. 2003. *Santería Enthroned: Art, Ritual, and Innovation in an Afro-Cuban Religion*. Chicago: University of Chicago Press.

Cabezas, Amalia. 2006. "The Eroticization of Labor in Cuba's All-Inclusive Resorts: Performing Race, Class, and Gender in the New Tourist Economy." *Social Identities* 12(5): 507–521.

Cabezas, Amalia. 2009. *Economies of Desire: Sex and Tourism in Cuba and the Dominican Republic*. Philadelphia: Temple University Press.

Campos, Roberto F. 2012a. "Find Excitement and Adventure in Cuban Waters." *Cuba Plus* 21: 16–17.

Campos, Roberto F. 2012b. "Cuban Tourism Likely to Grow Despite U.S. Economic Pressures." *The Havana Reporter*. II(10): 2.

Carter, Thomas F. 2008. "Of Spectacular Phantasmal Desire: Tourism and the Cuban State's Complicity in the Commodification of Its Citizens." *Leisure Studies* 27: 3, 241–257.

Cohen, Erik. 1979. "A Phenomenology of Tourist Experiences." *Sociology* 13: 179–201.

"Cuba: The Accidental Eden." 2010. Documentary film. Season 29, Episode 1, of PBS "Nature" television series. Writers Kelly Kraemer, Sam Rubinoff, and Doug Shultz. First aired September 26, 2010.

Daniel, Yvonne. 2010. "The Economic Vitamins of Cuba: Sacred and Other Dance Performance." In *Rhythms of the Afro-Atlantic World: Rituals and Remembrances*, edited by Mamadou Diouf and Ifeoma Kiddoe Nwankwo. Ann Arbor: University of Michigan Press.

Delgado, Kevin. 2009. "Spiritual Capital: Foreign Patronage and the Trafficking of Santería." In *Cuba in the Special Period: Culture and Ideology in the 1990s*, edited by Ariana Hernandez-Reguant. Hampshire, UK: Palgrave Macmillan.

Graburn, Nelson. 1989. "Tourism: The Sacred Journey." In *Hosts and Guests: The Anthropology of Tourism*, 2d ed., edited by Valene Smith. Philadelphia: University of Pennsylvania Press.

Guzman, Graciela. 2012. "Tourism's Best Year in Cuba." *Cuba Plus* 21: 24.

Hagedorn, Katherine. 2001. *Divine Utterances: The Performance of Afro-Cuban Santería*. Washington, DC: Smithsonian Institution Press.

Hernandez-Reguant, Ariana, ed. 2009. *Cuba in the Special Period: Culture and Ideology in the 1990s*. Hampshire, UK: Palgrave Macmillan.

Kempadoo, Kamala, ed. 1999. *Sun, Sex, and Gold: Tourism and Sex Work in the Caribbean*. Lanham, MD: Rowman and Littlefield.

Kim, Hyounggon, and Tazim Jamal. 2007. "Tourist Quest for Existential Authenticity." *Annals of Tourism Research* 34(1): 181–207.

Knauer, Lisa Maya. 2009. "Audiovisual Remittances and Transnational Subjectivities." In *Cuba in the Special Period: Culture and Ideology in the 1990s*, edited by Ariana Hernandez-Reguant. Hampshire, UK: Palgrave Macmillan.

MacCannell, Dean. 1976. *The Tourist: A New Theory of the Leisure Class*. London: Macmillan.

McCabe, Scott. 2005. "Who Is a Tourist? A Critical Review." *Tourist Studies* 5(1): 85–106.

Montserrat, Patty. 2012. "New Jewels of Cuban Tourism." *Cuba Plus* 21: 20–23.

Pattullo, Polly. 2005. *Last Resorts: The Cost of Tourism in the Caribbean*. London: Latin America Bureau.

Pozo Fernández, Alberto. 1993. *Cuba y el turismo: Actualidad y perspectivas de nuestra industria turística*. Havana: Editora Política.

Ritter, Archibald R. M. 2003. "An Overview of Cuba's Economy in the 2000s: Recuperation and/or Relapse." *Carleton Economic Paper*. February 2003. Department of Economics, Carleton University.

Ritter, Archibald R. M. 2010. "Shifting Realities in 'Special Period' Cuba." *Latin American Research Review* 45(3): 229–238. Pittsburgh, PA: University of Pittsburgh.

Routon, Kenneth. 2011. *Hidden Powers of State in the Cuban Imagination*. Gainesville: University Press of Florida.

Sanchez, Peter M., and Kathleen M. Adams. 2010. "The Janus-Faced Character of Tourism in Cuba." In *Tourists and Tourism: A Reader*, 2d ed., edited by Sharon Bohn Gmelch. Long Grove, IL: Waveland Press.

Schwartz, Rosalie. 1997. *Pleasure Island: Tourism and Temptation in Cuba*. Lincoln, NE: University of Nebraska Press.

Sheller, Mimi. 2003. *Consuming the Caribbean: From Arawaks to Zombies.* London: Routledge.

Taylor, J. 2001. "Authenticity and Sincerity in Tourism." *Annals of Tourism Research* 28: 7–26.

Turner, Victor. 1973. "The Center Out There: Pilgrim's Goal." *History of Religion* 12: 191–230.

Wang, N. 1999. "Rethinking Authenticity in Tourism Experience." *Annals of Tourism Research* 26(2): 349–370.

Zurbano, Roberto. 2013. "For Blacks in Cuba, the Revolution Hasn't Begun." *New York Times, Sunday Review.* March 24.

Afterword

JOCELYNE GUILBAULT ■

For many people, tourism is synonymous with the Caribbean. Given the ubiquitous performance of music in this region, it may thus be surprising that until recently, so few scholars have addressed the relation between music and tourism in the circum-Caribbean. Timothy Rommen is right to ask at the beginning of this book why it took so long for ethnomusicologists to see this research paradigm not only as viable, but as central to many of the questions typically asked in the field "about representation; local, national, and regional identifications; aesthetics; race; gender; ethnicity; and class" (see Introduction, this volume). After similarly pointing out the anthropologists' lack of concern about tourism until the late 1980s, Malcolm Crick (1989, 311) goes further by asking critical rhetorical questions to make his case:

> Is it that anthropologists, because we study "them" and not "us," have regarded tourists as someone else's concern? Is it that academic personalities find it difficult to take as a serious area of research a phenomenon so bound up with leisure and hedonism? A social psychologist has suggested that the relative neglect of tourism in the behavioral sciences relates to deeply embedded values in Western society concerning work and play (Pearce 1982, 1–2). But is there an even more basic emotional avoidance at work for anthropological researchers—namely, that tourists appear, in some aspects, to be our own distant relatives?"[1]

Some of these suggestions may partly explain why, apart from a few notable exceptions noted in Rommen's Introduction, most ethnomusicologists focusing on the Caribbean have until the early 1990s failed to engage this important field of enquiry. But as insightful as they may be, these suggestions do not tell the whole story. The independence movements that swept the English-speaking Caribbean from the early 1960s onwards, as well as the effects of their aftermath until the late 1980s,[2] I want to argue, were also deeply agentive in deterring researchers from engaging research on tourism. With very few monographs on the musical traditions of most islands, cultural officers hired by newly elected governments, nationalists, and social activists all worked to document and archive the local musical traditions through whom the population could identify itself. They organized musical competitions at schools, among workers of various associations, and nationally to feature and nurture the practice of "local" music. They also began to publish and circulate educational material to teach younger generations about the history of these practices—all in the spirit of the nation-building process. The national projects then were all about fostering self-pride and self-valorization. They were about developing a better knowledge and an appreciation of the country's cultural riches. While simultaneously developing tourism to boost the GNP, efforts deployed to cater for tourism were politically downplayed in terms of research priorities.

In addition to the highly charged political climate following the independence of many countries in the region, at least two other important factors may also help explain the neglect of studies focusing on the interrelation of music and tourism in the Caribbean. Apart from Cuba and Haiti, most music studies by local researchers in the aftermath of independence focused mainly on lyrics—based on the belief that in expressive arts, this is where politics is waged. In so doing, most local publications eschewed not only the music per se, but also the contexts in which local music was performed and their influence of the performances. In addition, relative to a region that counts at least twenty-eight island nations, up to the late 1980s few non-Caribbean ethnomusicologists and anthropologists studied Caribbean musical practices. As I explained elsewhere (Guilbault 1991), the persistent quest in ethnomusicology to study "authentic" traditional or classical musics from other countries implicitly, if not explicitly, translated into a near total disregard not only for hybrid musics—which characterize most Caribbean musics—but also for mass-mediated popular musics until the early 1990s. As a result, it could be suggested, very few ethnomusicologists considered the Caribbean worthy of study for the greater part of the twentieth Century.

But the situation has now dramatically changed. First, following the emergence of gender studies and the influence of cultural studies throughout the region,[3] which recognizes performing arts as participating in the elaboration of cultural politics, many scholars from the Caribbean have since the 1990s published numerous books and articles on traditional and popular musics in the region. Second, influenced by postmodernism, globalization, and postcolonial studies, the new focus on hybrid and cosmopolitan practices in academia viewed as endemic to the late twentieth and twenty-first century human condition has sparked interest among ethnomusicologists and led dozens to now focus on Caribbean musics.

Seizing upon the fact that there are now a sizeable number of researchers addressing Caribbean musics and that tourism has acquired an unprecedented economic importance in the region, the publication of this book on music and tourism in the circum-Caribbean comes at a propitious historical moment. Through richly detailed ethnographies, it details how in the context of tourism, music enables diverse and contrasting types of encounters and affects social relations locally, regionally, and internationally. It reveals how music acts in many contrasting capacities: how it intervenes as a cultural broker, generates income, and also produces pleasure; how it features local and cosmopolitan knowledge; how in some cases it serves as a spiritual medium; and how it turns political and private interests into economic possibilities as well as, inadvertently, social liabilities.

IS ENTERTAINMENT FOR TOURISTS A SPECIAL CASE?

The question is, what makes entertainment for tourists unique or different from other types of entertainment in the music business? It could be argued that they all have one thing in common: they are based on an odd relationship. As Crick puts it, "one member is at play, one is at work." Speaking about the tourist-local relationship and tourism in the postcolonial world in particular, he adds, "one has economic assets and little cultural knowledge, the other has cultural capital but little money" (1989, 331). While it does not apply to all tourists (some have more knowledge about the places they visit and the musics they hear than others) and to all musicians (some musicians in the islands have managed to create a decent income for themselves), this remark nonetheless points to what distinguishes entertainment for tourism in the circum-Caribbean: its postcolonial history and the vexed relationships it has entailed with the so-called "First World." In Crick's own wording, "the very possibility [of tourism in the region] . . . is securely rooted in the real world of gross political and economic inequalities between nations and classes" (334).[4]

It is thus not surprising to read how, based on this premise, many authors in this book are concerned with issues that are directly connected to the postcolonial condition. Without necessarily specifying who the tourist is, the specter of the foreign tourist as white and from the affluent "First World," looms large in many essays included here. The "us and them" paradigm is often alluded to, and along with it many of the "who benefits?" questions and fears to which it is associated: Who gets most of the revenues in touristic destinations and touristic entertainment, the locals or the foreign-owned companies? Who is in the position to deploy agency, to decide on the choice of repertoire, to determine the number of musicians who will play, when, and how many times a week for the tourists (see chapters 8 and 9)?

As many authors report, even after several decades of political independence, the question of identity also continues to be a serious preoccupation for many locals in the circum-Caribbean. According to whose aesthetics and ethics is music for the tourists performed (see chapters 7, 8, and 9)? Bearing in mind how this question matters for the Caribbean postcolonial, several authors have addressed how the impact of tourism on local music is feared by many local scholars, critics, and social activists in relation to at least two main issues: the folklorization and the commoditization of local musical practices. Folklorization is viewed as freezing in time and space musical practices for the sake of the (white) tourist's search for exoticism. In turn, commoditization is conceived as leading local musicians to dilute local music aesthetics in order to turn them into objects of mass consumption and to engage in crass-commercialism for the sake of mass tourism. The underlying concerns here—as much, it seems, for the writers of some of the essays in this volume as for many local critics—have to do with cultural identity and authenticity. But like several tourism researchers, I wonder: are tourists being chosen as conspicuous scapegoats for the cultural changes that people are witnessing?[5] I want to quote Crick (1989, 336) at length here for the points he makes puts in perspective the ineluctable dynamics of culture:

> For a start, in most cases we are dealing with societies with centuries of exposure to a whole range of economic, political, and cultural influences from the West. Long before tourism, those cultures were changing, including in directions that reflected their own understandings of the nature of Western societies (Marcus 1980). Besides, what in a culture is *not* staged? What does cultural authenticity consist of? As [D.] Greenwood states, all cultures "are in the process of 'making themselves up' all the time. In a general sense all culture is 'staged authenticity'" (1982, 27). That being so, if change is a permanent state, why should the staging bound up in tourism be regarded as so destructive, and why should the changes be seen in such a negative light? . . . One might additionally ask what is so abhorrent about inauthentic phenomena? As Simmel, a lucid explore of modernity, noted, phenomena we are disposed to call inauthentic or superficial very often reveal the nature of social reality. (Schmidt 1979, 465–466)

Clearly, as the authors of this book have indicated, tourism in the arts has a wide range of potentials. Commoditization may at times further (rather than inhibit) the survival of certain musical traditions (see chapter 2 and the Buena

Vista phenomenon) or stimulate the development of new musical styles (see chapter 1 and the modern mento concept).[6] Commoditization may also allow communication between island residents and diasporic communities that would not be possible otherwise (see chapter 4 and the production of cassette letters). It may also help tourists to develop a better appreciation of the music and of the people they are planning to visit by having access to recordings prior to their travels (see chapters 2 and 3). While the negative impact of commoditization triggered by tourism may be real (as chapters 6 and 10 point out, in relation to the commoditization of the black bodies and female ones in particular), tourism may not be the sole factor that has led to the current widely spread social problems in some areas of the circum-Caribbean. As rightly acknowledged in chapters 6 and 10, chronic unemployment, gender inequities, and lack of access to education may also have contributed to the attitudes and behaviors of people involved in the tourist industry.

REVEALING ETHNOGRAPHIES: NEW THEORETICAL HORIZONS AND NEW FINDINGS

Who's the Tourist and Who's the Local?

It is undeniable, as Shelagh J. Squire aptly puts it, that "tourism plays an important role in many people's lives" (1994, 3). What the essays of this book have shown is *how* this has been the case. One of the significant contributions that the authors' detailed ethnographic studies make is first to destabilize the caricatured ways in which the "tourist" and the "local" have often been defined. The "tourist" is not just the excessive and hedonist consumer and the sexual predator, the "ugly" tourist that many previous studies have often evoked—even though that kind of tourist still exists, as Hutchinson and Lamen have shown in chapters 6 and 10. As Katherine Hagedorn's narrative in chapter 11 aptly reveals, the tourist can also be a learner, a spiritual seeker, as well as a lover of a musical tradition typical to one country in the circum-Caribbean. And as she further explains, the tourist by definition is not only a foreigner. It can also be a local resident who is a "stranger to" some musical traditions in her own country (see chapter 9). The tourist can also be a "nostalgic" in search of a former time and past musical traditions (see chapter 2). As Matthew Smith importantly illustrates in chapter 5, the tourist can also be the musician involved in intraregional touring, a neighbor. In addition, the tourist can be a member of the diasporic community in New York or Miami or a "returnee" to the island after having lived abroad for many years, as chapters 4 and 6 have eloquently shown. Even though some authors in this book still hang on to this terminology to make some analytical points, most conclusively demonstrate that the use of the binary categories of "domestic" versus "international," and of "insider" versus "outsider" may be quite misleading. The complex mobilities of people in terms of geographic location, knowledge, sensibility, aesthetics, and ethics must not only be recognized but also traced to account for the diverse and contrasting positionings of what is referred to as the "tourist."

With a similar critical outlook, the authors of this book help redefine the "local," too often presented in academic studies as the passive, submissive, and perpetual "victim" of tourism.[7] Daniel Neely in chapter 1, for instance, provides a telling account of how musicians playing for tourists often act as savvy strategists. Remember his description of how some Jamaican musicians strategically changed the names of the musical style they were playing from mento to calypso or simply adopted the latter music to tap on the calypso craze of the late 1930s to the late 1950s to their greatest commercial advantage in holiday resorts and touristic hotels. Think also about how Oliver Greene in chapter 7 turns our attention to leading members of a Belizian community as cultural and commercial entrepreneurs in his description of the Garinagu Settlement Day in Belize—a festival the Garinagu created by and for themselves and which they continue to organize and control for their own cultural, social, and financial interests. For his part, Jerome Camal in chapter 8 clearly shows that the "locals" can and do make choices about who their festivals should attract first and foremost—even if at times, it is at a great cost, financially and otherwise. For the organizers of the festival gwoka, Camal recounts, the socio-political stakes of this festival are more important than the potential financial benefits they could gain by linking their festival musical events to a hotel circuit. As noted by Vincenzo Perna in chapter 2, whether it is through the Buena Vista music evoking the past or the sexy dancing on Timba "burning beats," the play *of* and *on* difference in Cuba and, arguably, in most countries in the circum-Caribbean—has not been the exclusive affair of the foreign-owned hotel companies, the promoters of travel packages, or of the tourists. It has been an affair that has engaged as much the local tourist industry authorities, the musicians, and the dancers partaking in that industry (see also chapter 9). Tourism—its dynamics and impact—must thus be viewed as the responsibility of all these entities.

Different Contact Zones, Different Types of Music, and Different Types of Relationships

One of the great merits of this collection of ethnographic studies is that it shows the importance of qualifying the reach of tourism on the local public. As several authors have noted, the reach is uneven. The diverse cases included in this book aptly demonstrate how the different touristic sites or contact zones favor different types of musics and different types of encounters or relationships. A sacred spectacle such as the Afro-Cuban Regla de Ocha, a festival around a musical tradition such as the Second line in New Orleans, a community festival such as the festival gwoka: they each attract different kinds of publics—albeit at times overlapping. They encourage contacts among the organizers, performers, and attendees that are allegedly different by the sheer nature of what they each require (or do not require)—a specific kind of knowledge (religious, musical, or linguistic), musical sensibility, or political engagement. In the same way, looking at a hotel show of folkloric dance and music versus going to a nightclub not only to hear, but also to dance with other people on the music performed by a deejay, usually encourage different kinds of relationships among audience members and performers. To give another example: touring to play for and to learn from the people one visits—as was noted by Smith in chapter 5—significantly differs from the other types of contact zones mentioned above. The point here is that the authors of this book powerfully show how the impact of tourism needs to be historically situated, and carefully assessed in relation to not only the ways it interacts with the musical traditions performed in the country, but also the workers that tourism recruits, for how long, where, and when, as well as the socioeconomic and political environments in which tourism takes place.

In relation to the impact of tourism on local musical practices in particular, as Mimi Sheller insightfully writes, "the complex mobilities that [have] informed the production and circulation of Caribbean music cultures" since the beginning of the twentieth century has been such that "there is no clear distinction . . . between "authentic" culture and "commercial" performance; they are always in touch with each other" (see chapter 3). What is at stake and needs to be examined, as Ruthie Meadows suggests in chapter 9, is whether the "presentational intent" of the organizers of festivals aimed at tourists play on a selective difference that perpetuates the erasure of social problems (racism, sexism, segregation, poverty) or that helps improve the lives of the very people that are at the heart of what and of who is performed. What is, however, also important to recognize is how so-called "authentic" culture is not by default antithetical to commercial ventures. As Largey indicates, it is thanks to the production of cassette letters from Haiti featuring the music of rara bands and what he dubs "the affective power of technology" that diasporic intimacies may be nurtured and reinforced.

FOR FURTHER EXPLORATIONS

The socioeconomic and political importance that tourism has acquired in the circum-Caribbean cannot be overlooked; the central role that music plays in this industry, in its turn, cannot be overestimated. More detailed ethnographic studies such as those presented in this volume are needed, even nearly thirty years after Cohen's injunction, "to bring theory and empirical research closer together" (1984, 388). More ethnographic perspectives must be integrated to bring the study of music and tourism more fully into postmodern dialogues (Squire 1994, 12). We still hear too little the voice of the locals. How do they negotiate their own motivations and dispositions with the complex demands and expectations of tourists?[8] What does the diasporic subject from its multi-sited senses of home and multiple senses of belonging looking directly and sideways at tourism in the Caribbean have (and would like) to say? Furthermore, as Stronza puts it, "We [also continue to] know practically nothing . . . about the impacts of tourism on the tourists themselves. How are they affected by what they see, do, experience during their travels?" (2001, 263). The "encounter" is one site only; the aftermath, at and beyond the site of encounter is something else. This points to the need for grounding tourism studies in multi-sited theory, method, and practice.[9]

In the same vein, further attention must be given to the dialogues between the locals and the visiting groups, between the officers of the Ministry of tourism and the tour promoters, and between the hotel owners and the musicians. What types of musical expectations are taken for granted, what types of musical presentations are fought over, and what invented traditions are being proposed? More questions must indeed be asked about the international tourism network. What are the organizations and who are the leading voices that contribute to construct and inform the tourists? What are the interconnections that exist among the different parties involved, and what types of cultural politics and economic campaigns do they each wage to maximize their own gains? What kinds of media texts, images, or recordings are produced and circulated to promote a country's music and culture, and to what effects for the tourists and the tourist receivers?

The essays assembled in this book have productively focused on specific historical moments to examine music and tourism in the Caribbean region. However, if we agree that, "Industrial restructuring . . . will alter not only the tourist services created but also the relationship between producers and consumers of tourism products, and how meanings of the tourist experience are negotiated by various agencies" (Squire 1994, 8), the question that must now be addressed is this: What are the changes in the musical production dedicated to the tourism industry and in the tourist consumption of music that have occurred over the past ten years, twenty years, or fifty years in the circum-Caribbean? Such diachronic studies would contribute handsomely to our critical understandings of the social processes, patterns, and politics of representation that have been enacted in the musical performances for tourists.

This book could be read as a call to arms. It is an important corrective to the tendency to marginalize the role of tourism in Caribbean ethnomusicology. But what would it mean to take music and tourism studies not simply as an additional area of focus at the end of the day, but as the critical starting point, as the first chapter one must write to begin examining twentieth-century Caribbean musical histories of encounters? What would happen if the twentieth-century "tourist other" and the historicized already complex character of the "Caribbean local" were described as co-present and co-producers of many of the contemporary musical practices? Tourists and tourism then would be consistently woven into the analysis of the colonial and the postcolonial, the local and the global, the national and the transnational, and the very idea of the past into the present, that is, tradition. In what ways would addressing music and tourism as formative of the musical sensibilities, aesthetics, and ethics of style help us reimagine the very project of Caribbean ethnomusicology? Put another way, how would the study of music and tourism help shape postcolonial ethnomusicology in the Caribbean?

If music and tourism studies are indeed considered part of postcolonial queries, then could a comparative framework and an explicit set of critical questions be formulated to revisit how the contemporary histories of circum-Caribbean musical traditions have been told? How the local and tourist voices have interacted? How the histories of tourism in the islands have shared and yet responded to pressures of specific geographies, socioeconomic conditions, and international political relations? The insights made possible by the thick ethnographies included in this volume open a window onto the distinct modes of representation, mixes of sounds, and ethical behaviors that the complex and varied cultural politics of tourism have generated in some parts of the circum-Caribbean. The next step needs to show why the study of music and tourism is central to postcolonial ethnomusicology in and of the circum-Caribbean, and what postcolonial ethnomusicology in and of the region can contribute to further the theoretical development of tourism studies.

NOTES

1. For further elaboration on the similarities between anthropologists and tourists, see Stronza (2001, 261).
2. It is important to remember that many Caribbean islands gained their independence from the United Kingdom late in the twentieth century: Dominica in 1978, St. Lucia in 1979, and the twin-islands of Antigua and Barbuda in 1981, to name only these few.
3. Following the Birmingham School that for years had at its helm Stuart Hall—incidentally, a Jamaican scholar who has worked all his life in England—there are now Departments of cultural studies at the University of the West Indies in its three campuses, at Mona in Jamaica, St. Augustine in Trinidad, and Cave Hill in Barbados.

4. In this quote, I understand the author's reference to "the very possibility [of tourism in the region]" to mean "the very possibility to travel to the region"—the implications being that to do so, one has to have not only some financial capital that the "Caribbean local resident" presumably does not have, but also, by extension, the time to engage in leisure activities. As Martin Stokes aptly remarks, to define tourism as simply a leisure activity has been critically revisited. For an elaboration of how leisure in the post-industrial world has become a site, or better put, a "work" of self-fashioning, see his excellent essay "Music, Travel and Tourism" (1999).
5. Here I am paraphrasing Crick writing, "As several authors have argued . . . tourists may have been chosen as conspicuous scapegoats" (1989, 335).
6. For a critical view of commoditization in the context of tourism studies, see Cohen (1984, 387–388).
7. For further elaboration on the subject, see Bendix (1989), Mansperger (1995), Pattullo (1996), and Desmond (1999).
8. For further elaboration on the subject, see Stokes (1999, 143–145).
9. For further elaboration on the subject, see Marcus (1995).

REFERENCES

Bendix, Regina. 1989. "Tourism and Cultural Displays: Inventing Traditions for Whom?" *Journal of American Folklore* 102: 131–146.
Cohen, Erik. 1984. "The Sociology of Tourism: Approaches, Issues, and Findings." *Annual Review of Sociology* 10: 373–392.
Crick, Malcolm. 1989. "Representations of International Tourism in the Social Sciences: Sun, Sex, Sights, Savings, and Servility." *Annual Review of Anthropology* 18: 307–344.
Desmond, Jane C. 1999. *Staging Tourism*. Chicago: University of Chicago Press.
Greenwood, D. 1982. "Cultural 'Authenticity.'" *Cultural Survival Quarterly* 6(3): 27–28.
Guilbault, Jocelyne. 1991. "Ethnomusicology and the Study of Music in the Caribbean." *Studies in Third World Societies* 45: 117–140.
Mansperger, Mark C. 1995. "Tourism and Cultural Change in Small-Scale Societies." *Human Organization* 54: 87–94.
Marcus, George E. 1980. "The Ethnographic Subject as Ethnographer: A Neglected Dimension of Anthropological Research." *Rice University Studies* 66: 55–68.
——. 1995. "Ethnography in/of the World System: The Emergence of Multi-Sited Ethnography." *Annual Review of Anthropology* 24: 95–117.
Pattullo, Polly. 1996. *Last Resorts: The Cost of Tourism in the Caribbean*. London: Cassell.
Pearce, Philip L. 1982. *The Social Psychology of Tourist Behavior*. Oxford: Pergamon.
Schmidt, Catherine J. 1979. "The Guided Tour: Insulated Adventure." *Urban Life* 7: 441–467.
Squire, Shelagh J. 1994. "Accounting for Cultural Meanings: The Interface Between Geography and Tourism Studies Re-examined." *Progress in Human Geography* 18: 1.
Stokes, Martin. 1999. "Music, Travel and Tourism: An Afterword." *The World of Music* 41(3): 141–155.
Stronza, Amanda. 2001. "Anthropology of Tourism: Forging New Ground for Ecotourism and Other Alternatives." *Annual Review of Anthropology* 30: 261–283.